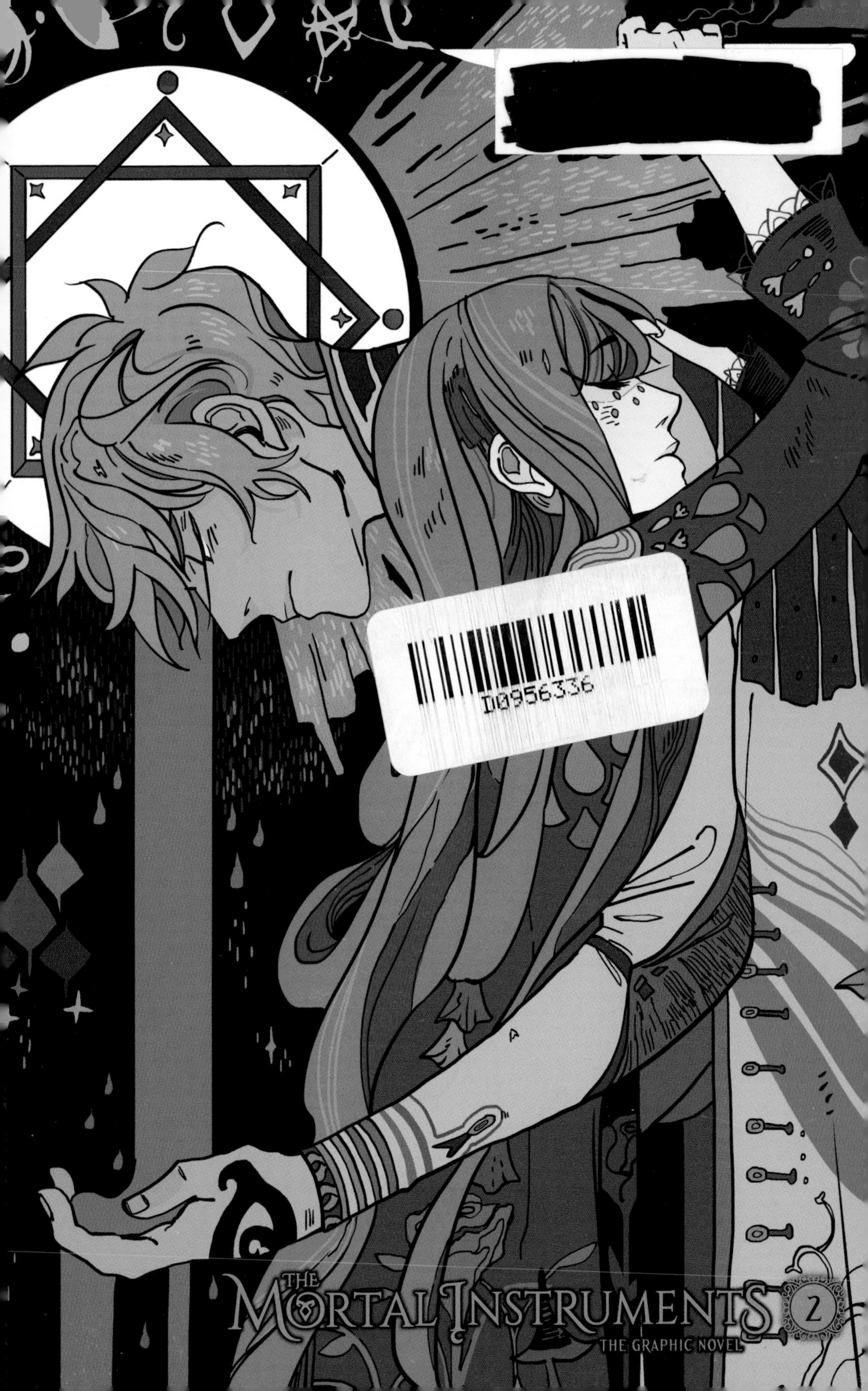
THE MORTAL INSTRUMENTS 2
THE GRAPHIC NOVEL

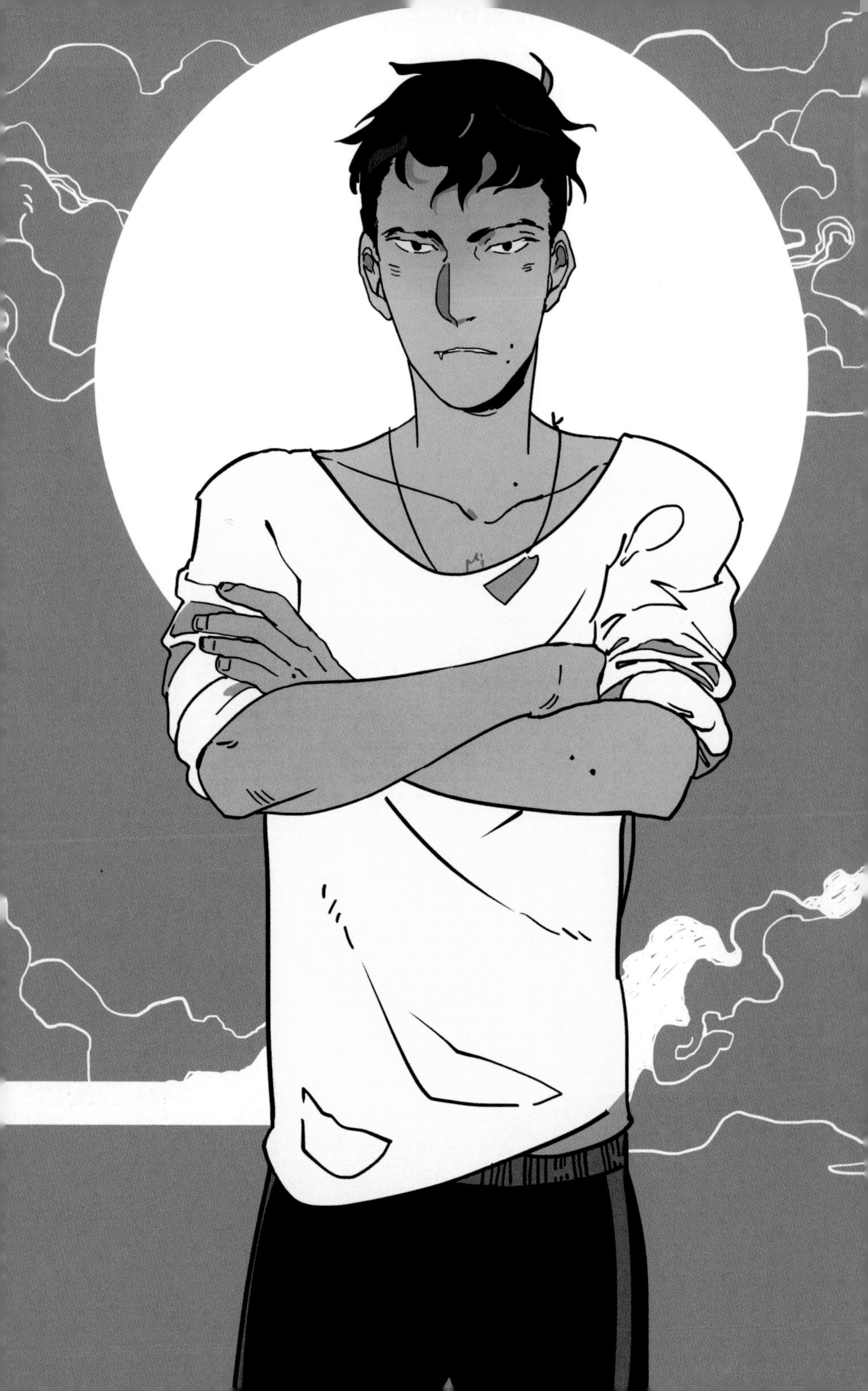

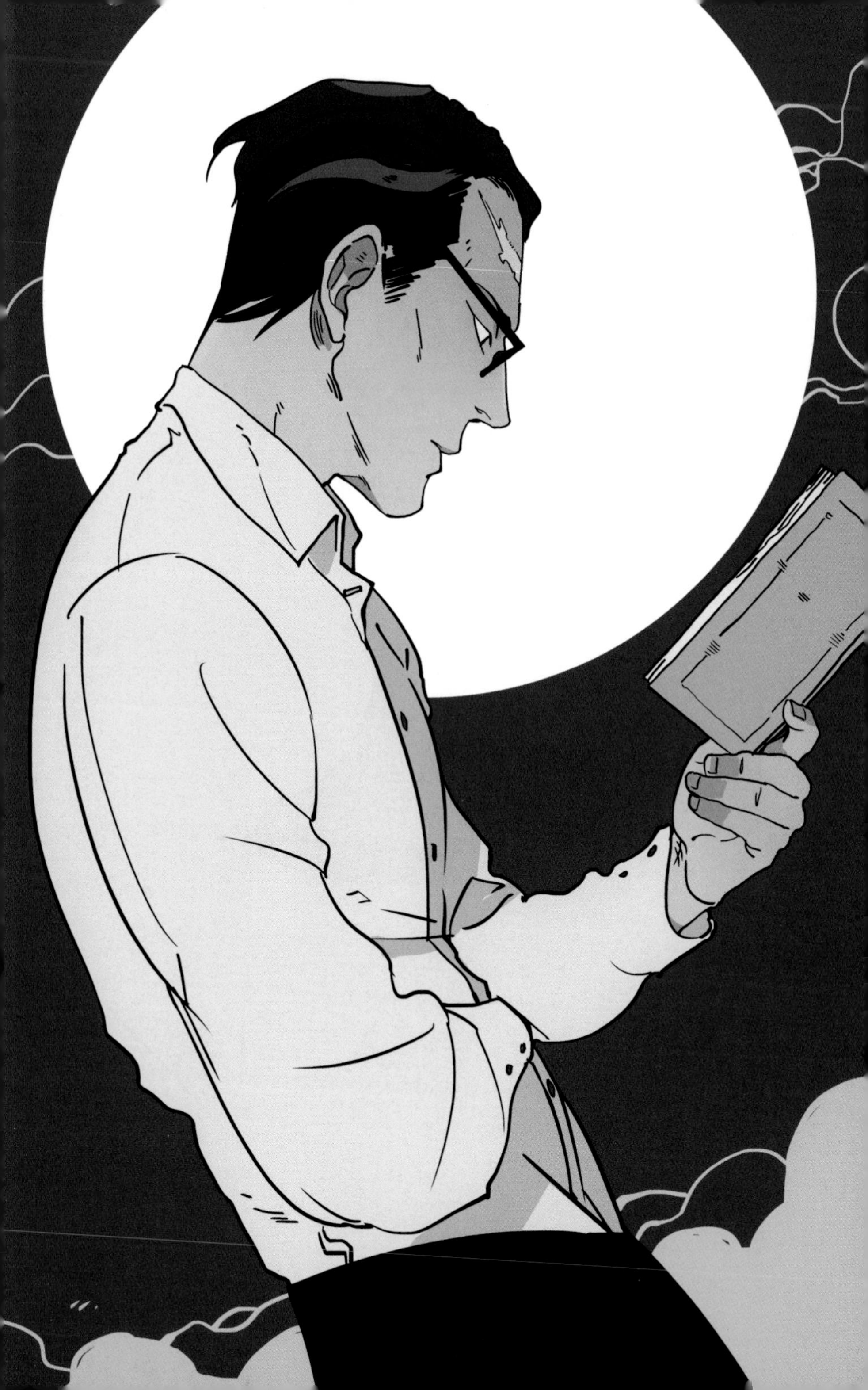

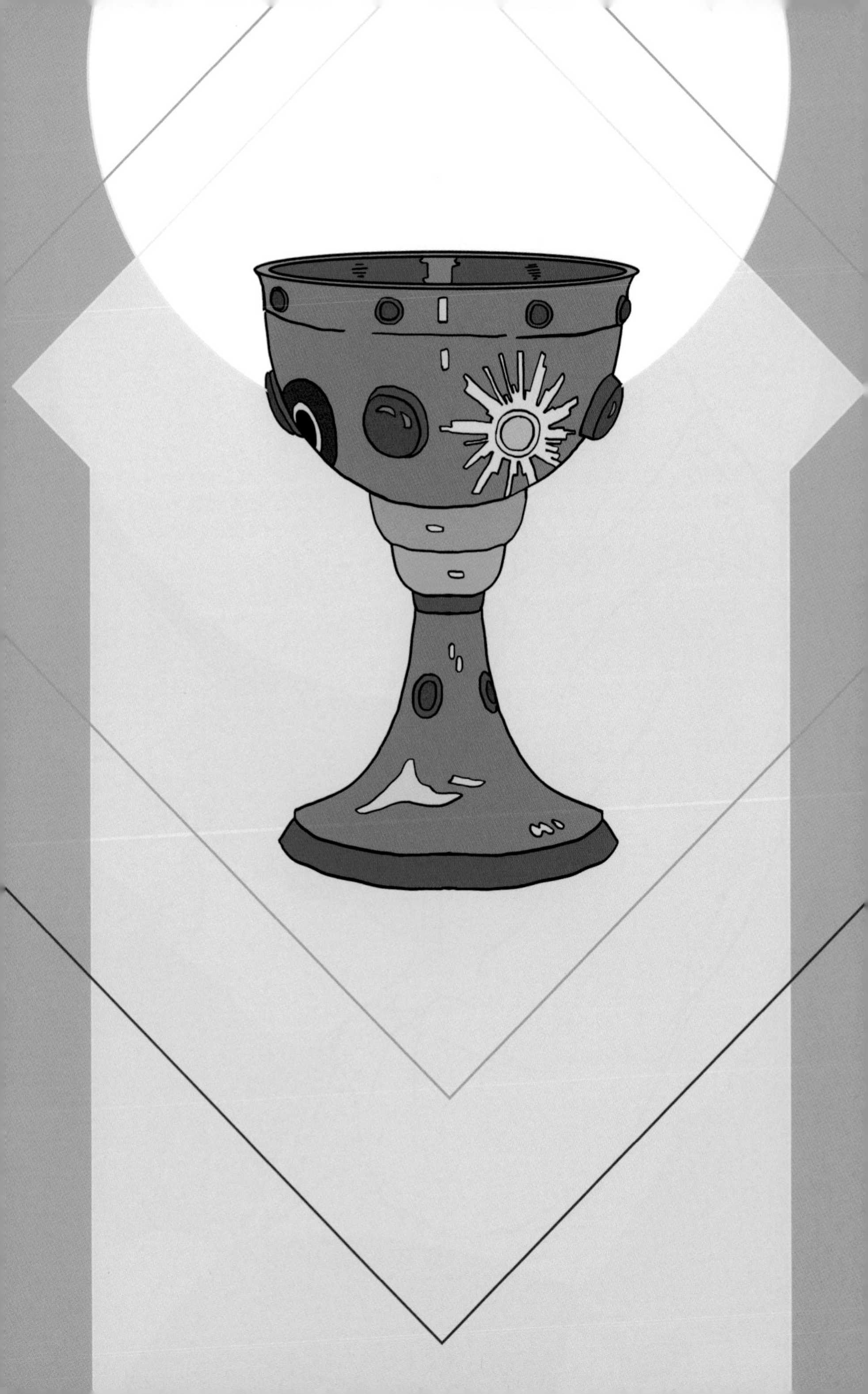

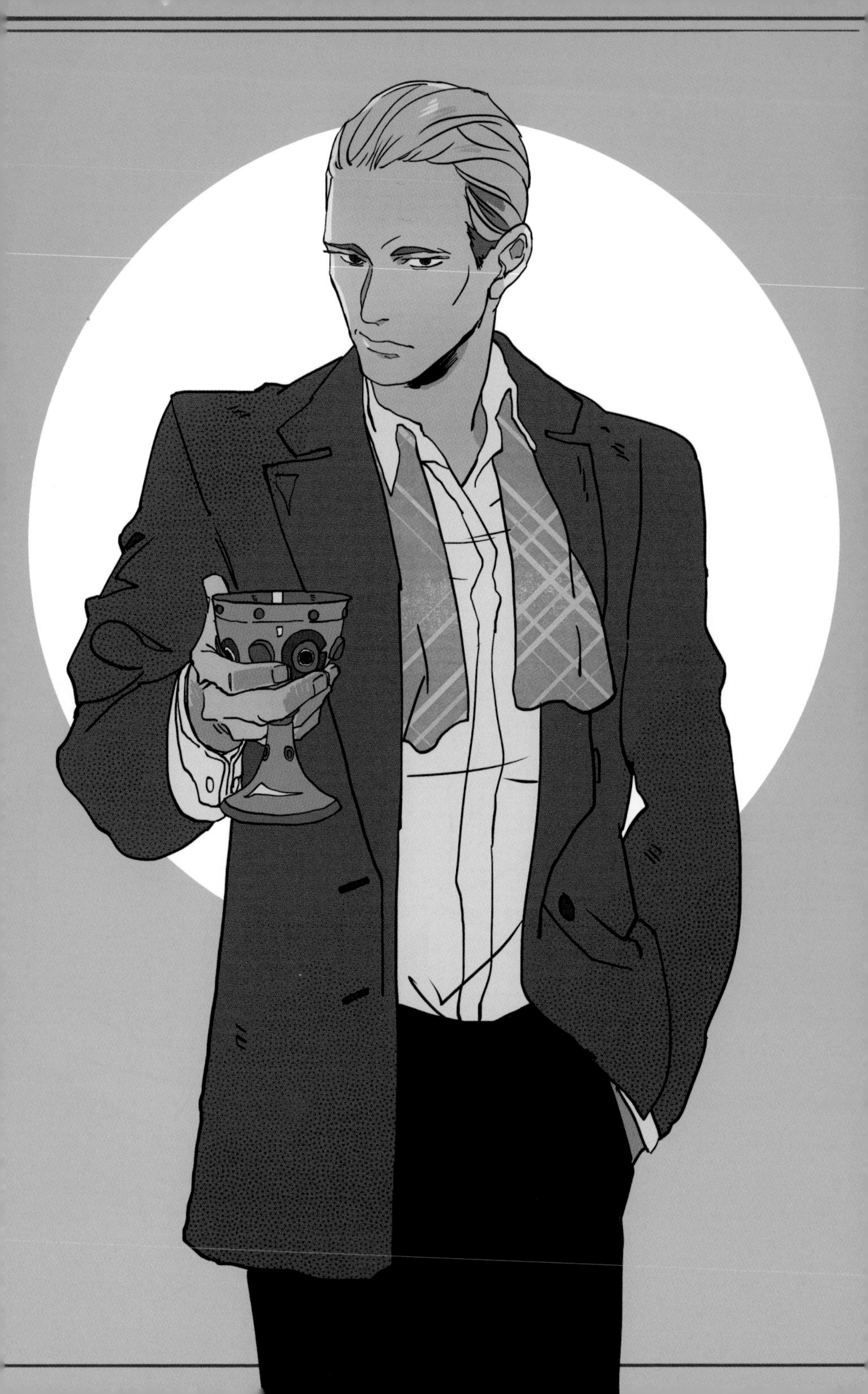

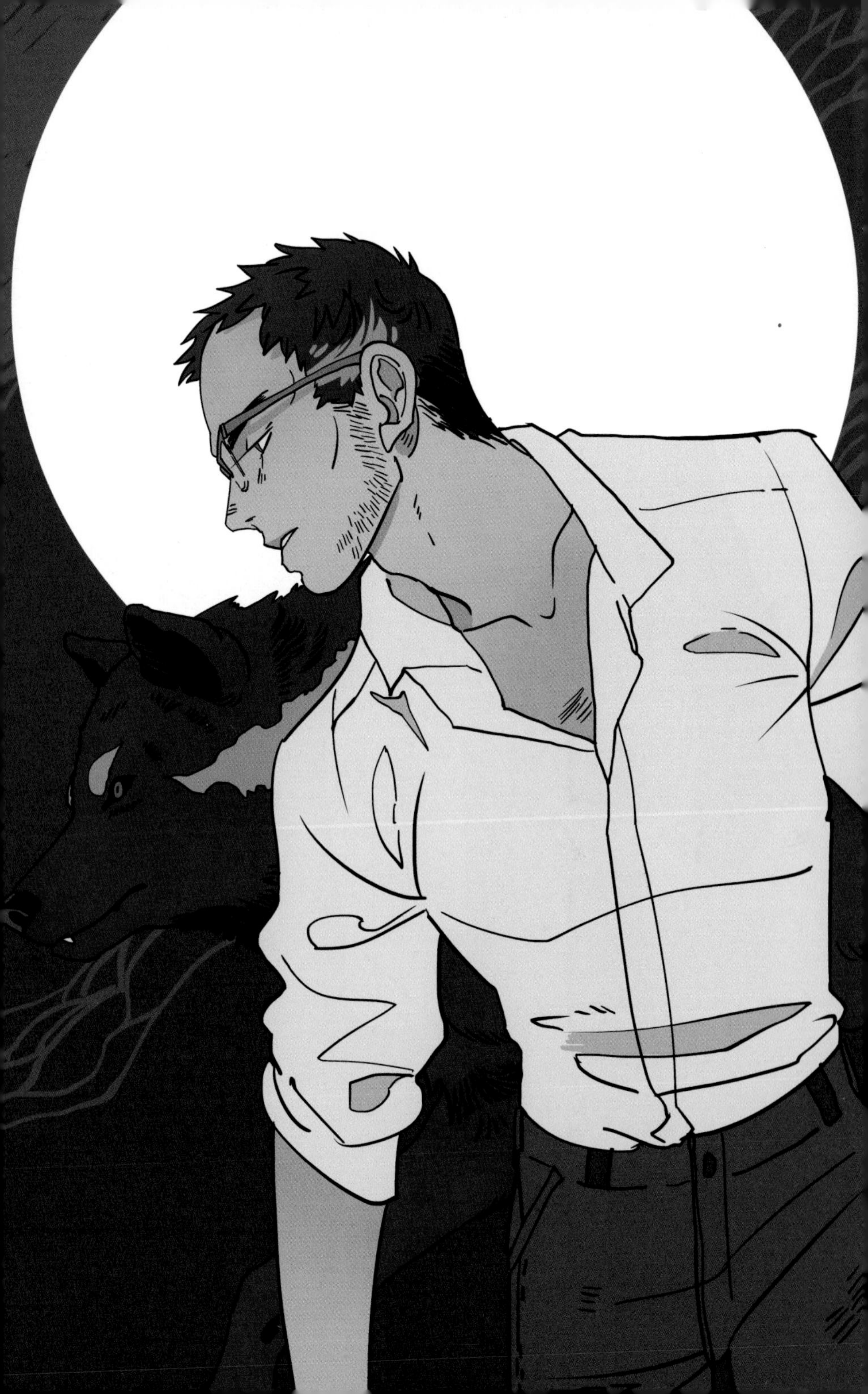

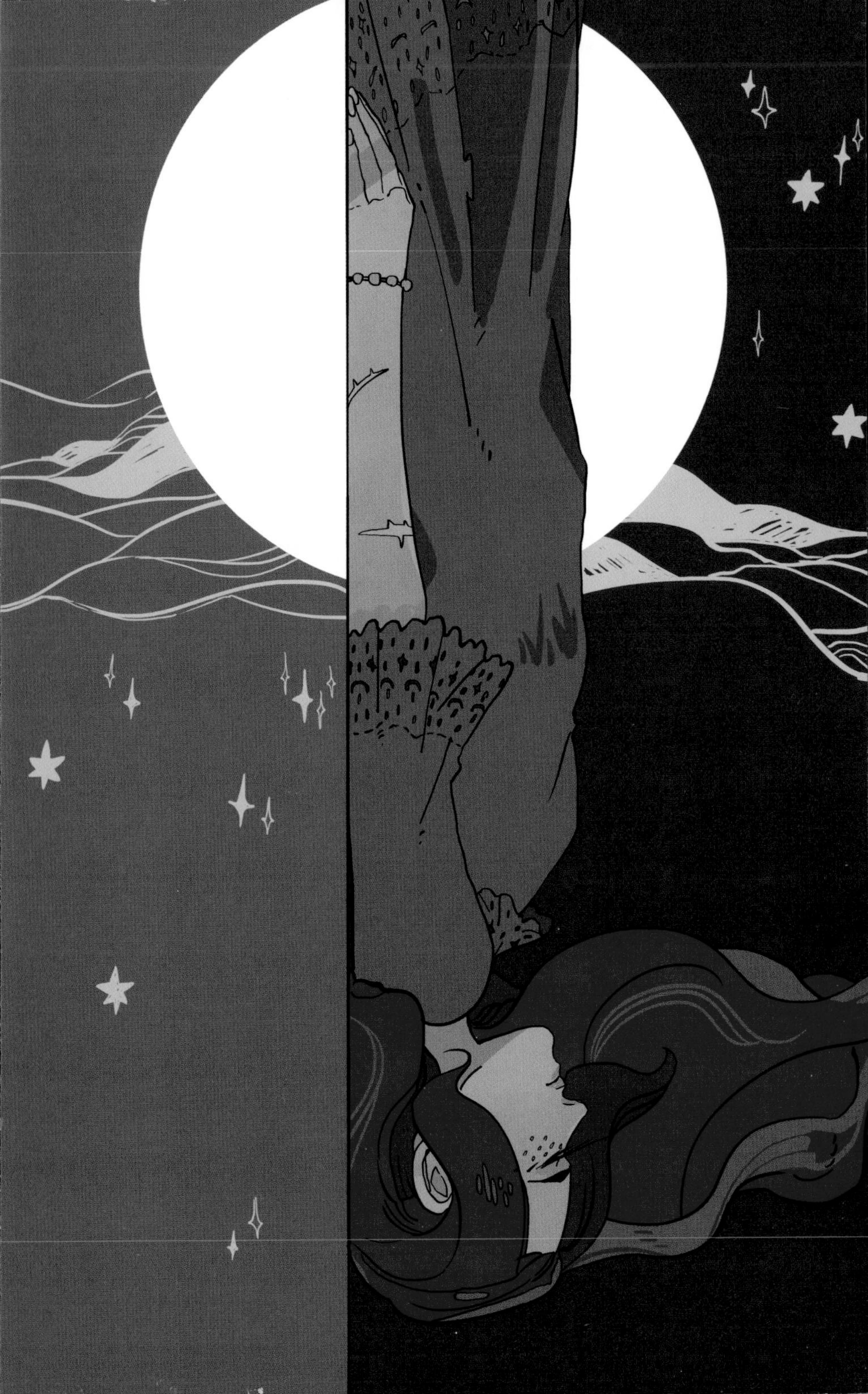

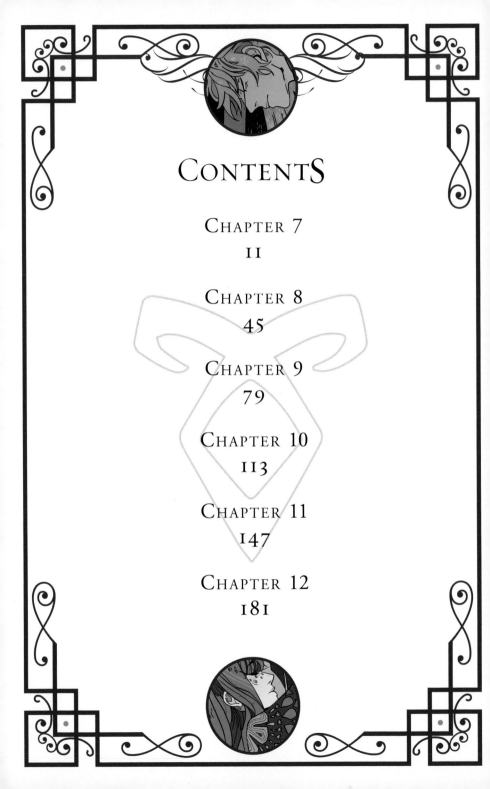

Contents

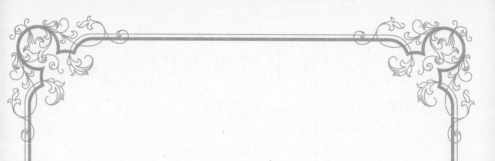

THE MORTAL INSTRUMENTS
THE GRAPHIC NOVEL

STORY BY
CASSANDRA CLARE ART BY
CASSANDRA JEAN

THE MORTAL INSTRUMENTS ②
THE GRAPHIC NOVEL

CASSANDRA CLARE
CASSANDRA JEAN

Art and Adaptation: Cassandra Jean
Lettering: JuYoun Lee

Yen Press
1290 Avenue of the Americas
New York, NY 10104

Visit us at yenpress.com
facebook.com/yenpress
twitter.com/yenpress
yenpress.tumblr.com
instagram.com/yenpress

First Yen Press Edition: October 2018

Yen Press is an imprint of Yen Press, LLC.
The Yen Press name and logo are trademarks of Yen Press, LLC.

The publisher is not responsible for websites (or their content) that are not owned by the publisher.

Library of Congress Control Number: 2017945496

ISBNs: 978-0-316-46582-3 (paperback)
978-1-9753-0288-7 (ebook)

10 9 8 7 6 5 4 3 2 1

WOR

Printed in the United States of America

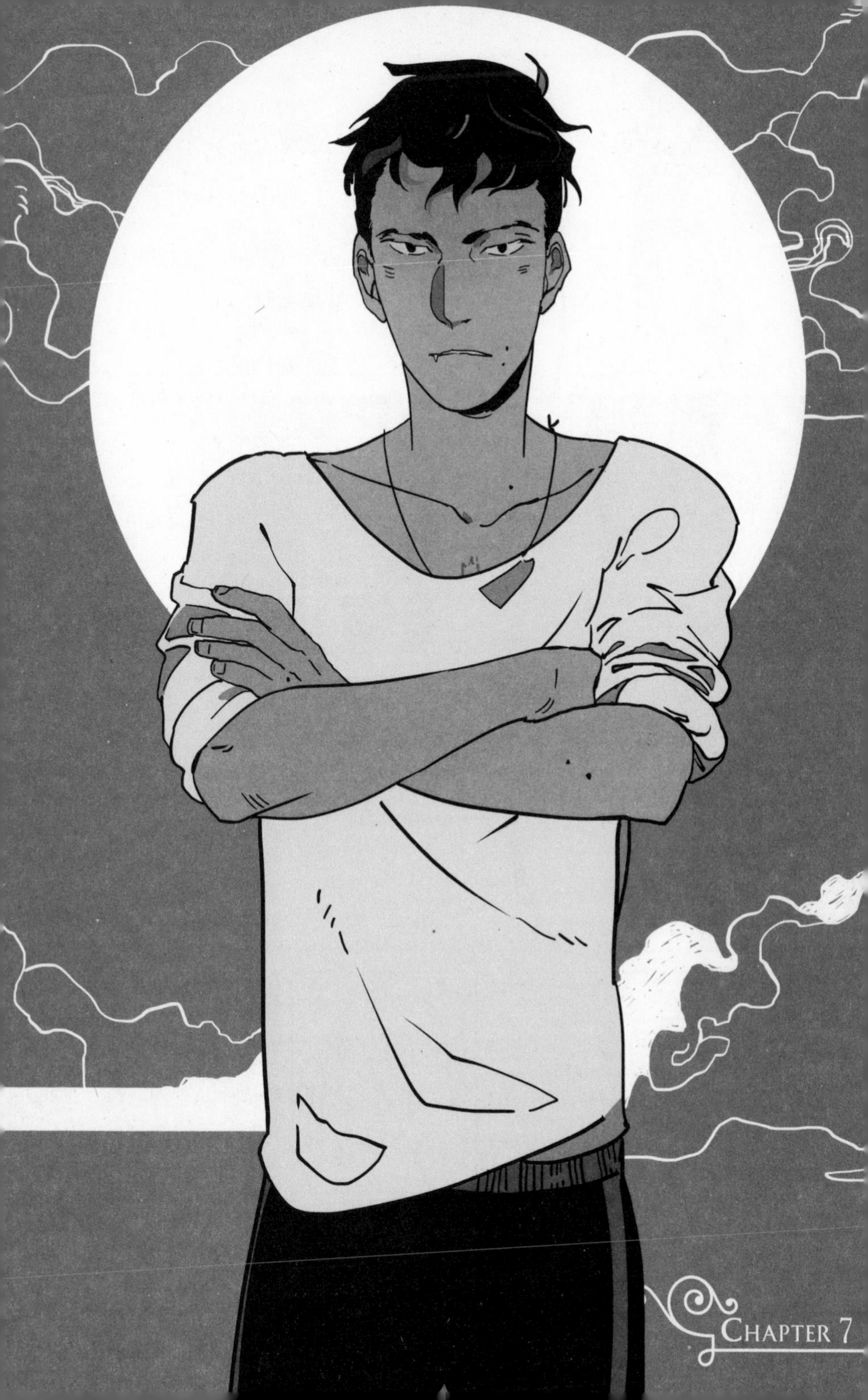

Chapter 7

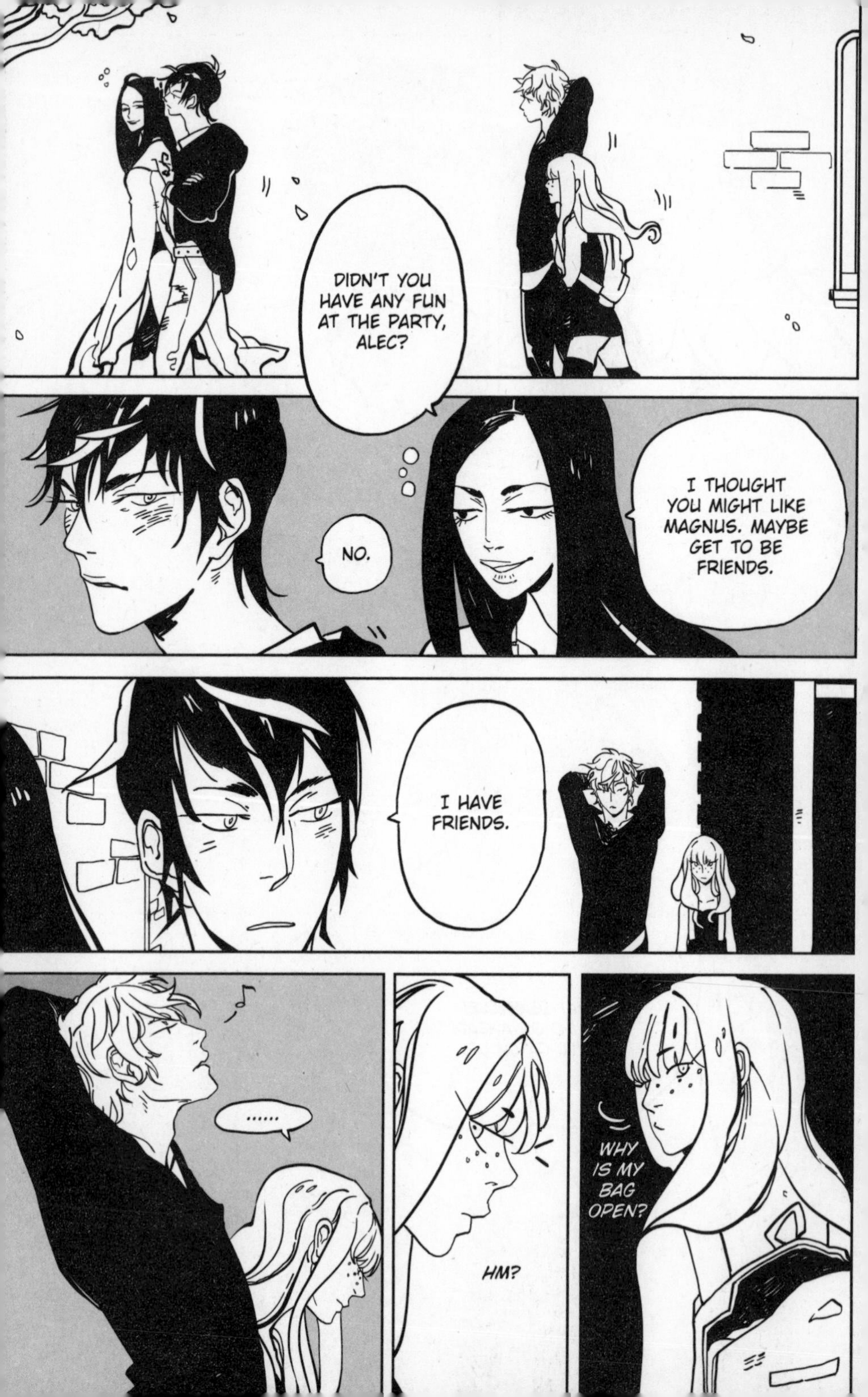
DIDN'T YOU HAVE ANY FUN AT THE PARTY, ALEC?
NO.
I THOUGHT YOU MIGHT LIKE MAGNUS. MAYBE GET TO BE FRIENDS.
I HAVE FRIENDS.
......
HM?
WHY IS MY BAG OPEN?

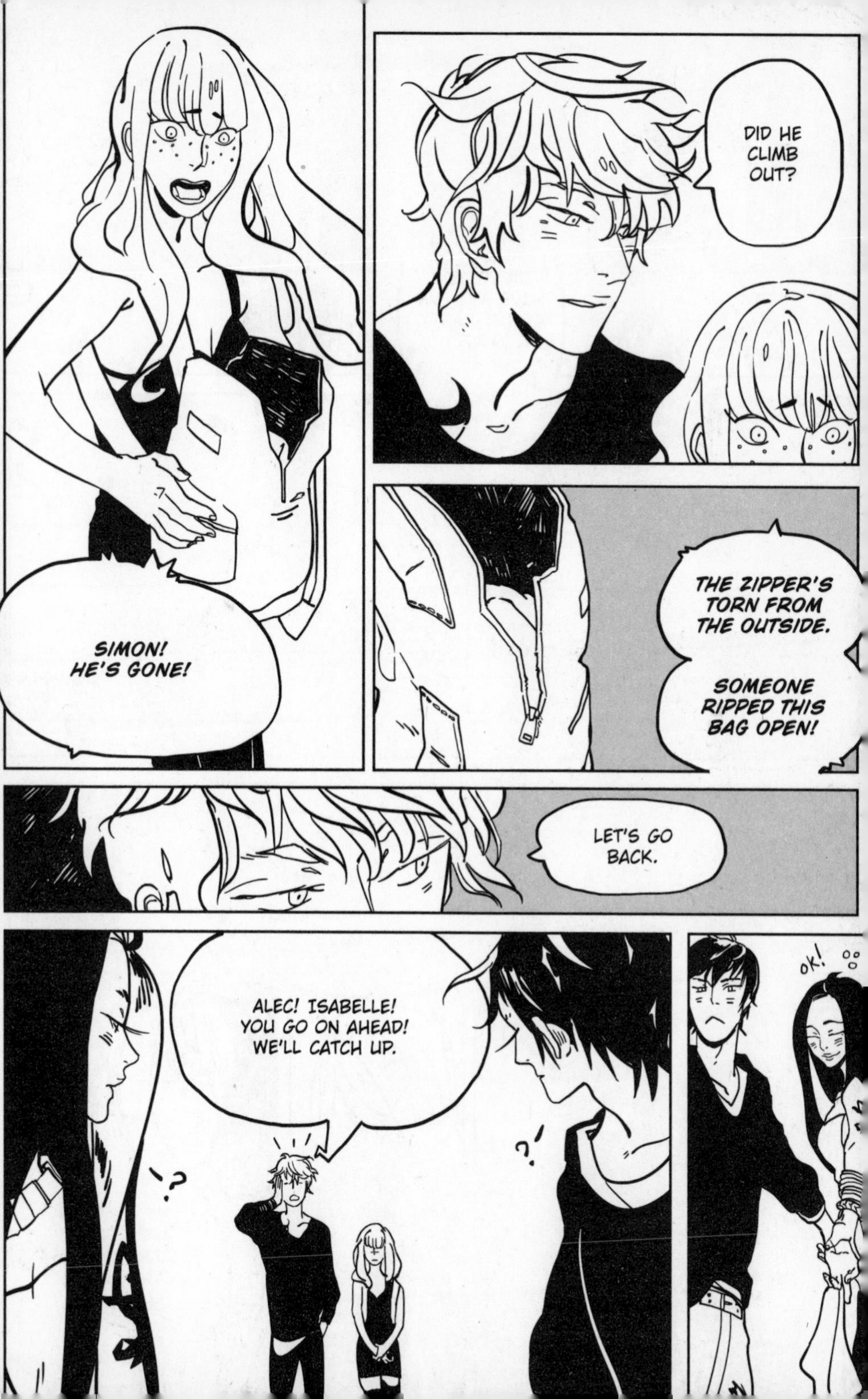
SIMON! HE'S GONE!
DID HE CLIMB OUT?
THE ZIPPER'S TORN FROM THE OUTSIDE.
SOMEONE RIPPED THIS BAG OPEN!
LET'S GO BACK.
ALEC! ISABELLE! YOU GO ON AHEAD! WE'LL CATCH UP.
OK!

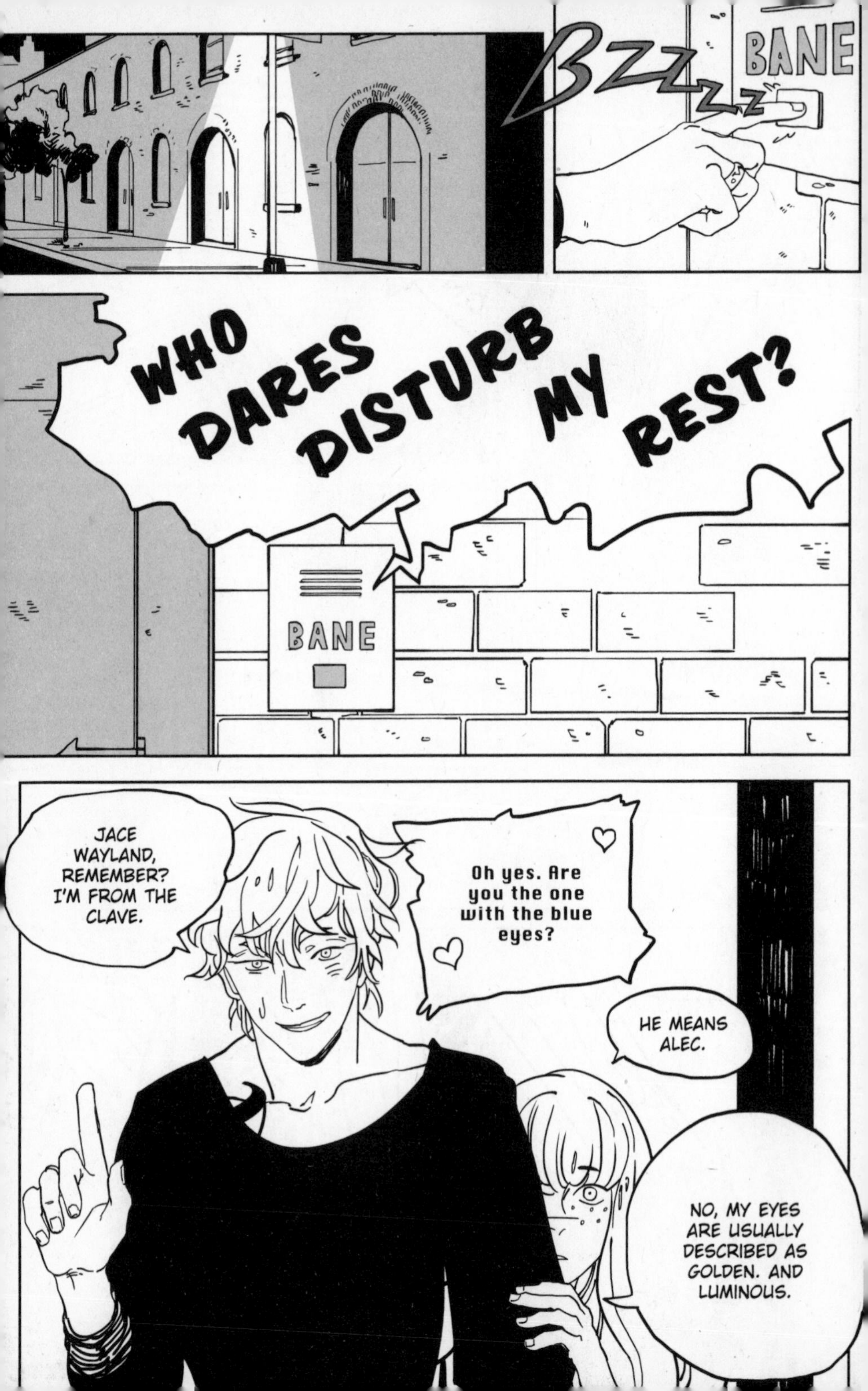
BZZZZ
BANE
WHO DARES DISTURB MY REST?
BANE
JACE WAYLAND, REMEMBER? I'M FROM THE CLAVE.
Oh yes. Are you the one with the blue eyes?
HE MEANS ALEC.
NO, MY EYES ARE USUALLY DESCRIBED AS GOLDEN. AND LUMINOUS.

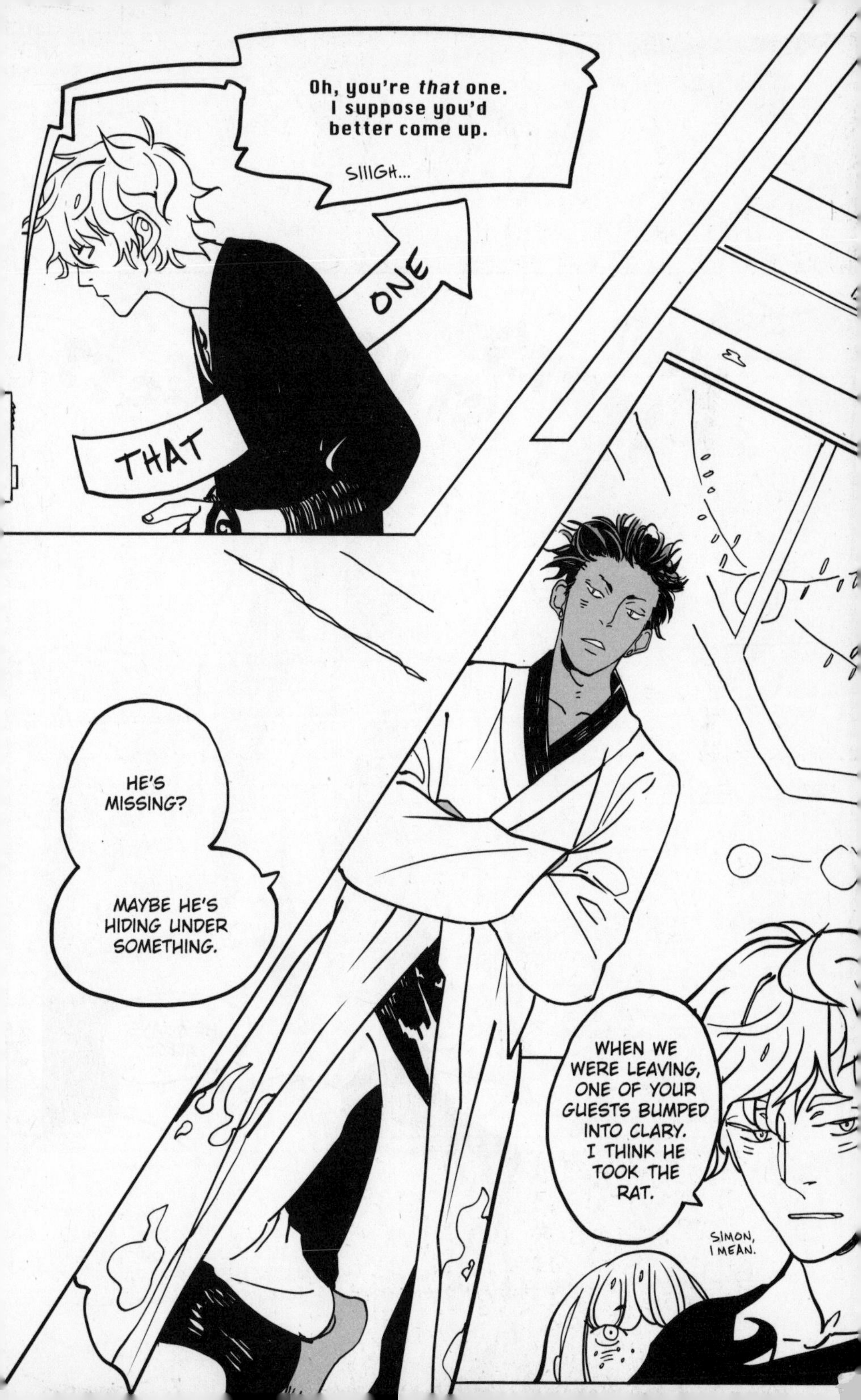
Oh, you're *that* one. I suppose you'd better come up.
SIIIGH...
THAT
ONE
HE'S MISSING?
MAYBE HE'S HIDING UNDER SOMETHING.
WHEN WE WERE LEAVING, ONE OF YOUR GUESTS BUMPED INTO CLARY. I THINK HE TOOK THE RAT.
SIMON, I MEAN.

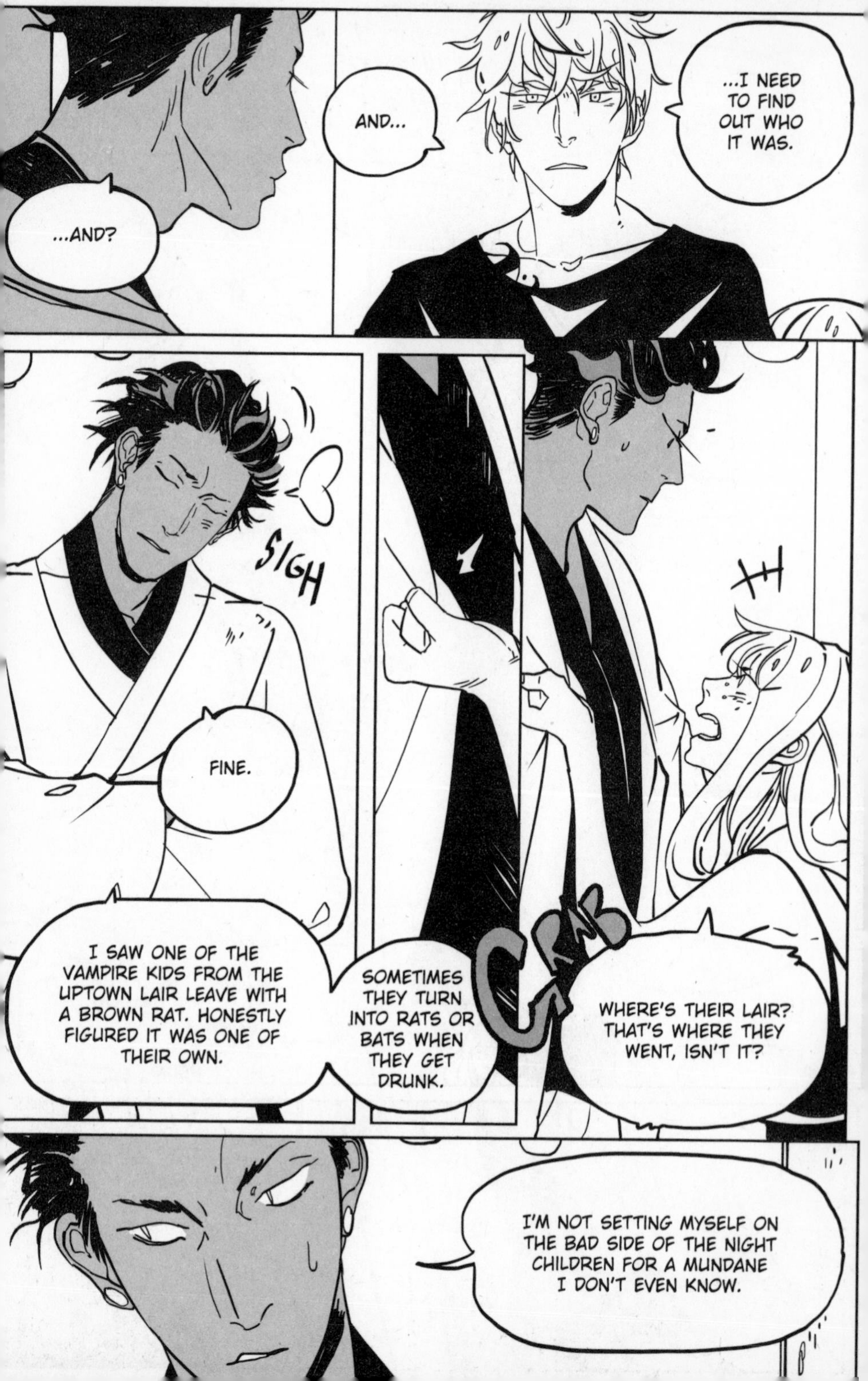
...AND?
AND...
...I NEED TO FIND OUT WHO IT WAS.
SIGH
FINE.
I SAW ONE OF THE VAMPIRE KIDS FROM THE UPTOWN LAIR LEAVE WITH A BROWN RAT. HONESTLY FIGURED IT WAS ONE OF THEIR OWN.
SOMETIMES THEY TURN INTO RATS OR BATS WHEN THEY GET DRUNK.
GRAB
WHERE'S THEIR LAIR? THAT'S WHERE THEY WENT, ISN'T IT?
I'M NOT SETTING MYSELF ON THE BAD SIDE OF THE NIGHT CHILDREN FOR A MUNDANE I DON'T EVEN KNOW.

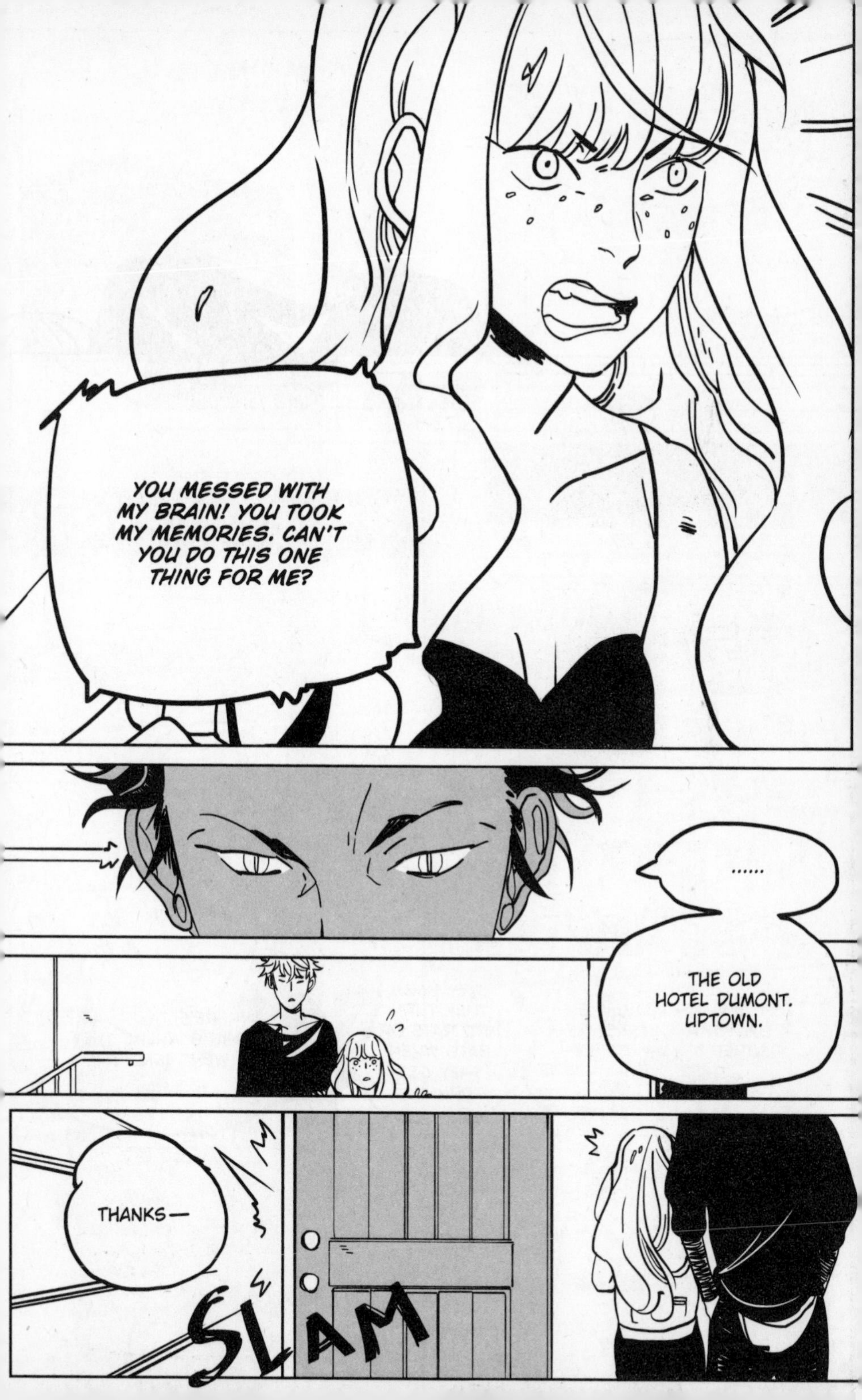
YOU MESSED WITH MY BRAIN! YOU TOOK MY MEMORIES. CAN'T YOU DO THIS ONE THING FOR ME?
......
THE OLD HOTEL DUMONT. UPTOWN.
THANKS—
SLAM

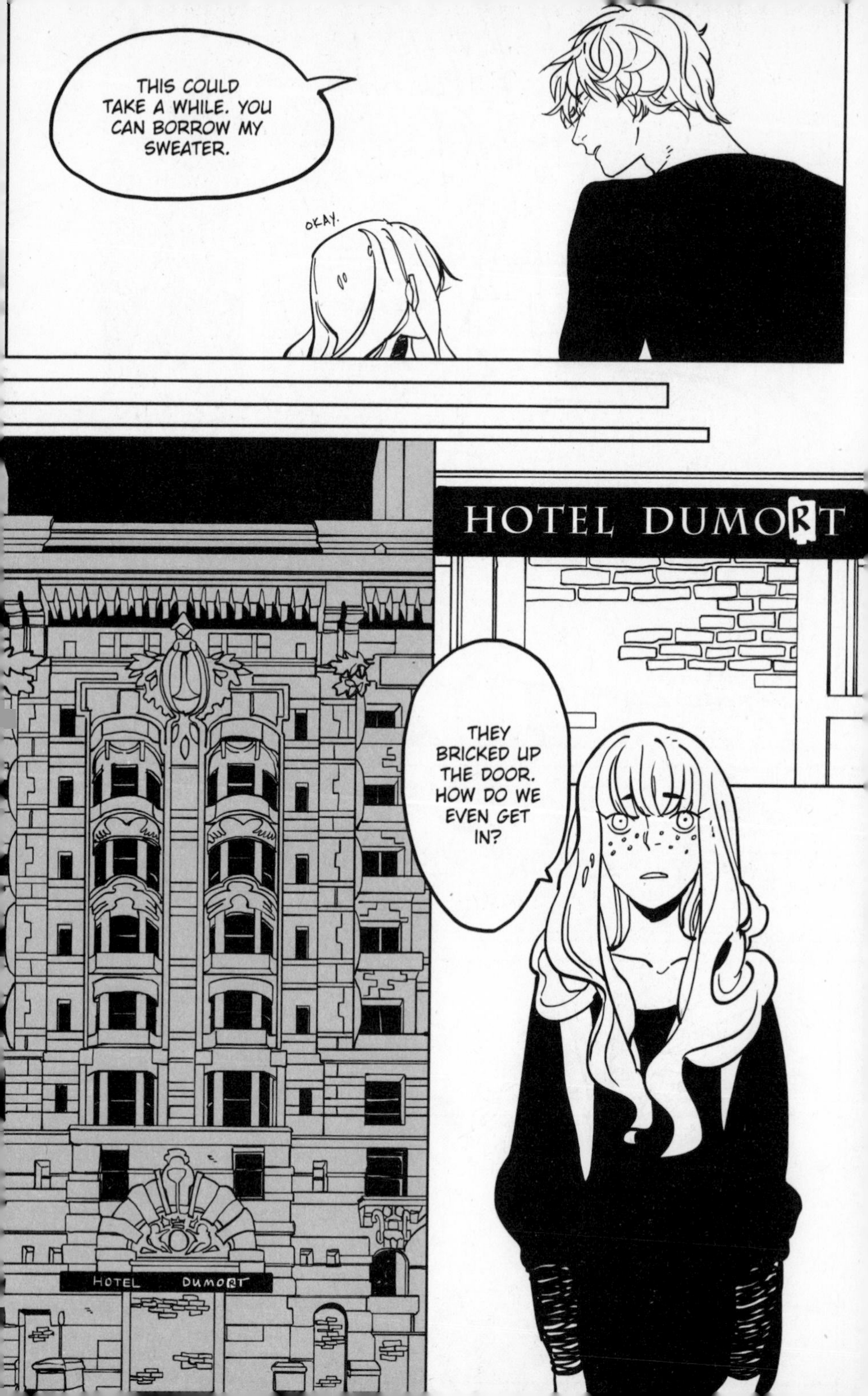
THIS COULD TAKE A WHILE. YOU CAN BORROW MY SWEATER.
OKAY.
HOTEL DUMORT
THEY BRICKED UP THE DOOR. HOW DO WE EVEN GET IN?
HOTEL DUMORT

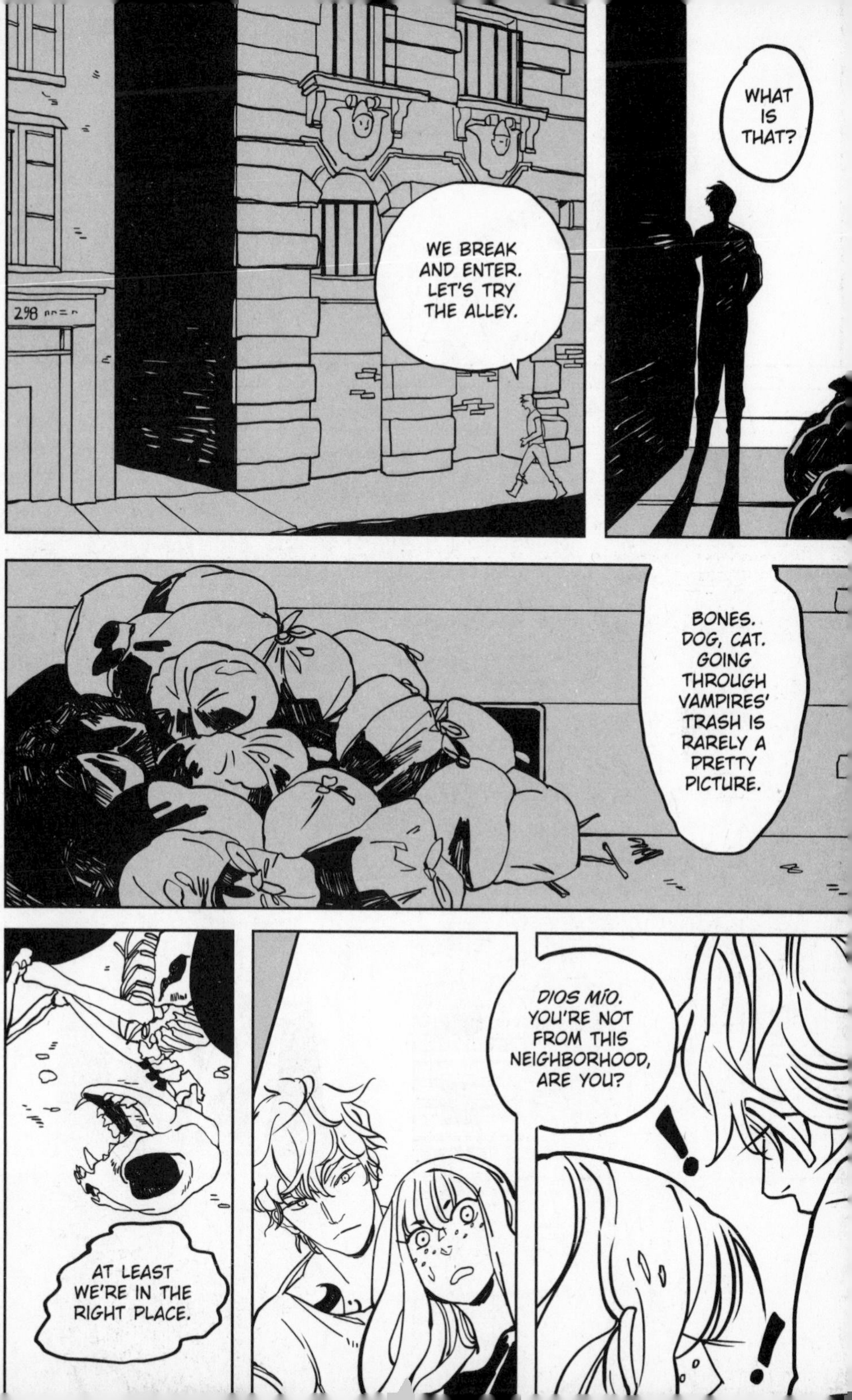
298
WE BREAK AND ENTER. LET'S TRY THE ALLEY.
WHAT IS THAT?
BONES. DOG, CAT. GOING THROUGH VAMPIRES' TRASH IS RARELY A PRETTY PICTURE.
AT LEAST WE'RE IN THE RIGHT PLACE.
DIOS MÍO. YOU'RE NOT FROM THIS NEIGHBORHOOD, ARE YOU?
!
!

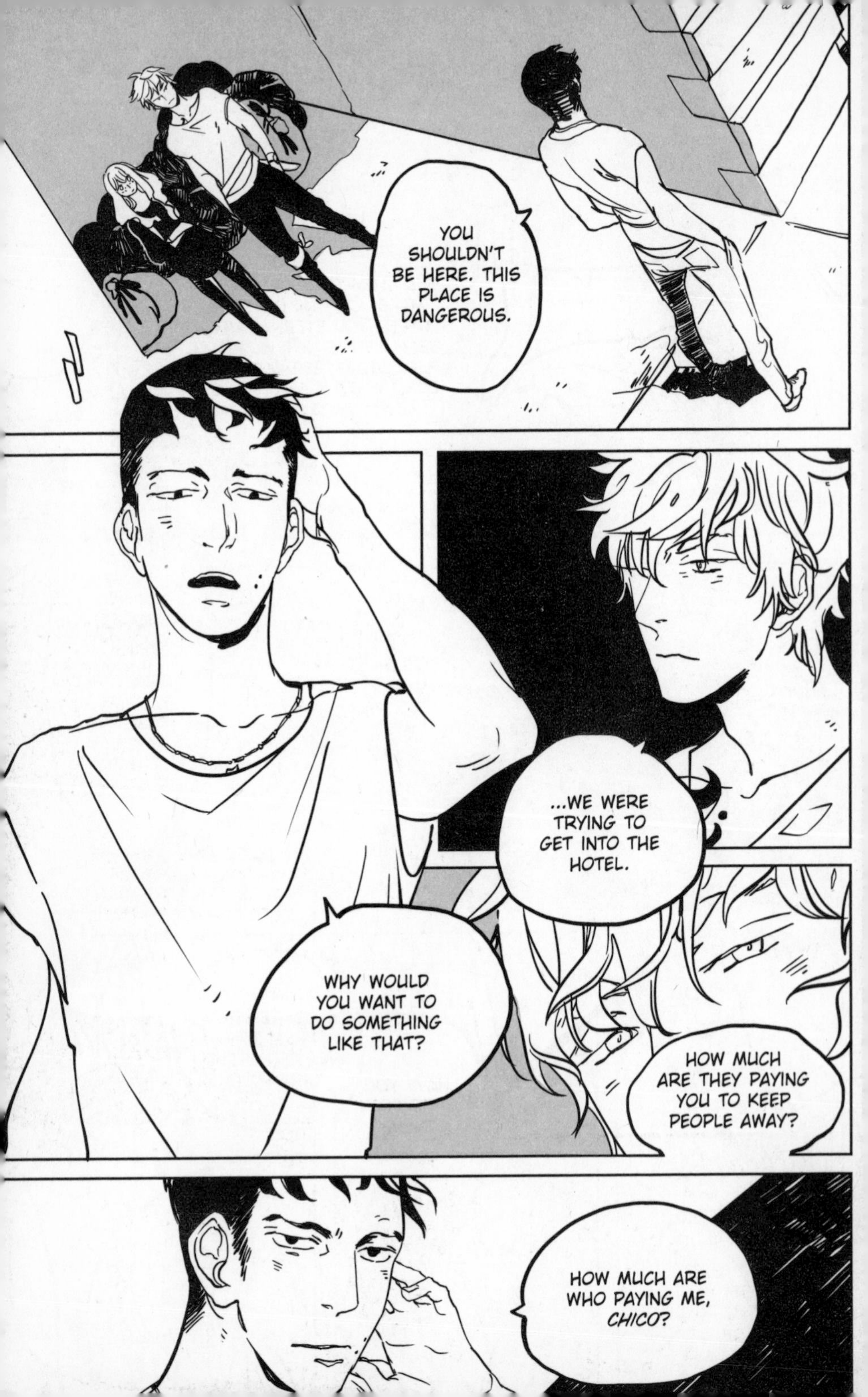
YOU SHOULDN'T BE HERE. THIS PLACE IS DANGEROUS.
...WE WERE TRYING TO GET INTO THE HOTEL.
WHY WOULD YOU WANT TO DO SOMETHING LIKE THAT?
HOW MUCH ARE THEY PAYING YOU TO KEEP PEOPLE AWAY?
HOW MUCH ARE WHO PAYING ME, *CHICO*?

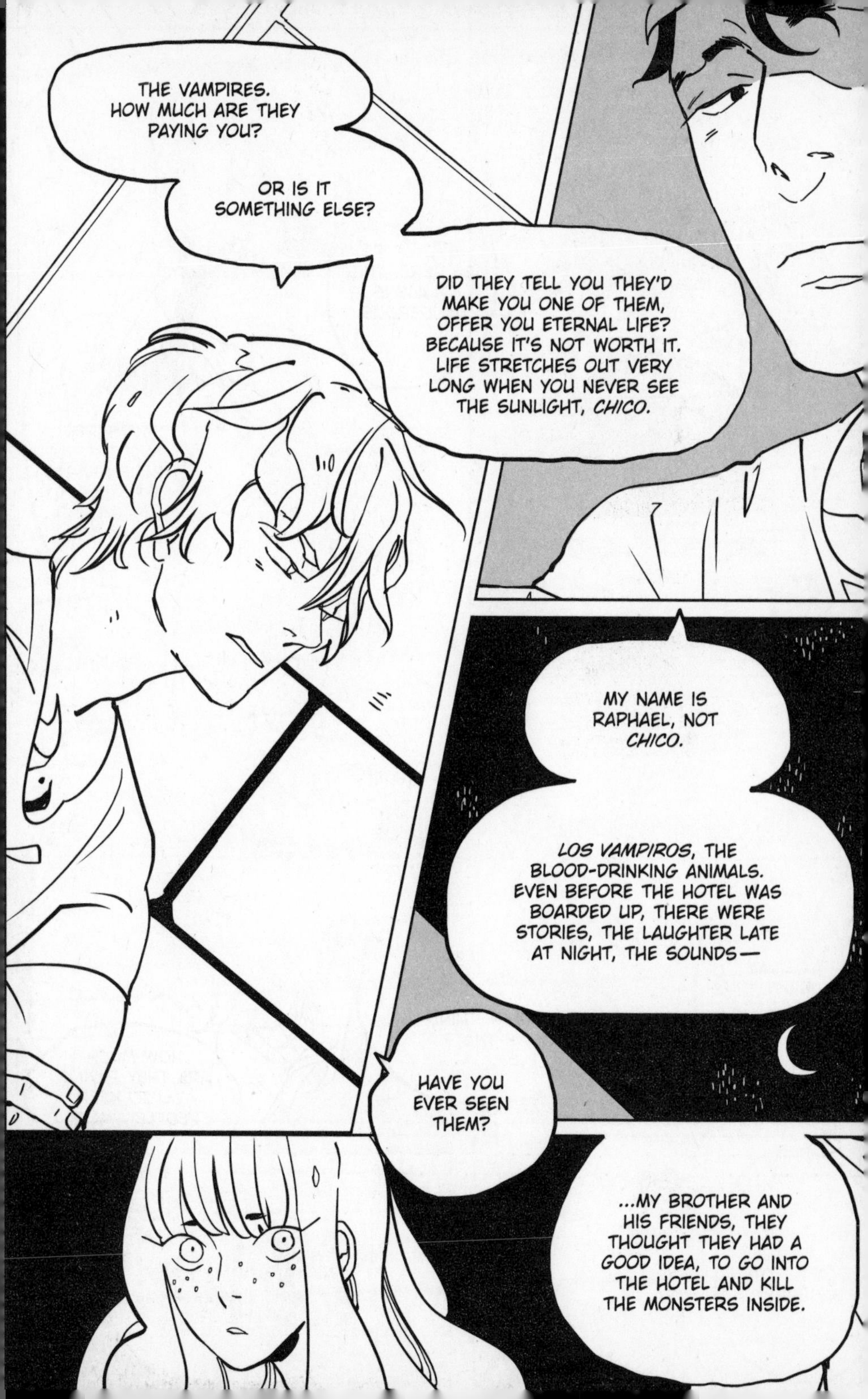
THE VAMPIRES. HOW MUCH ARE THEY PAYING YOU?
OR IS IT SOMETHING ELSE?
DID THEY TELL YOU THEY'D MAKE YOU ONE OF THEM, OFFER YOU ETERNAL LIFE? BECAUSE IT'S NOT WORTH IT. LIFE STRETCHES OUT VERY LONG WHEN YOU NEVER SEE THE SUNLIGHT, *CHICO.*
MY NAME IS RAPHAEL, NOT *CHICO.*
LOS VAMPIROS, THE BLOOD-DRINKING ANIMALS. EVEN BEFORE THE HOTEL WAS BOARDED UP, THERE WERE STORIES, THE LAUGHTER LATE AT NIGHT, THE SOUNDS—
HAVE YOU EVER SEEN THEM?
...MY BROTHER AND HIS FRIENDS, THEY THOUGHT THEY HAD A GOOD IDEA, TO GO INTO THE HOTEL AND KILL THE MONSTERS INSIDE.

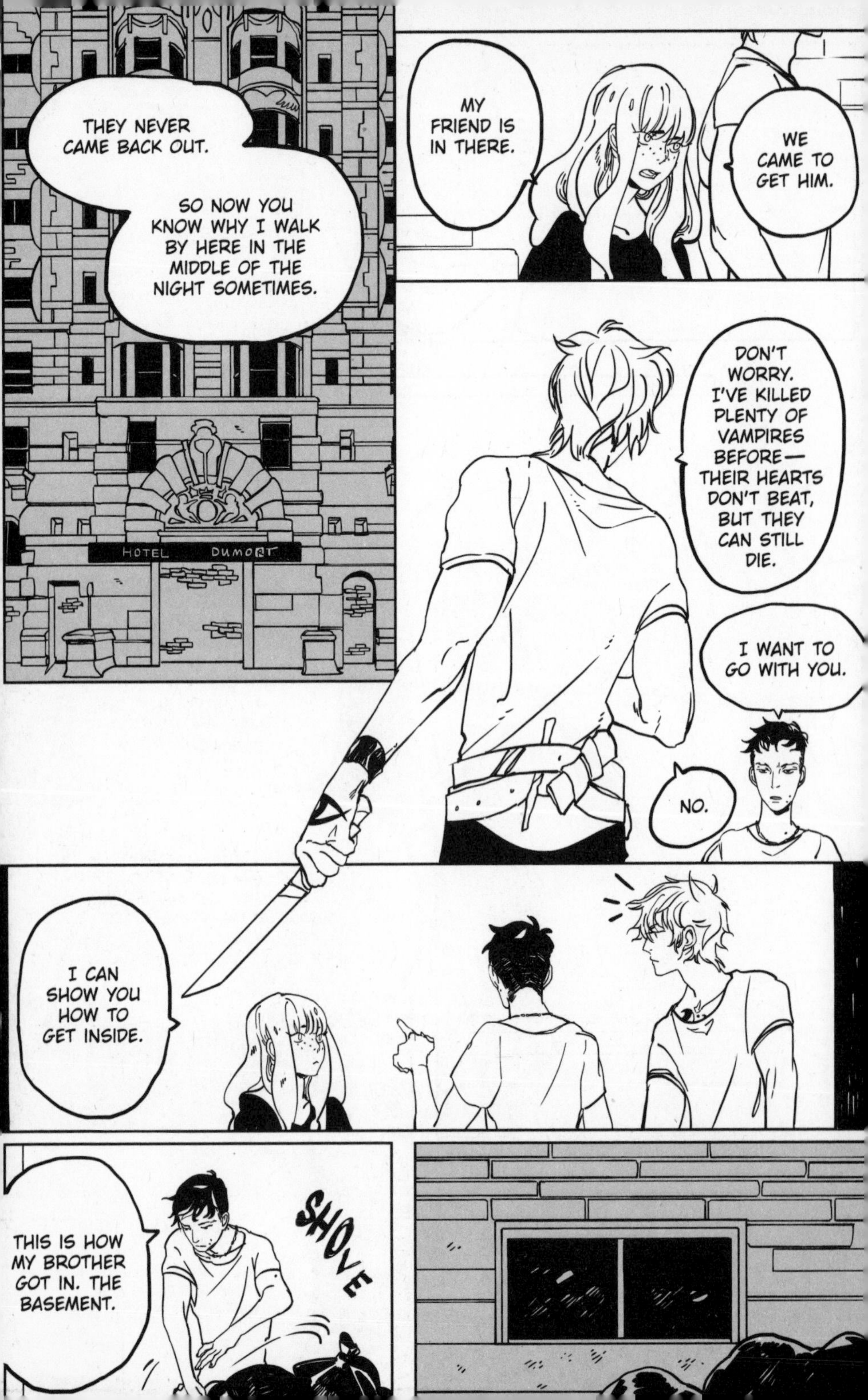
THEY NEVER CAME BACK OUT.
SO NOW YOU KNOW WHY I WALK BY HERE IN THE MIDDLE OF THE NIGHT SOMETIMES.
HOTEL DUMORT
MY FRIEND IS IN THERE.
WE CAME TO GET HIM.
DON'T WORRY. I'VE KILLED PLENTY OF VAMPIRES BEFORE—THEIR HEARTS DON'T BEAT, BUT THEY CAN STILL DIE.
I WANT TO GO WITH YOU.
NO.
I CAN SHOW YOU HOW TO GET INSIDE.
THIS IS HOW MY BROTHER GOT IN. THE BASEMENT.
SHOVE

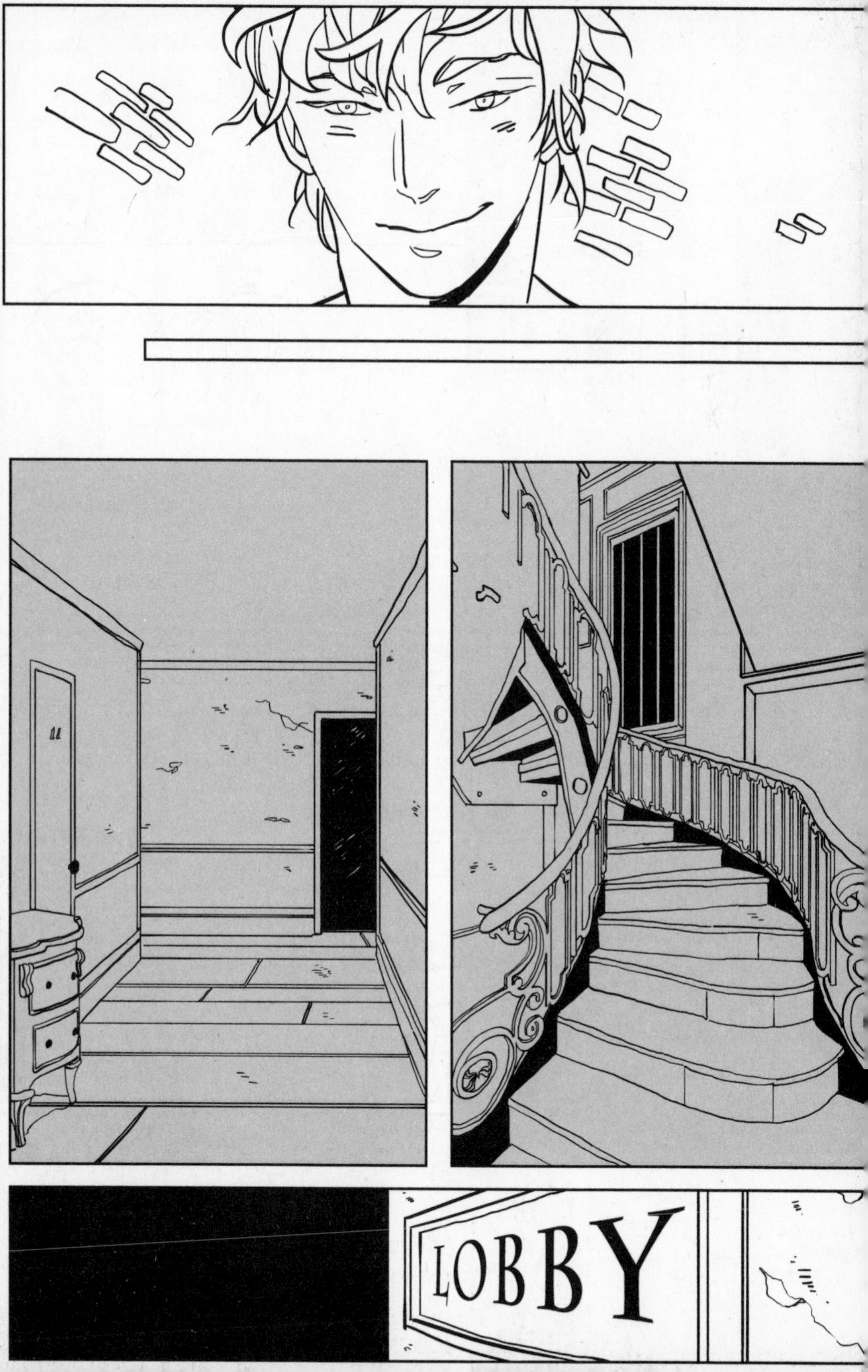
LOBBY

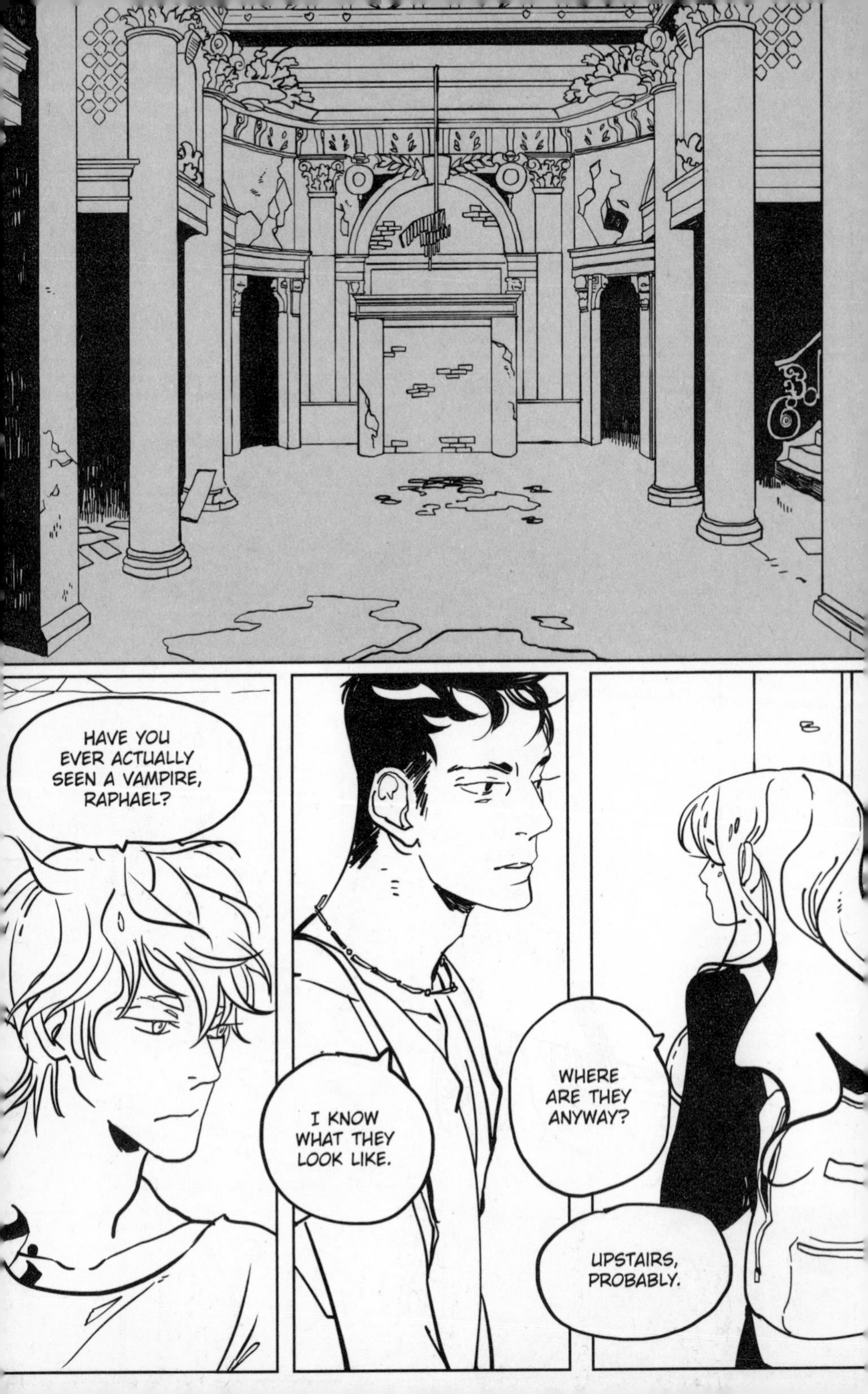
HAVE YOU EVER ACTUALLY SEEN A VAMPIRE, RAPHAEL?
I KNOW WHAT THEY LOOK LIKE.
WHERE ARE THEY ANYWAY?
UPSTAIRS, PROBABLY.

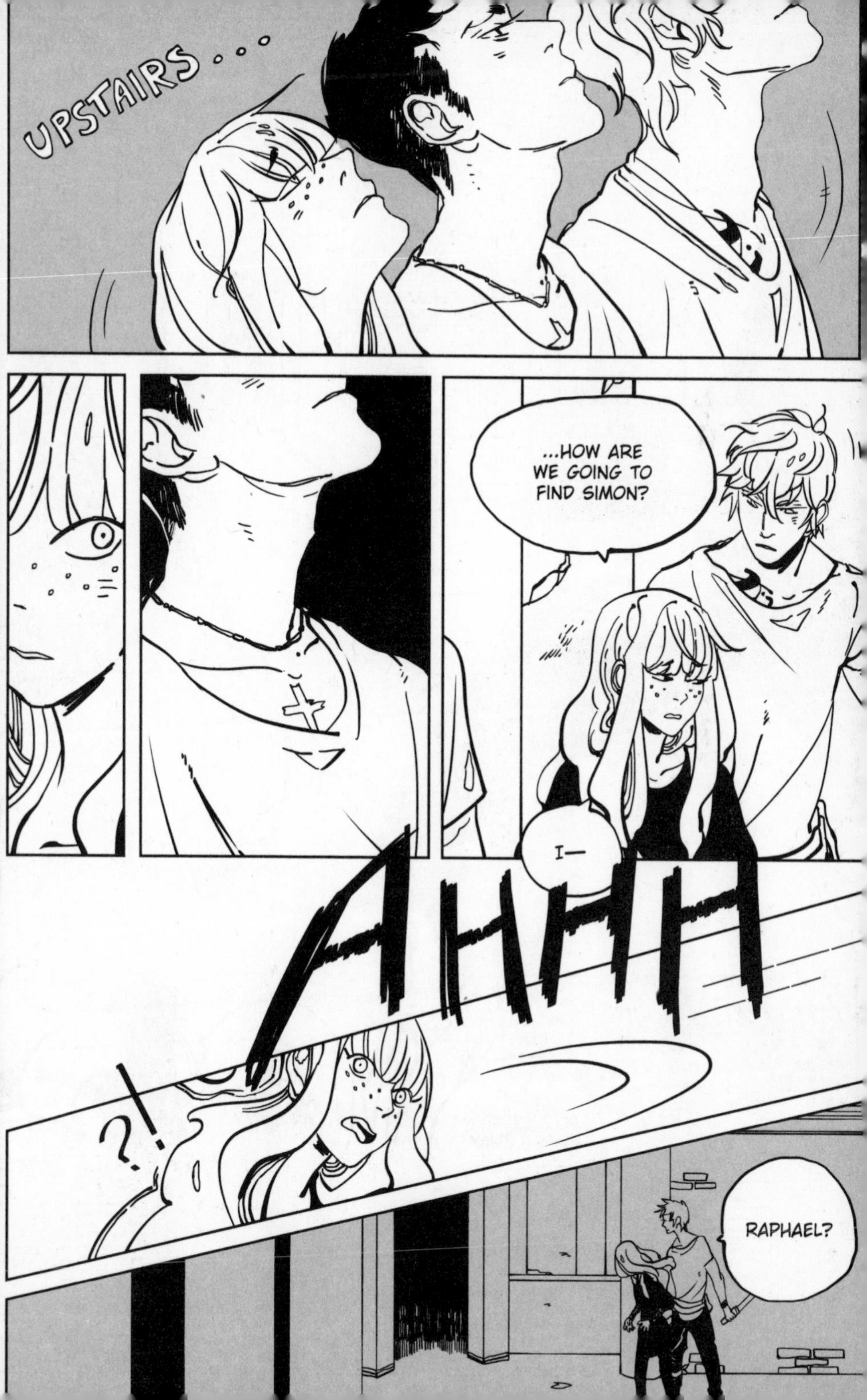
UPSTAIRS...
...HOW ARE WE GOING TO FIND SIMON?
I—
AHHH
?!
RAPHAEL?

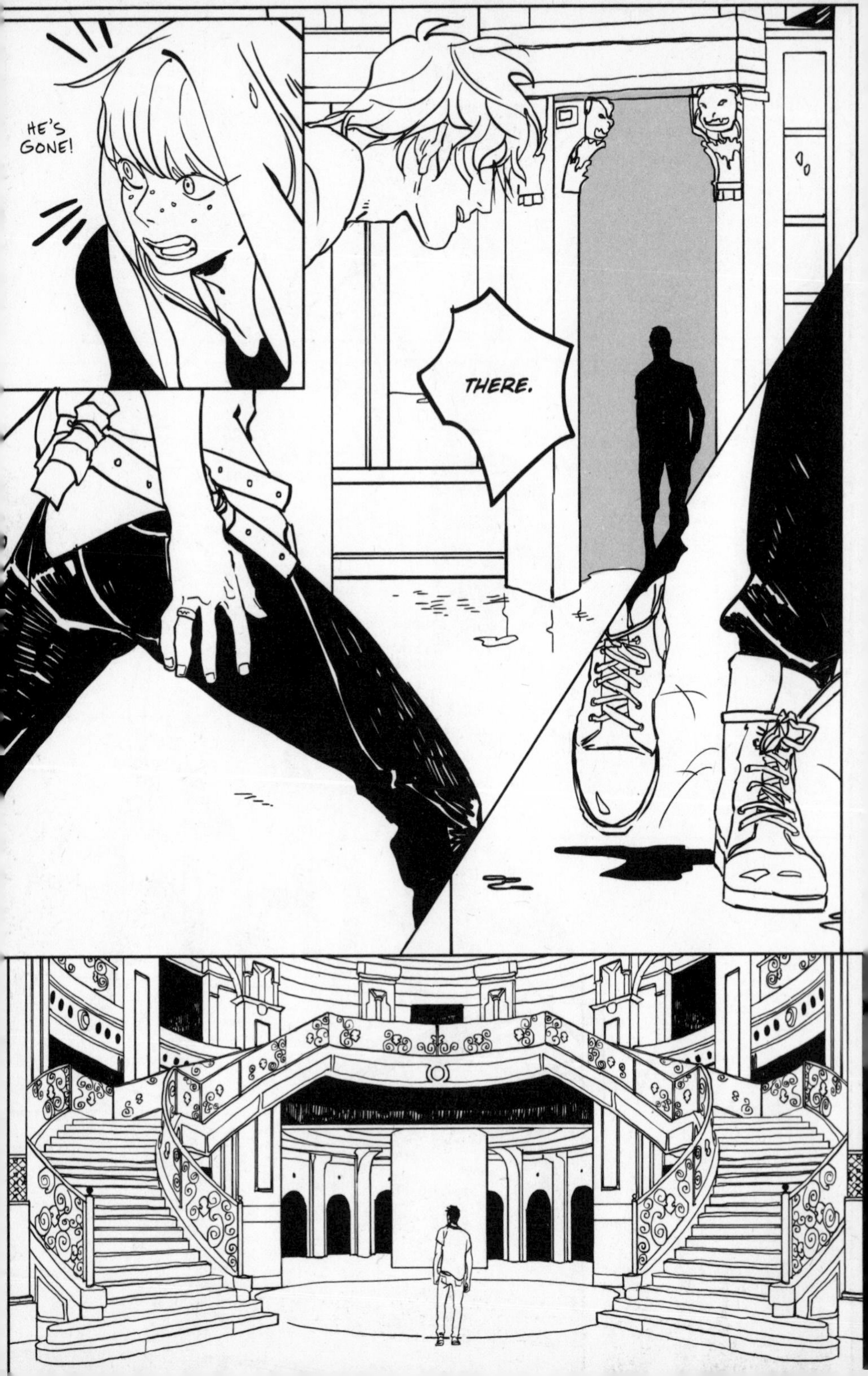
HE'S GONE!
THERE.

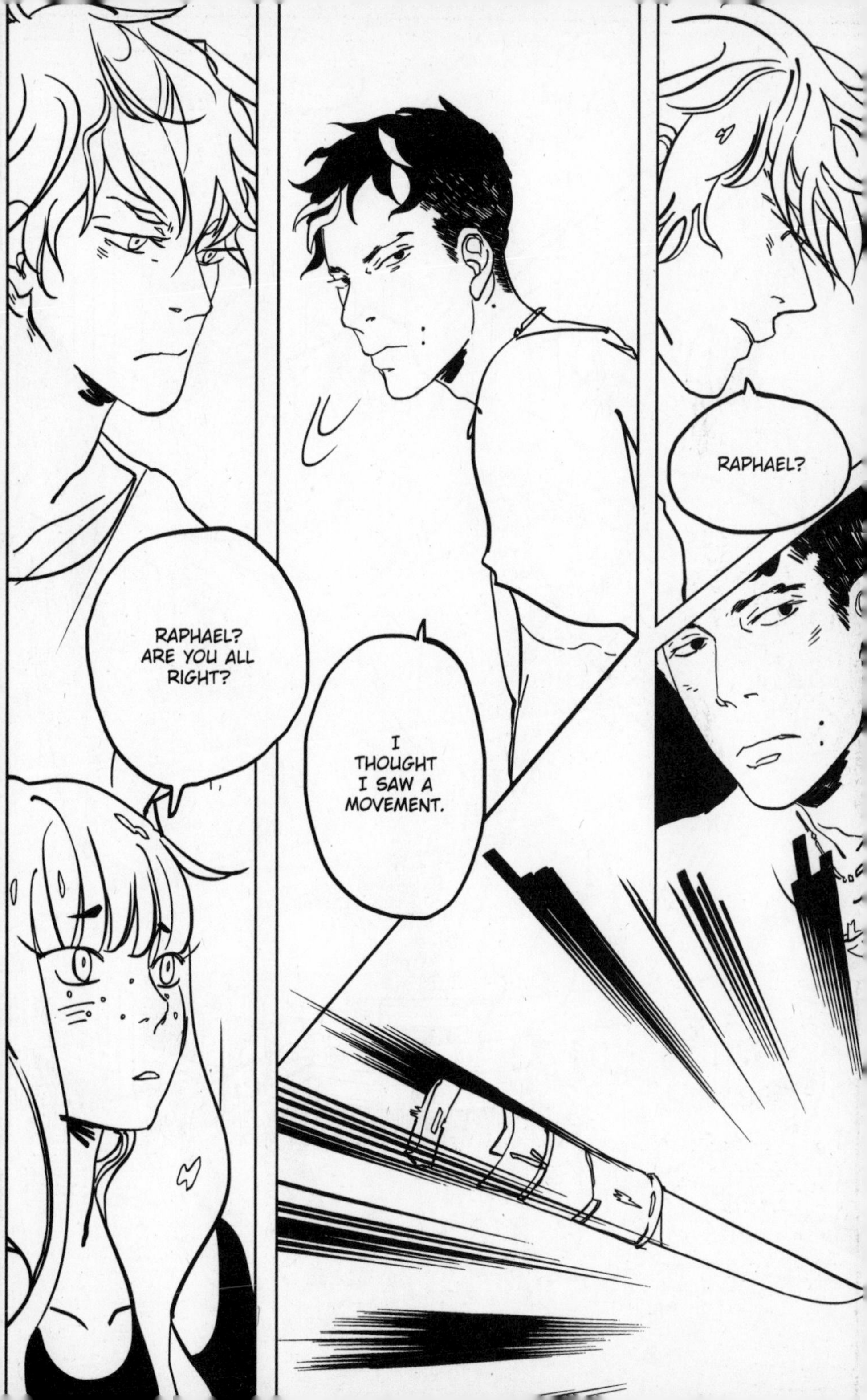
RAPHAEL? ARE YOU ALL RIGHT?
I THOUGHT I SAW A MOVEMENT.
RAPHAEL?

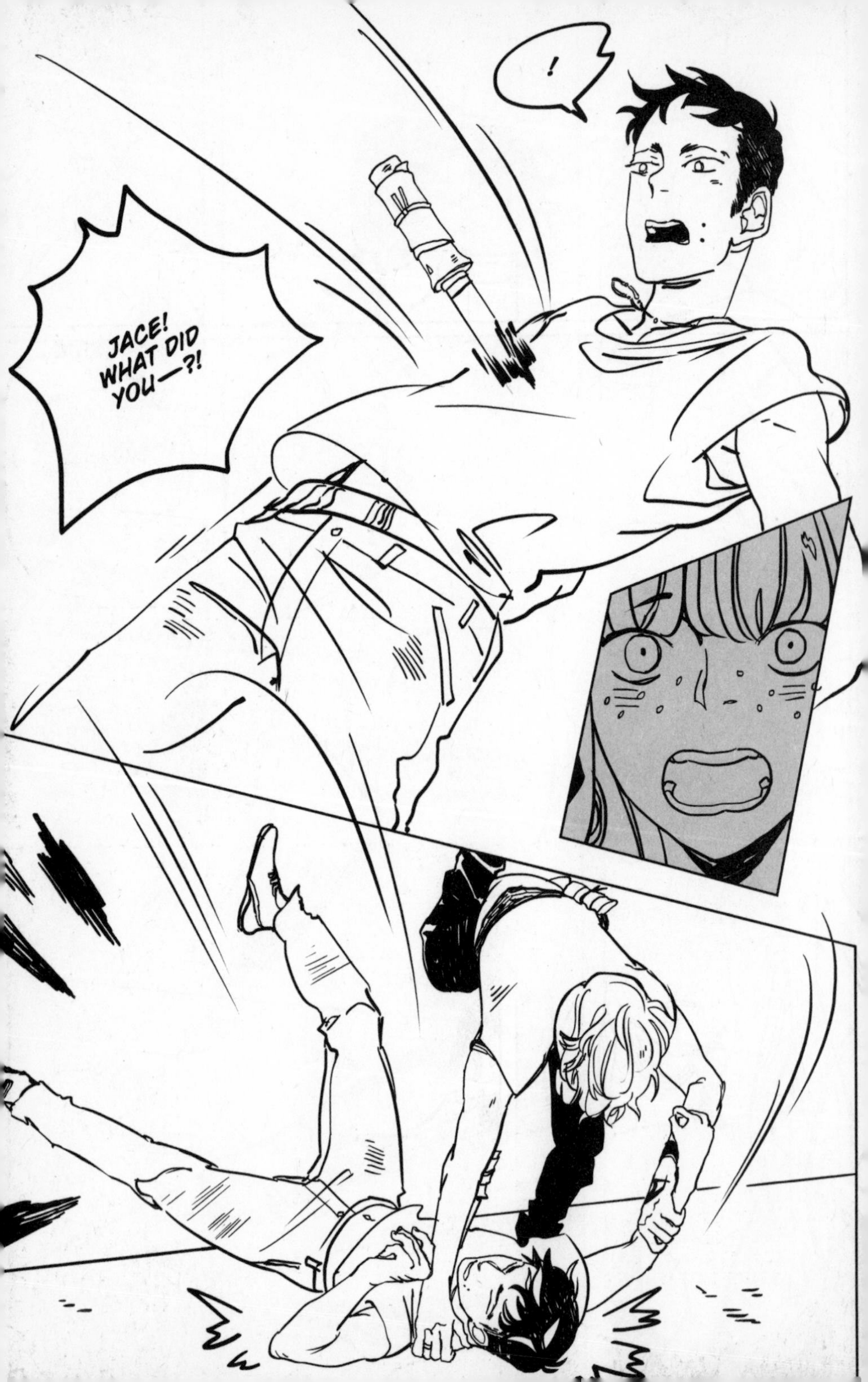
!
JACE! WHAT DID YOU—?!

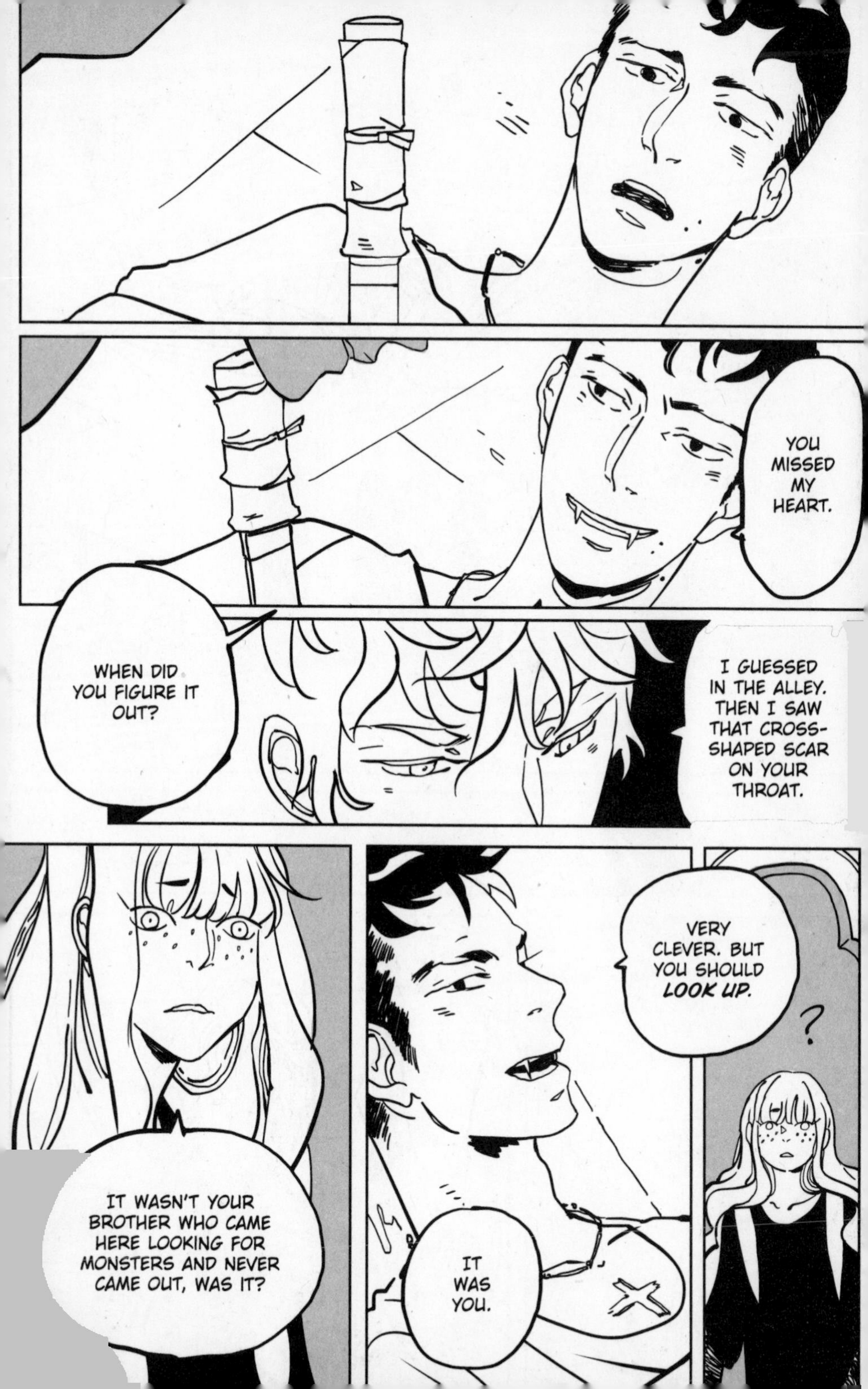
YOU MISSED MY HEART.
WHEN DID YOU FIGURE IT OUT?
I GUESSED IN THE ALLEY. THEN I SAW THAT CROSS-SHAPED SCAR ON YOUR THROAT.
IT WASN'T YOUR BROTHER WHO CAME HERE LOOKING FOR MONSTERS AND NEVER CAME OUT, WAS IT?
IT WAS YOU.
VERY CLEVER. BUT YOU SHOULD LOOK UP.
?

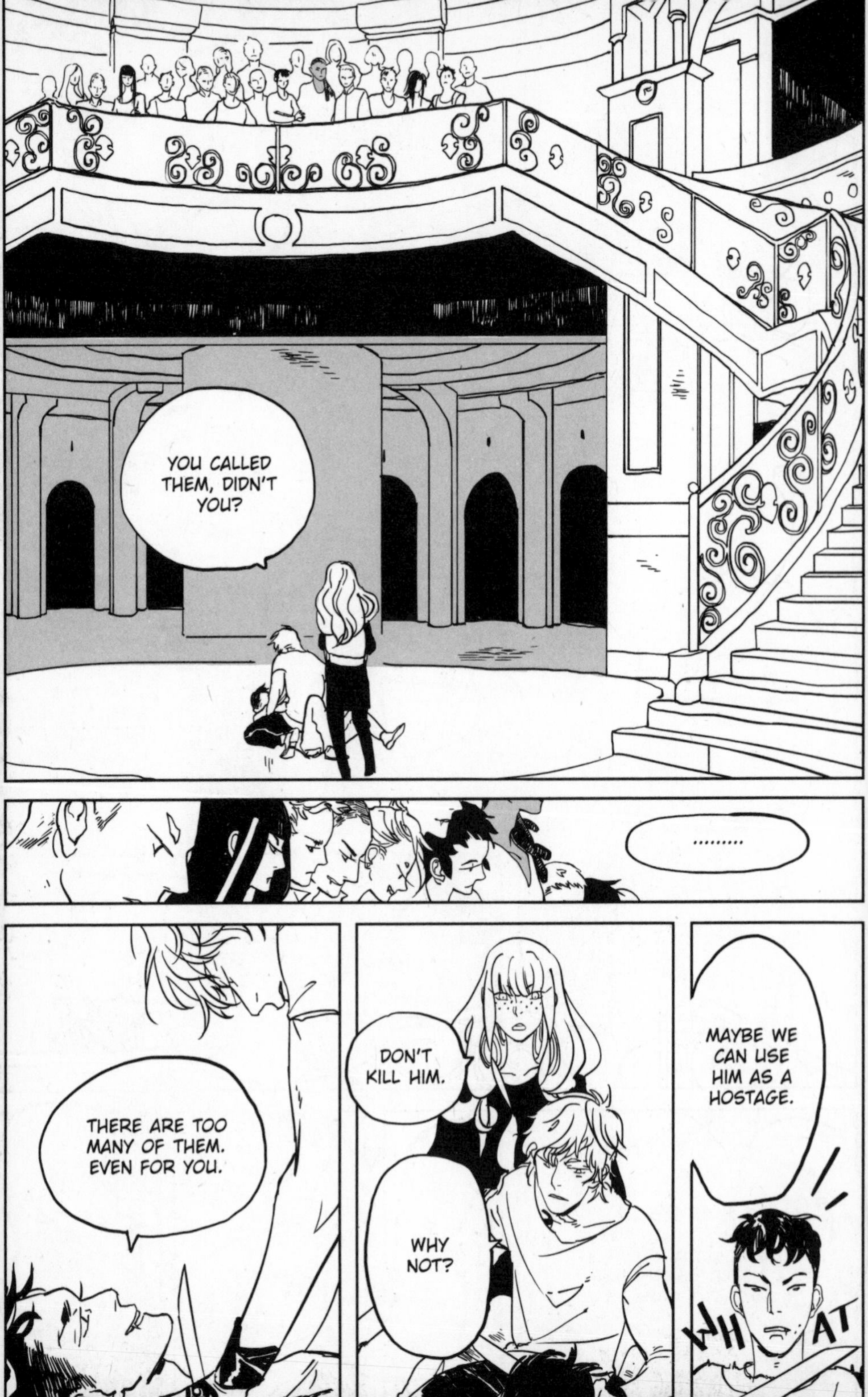
YOU CALLED THEM, DIDN'T YOU?
....
THERE ARE TOO MANY OF THEM. EVEN FOR YOU.
DON'T KILL HIM.
WHY NOT?
MAYBE WE CAN USE HIM AS A HOSTAGE.
WHAT

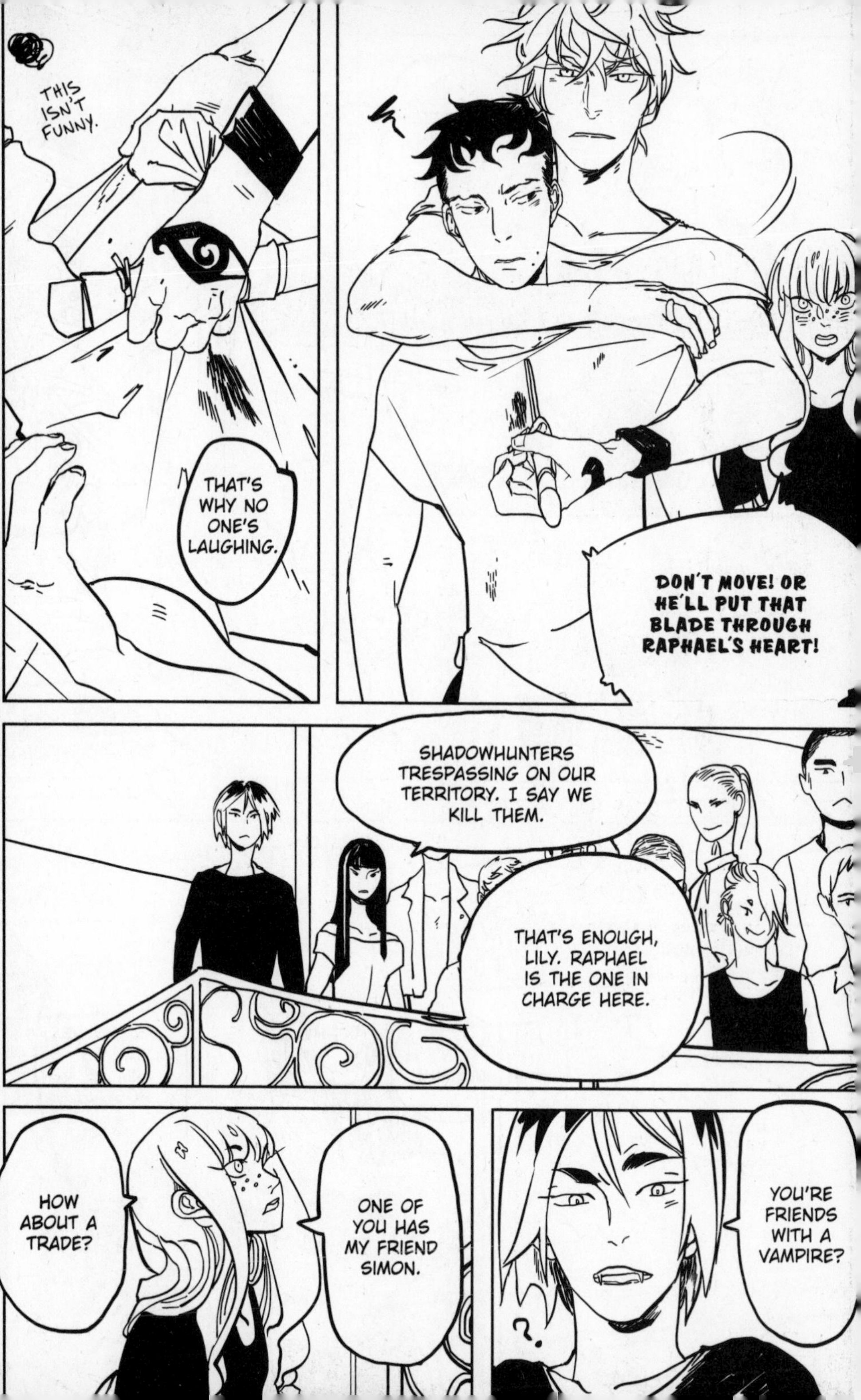
THIS ISN'T FUNNY.
THAT'S WHY NO ONE'S LAUGHING.
DON'T MOVE! OR HE'LL PUT THAT BLADE THROUGH RAPHAEL'S HEART!
SHADOWHUNTERS TRESPASSING ON OUR TERRITORY. I SAY WE KILL THEM.
THAT'S ENOUGH, LILY. RAPHAEL IS THE ONE IN CHARGE HERE.
HOW ABOUT A TRADE?
ONE OF YOU HAS MY FRIEND SIMON.
YOU'RE FRIENDS WITH A VAMPIRE?

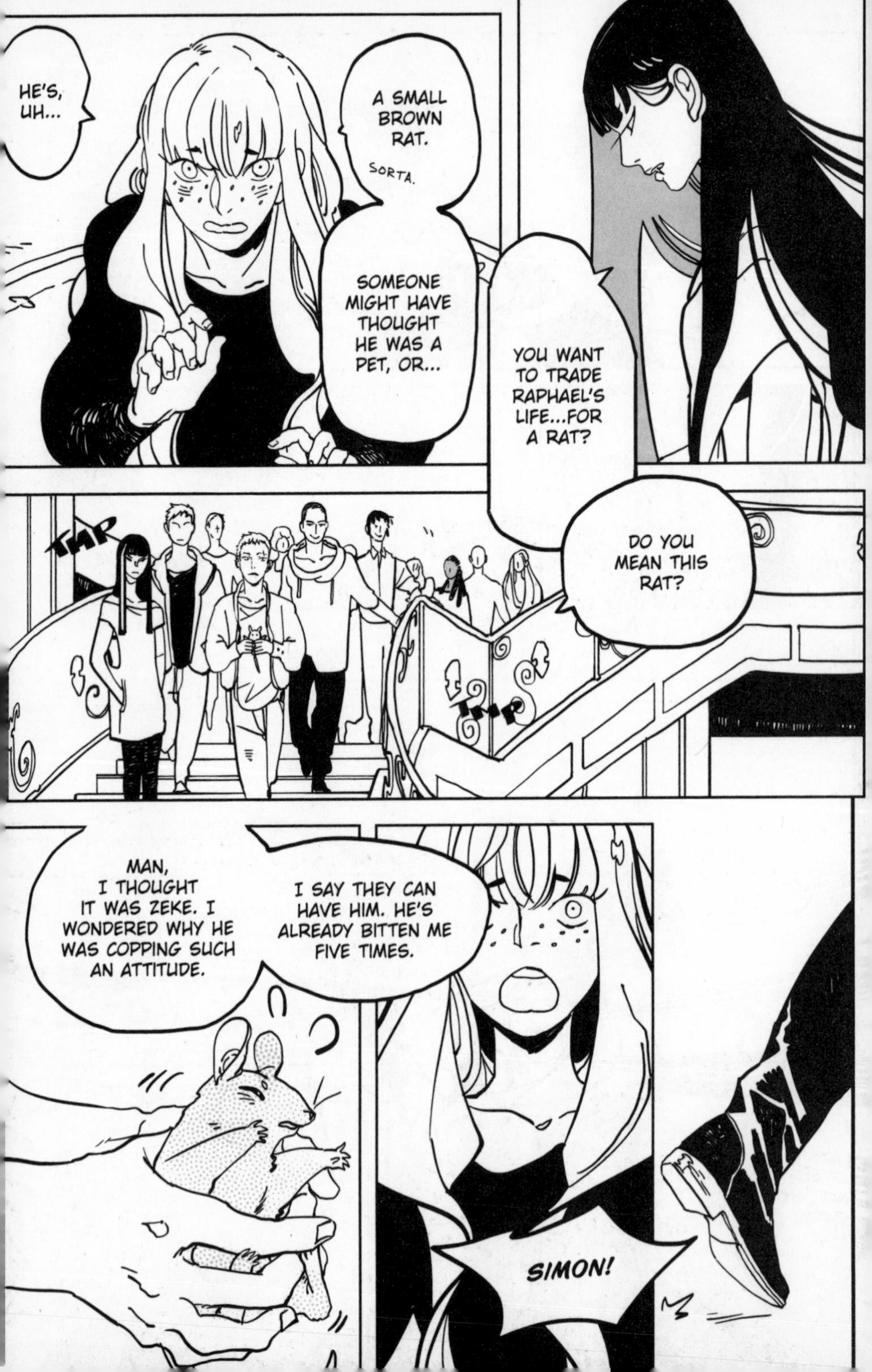
HE'S, UH...
A SMALL BROWN RAT.
SORTA.
SOMEONE MIGHT HAVE THOUGHT HE WAS A PET, OR...
YOU WANT TO TRADE RAPHAEL'S LIFE...FOR A RAT?
TMP
DO YOU MEAN THIS RAT?
TMP
MAN, I THOUGHT IT WAS ZEKE. I WONDERED WHY HE WAS COPPING SUCH AN ATTITUDE.
I SAY THEY CAN HAVE HIM. HE'S ALREADY BITTEN ME FIVE TIMES.
SIMON!

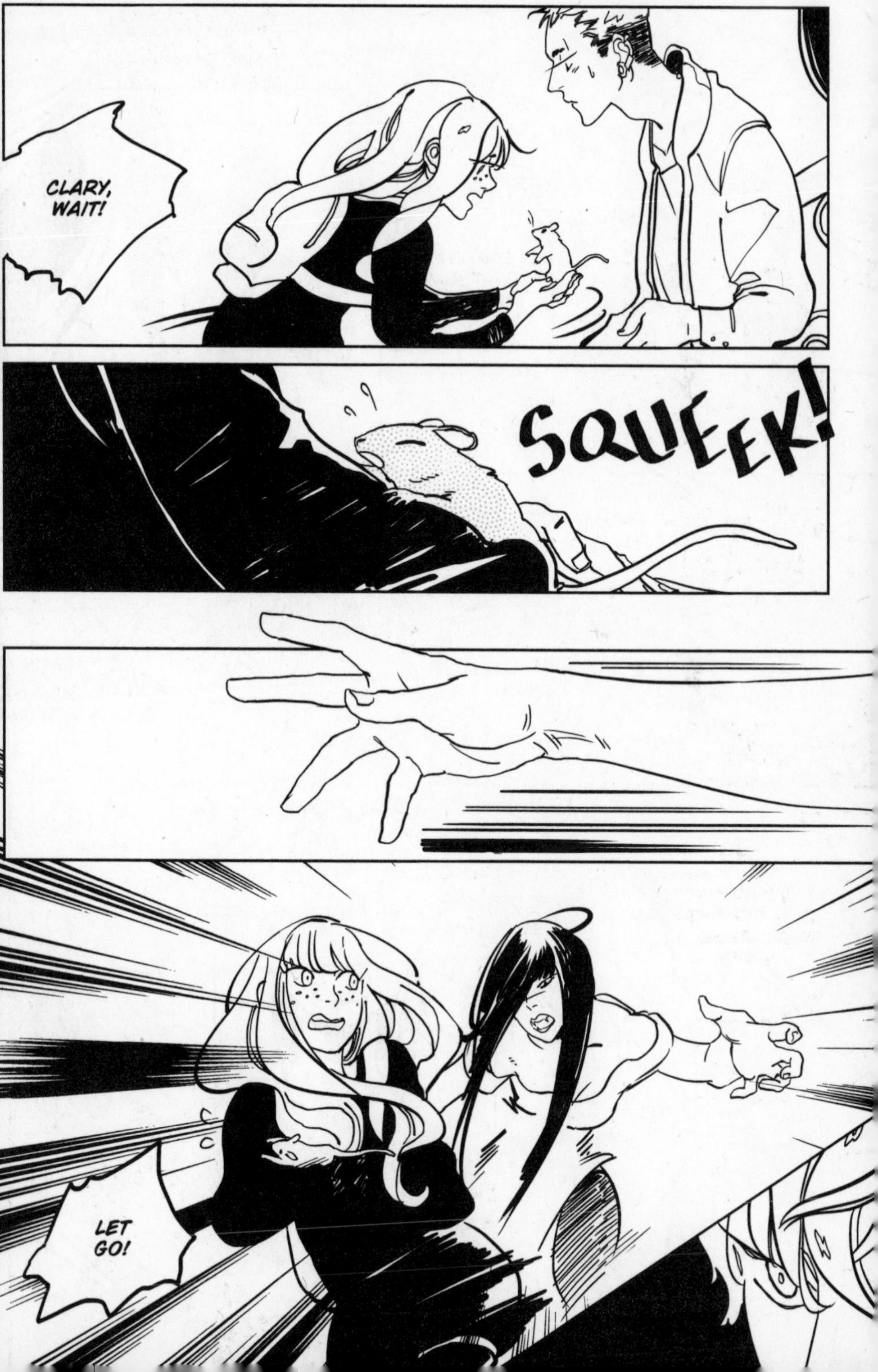
CLARY, WAIT!
SQUEEEK!
LET GO!

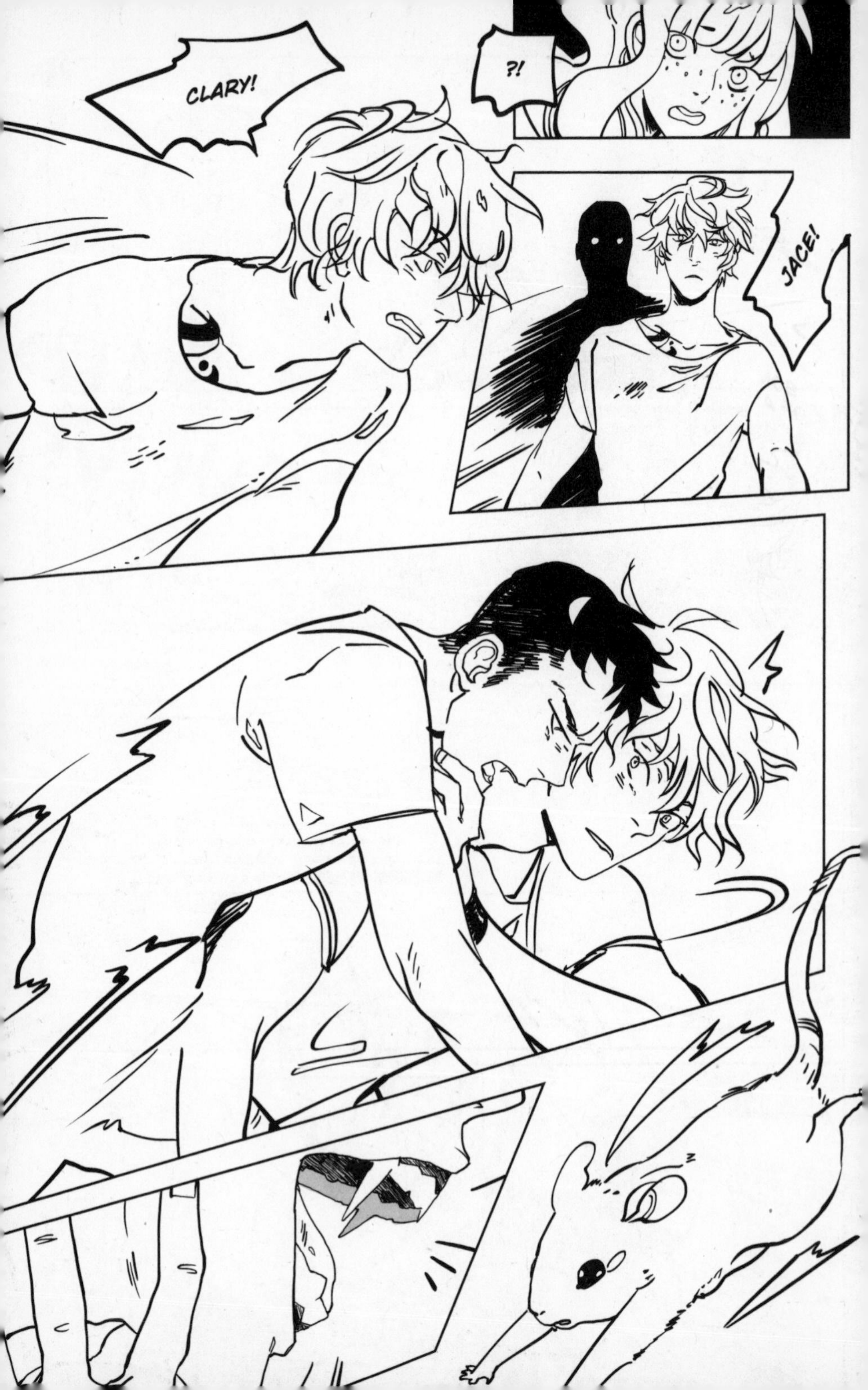
CLARY!
?!
JACE!

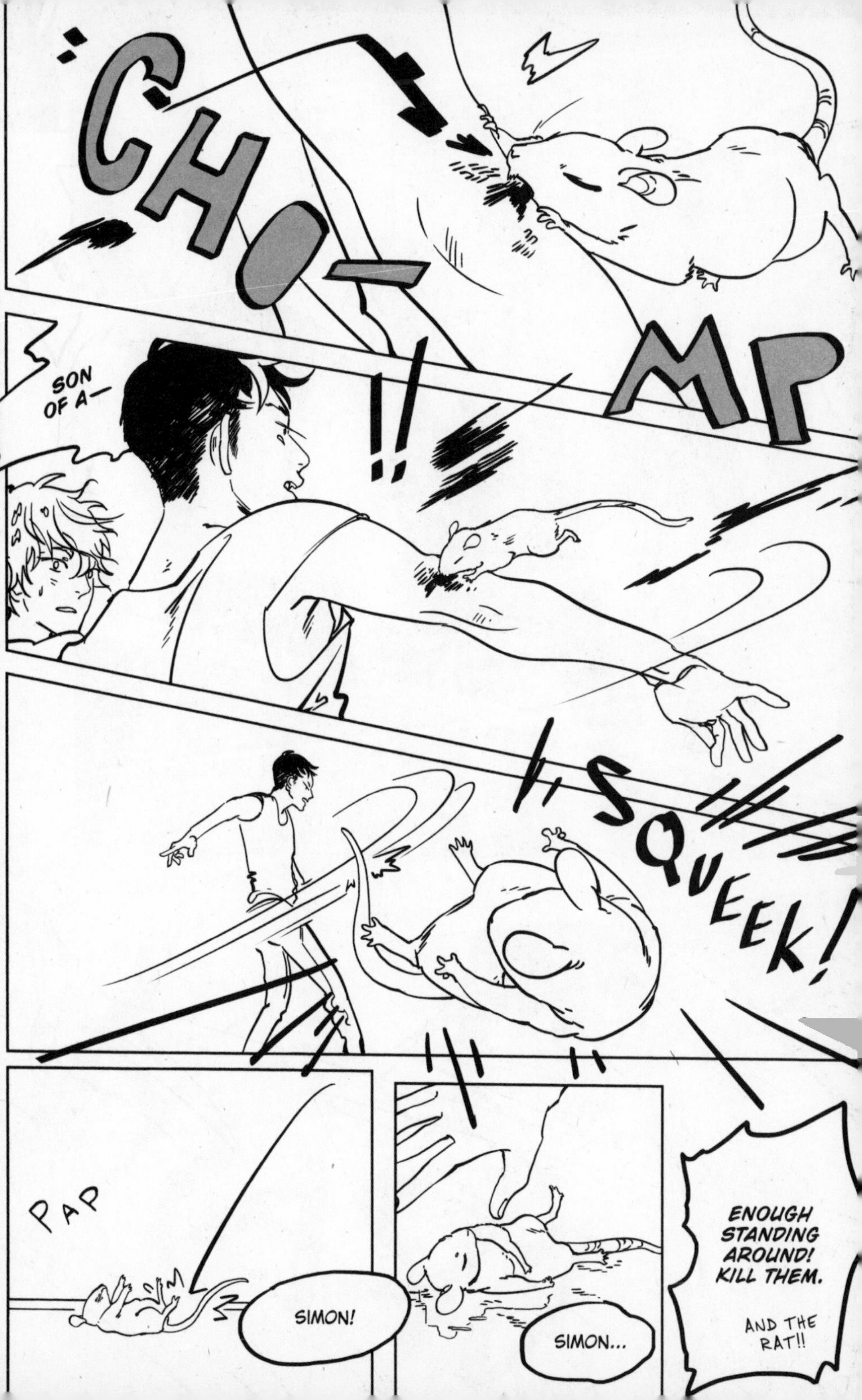
CHOMP
SON OF A—
!!
SQUEEK!
PAP
SIMON!
SIMON...
ENOUGH STANDING AROUND! KILL THEM.
AND THE RAT!!

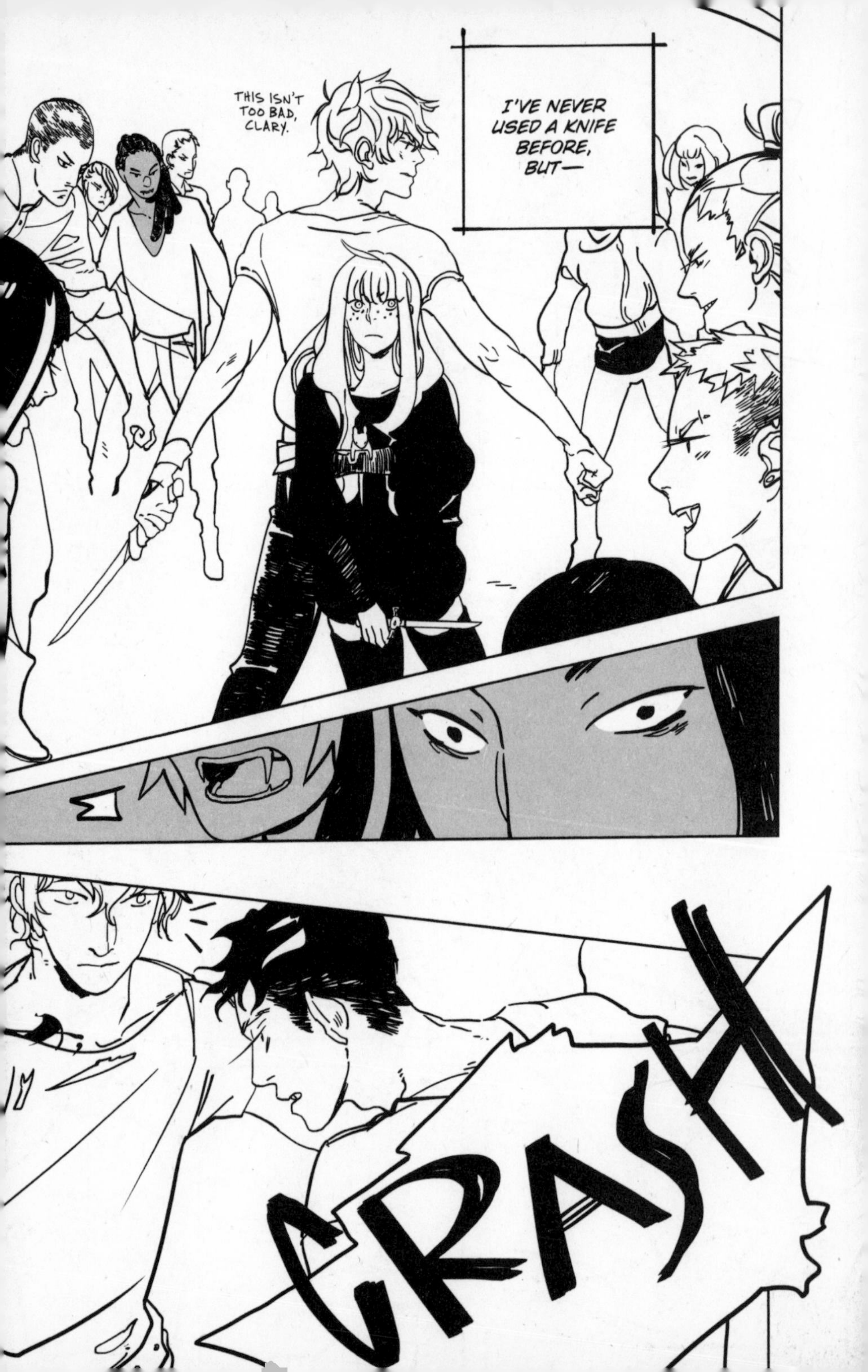
THIS ISN'T TOO BAD, CLARY.
I'VE NEVER USED A KNIFE BEFORE, BUT—
CRASH

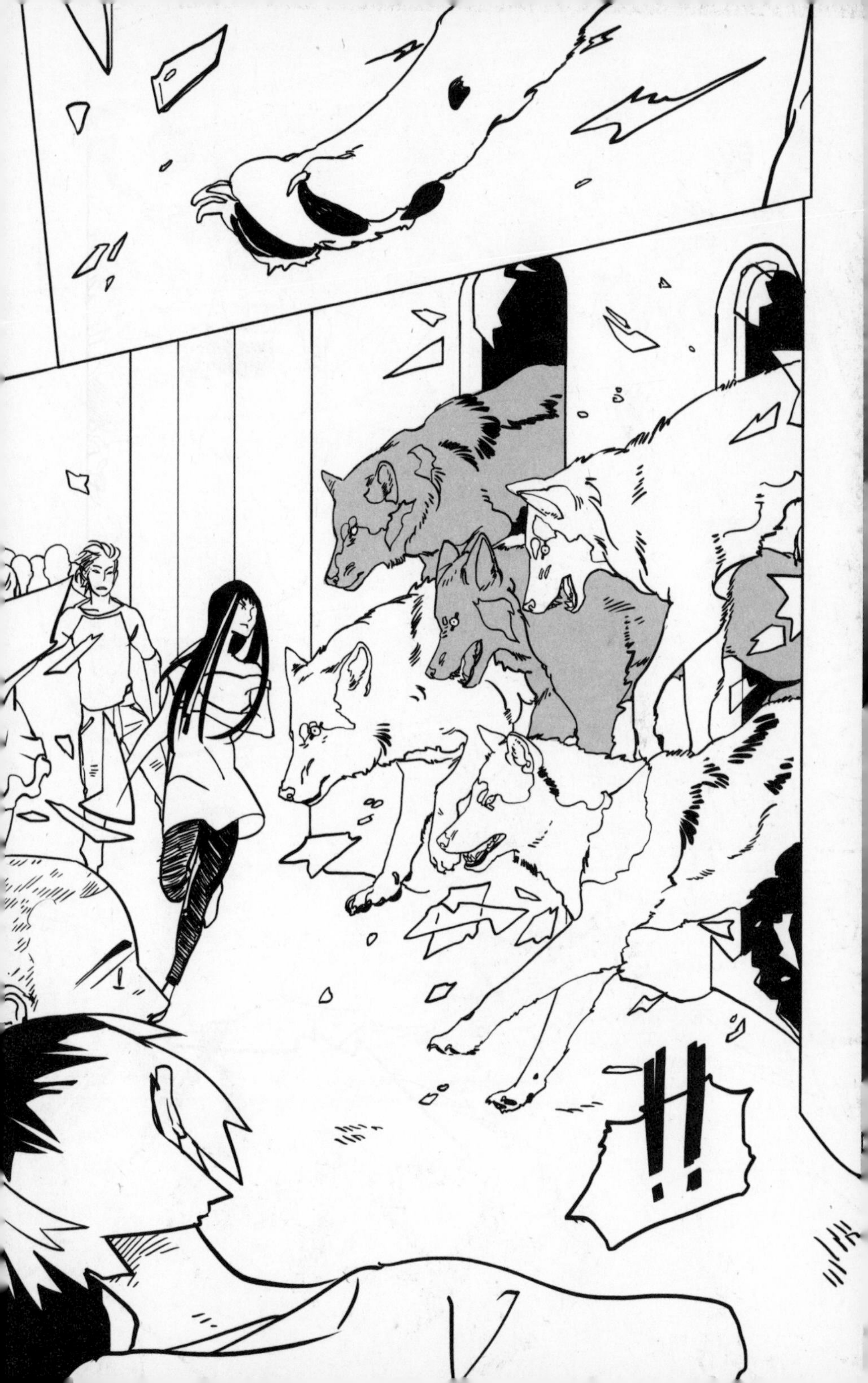
!!

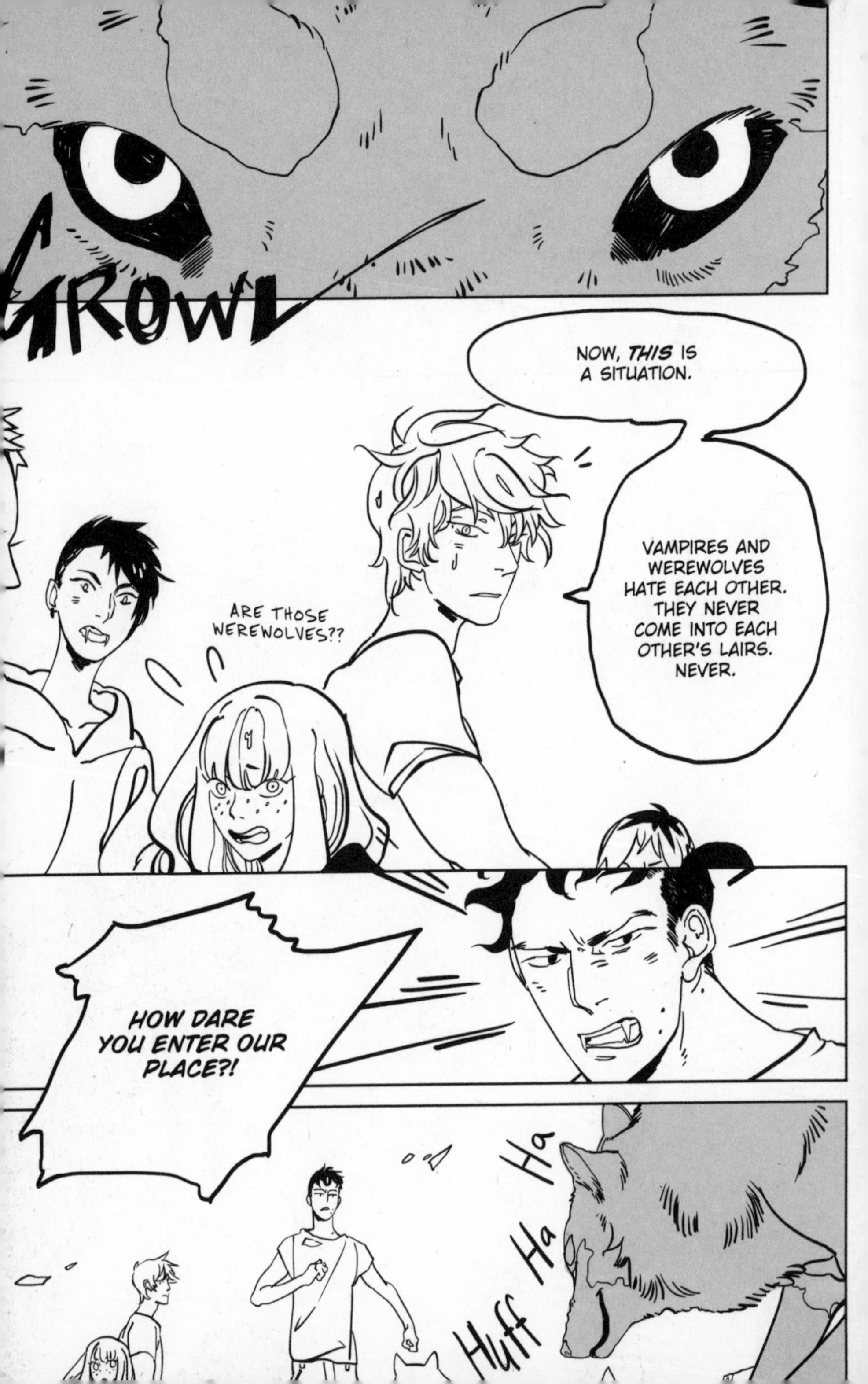
GROWL
NOW, THIS IS A SITUATION.
ARE THOSE WEREWOLVES??
VAMPIRES AND WEREWOLVES HATE EACH OTHER. THEY NEVER COME INTO EACH OTHER'S LAIRS. NEVER.
HOW DARE YOU ENTER OUR PLACE?!
Ha
Ha
Huff

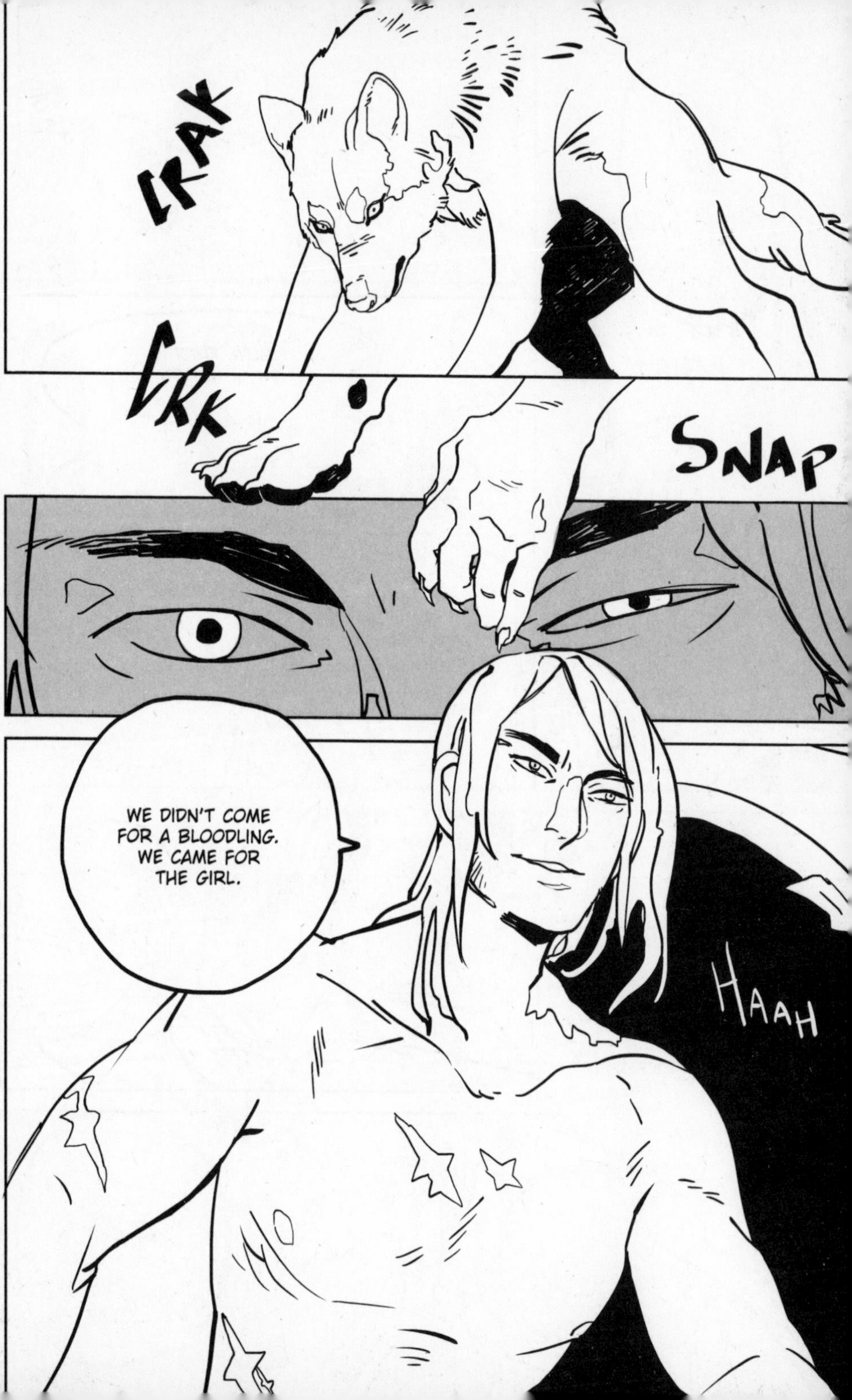
CRAK
CRK
SNAP
WE DIDN'T COME FOR A BLOODLING. WE CAME FOR THE GIRL.
HAAH

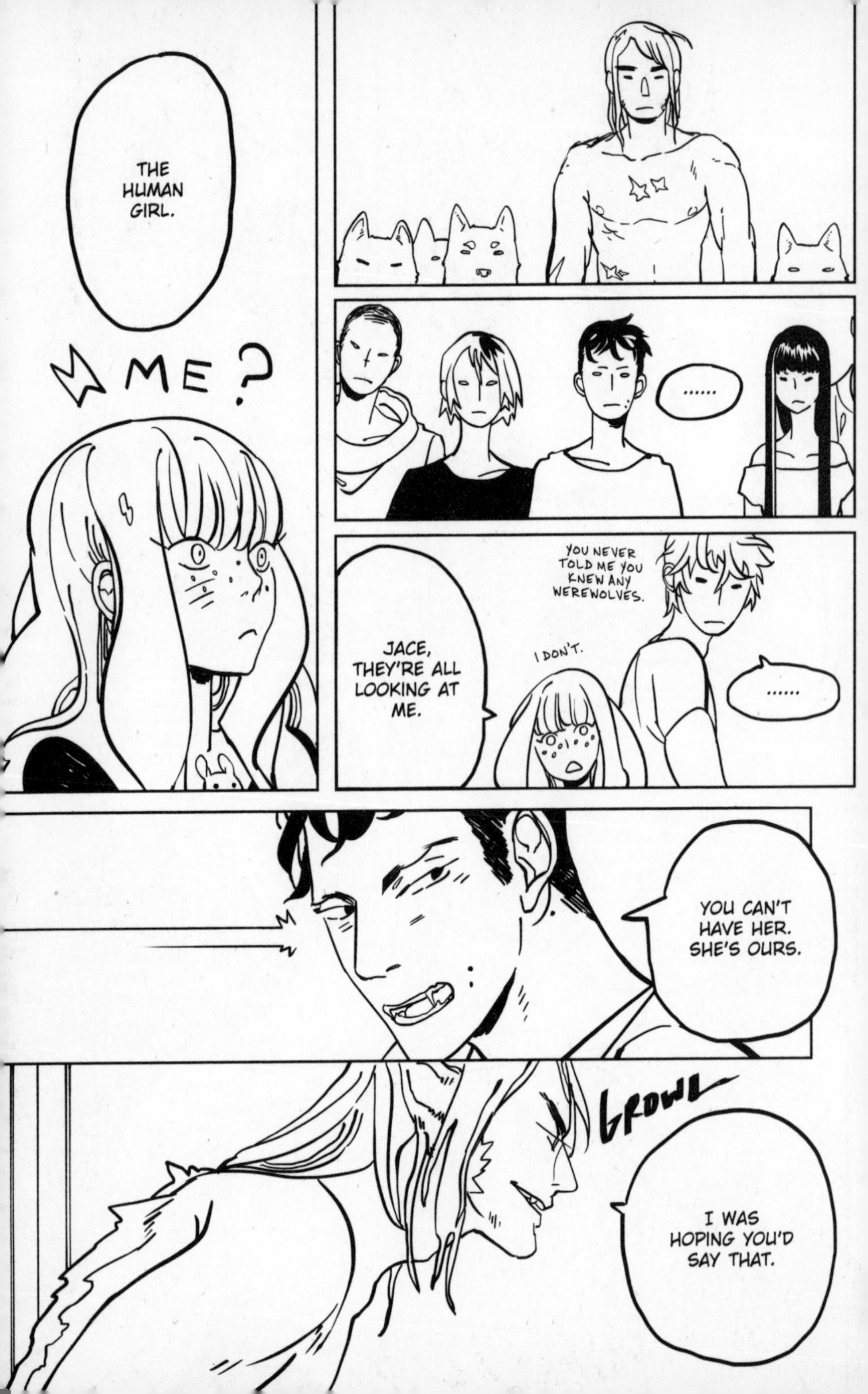
THE HUMAN GIRL.
ME?
......
JACE, THEY'RE ALL LOOKING AT ME.
YOU NEVER TOLD ME YOU KNEW ANY WEREWOLVES.
I DON'T.
......
YOU CAN'T HAVE HER. SHE'S OURS.
GROWL
I WAS HOPING YOU'D SAY THAT.

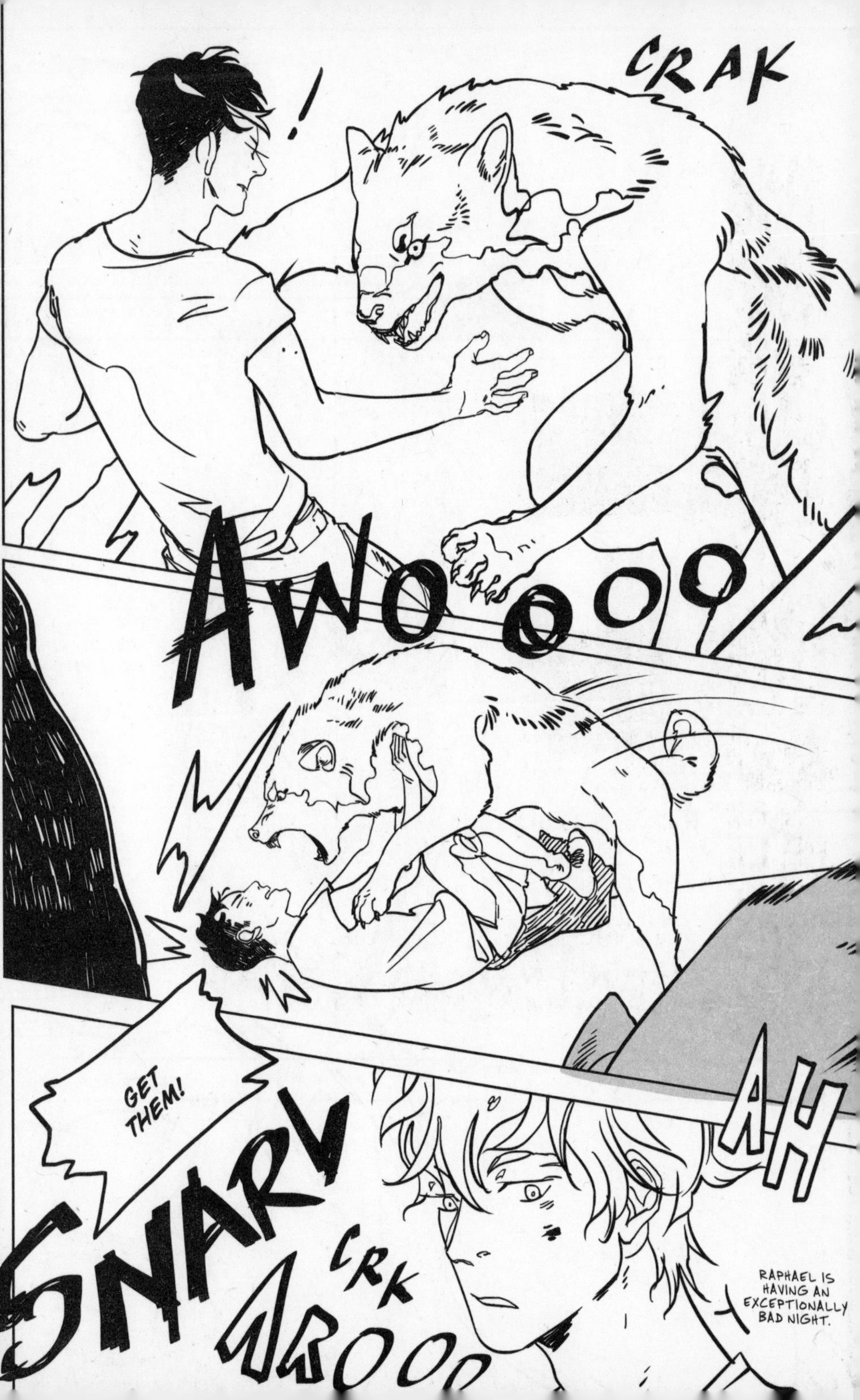
!
CRAK
AWOOOOO
GET THEM!
SNARL
CRK
AROOO
AH
RAPHAEL IS HAVING AN EXCEPTIONALLY BAD NIGHT.

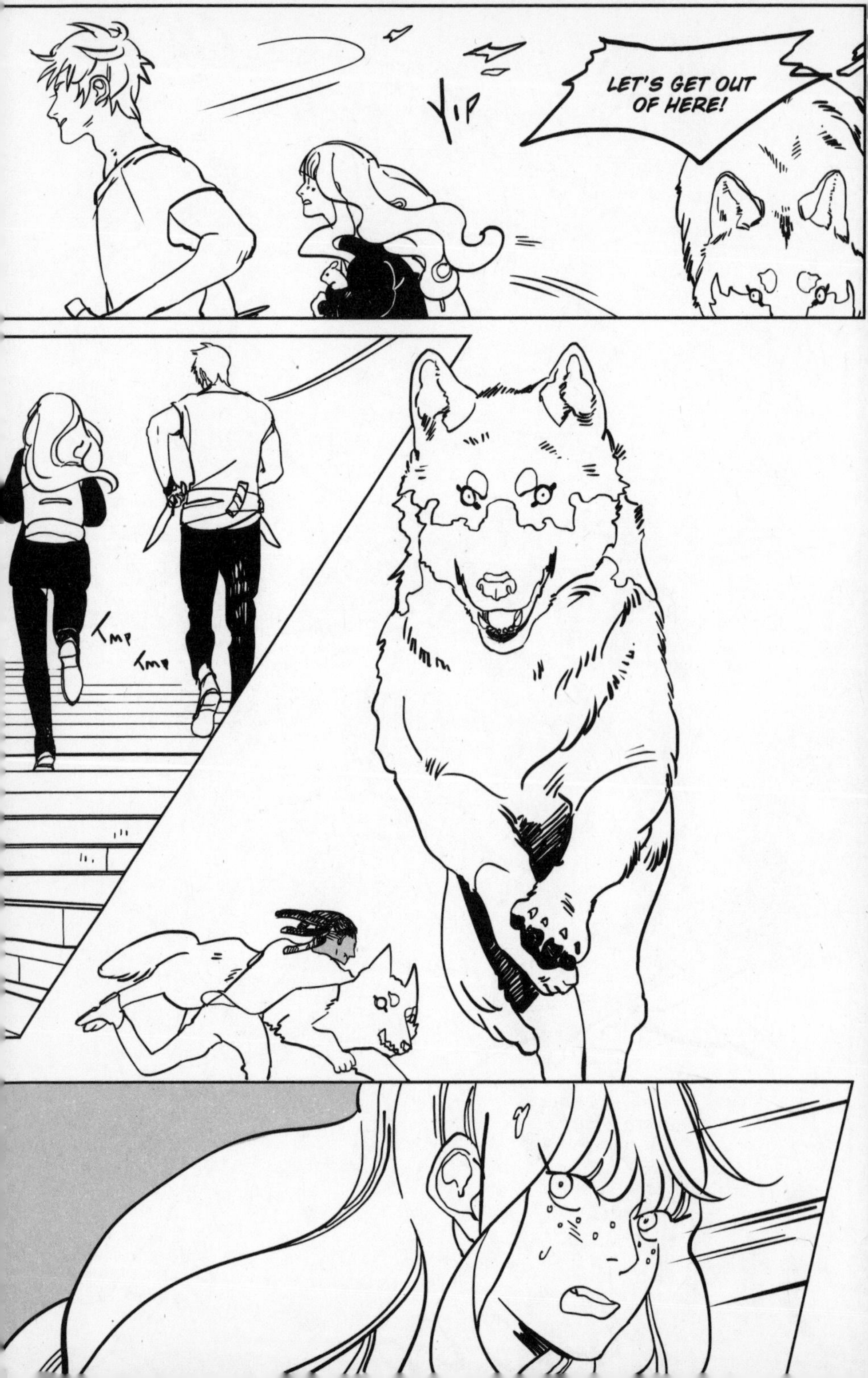

YIP
LET'S GET OUT OF HERE!
TMP
TMP

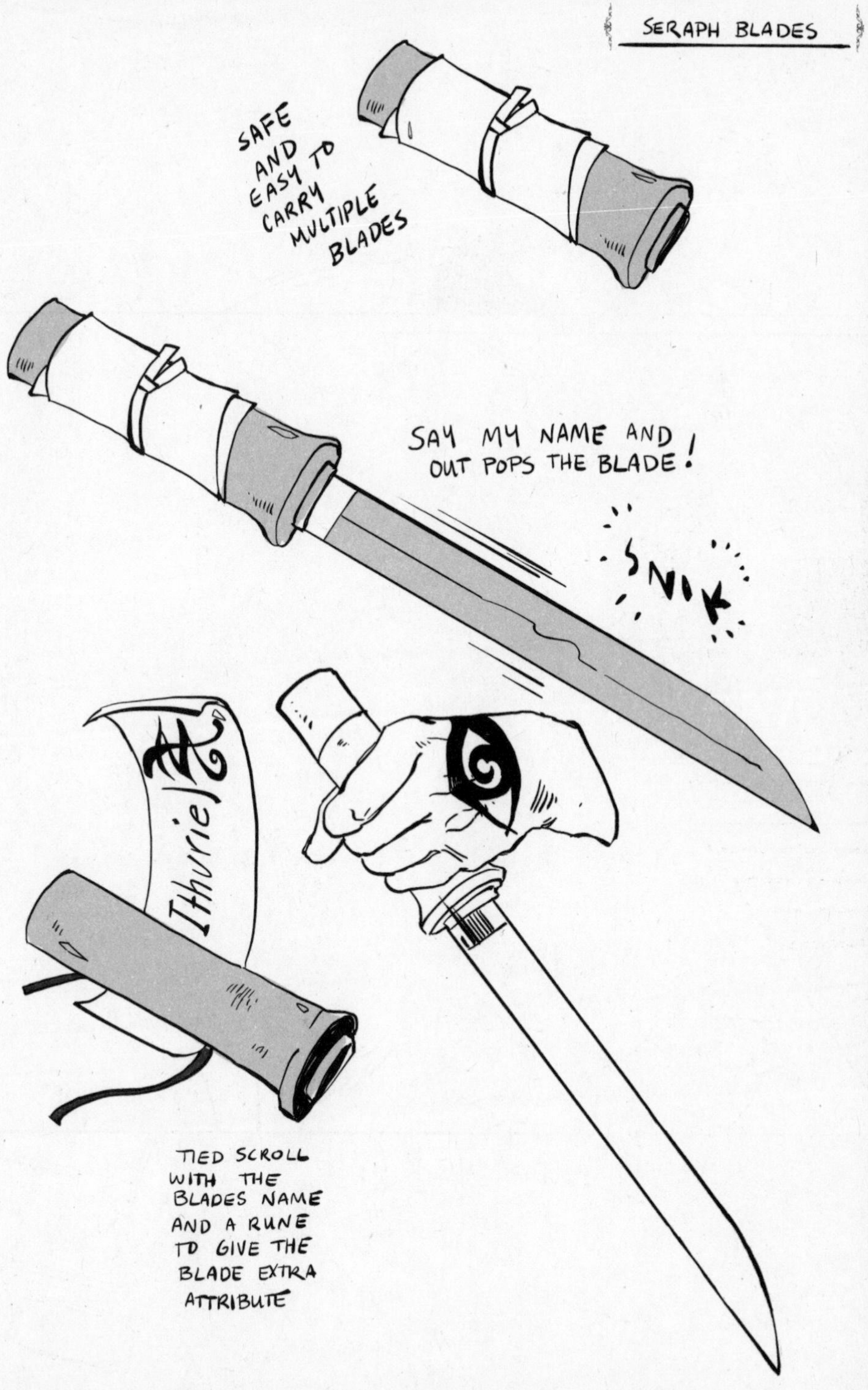
SERAPH BLADES
SAFE AND EASY TO CARRY MULTIPLE BLADES
SAY MY NAME AND OUT POPS THE BLADE!
SNIK
Ithuriel
TIED SCROLL WITH THE BLADES NAME AND A RUNE TO GIVE THE BLADE EXTRA ATTRIBUTE

THE MORTAL INSTRUMENTS

THE GRAPHIC NOVEL

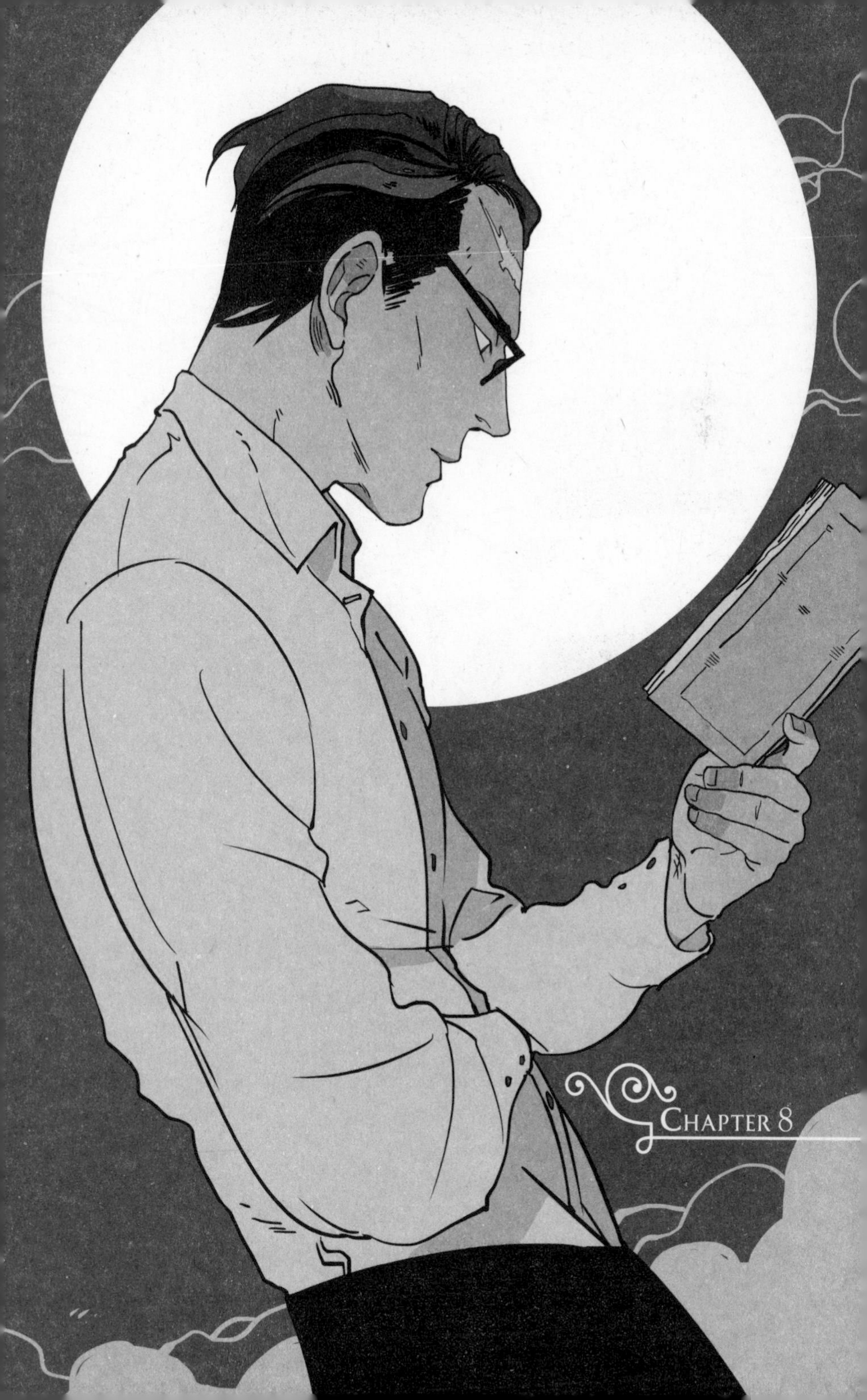

Chapter 8

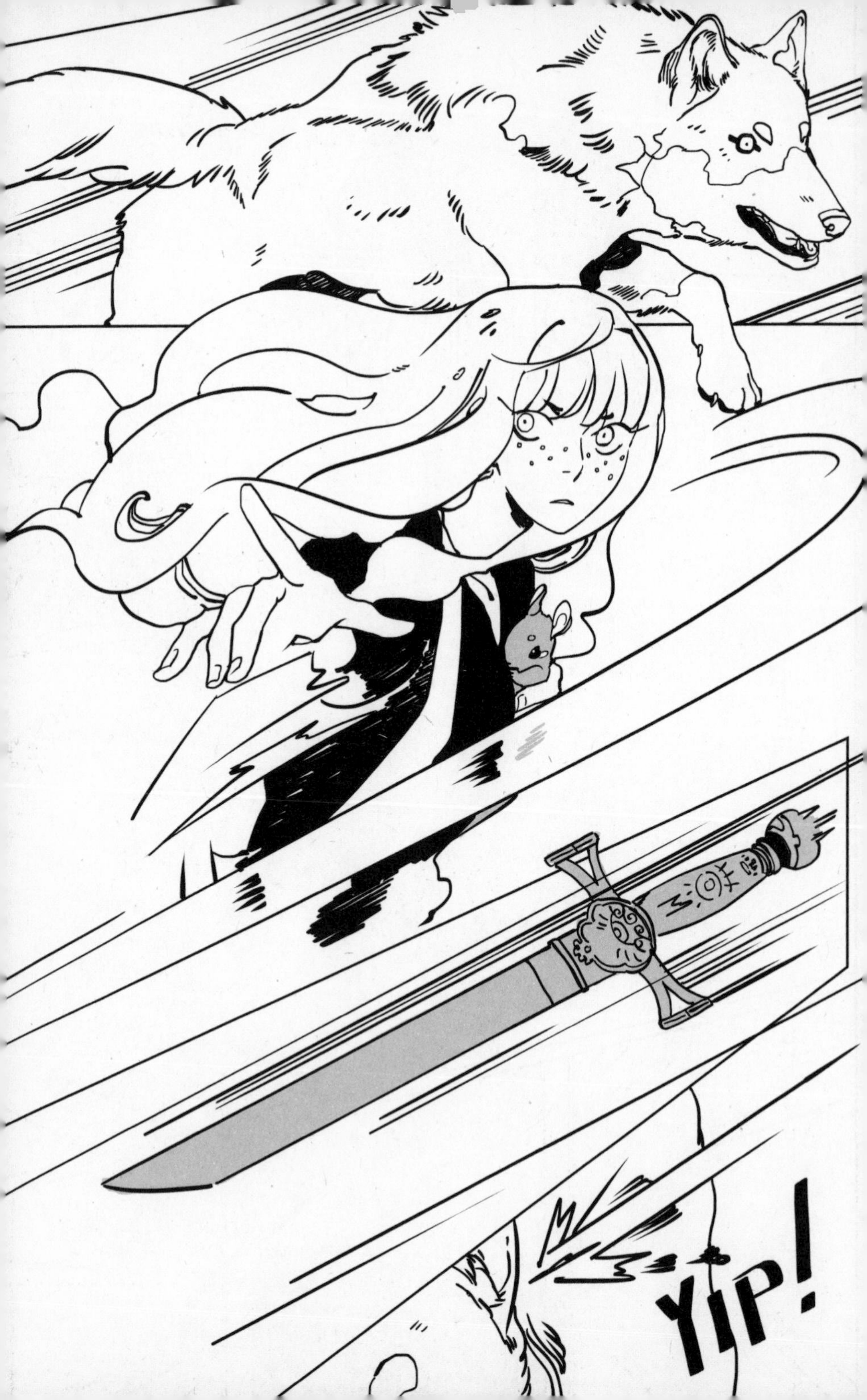
YIP!

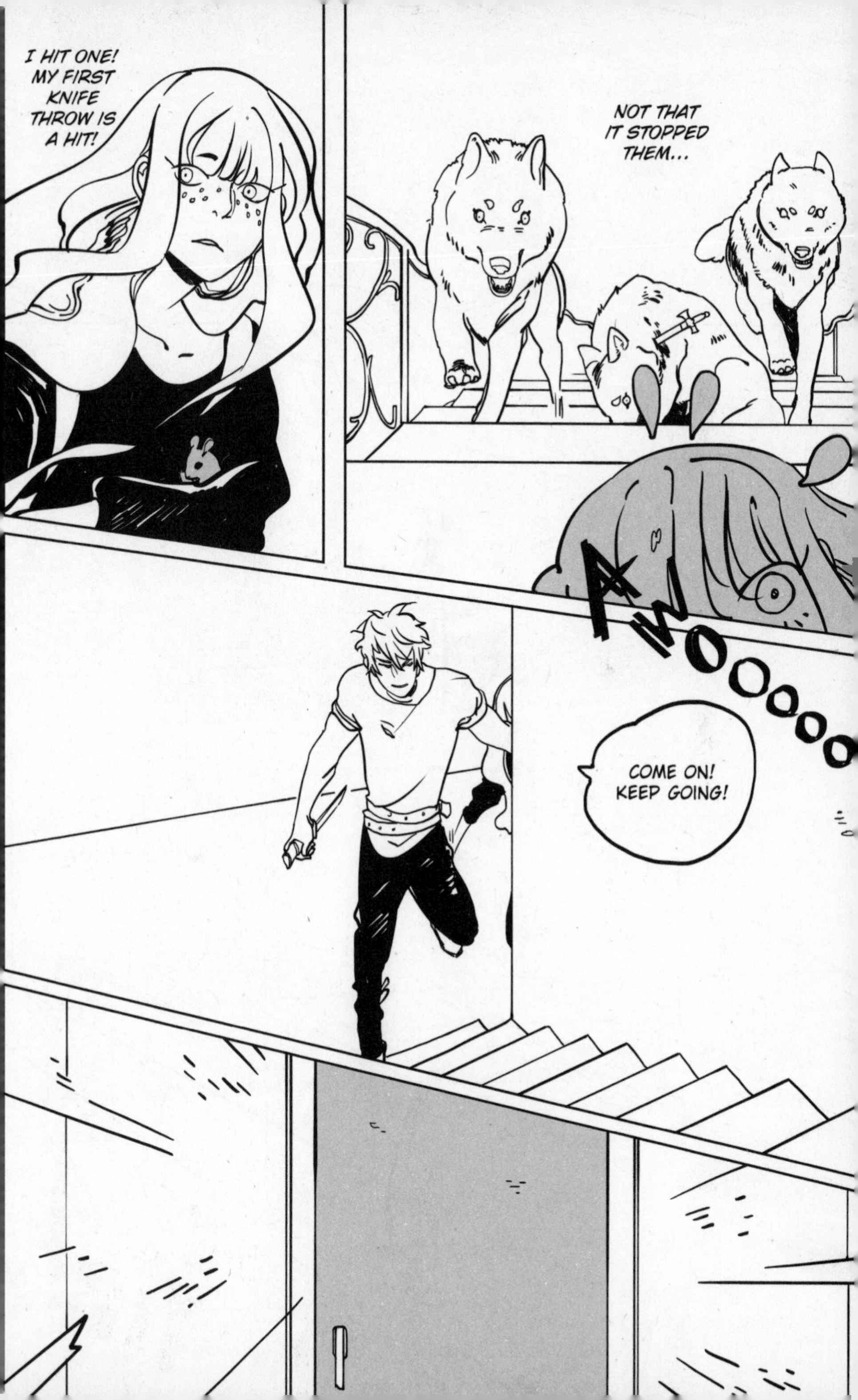
I HIT ONE! MY FIRST KNIFE THROW IS A HIT!
NOT THAT IT STOPPED THEM...
AWOOOOOO
COME ON! KEEP GOING!

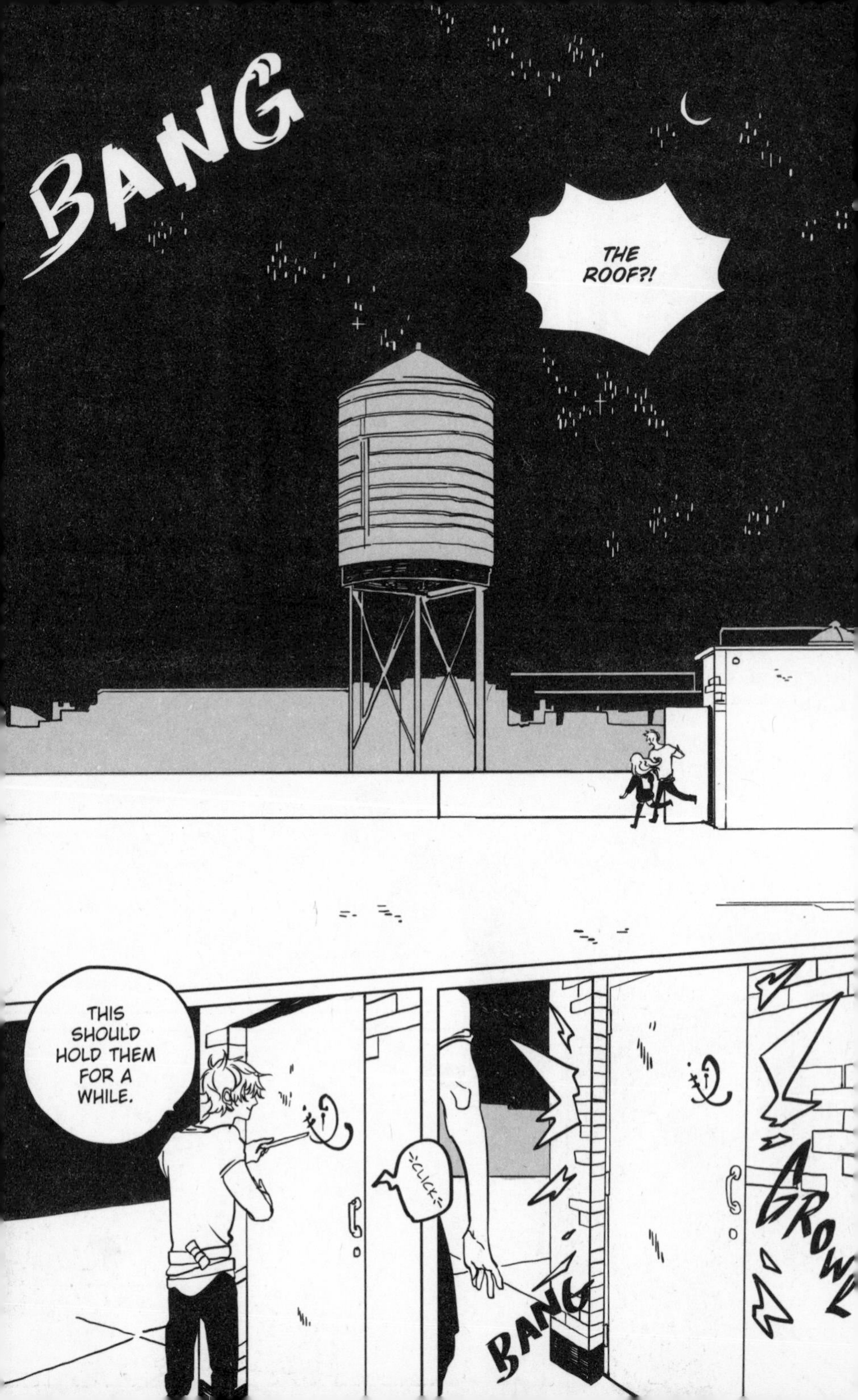
BANG
THE ROOF?!
THIS SHOULD HOLD THEM FOR A WHILE.
CLICK
BANG
GROWL

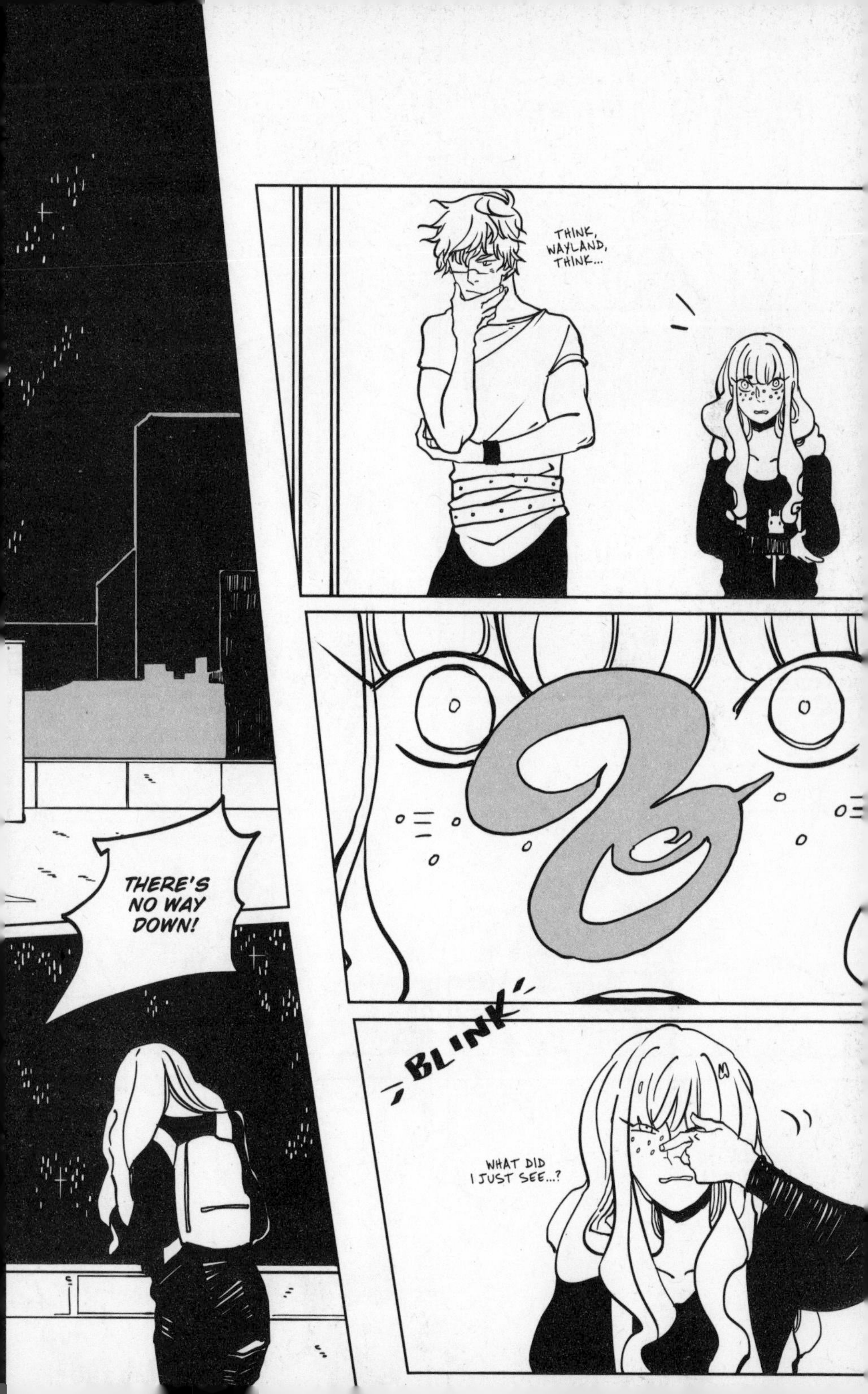
THINK, WAYLAND, THINK...
THERE'S NO WAY DOWN!
BLINK
WHAT DID I JUST SEE...?

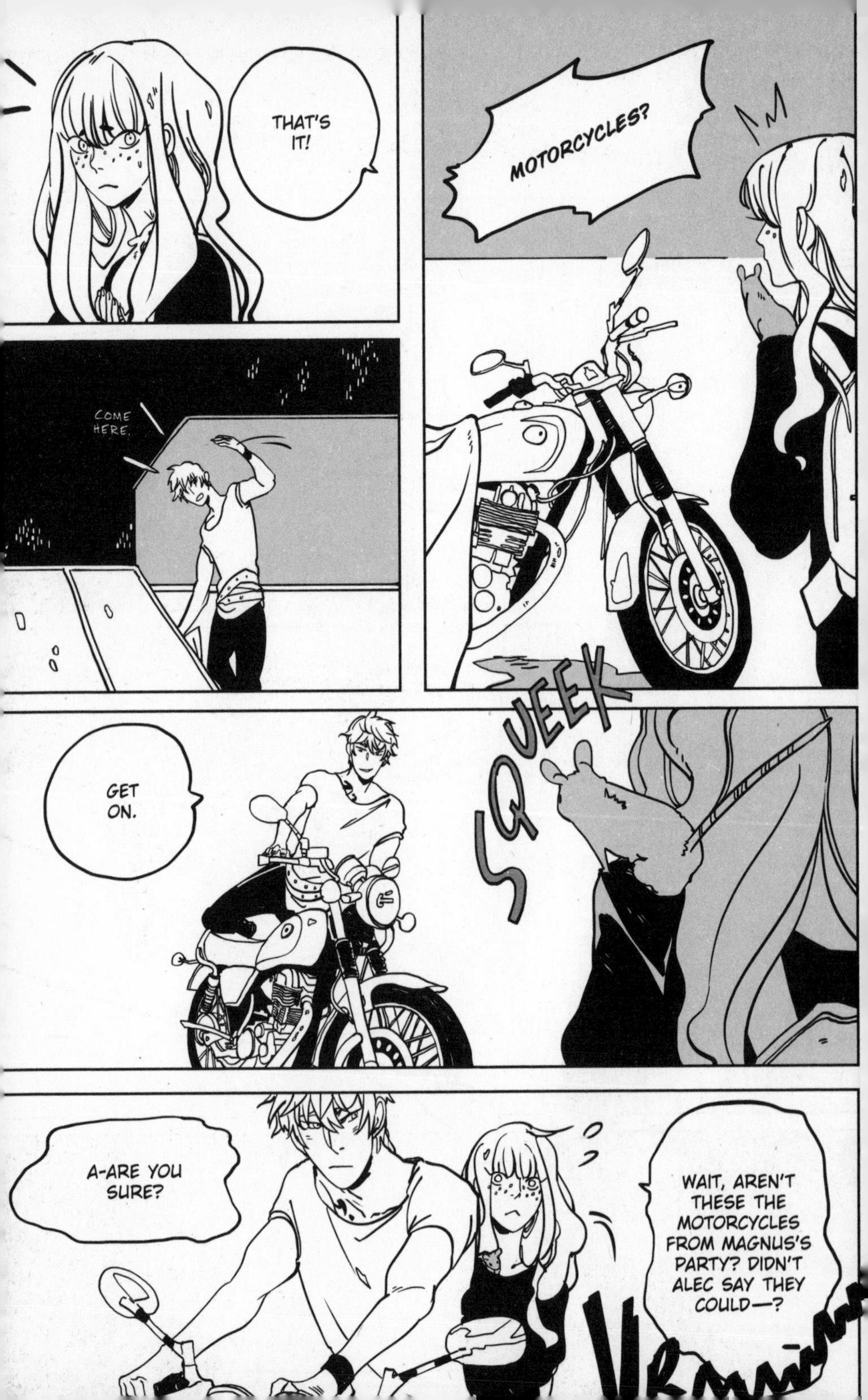
THAT'S IT!
COME HERE.
MOTORCYCLES?
GET ON.
SQUEEK
A-ARE YOU SURE?
WAIT, AREN'T THESE THE MOTORCYCLES FROM MAGNUS'S PARTY? DIDN'T ALEC SAY THEY COULD—?

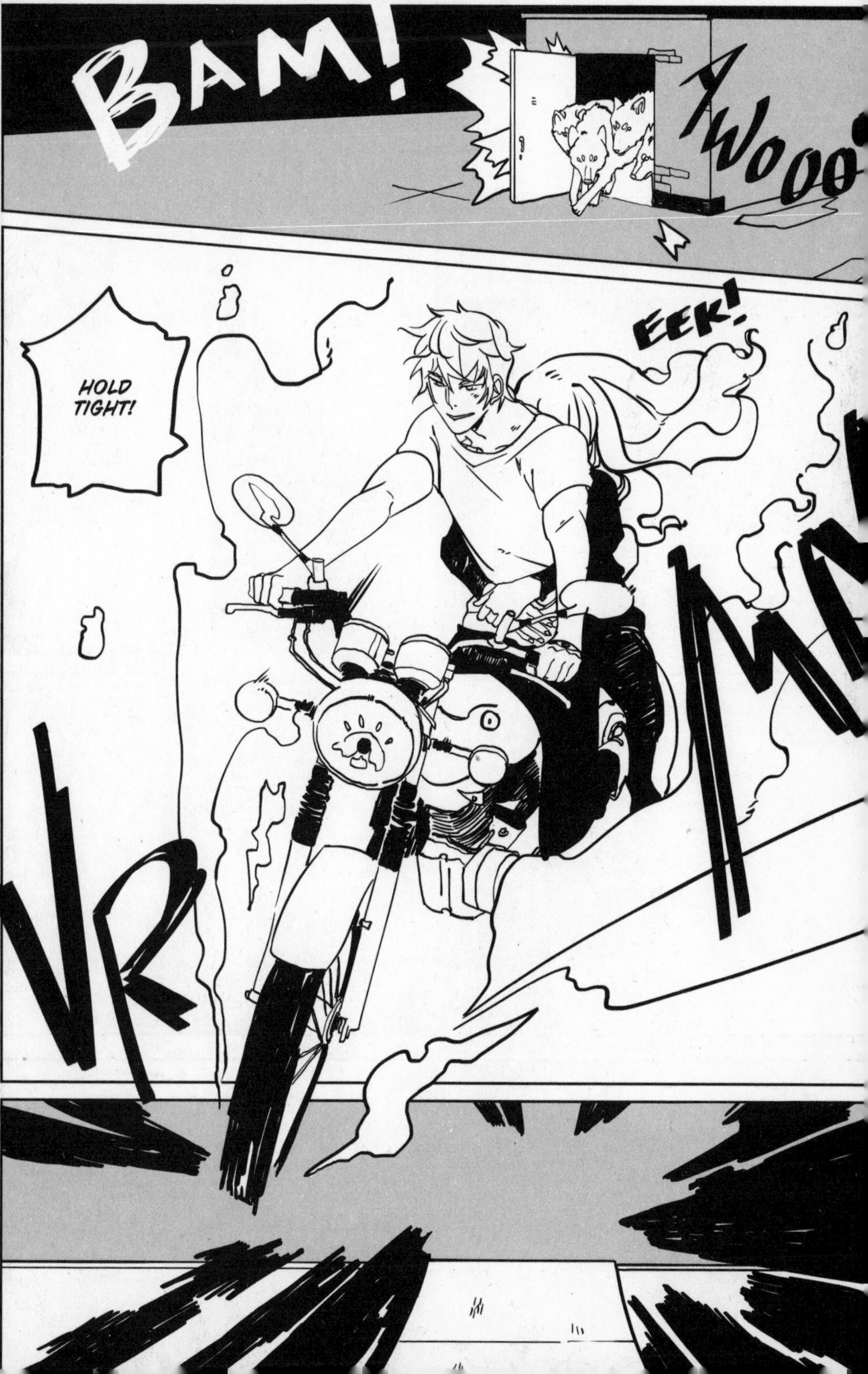
BAM!
AWOOO
HOLD TIGHT!
EEK!

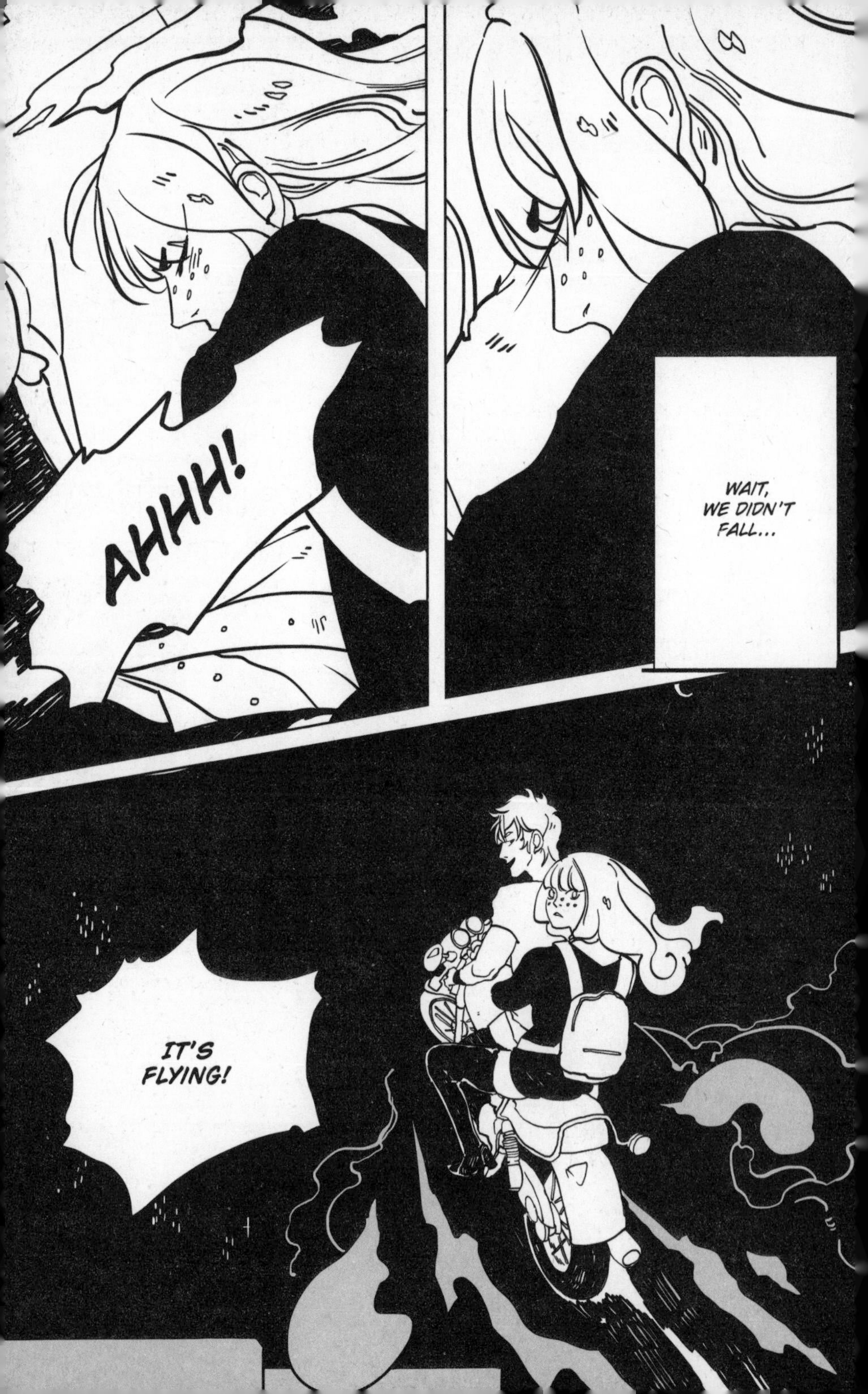
AHHH!
WAIT, WE DIDN'T FALL...
IT'S FLYING!

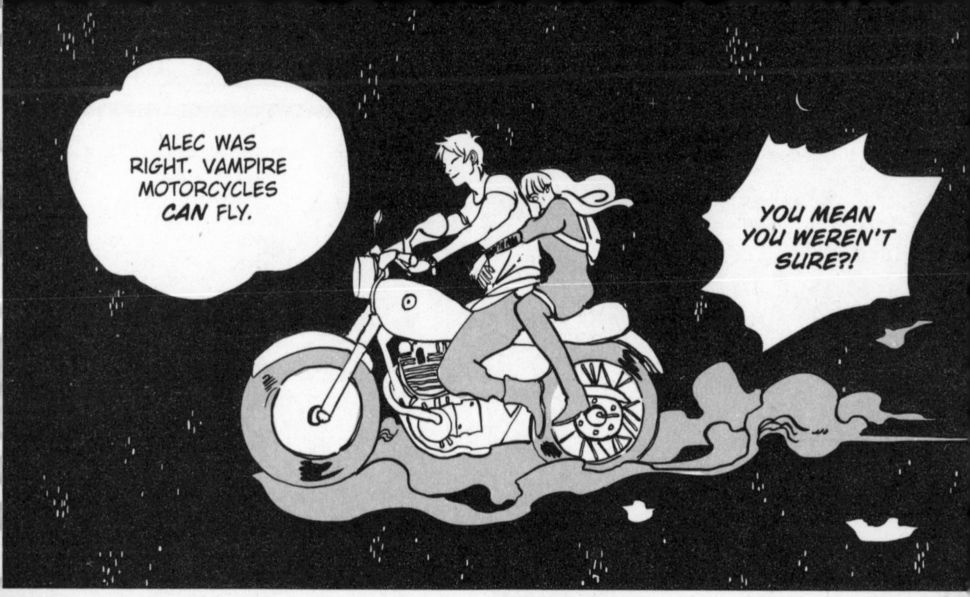
ALEC WAS RIGHT. VAMPIRE MOTORCYCLES *CAN* FLY.
YOU MEAN YOU WEREN'T SURE?!

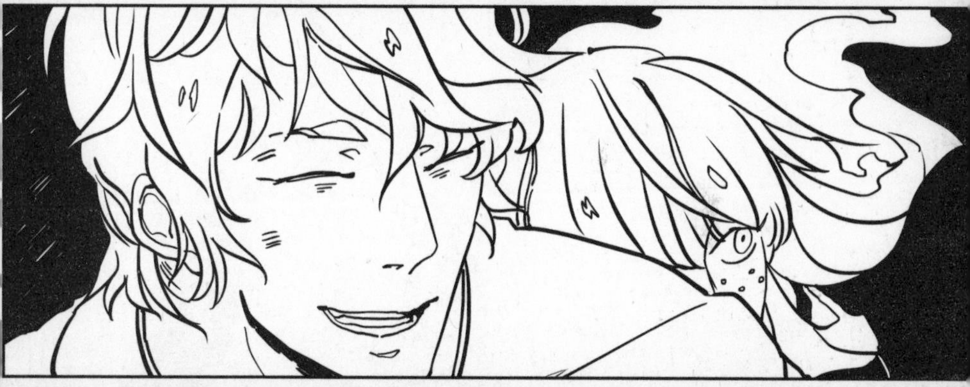

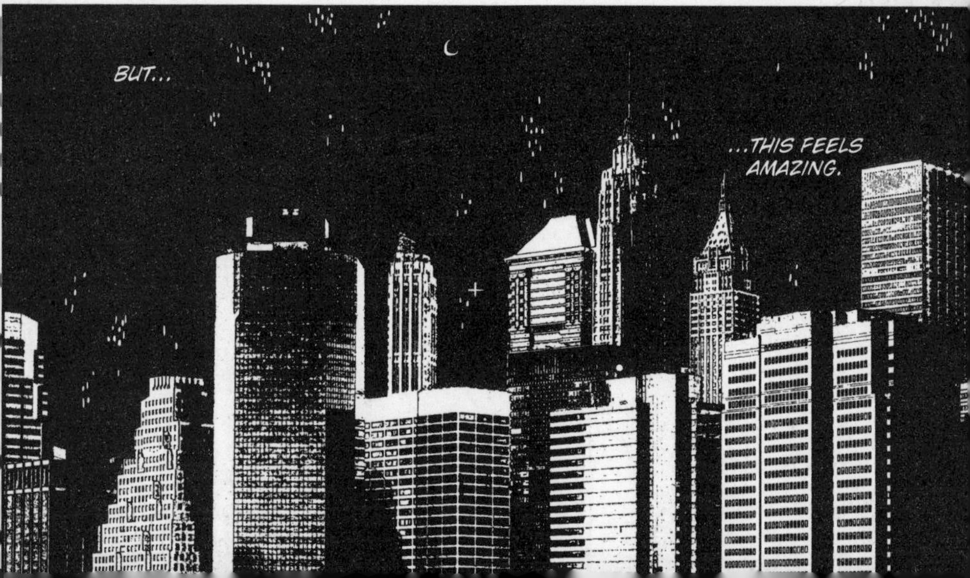
BUT...
...THIS FEELS AMAZING.

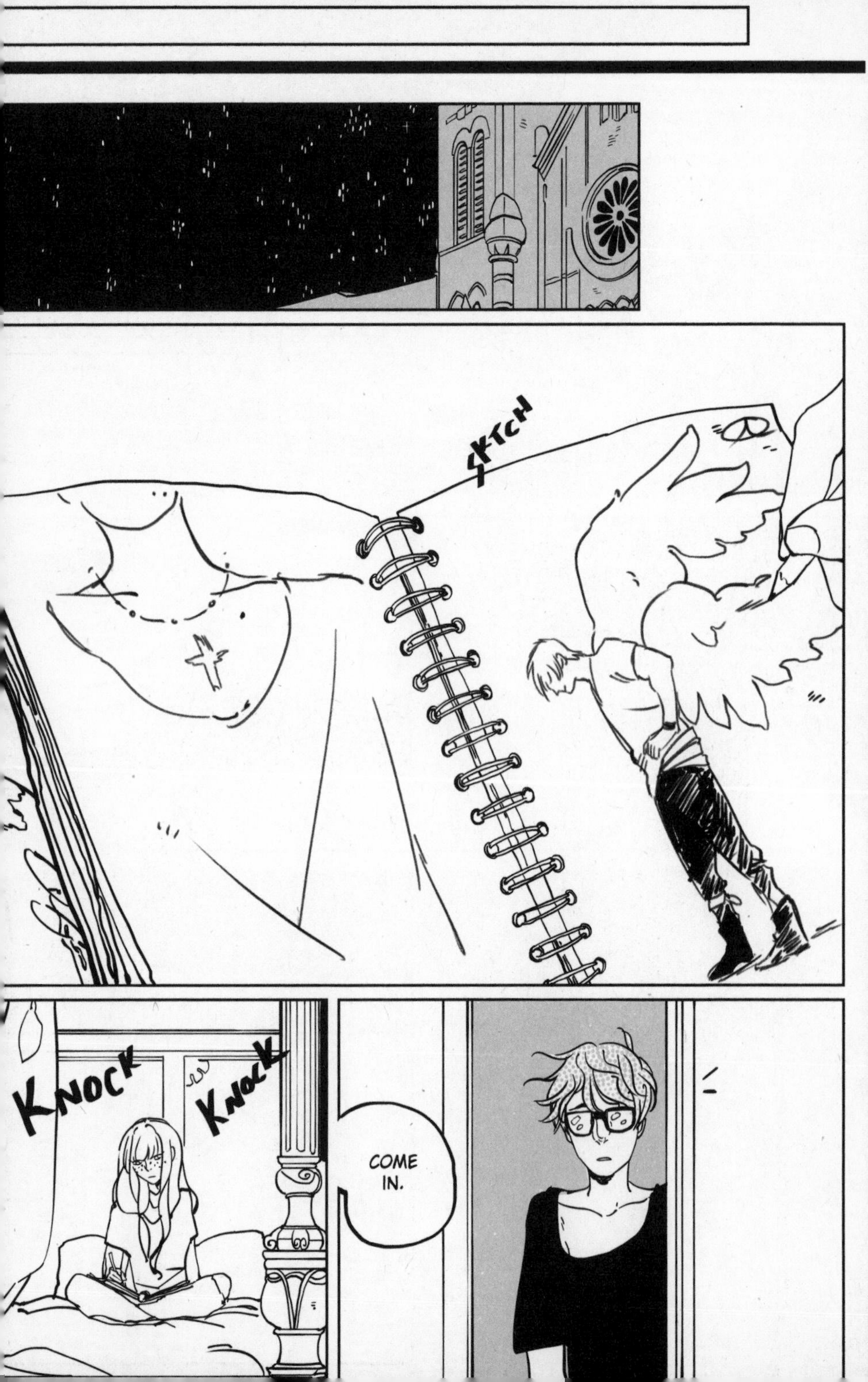
SKTCH
KNOCK
KNOCK
COME IN.

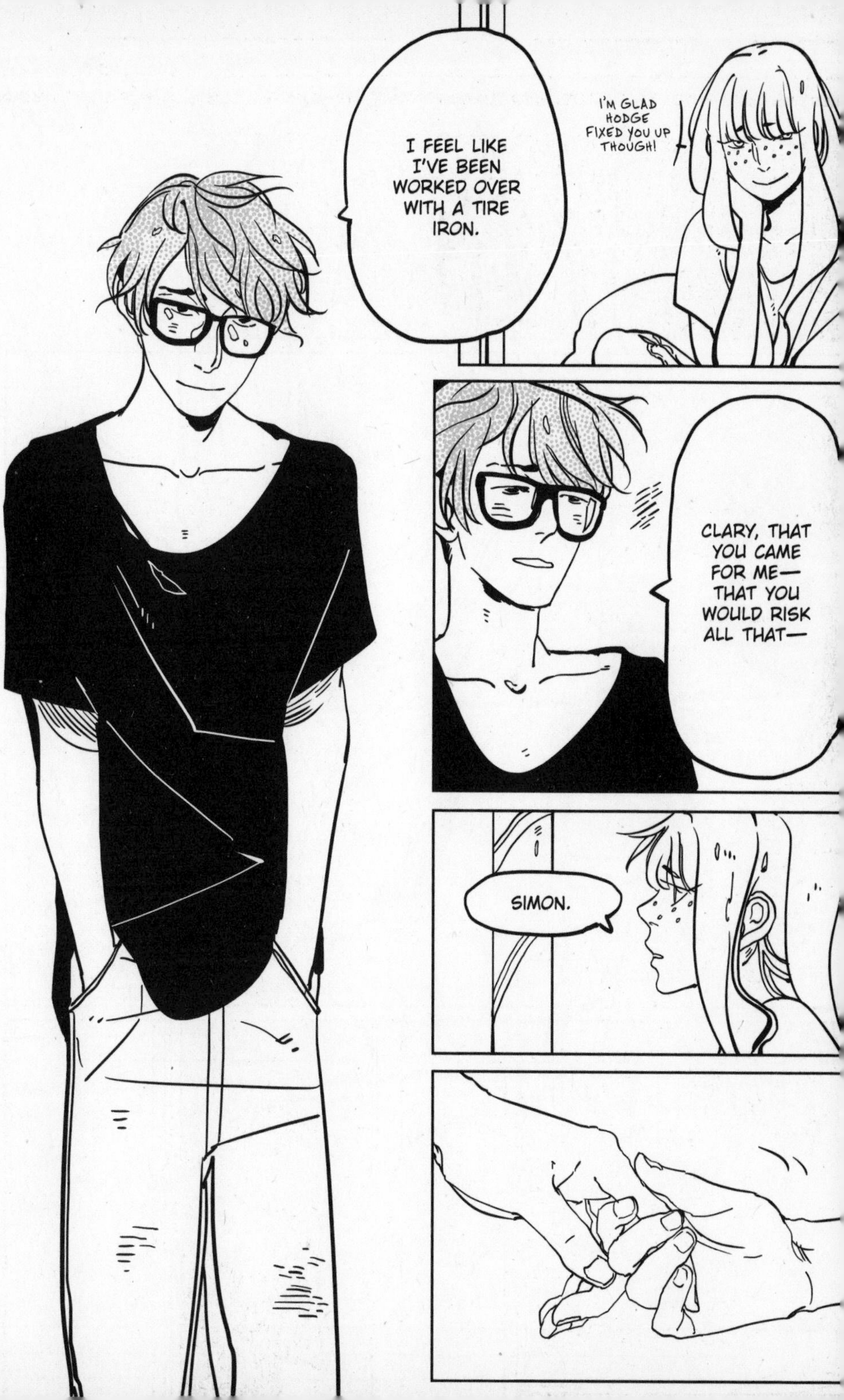
I FEEL LIKE I'VE BEEN WORKED OVER WITH A TIRE IRON.
I'M GLAD HODGE FIXED YOU UP THOUGH!
CLARY, THAT YOU CAME FOR ME— THAT YOU WOULD RISK ALL THAT—
SIMON.

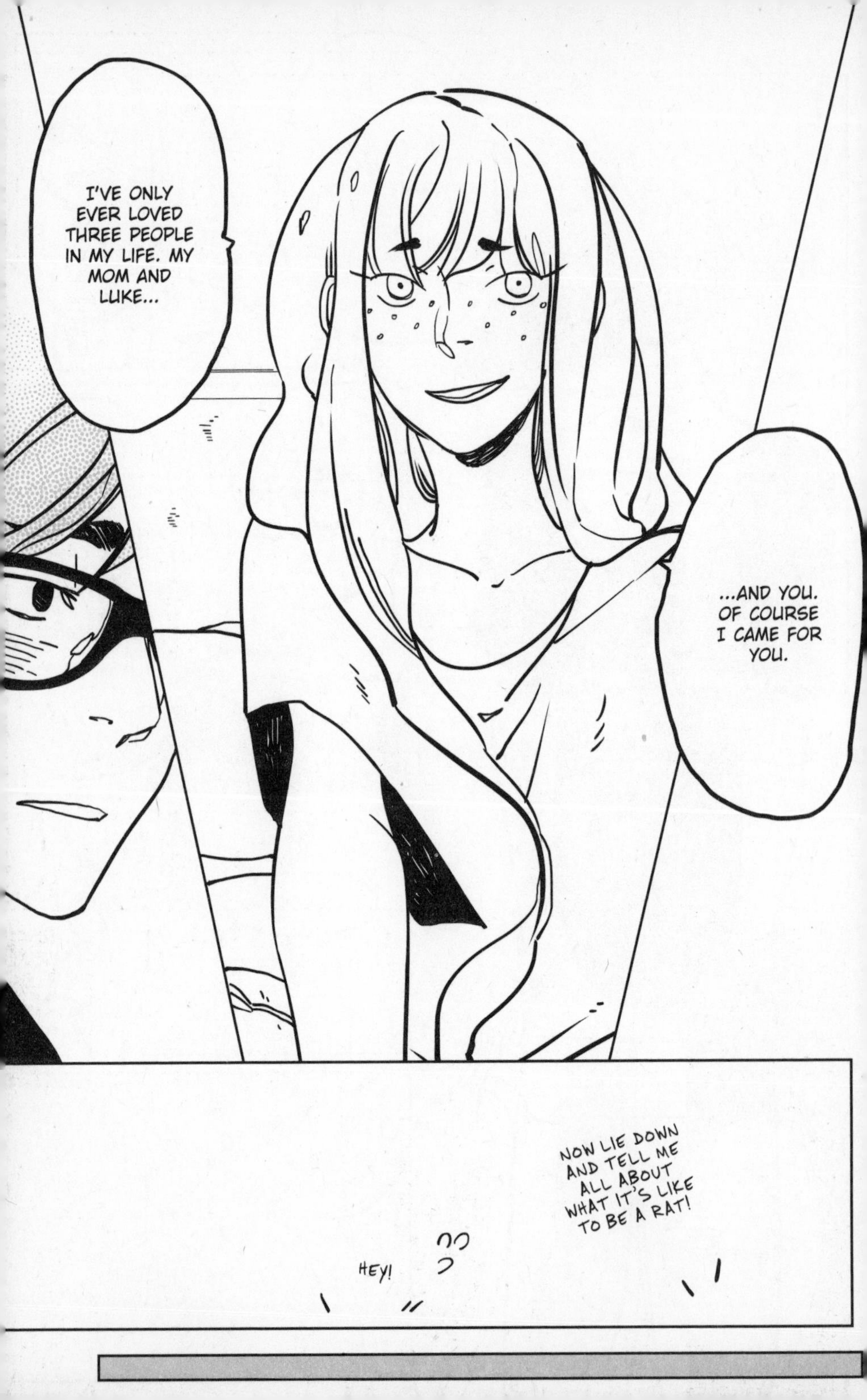
I'VE ONLY EVER LOVED THREE PEOPLE IN MY LIFE. MY MOM AND LUKE...
...AND YOU. OF COURSE I CAME FOR YOU.
NOW LIE DOWN AND TELL ME ALL ABOUT WHAT IT'S LIKE TO BE A RAT!
HEY!

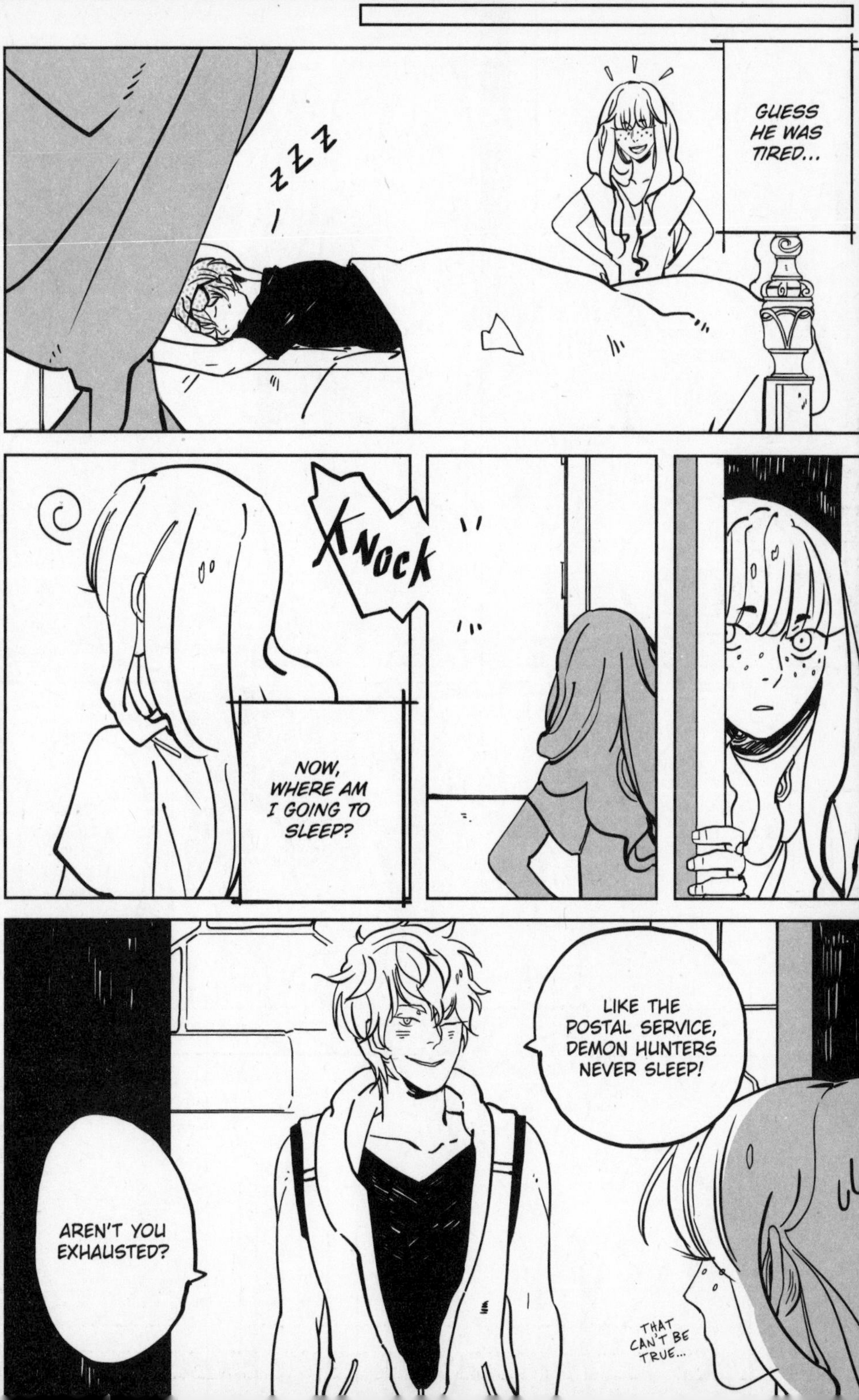
ZZZ
GUESS HE WAS TIRED...
NOW, WHERE AM I GOING TO SLEEP?
KNOCK
LIKE THE POSTAL SERVICE, DEMON HUNTERS NEVER SLEEP!
AREN'T YOU EXHAUSTED?
THAT CAN'T BE TRUE...

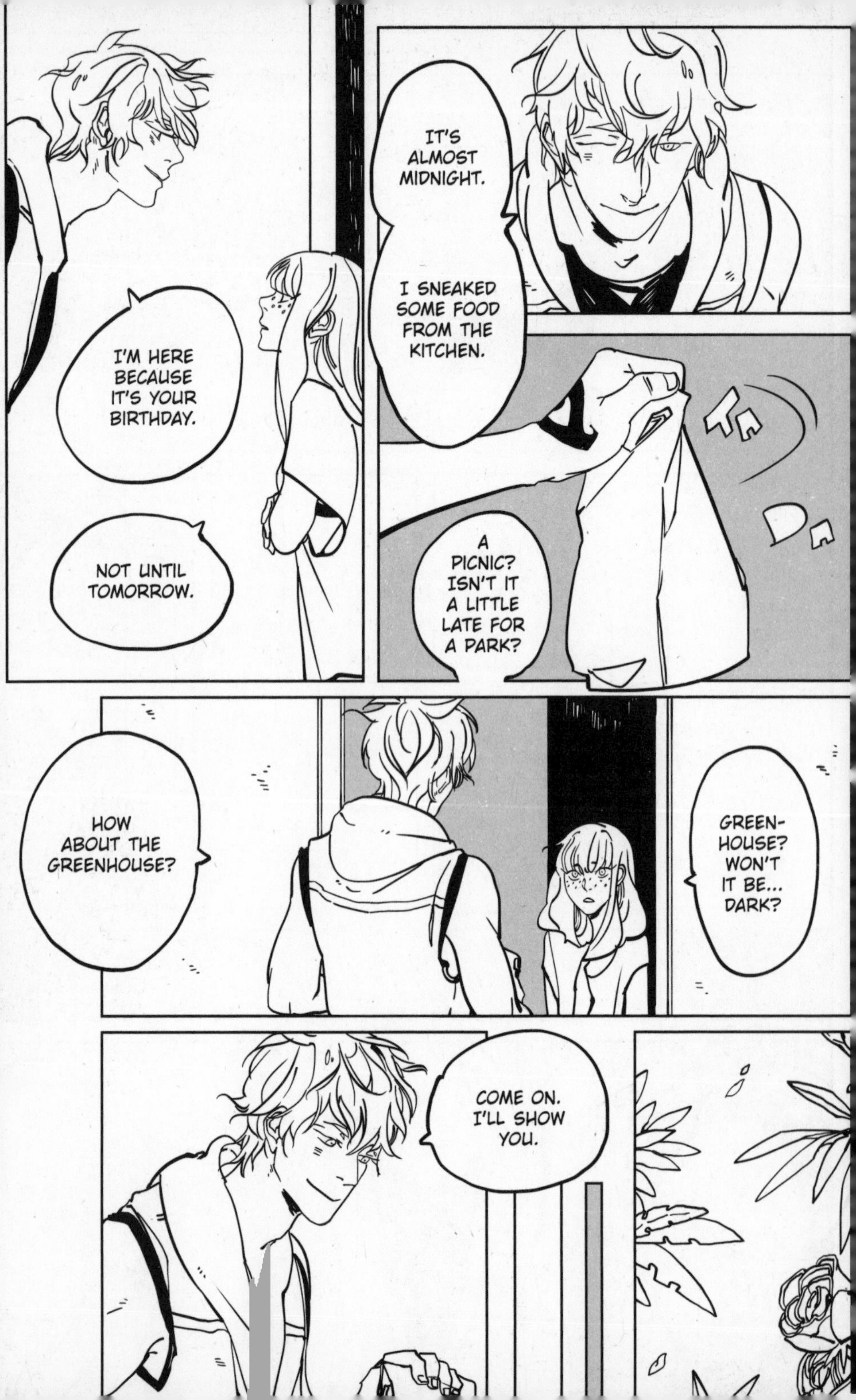
I'M HERE BECAUSE IT'S YOUR BIRTHDAY.
NOT UNTIL TOMORROW.
IT'S ALMOST MIDNIGHT.
I SNEAKED SOME FOOD FROM THE KITCHEN.
TA
DA
A PICNIC? ISN'T IT A LITTLE LATE FOR A PARK?
HOW ABOUT THE GREENHOUSE?
GREEN-HOUSE? WON'T IT BE... DARK?
COME ON. I'LL SHOW YOU.

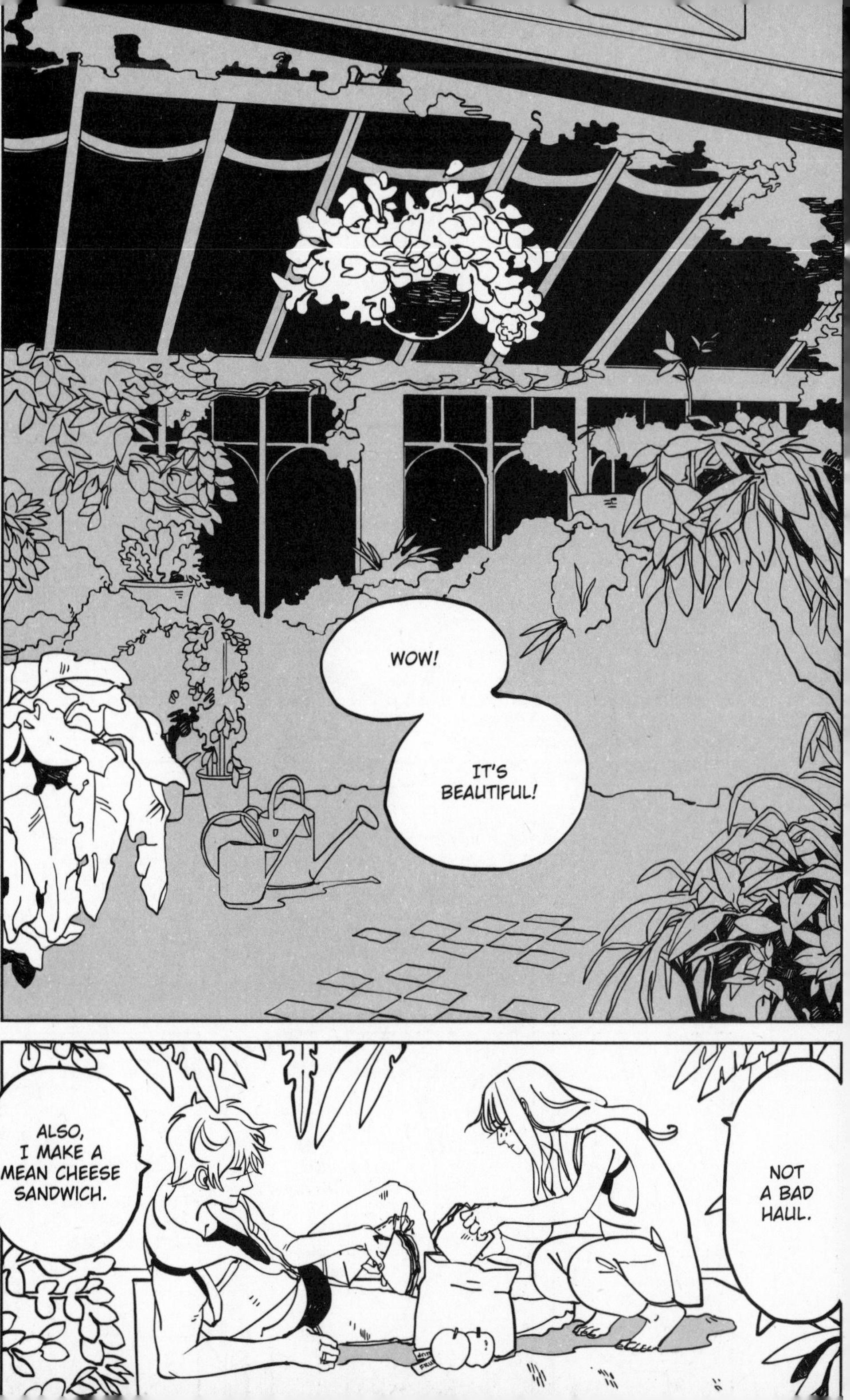
WOW!
IT'S BEAUTIFUL!
ALSO, I MAKE A MEAN CHEESE SANDWICH.
NOT A BAD HAUL.

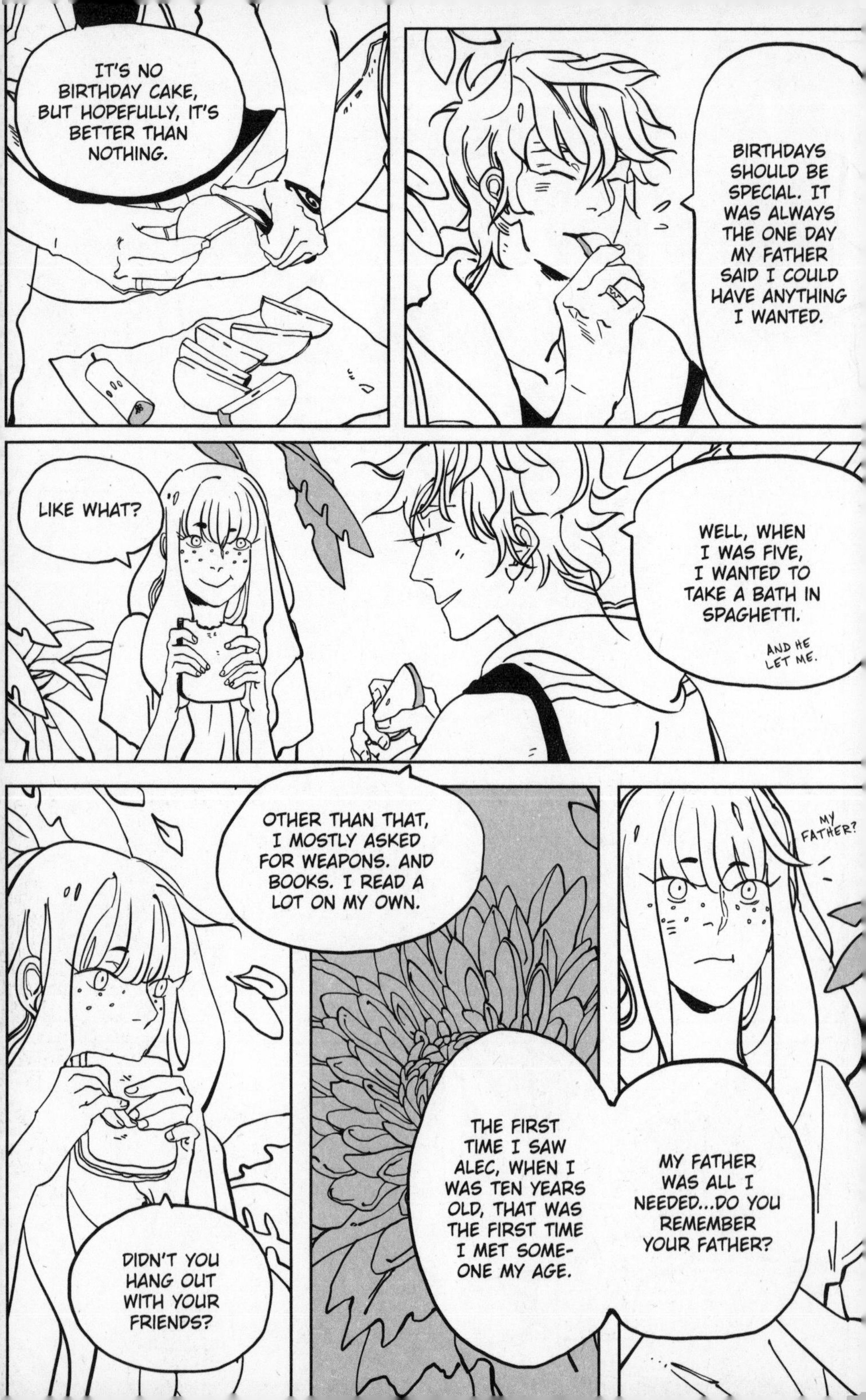
IT'S NO BIRTHDAY CAKE, BUT HOPEFULLY, IT'S BETTER THAN NOTHING.
BIRTHDAYS SHOULD BE SPECIAL. IT WAS ALWAYS THE ONE DAY MY FATHER SAID I COULD HAVE ANYTHING I WANTED.
LIKE WHAT?
WELL, WHEN I WAS FIVE, I WANTED TO TAKE A BATH IN SPAGHETTI.
AND HE LET ME.
OTHER THAN THAT, I MOSTLY ASKED FOR WEAPONS. AND BOOKS. I READ A LOT ON MY OWN.
DIDN'T YOU HANG OUT WITH YOUR FRIENDS?
THE FIRST TIME I SAW ALEC, WHEN I WAS TEN YEARS OLD, THAT WAS THE FIRST TIME I MET SOME-ONE MY AGE.
MY FATHER?
MY FATHER WAS ALL I NEEDED...DO YOU REMEMBER YOUR FATHER?

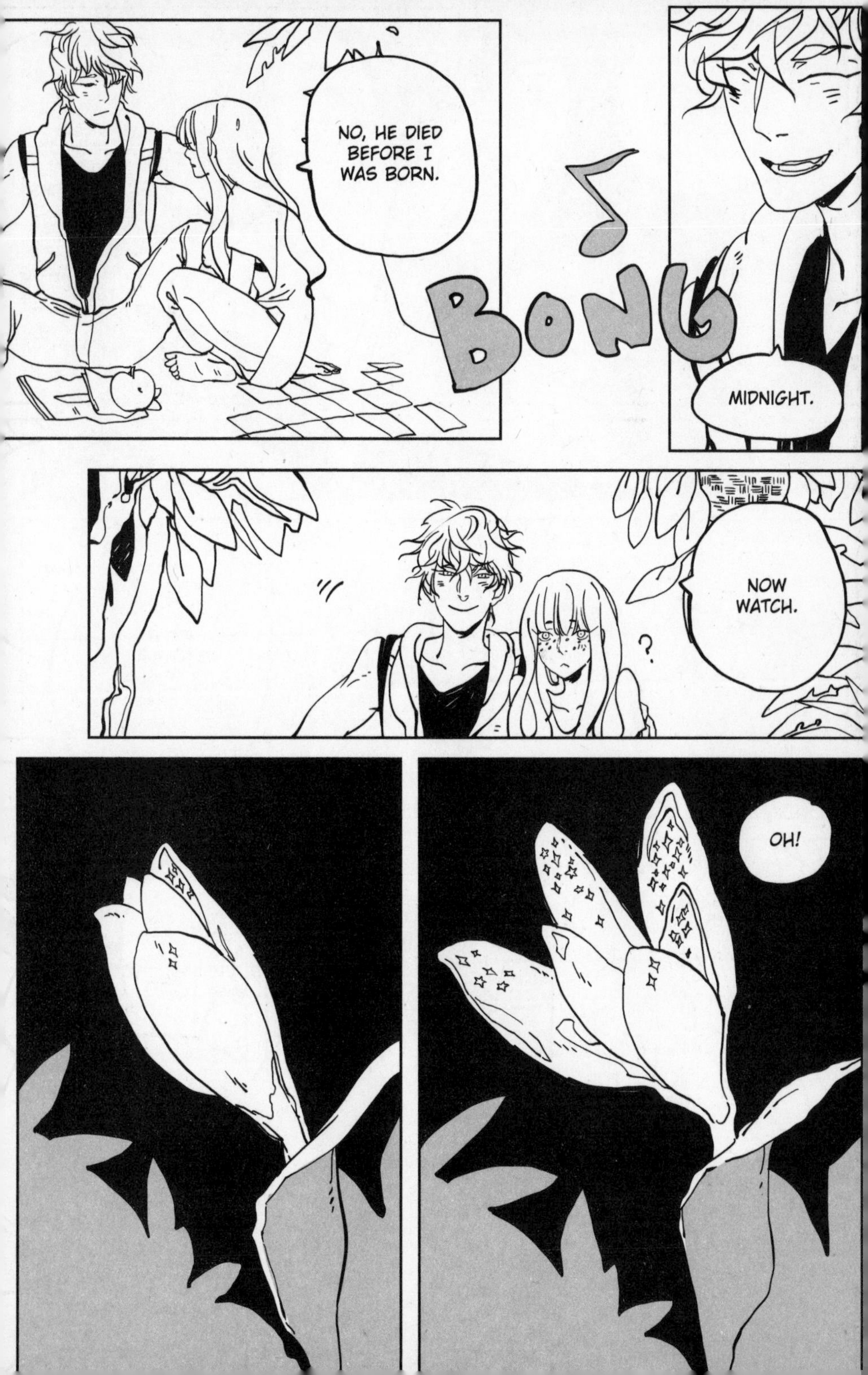
NO, HE DIED BEFORE I WAS BORN.
BONG
MIDNIGHT.
NOW WATCH.
?
OH!

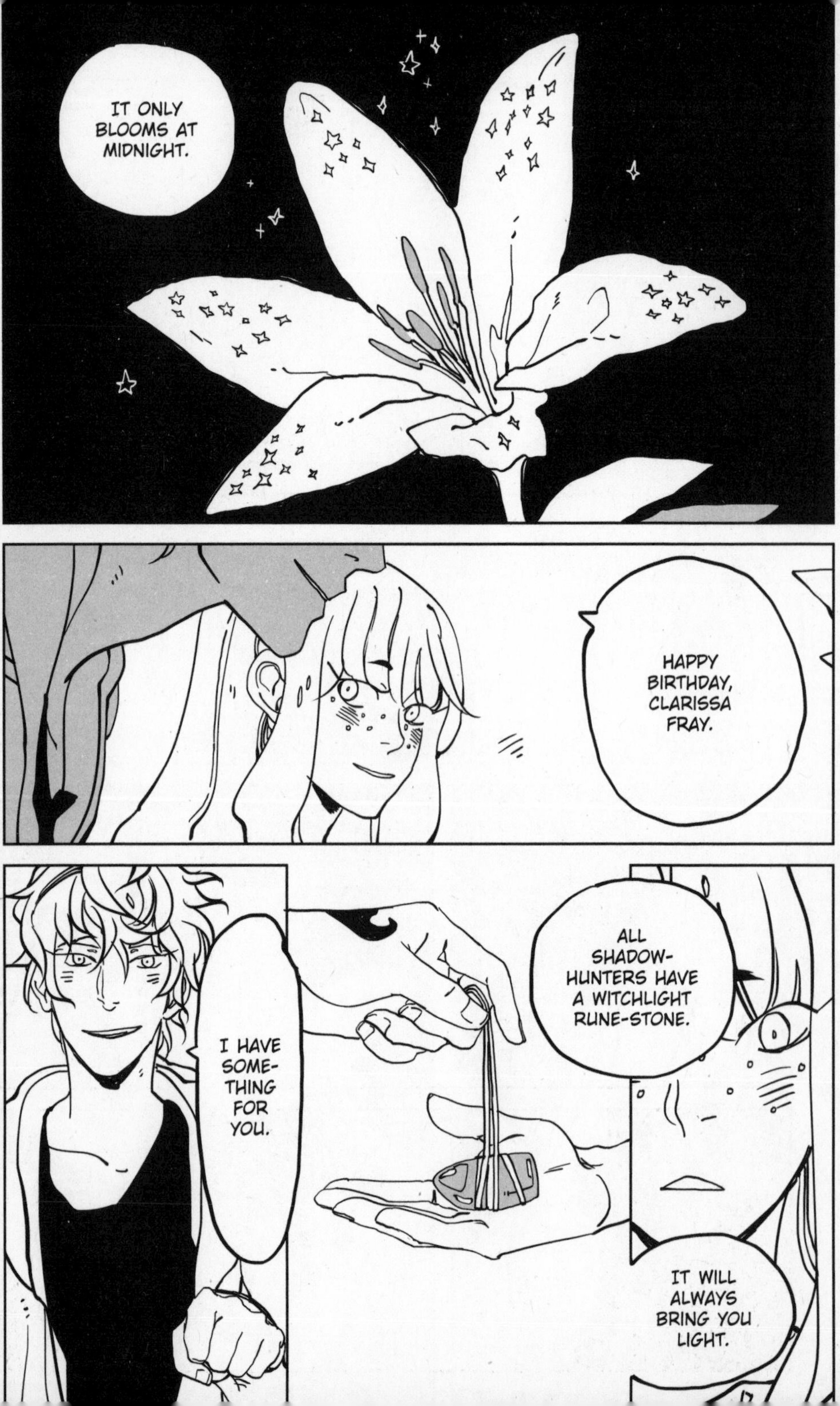
IT ONLY BLOOMS AT MIDNIGHT.
HAPPY BIRTHDAY, CLARISSA FRAY.
I HAVE SOME-THING FOR YOU.
ALL SHADOW-HUNTERS HAVE A WITCHLIGHT RUNE-STONE.
IT WILL ALWAYS BRING YOU LIGHT.

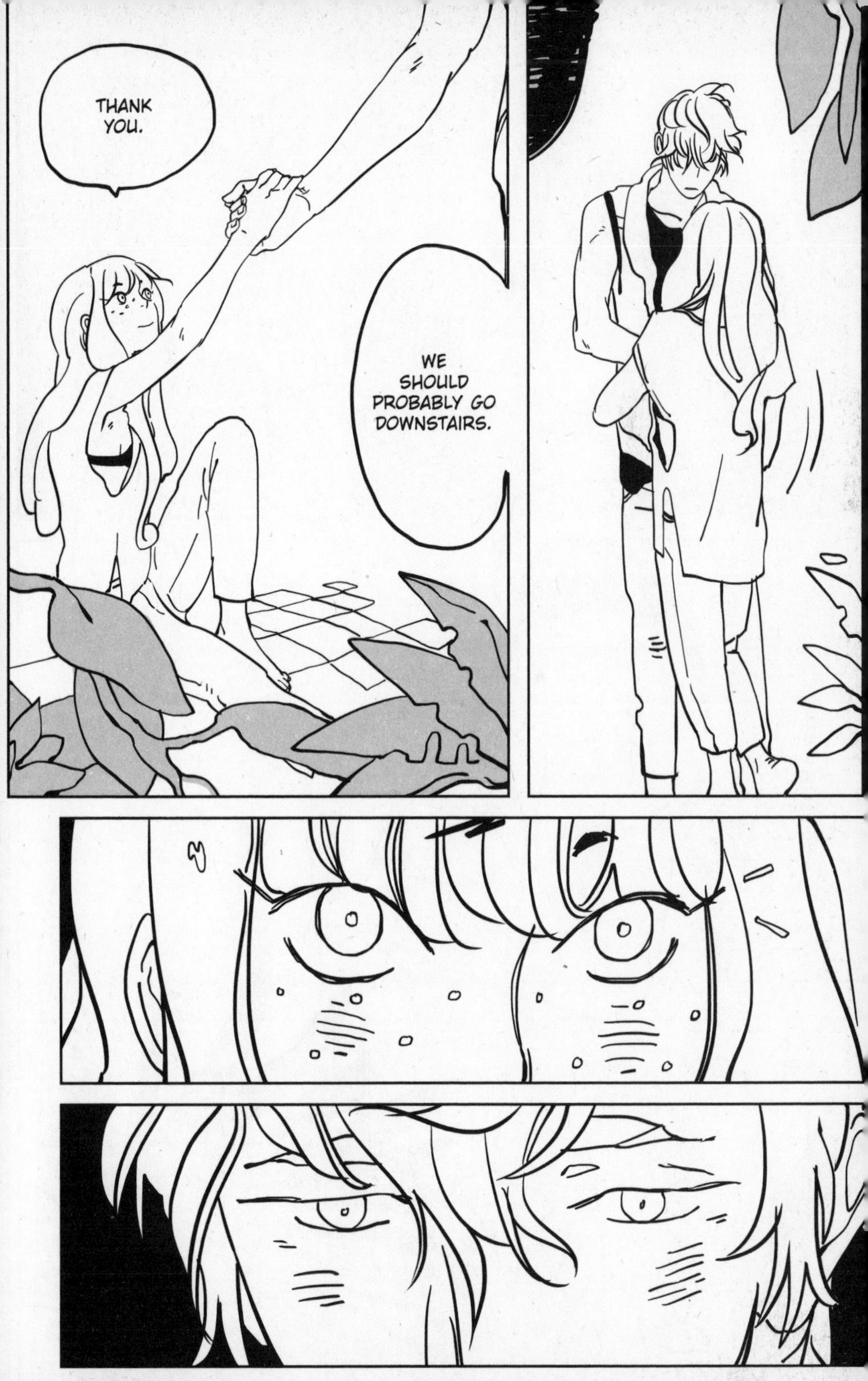
THANK YOU.
WE SHOULD PROBABLY GO DOWNSTAIRS.

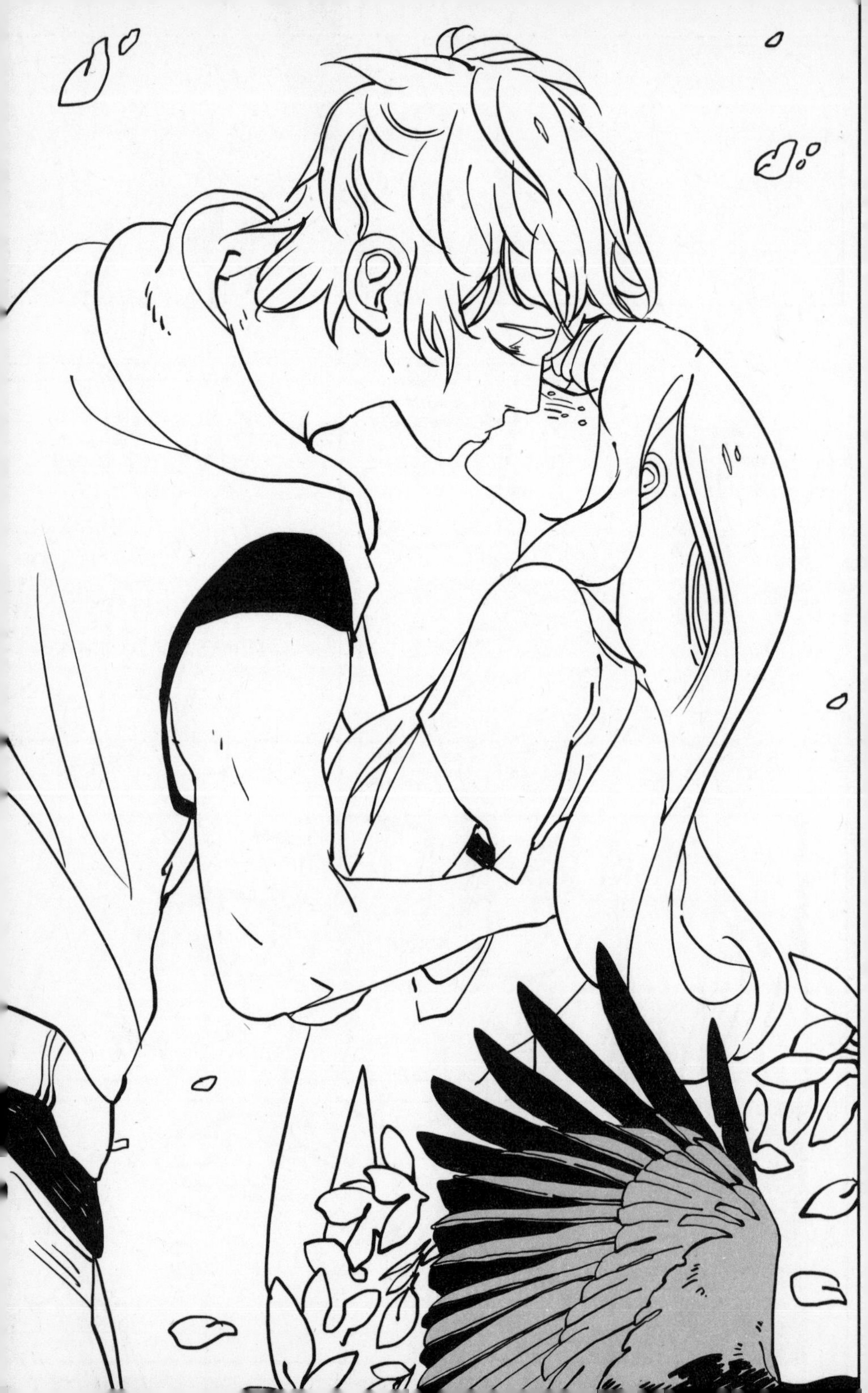

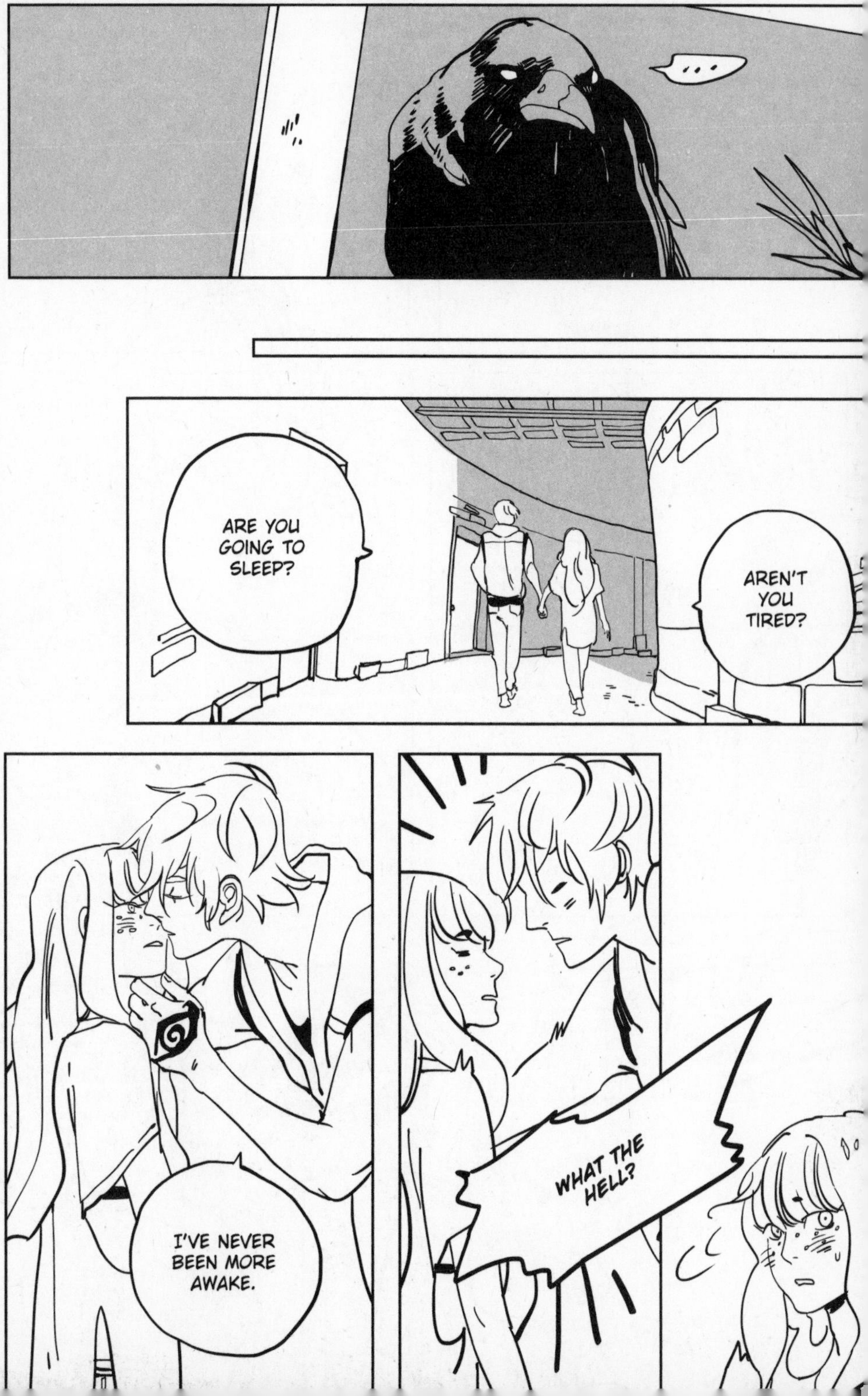
...
ARE YOU GOING TO SLEEP?
AREN'T YOU TIRED?
I'VE NEVER BEEN MORE AWAKE.
WHAT THE HELL?

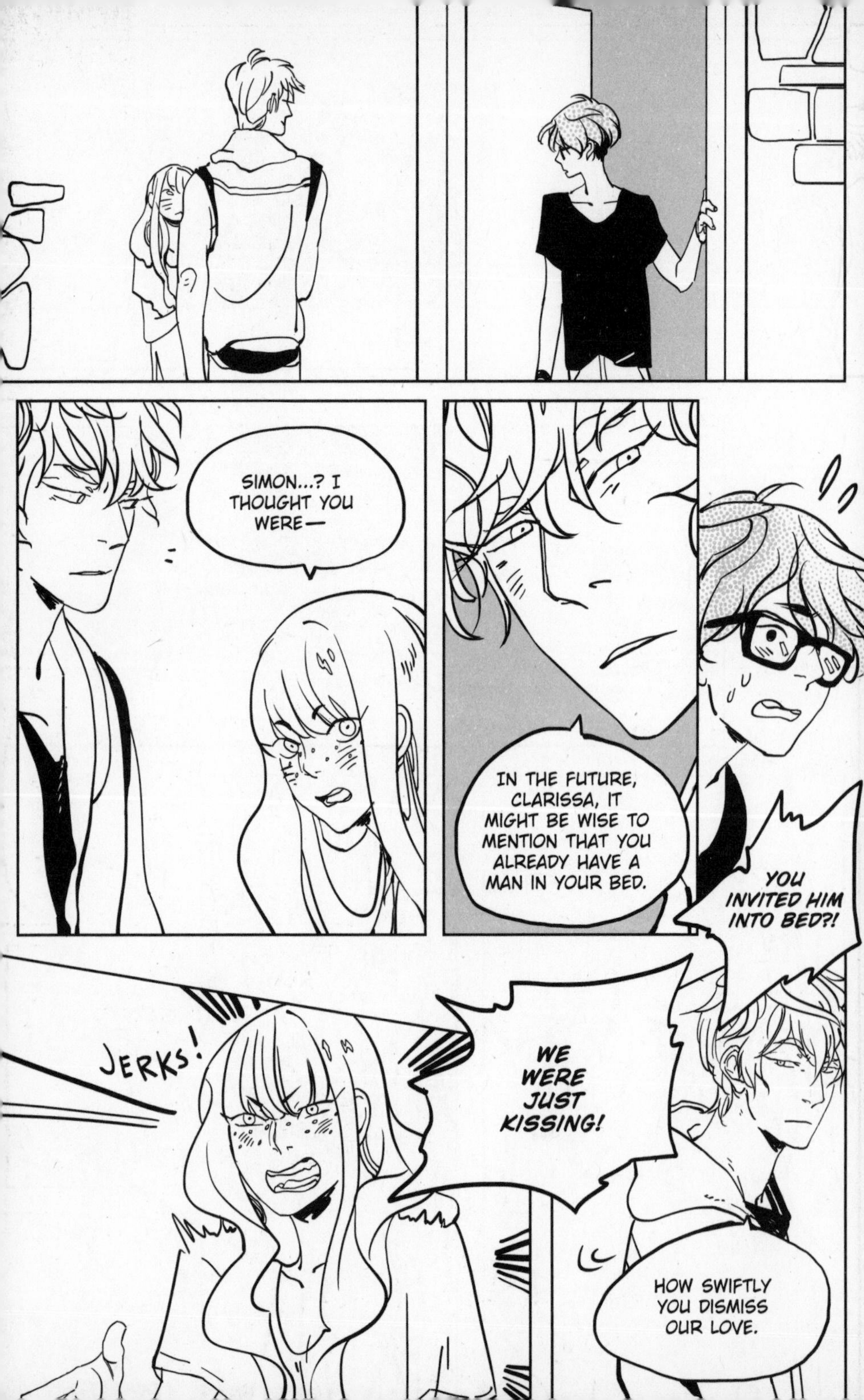
SIMON...? I THOUGHT YOU WERE—
IN THE FUTURE, CLARISSA, IT MIGHT BE WISE TO MENTION THAT YOU ALREADY HAVE A MAN IN YOUR BED.
YOU INVITED HIM INTO BED?!
JERKS!
WE WERE JUST KISSING!
HOW SWIFTLY YOU DISMISS OUR LOVE.

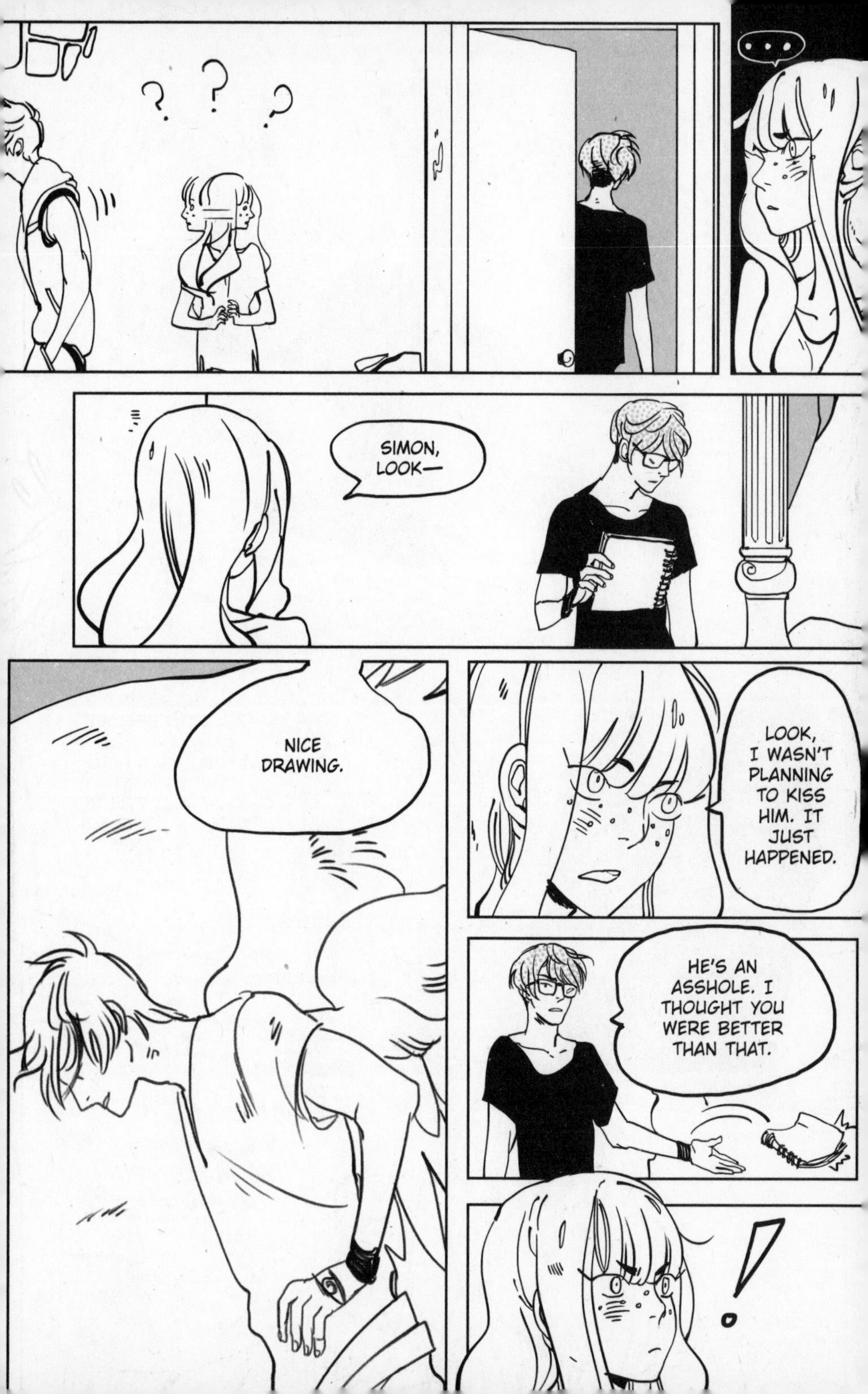
? ? ?
...
SIMON, LOOK—
NICE DRAWING.
LOOK, I WASN'T PLANNING TO KISS HIM. IT JUST HAPPENED.
HE'S AN ASSHOLE. I THOUGHT YOU WERE BETTER THAN THAT.
!

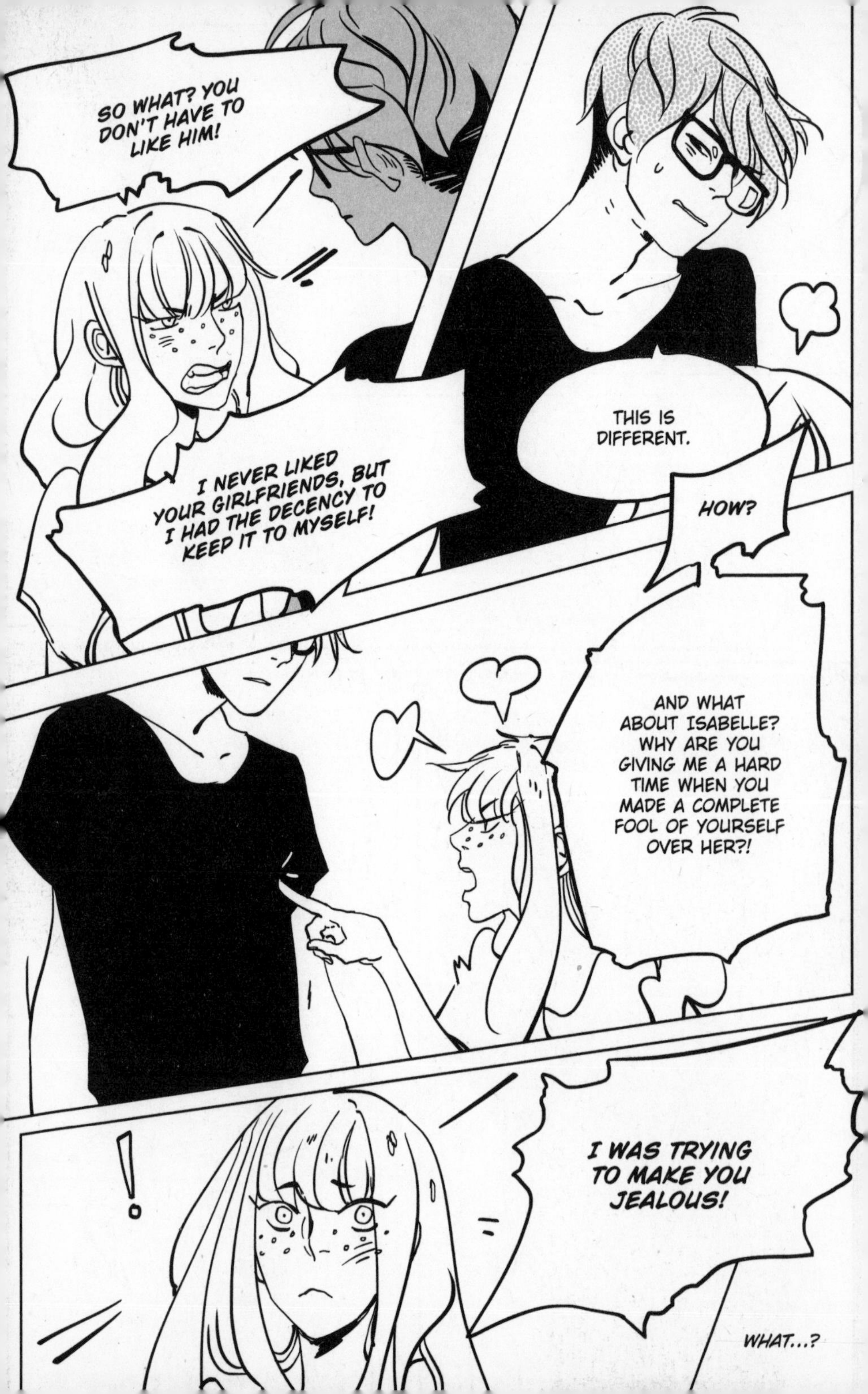
SO WHAT? YOU DON'T HAVE TO LIKE HIM!
I NEVER LIKED YOUR GIRLFRIENDS, BUT I HAD THE DECENCY TO KEEP IT TO MYSELF!
THIS IS DIFFERENT.
HOW?
AND WHAT ABOUT ISABELLE? WHY ARE YOU GIVING ME A HARD TIME WHEN YOU MADE A COMPLETE FOOL OF YOURSELF OVER HER?!
!
I WAS TRYING TO MAKE YOU JEALOUS!
WHAT...?

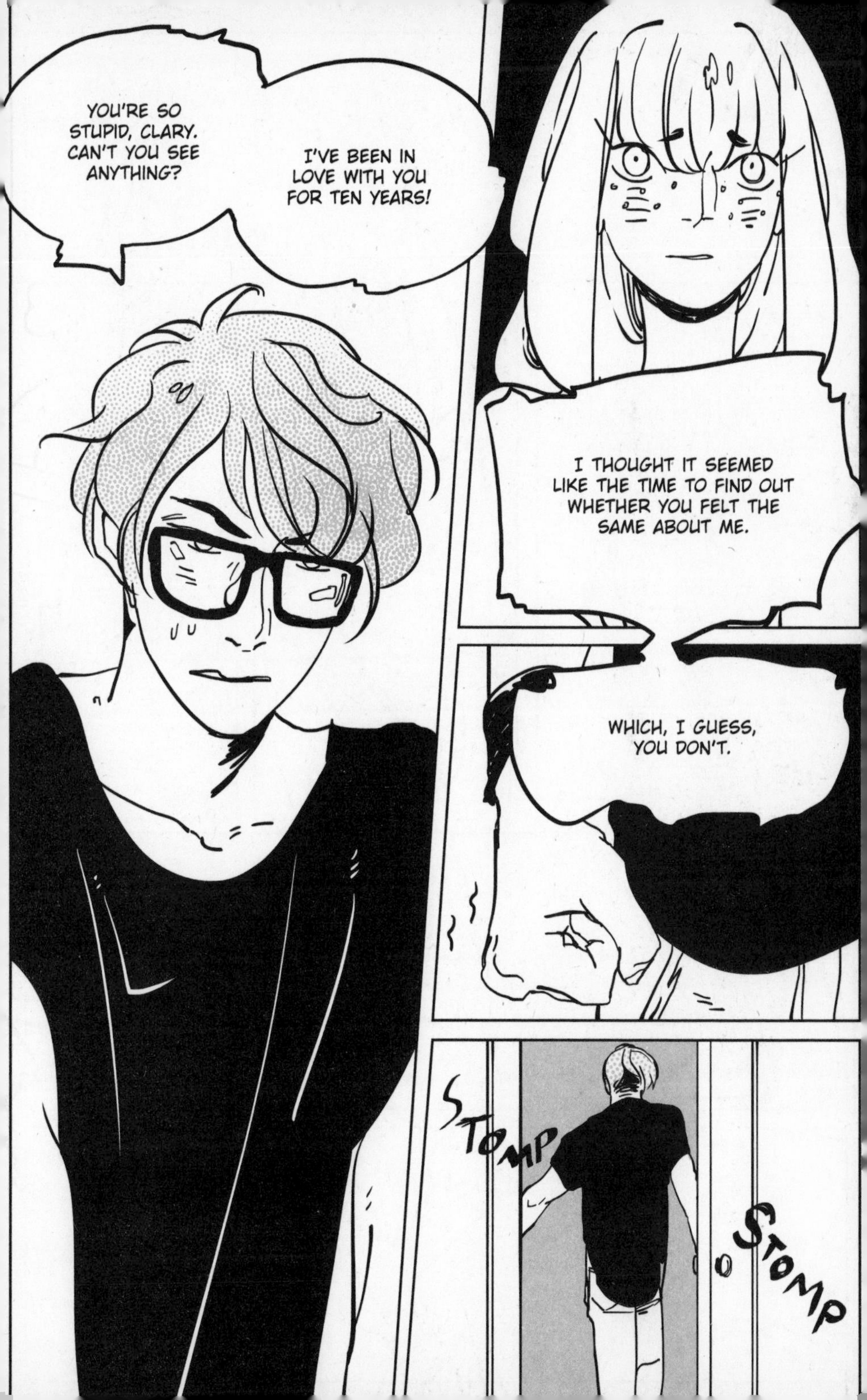
YOU'RE SO STUPID, CLARY. CAN'T YOU SEE ANYTHING?
I'VE BEEN IN LOVE WITH YOU FOR TEN YEARS!
I THOUGHT IT SEEMED LIKE THE TIME TO FIND OUT WHETHER YOU FELT THE SAME ABOUT ME.
WHICH, I GUESS, YOU DON'T.
STOMP
STOMP

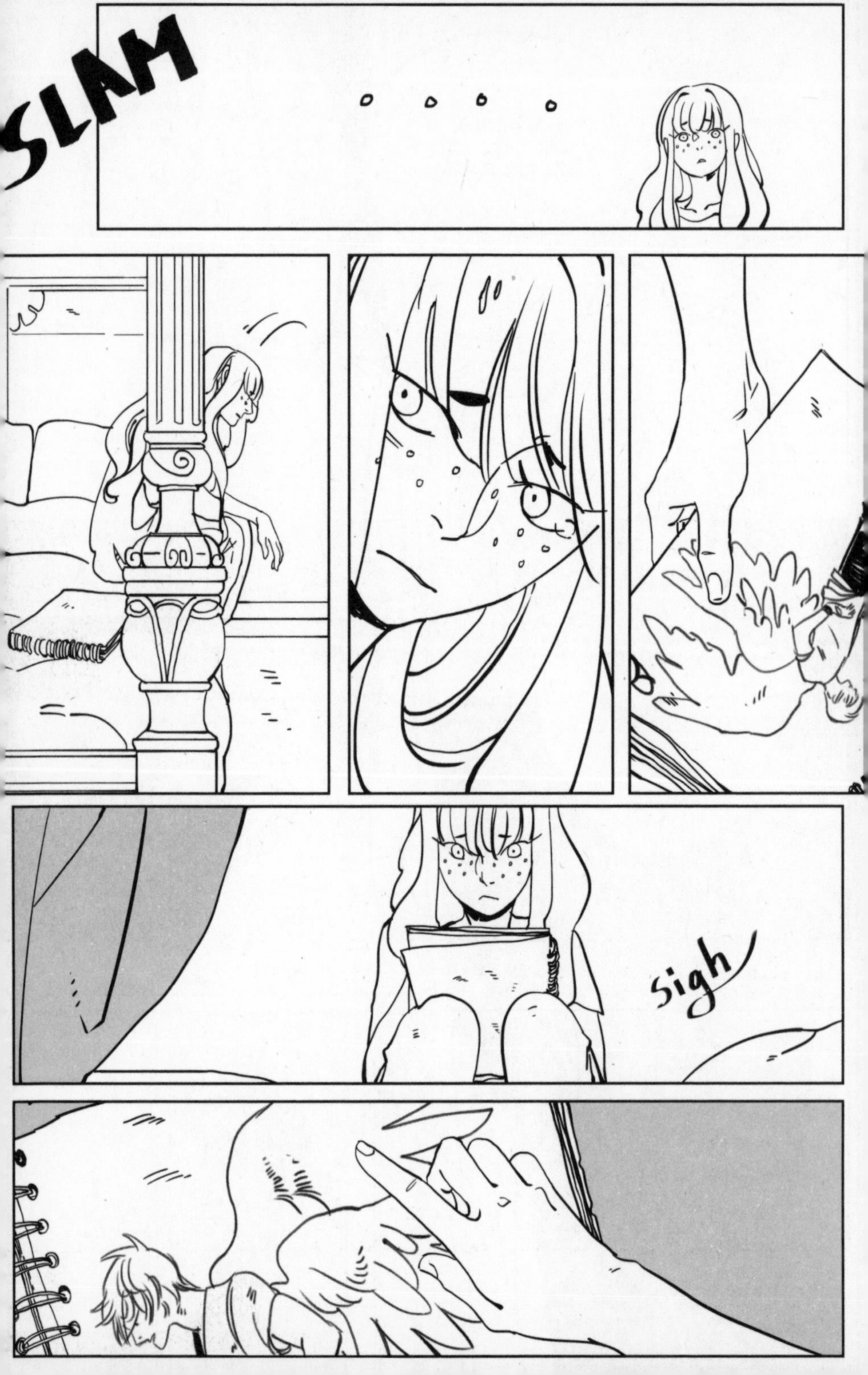
SLAM
. . . .
sigh

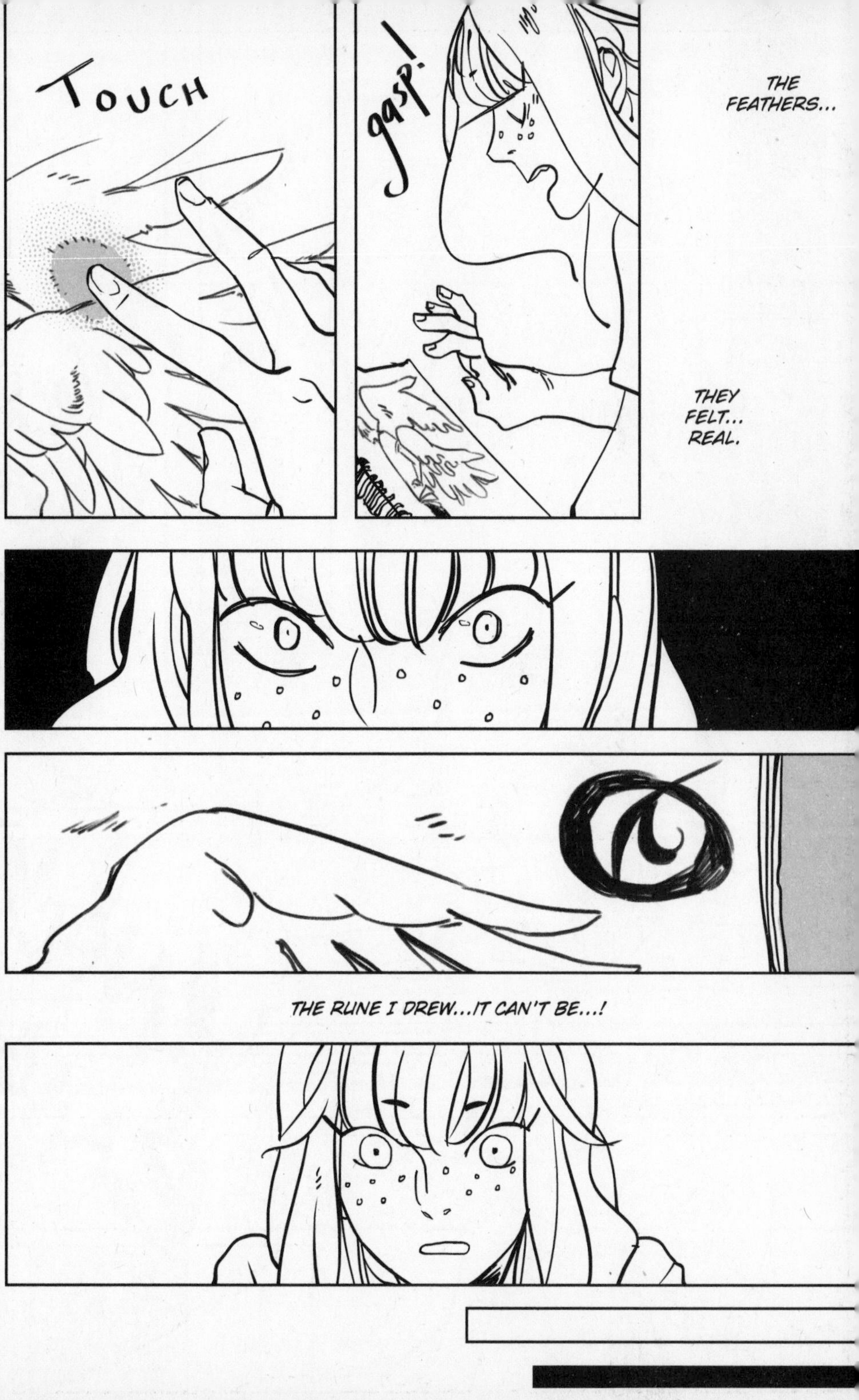
TOUCH
gasp!
THE FEATHERS...
THEY FELT... REAL.
THE RUNE I DREW...IT CAN'T BE...!

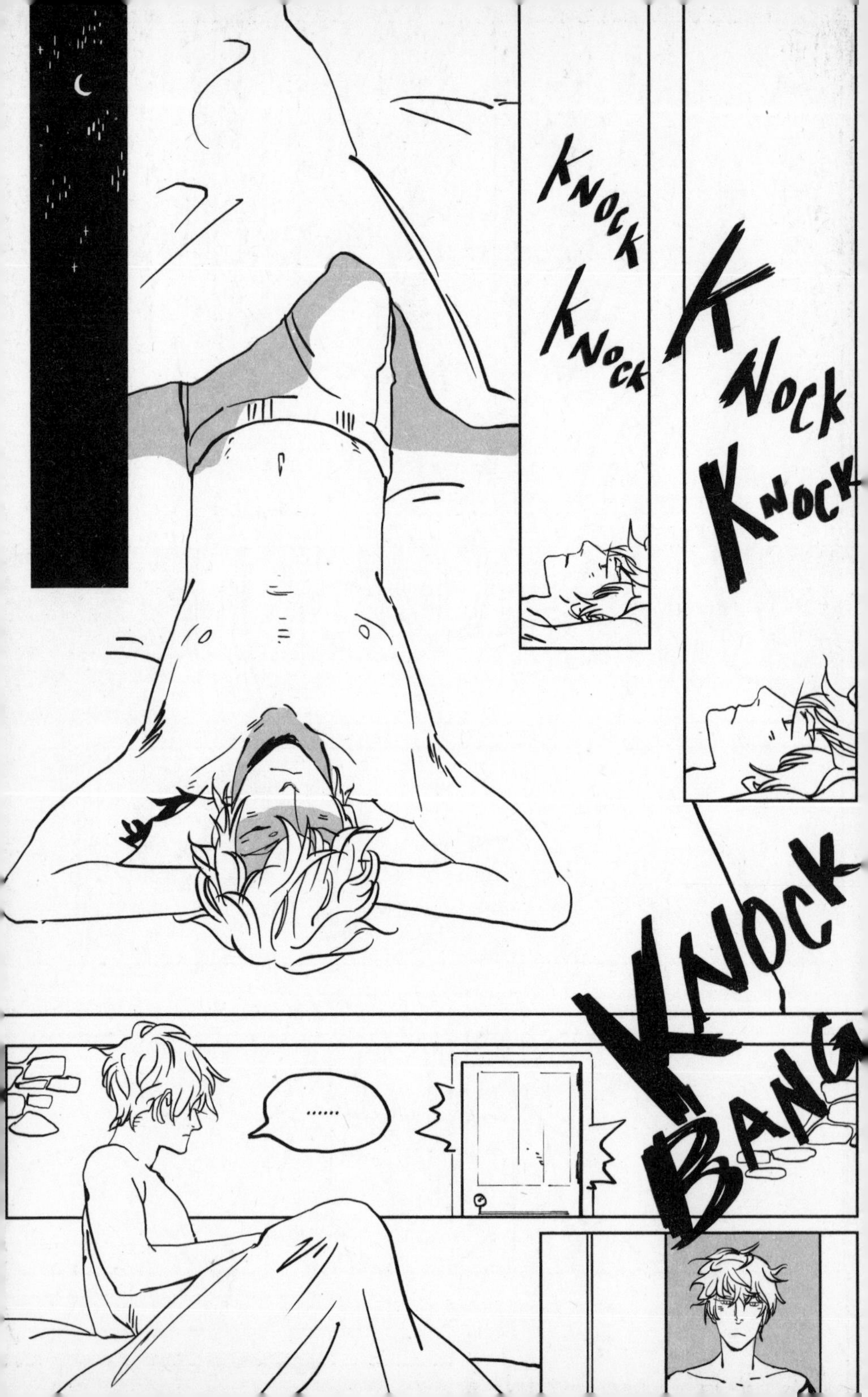

KNOCK KNOCK
KNOCK KNOCK
KNOCK
……
BANG

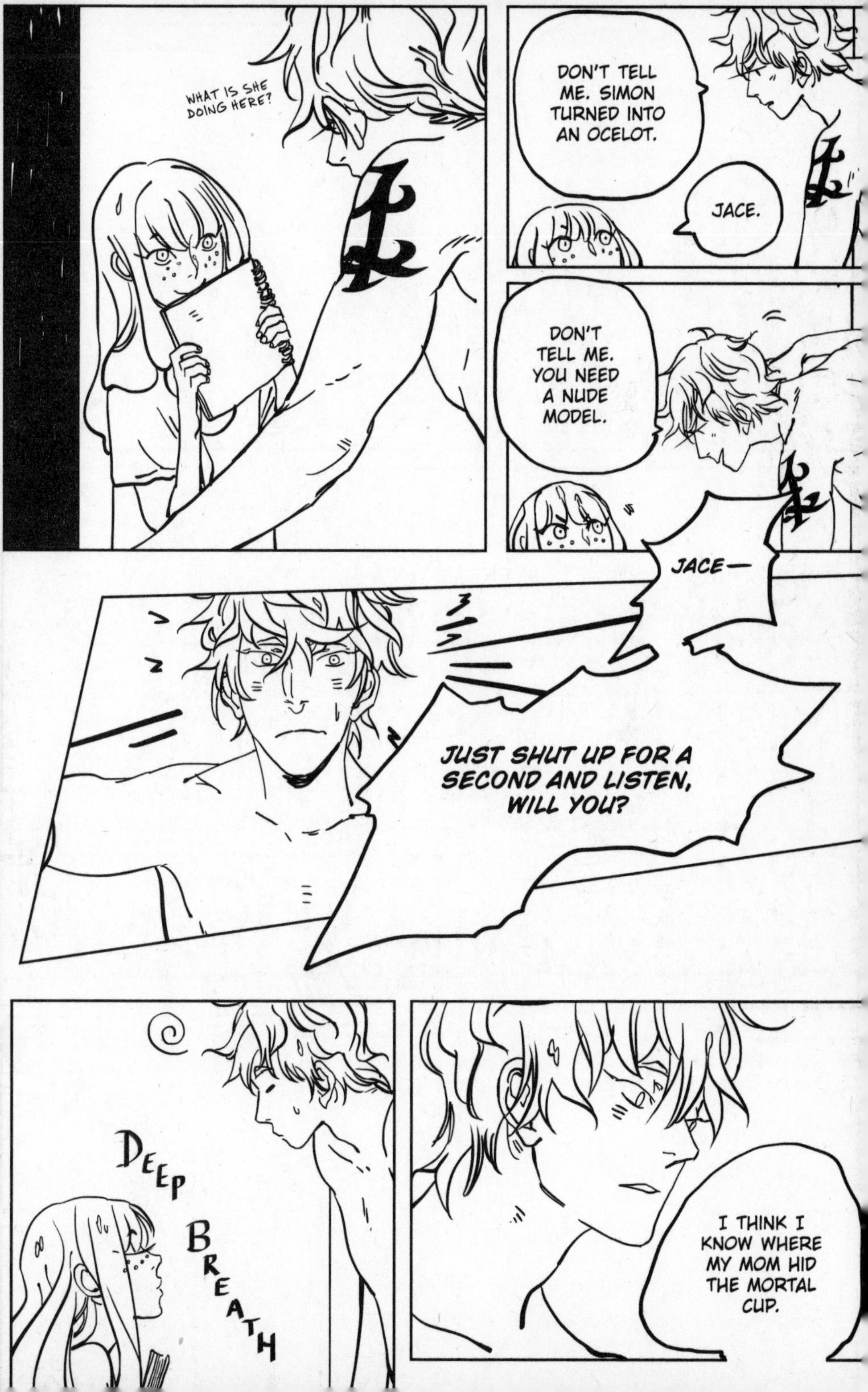
WHAT IS SHE DOING HERE?
DON'T TELL ME. SIMON TURNED INTO AN OCELOT.
JACE.
DON'T TELL ME. YOU NEED A NUDE MODEL.
JACE—
JUST SHUT UP FOR A SECOND AND LISTEN, WILL YOU?
DEEP BREATH
I THINK I KNOW WHERE MY MOM HID THE MORTAL CUP.

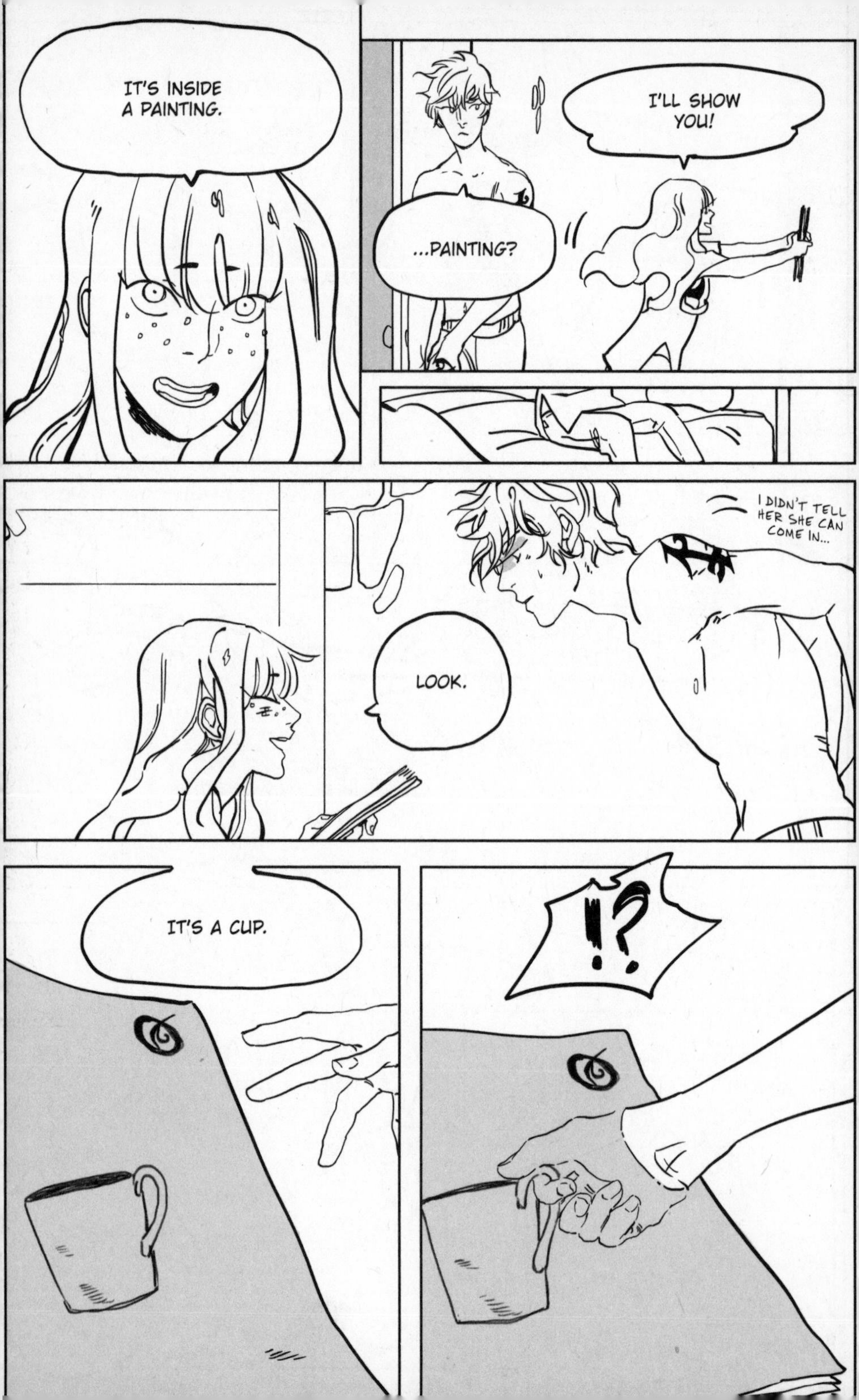
IT'S INSIDE A PAINTING.
...PAINTING?
I'LL SHOW YOU!
I DIDN'T TELL HER SHE CAN COME IN...
LOOK.
IT'S A CUP.
!?

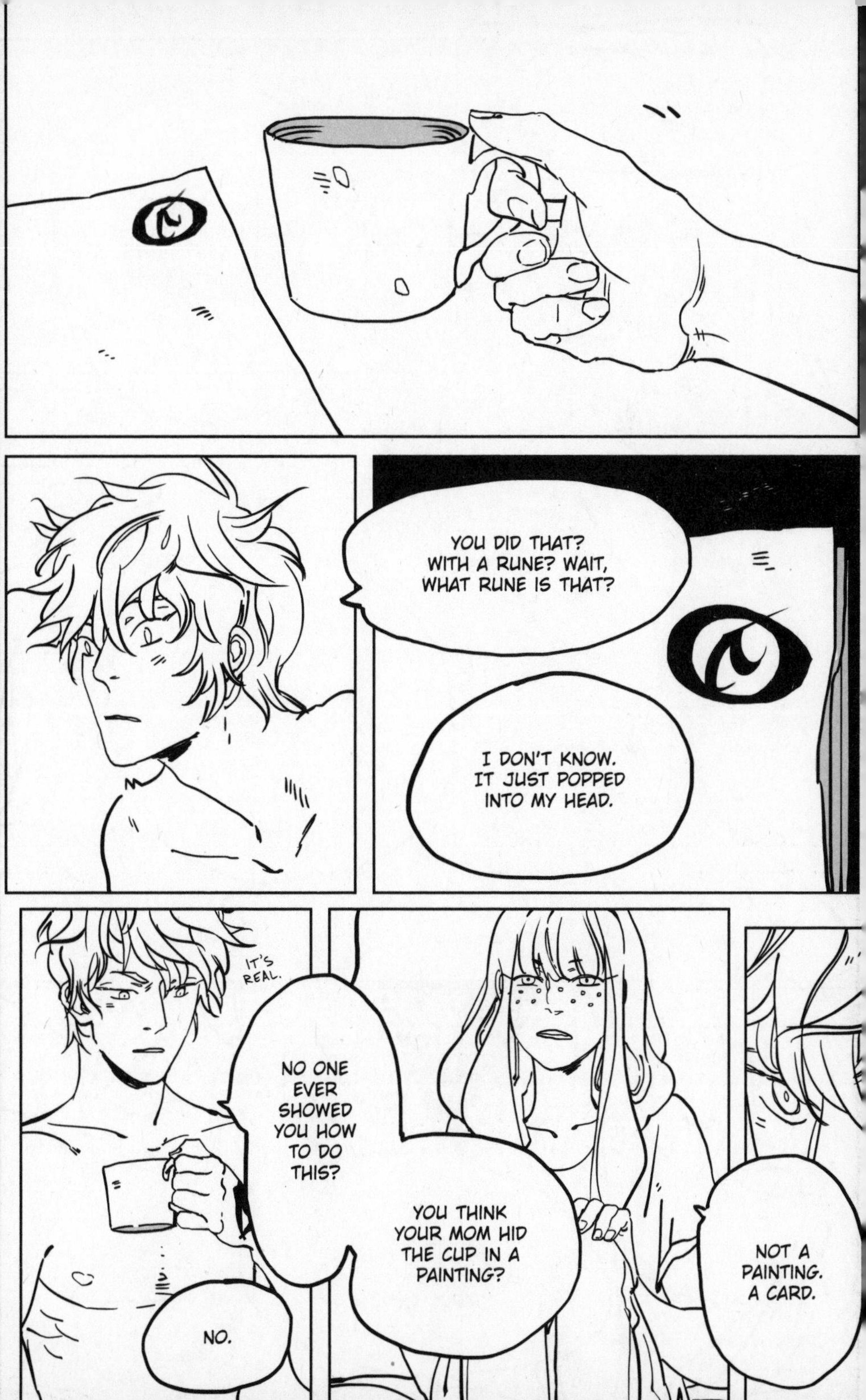
YOU DID THAT? WITH A RUNE? WAIT, WHAT RUNE IS THAT?
I DON'T KNOW. IT JUST POPPED INTO MY HEAD.
IT'S REAL.
NO ONE EVER SHOWED YOU HOW TO DO THIS?
NO.
YOU THINK YOUR MOM HID THE CUP IN A PAINTING?
NOT A PAINTING. A CARD.

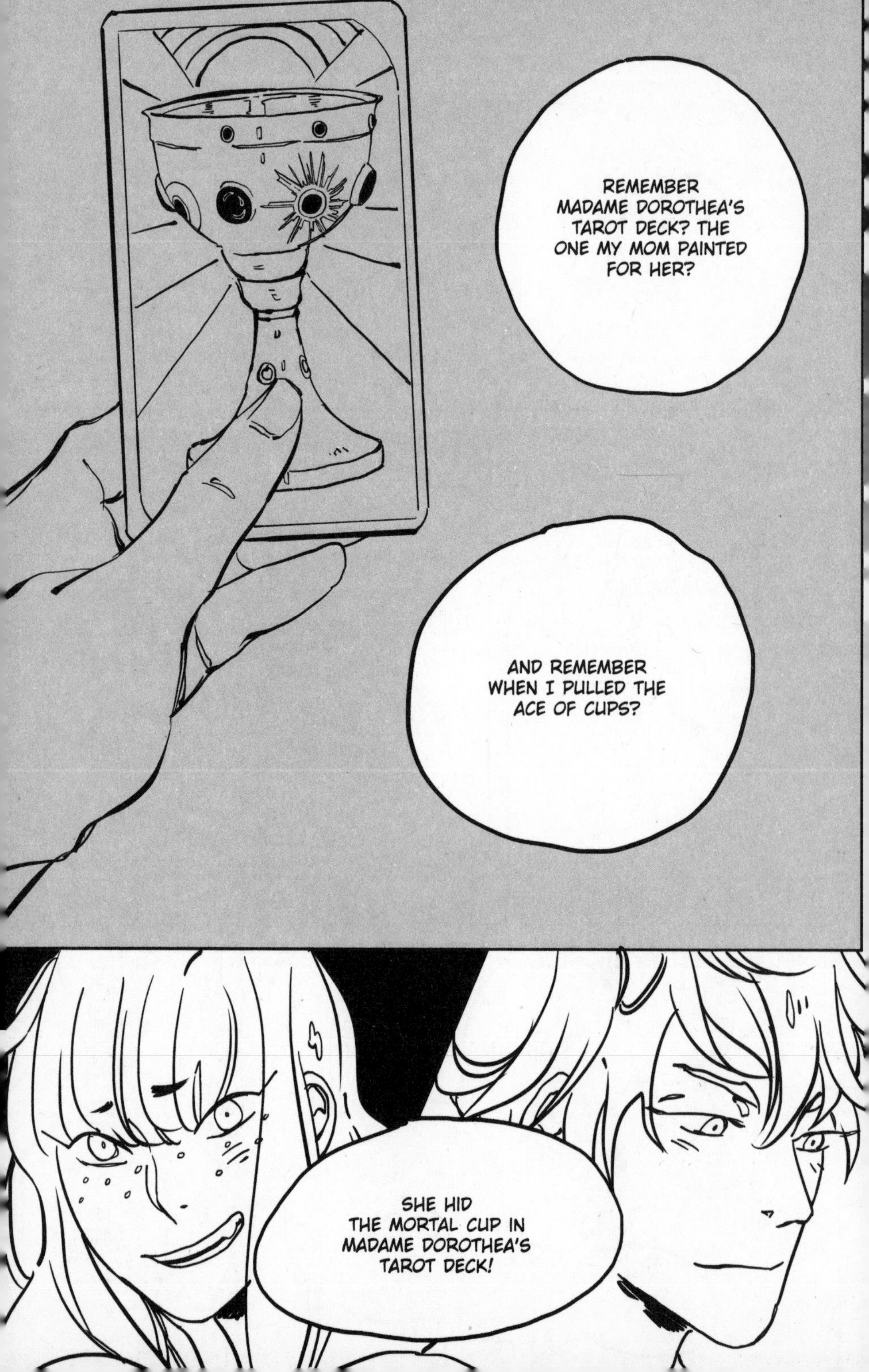
REMEMBER MADAME DOROTHEA'S TAROT DECK? THE ONE MY MOM PAINTED FOR HER?
AND REMEMBER WHEN I PULLED THE ACE OF CUPS?
SHE HID THE MORTAL CUP IN MADAME DOROTHEA'S TAROT DECK!

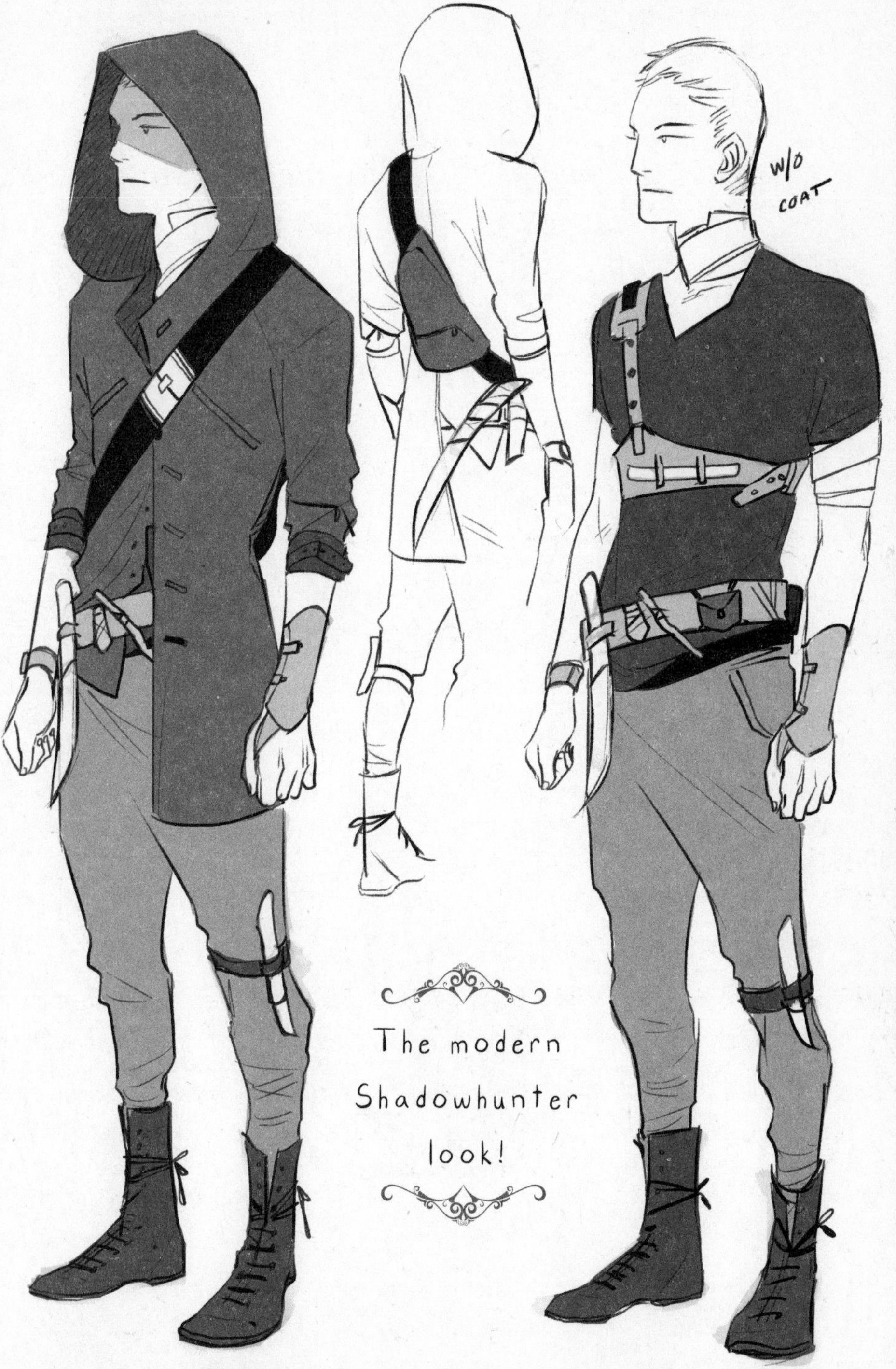
W/O COAT
The modern Shadowhunter look!

THE MORTAL INSTRUMENTS

THE GRAPHIC NOVEL

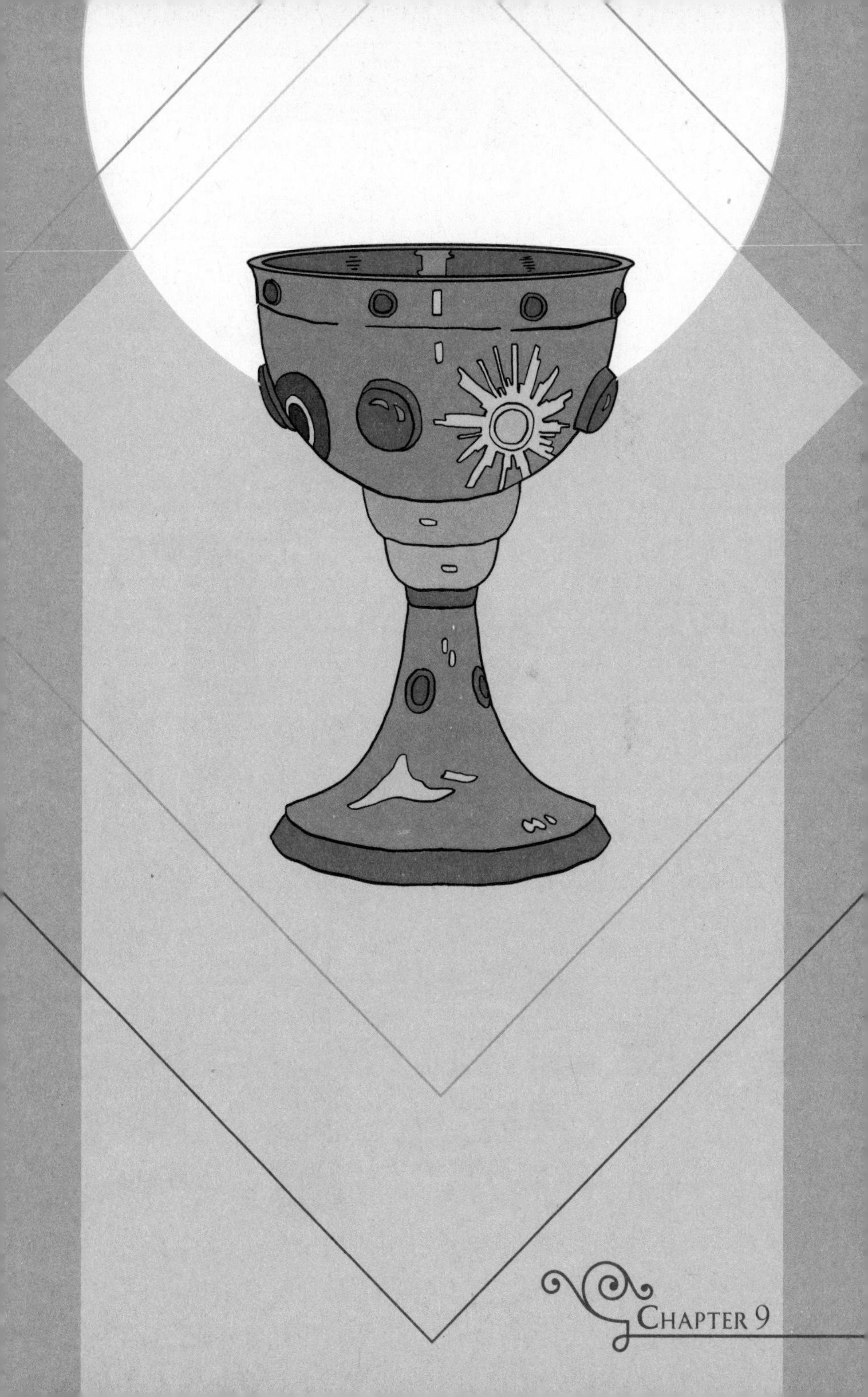

Chapter 9

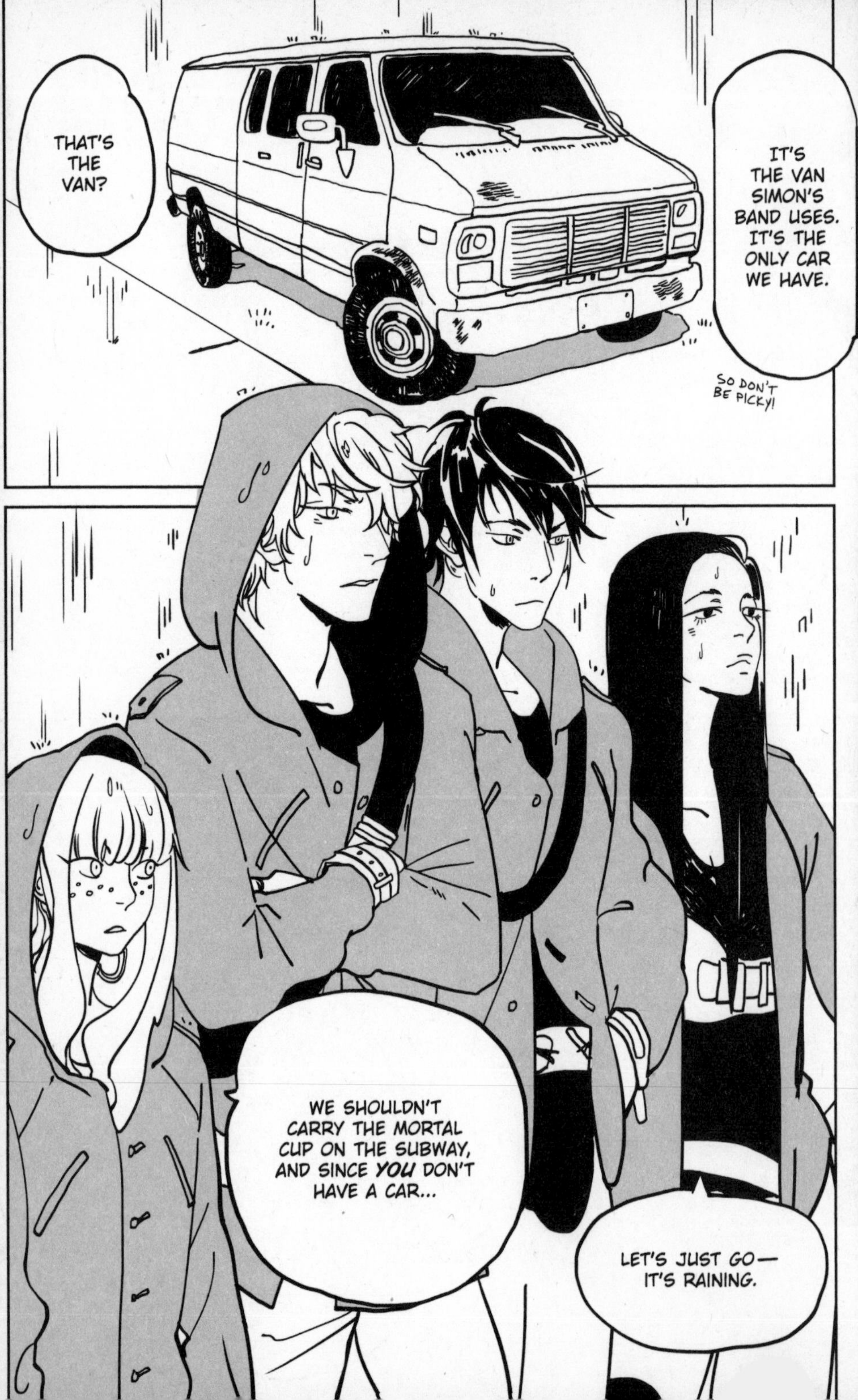
THAT'S THE VAN?
IT'S THE VAN SIMON'S BAND USES. IT'S THE ONLY CAR WE HAVE.
SO DON'T BE PICKY!
WE SHOULDN'T CARRY THE MORTAL CUP ON THE SUBWAY, AND SINCE *YOU* DON'T HAVE A CAR...
LET'S JUST GO— IT'S RAINING.

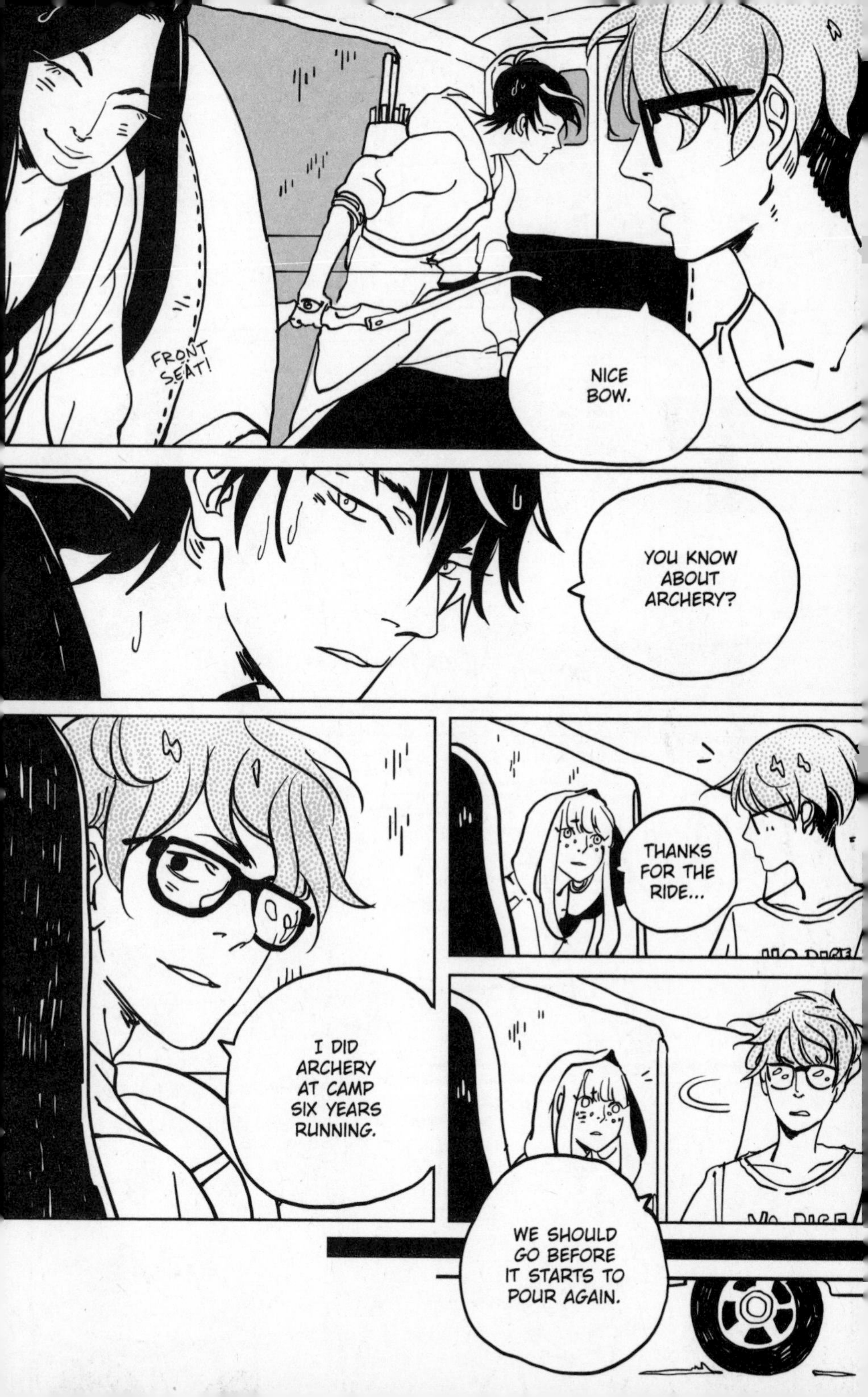
FRONT SEAT!
NICE BOW.
YOU KNOW ABOUT ARCHERY?
I DID ARCHERY AT CAMP SIX YEARS RUNNING.
THANKS FOR THE RIDE...
WE SHOULD GO BEFORE IT STARTS TO POUR AGAIN.

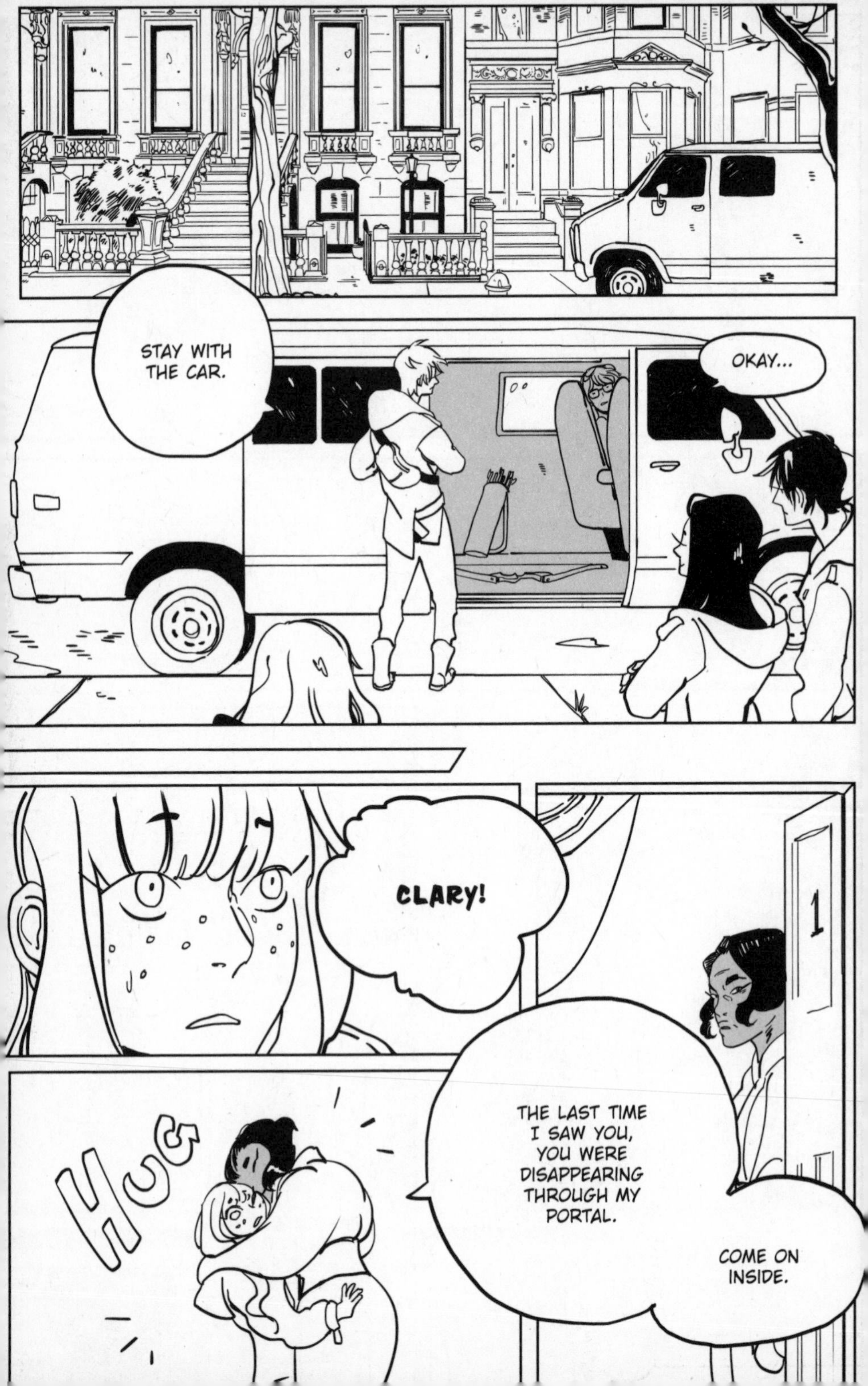
STAY WITH THE CAR.
OKAY...
CLARY!
1
HUG
THE LAST TIME I SAW YOU, YOU WERE DISAPPEARING THROUGH MY PORTAL.
COME ON INSIDE.

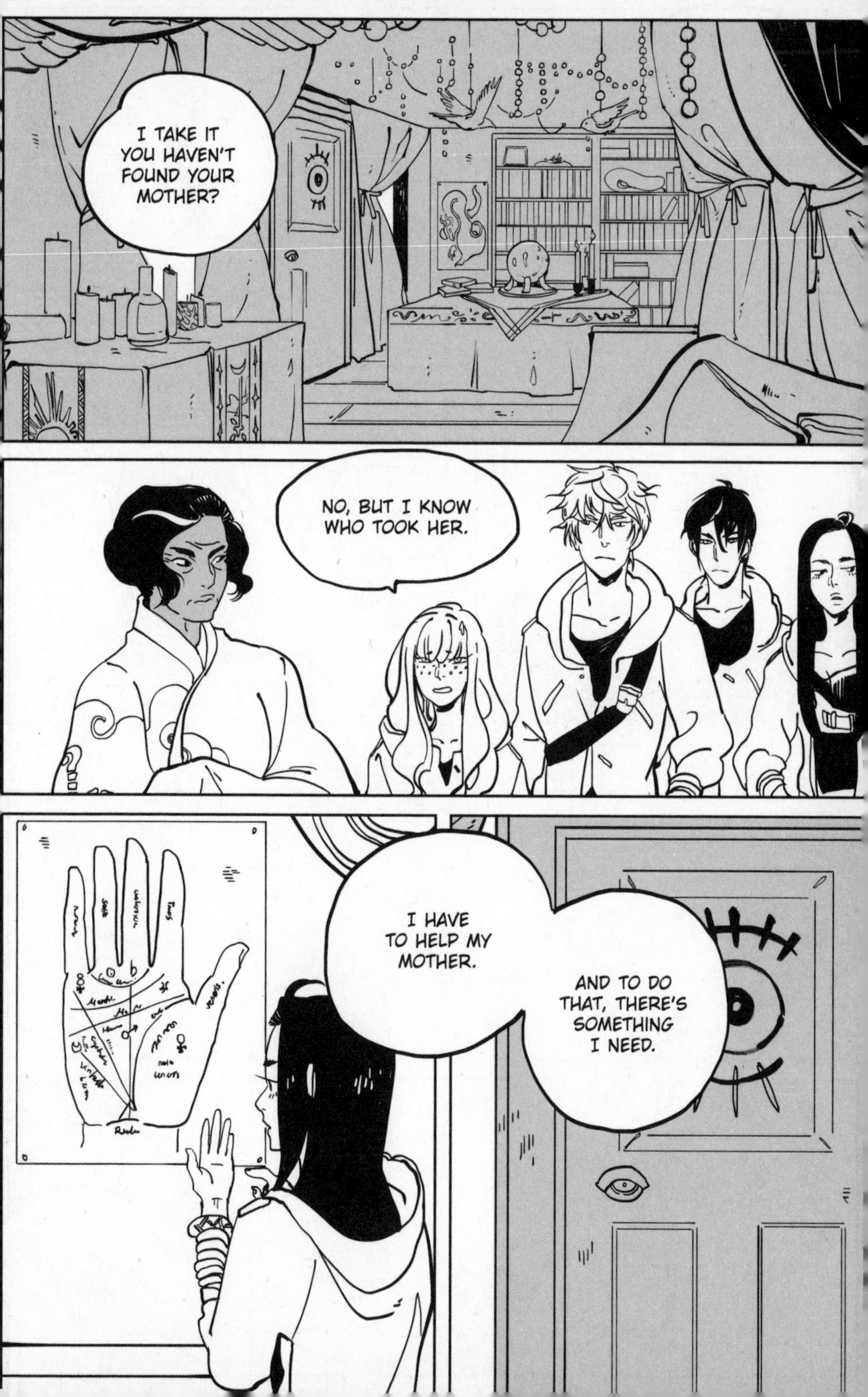
I TAKE IT YOU HAVEN'T FOUND YOUR MOTHER?
NO, BUT I KNOW WHO TOOK HER.
I HAVE TO HELP MY MOTHER.
AND TO DO THAT, THERE'S SOMETHING I NEED.

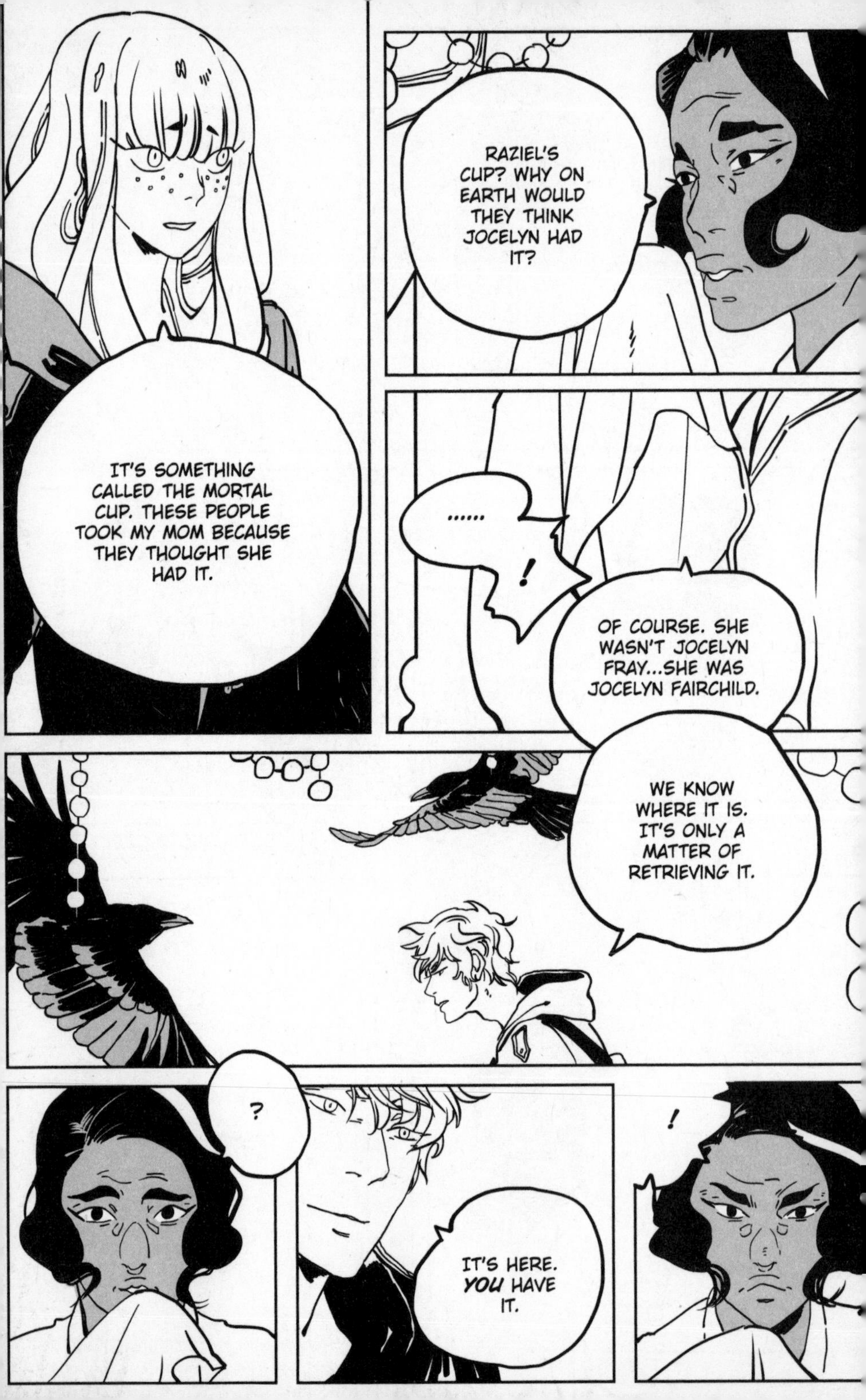
RAZIEL'S CUP? WHY ON EARTH WOULD THEY THINK JOCELYN HAD IT?
IT'S SOMETHING CALLED THE MORTAL CUP. THESE PEOPLE TOOK MY MOM BECAUSE THEY THOUGHT SHE HAD IT.
......
!
OF COURSE. SHE WASN'T JOCELYN FRAY...SHE WAS JOCELYN FAIRCHILD.
WE KNOW WHERE IT IS. IT'S ONLY A MATTER OF RETRIEVING IT.
?
IT'S HERE. *YOU* HAVE IT.
!

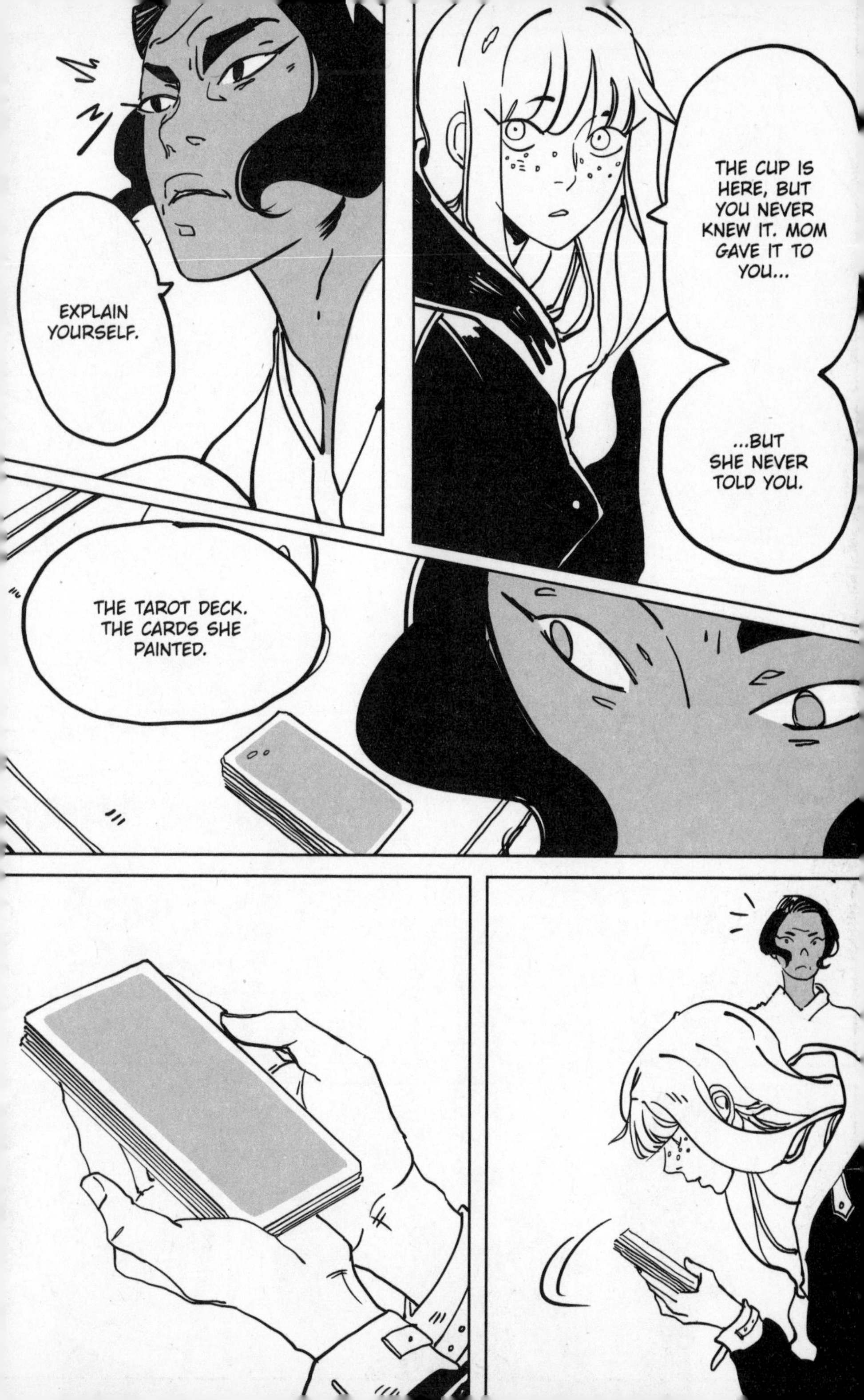
EXPLAIN YOURSELF.
THE CUP IS HERE, BUT YOU NEVER KNEW IT. MOM GAVE IT TO YOU...
...BUT SHE NEVER TOLD YOU.
THE TAROT DECK. THE CARDS SHE PAINTED.

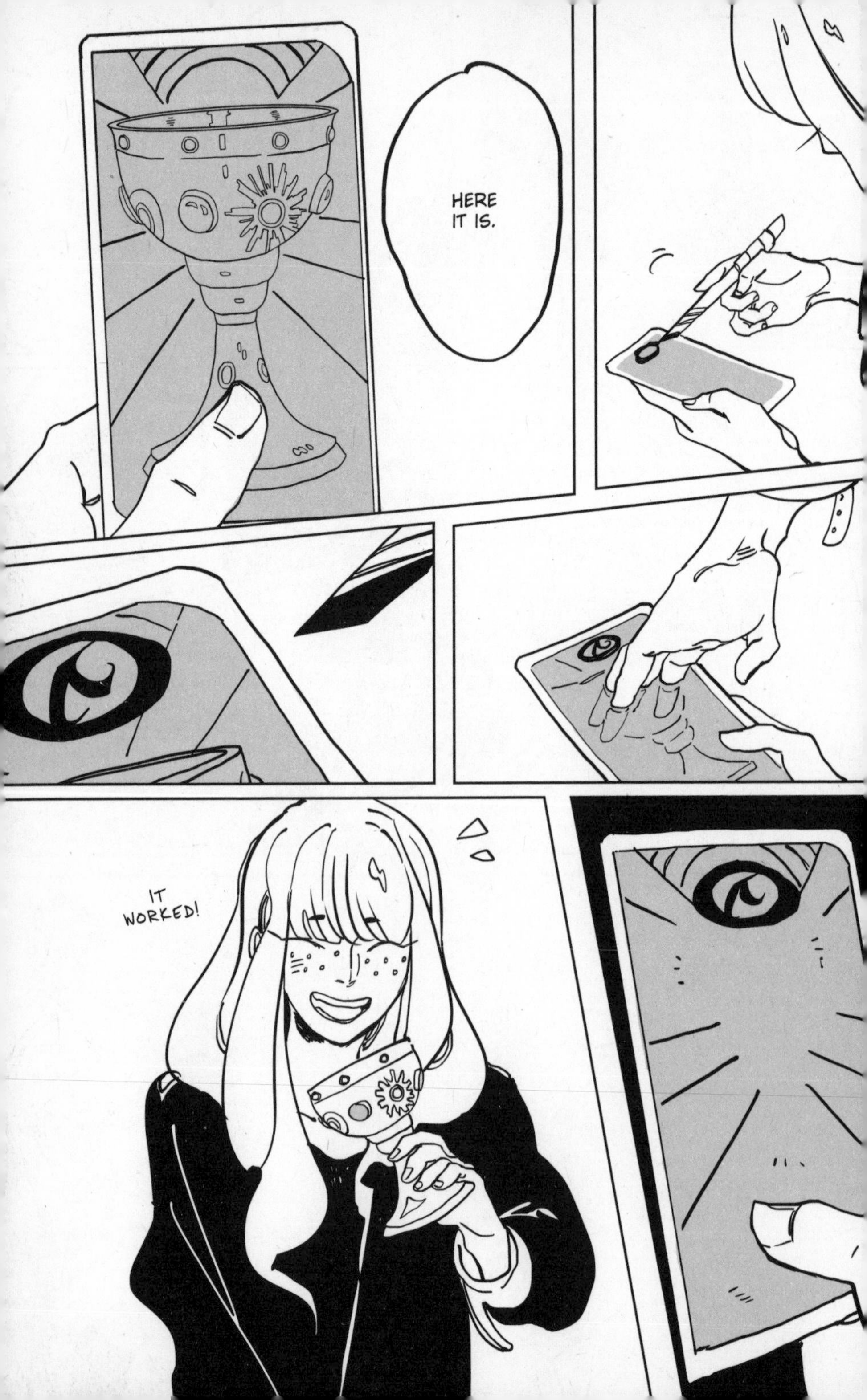
HERE IT IS.
IT WORKED!

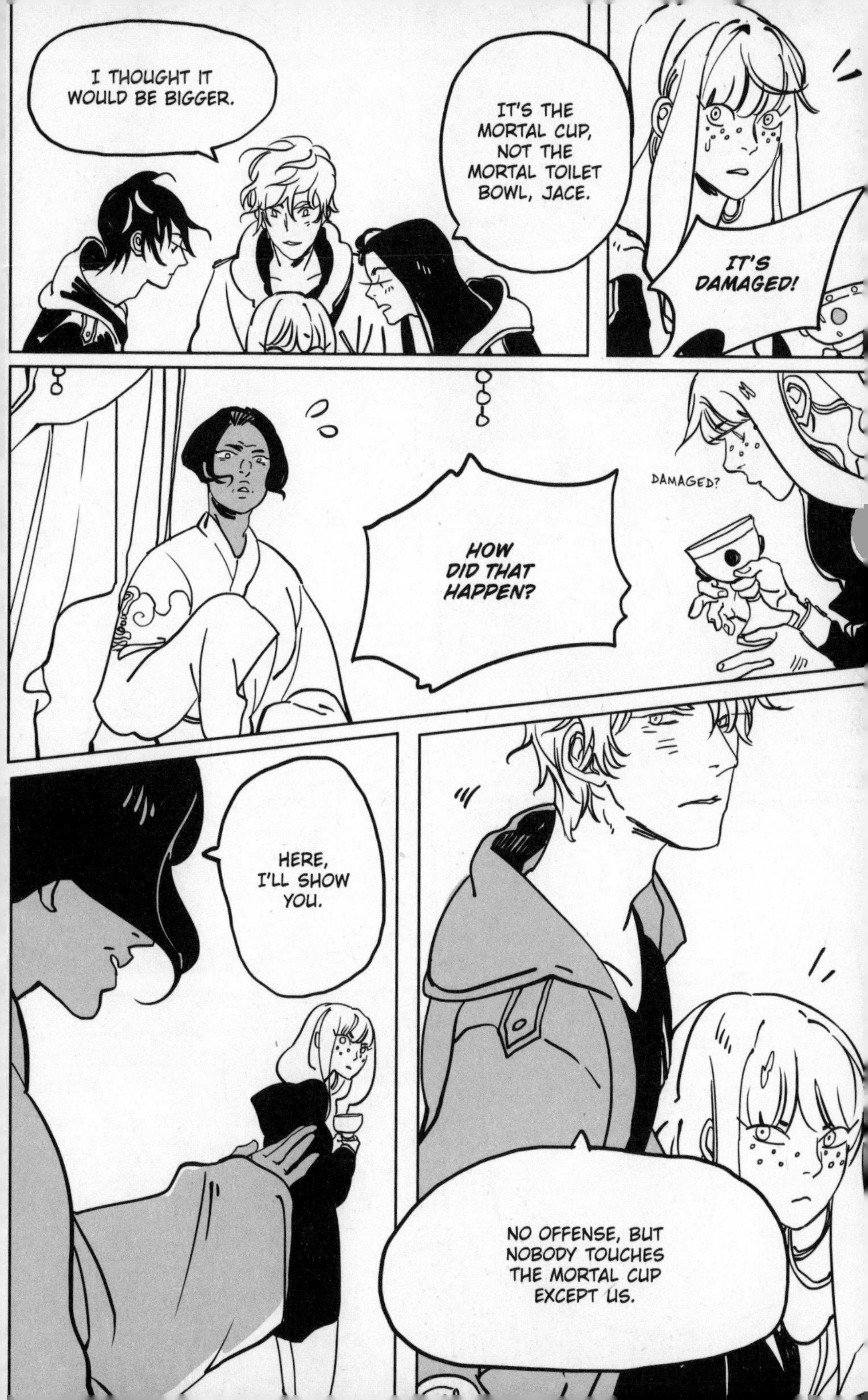
I THOUGHT IT WOULD BE BIGGER.
IT'S THE MORTAL CUP, NOT THE MORTAL TOILET BOWL, JACE.
IT'S DAMAGED!
HOW DID THAT HAPPEN?
DAMAGED?
HERE, I'LL SHOW YOU.
NO OFFENSE, BUT NOBODY TOUCHES THE MORTAL CUP EXCEPT US.

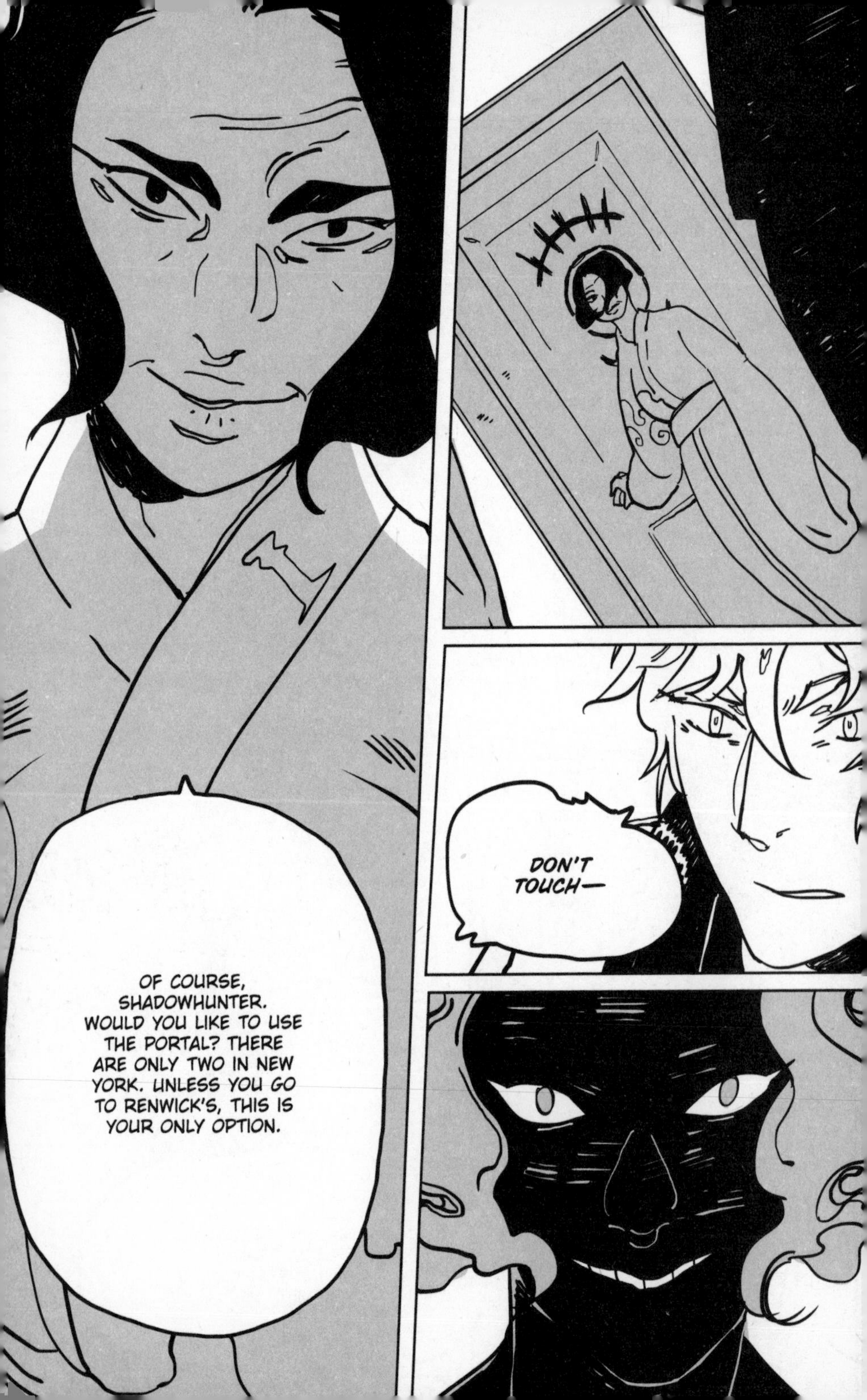
OF COURSE, SHADOWHUNTER. WOULD YOU LIKE TO USE THE PORTAL? THERE ARE ONLY TWO IN NEW YORK. UNLESS YOU GO TO RENWICK'S, THIS IS YOUR ONLY OPTION.
DON'T TOUCH—

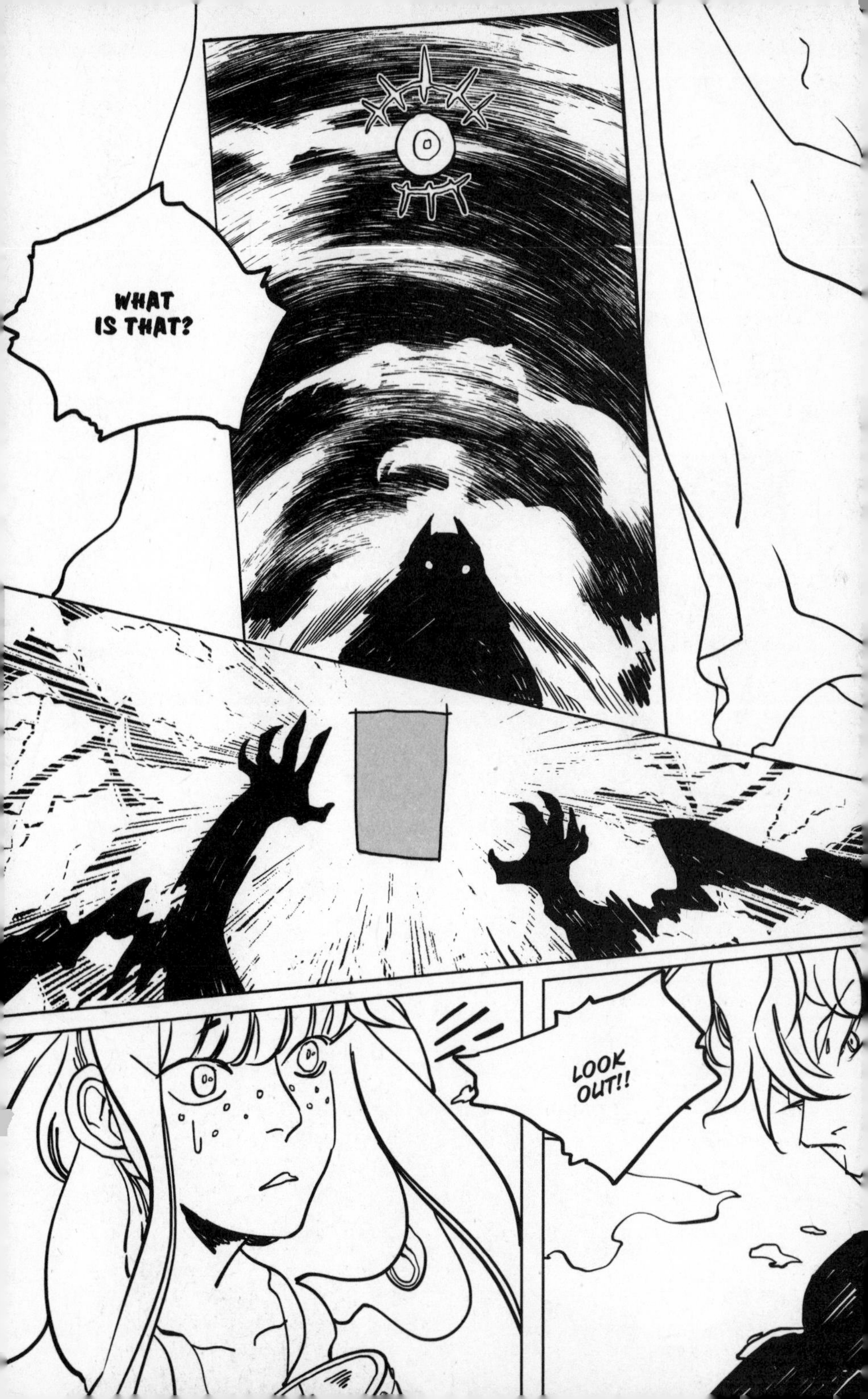
WHAT IS THAT?
LOOK OUT!!

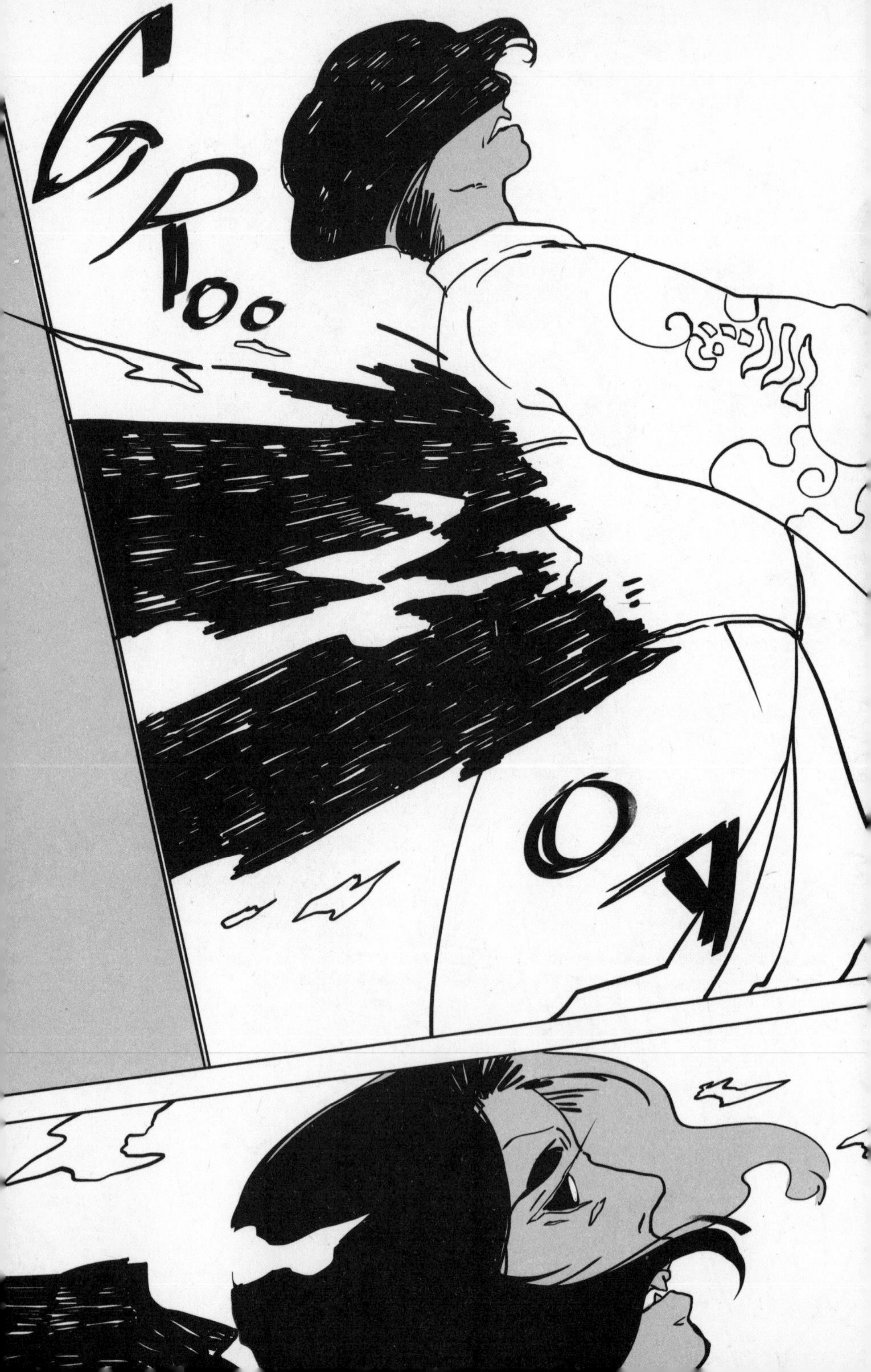
GROO

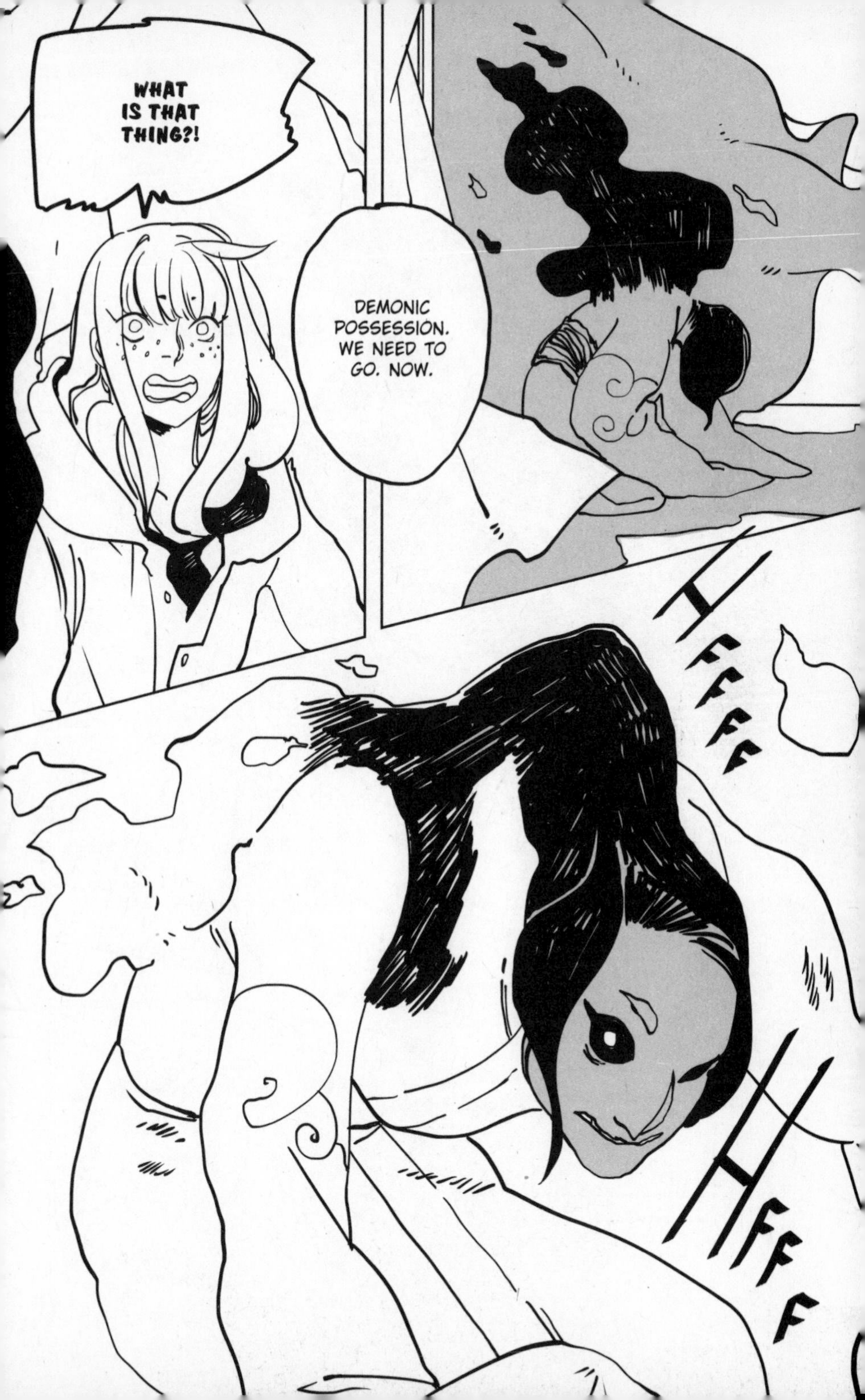
WHAT IS THAT THING?!
DEMONIC POSSESSION. WE NEED TO GO. NOW.
HFFFF
HHFFF

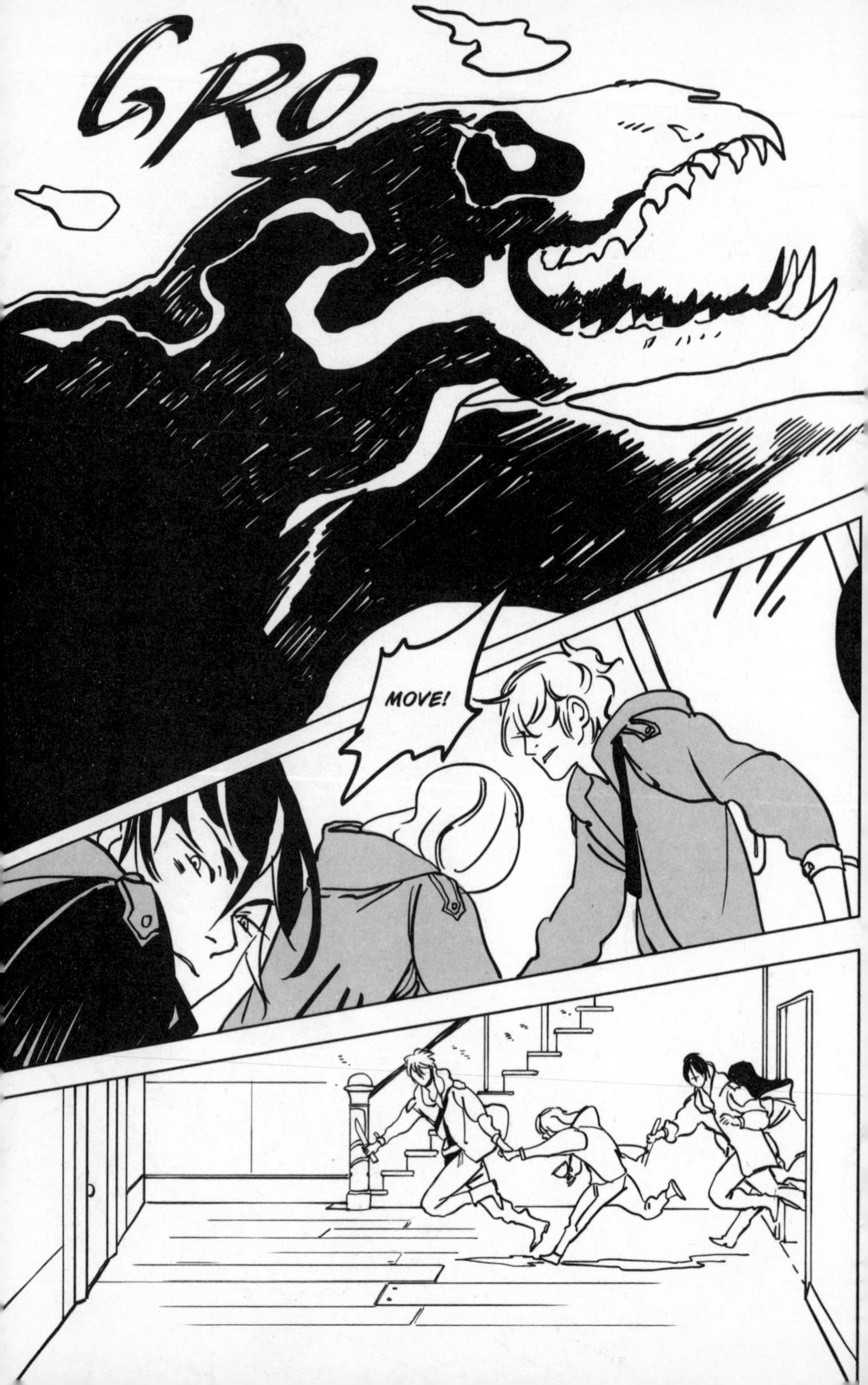
GRO
MOVE!

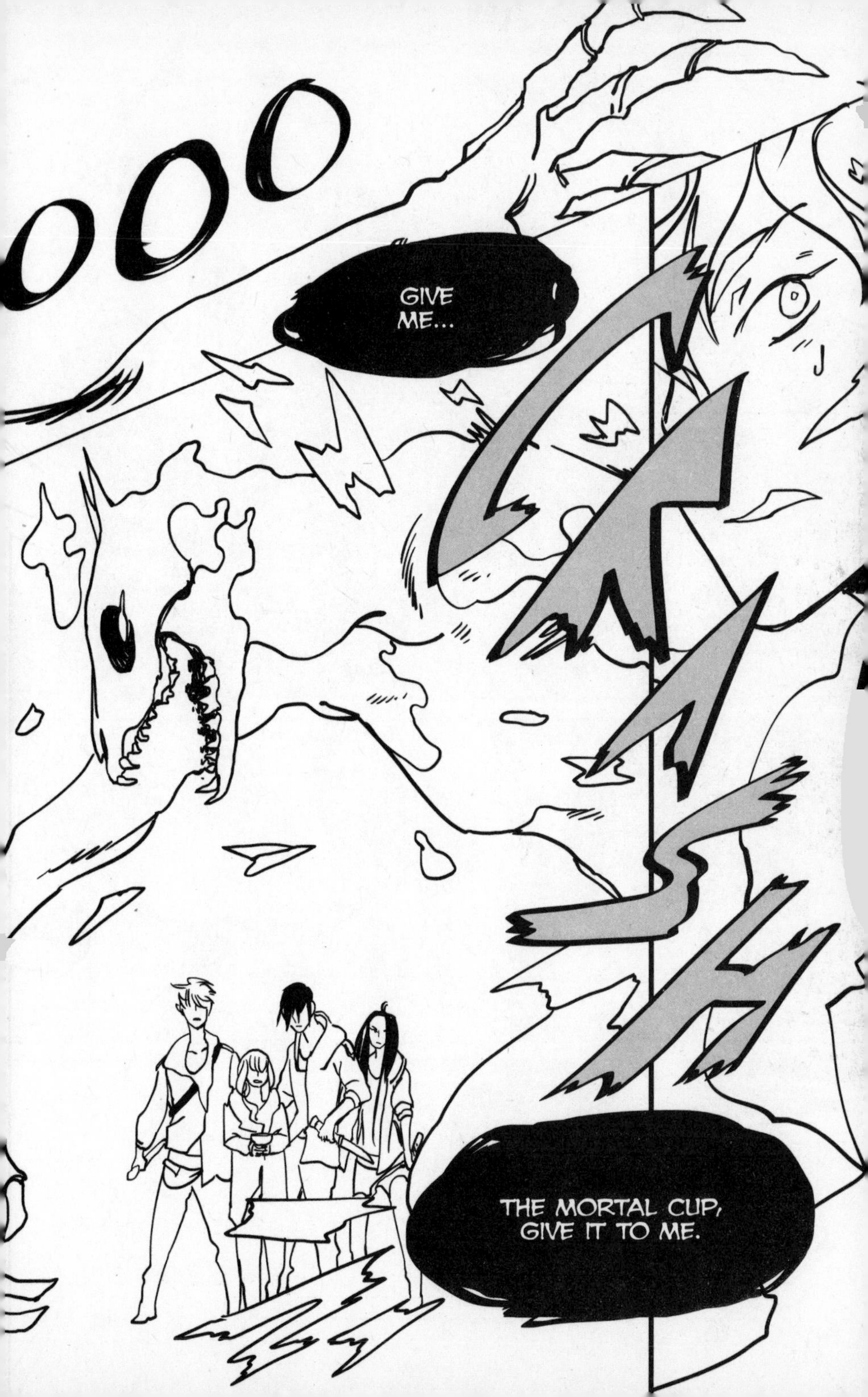
OOOO
GIVE ME...
CRASH
THE MORTAL CUP, GIVE IT TO ME.

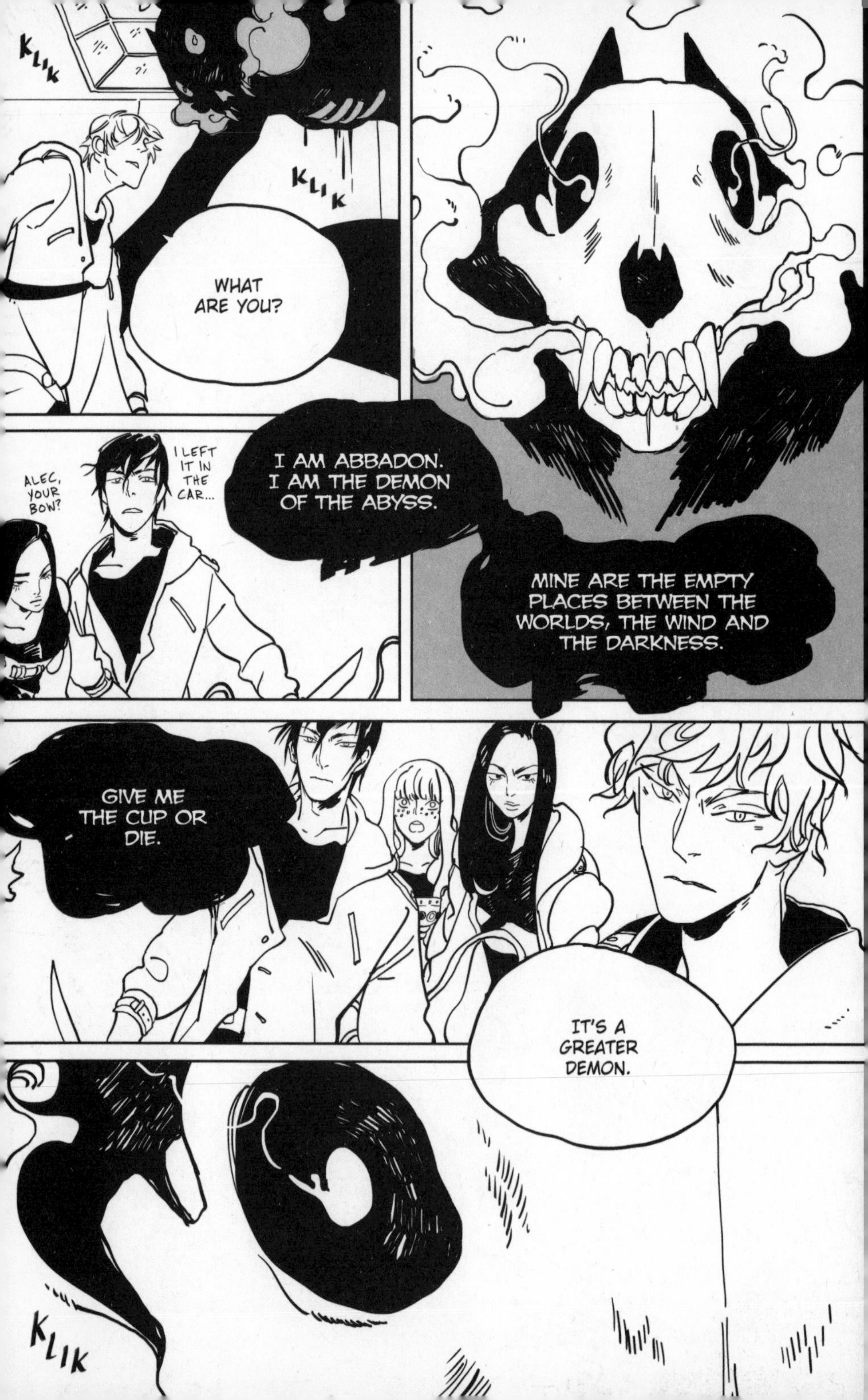
KLIK
KLIK
WHAT ARE YOU?
I AM ABBADON. I AM THE DEMON OF THE ABYSS.
MINE ARE THE EMPTY PLACES BETWEEN THE WORLDS, THE WIND AND THE DARKNESS.
ALEC, YOUR BOW?
I LEFT IT IN THE CAR...
GIVE ME THE CUP OR DIE.
IT'S A GREATER DEMON.
KLIK

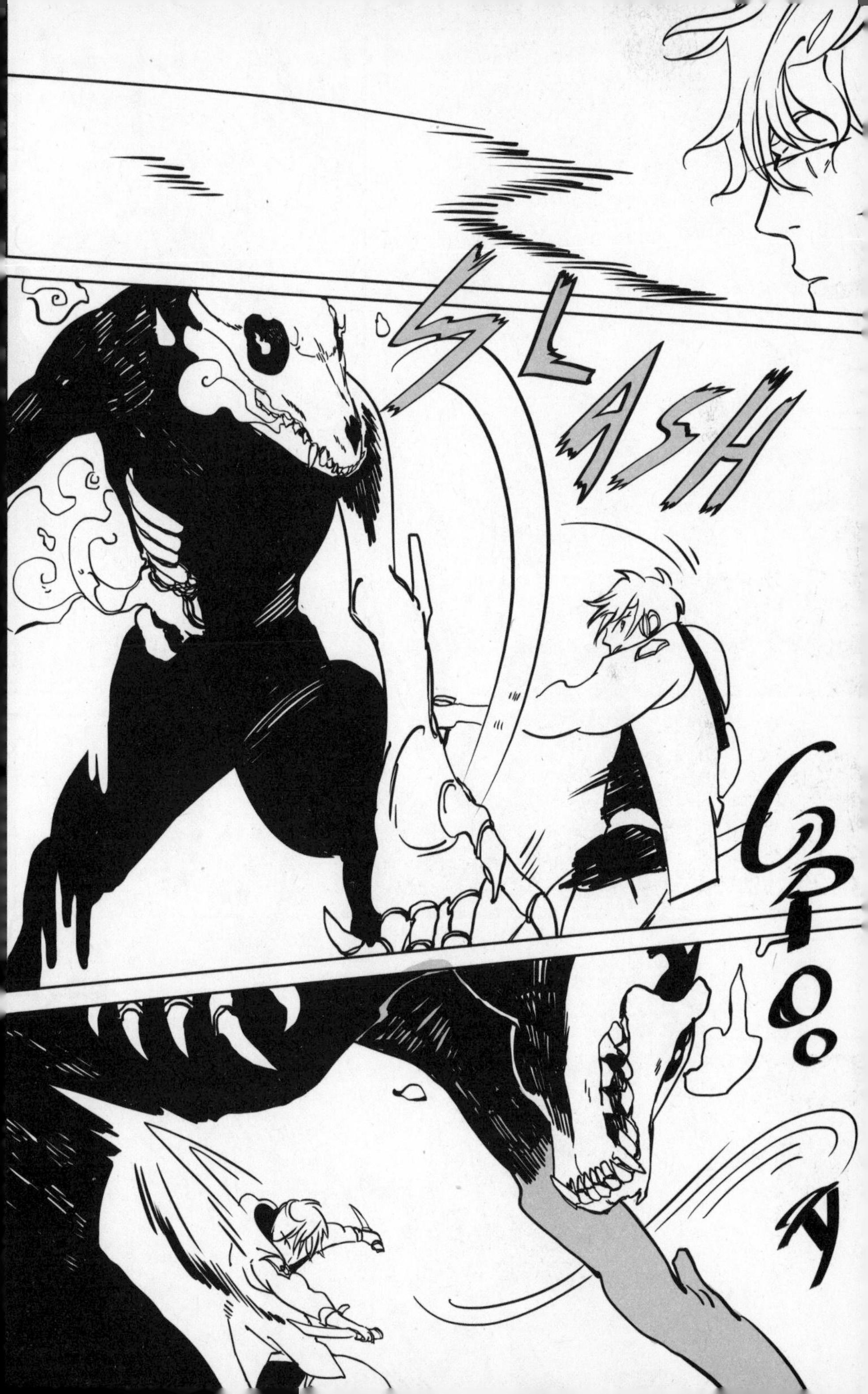
SLASH
GRIP

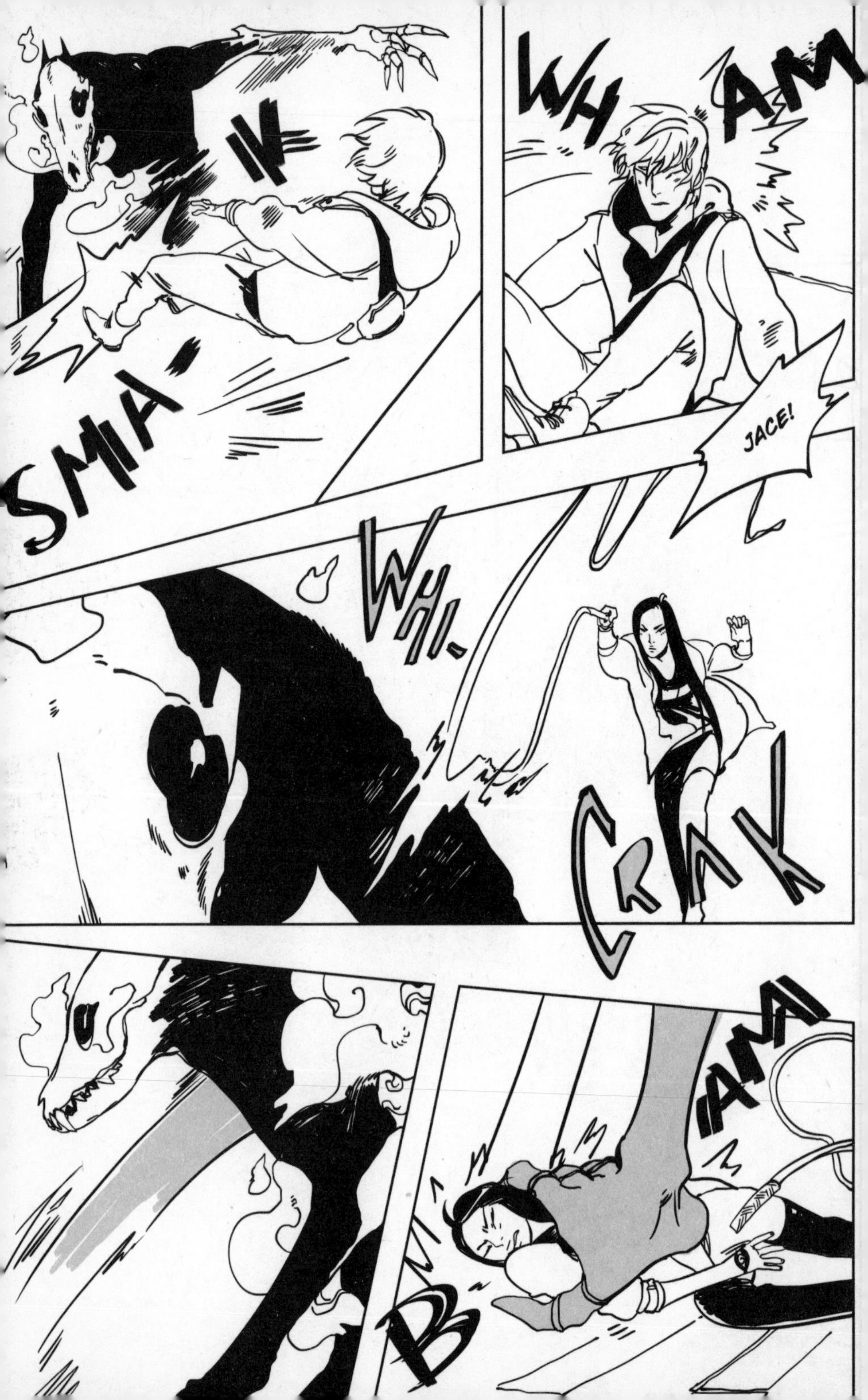
SMA-
WH AM
JACE!
WHI-
CRAK
BAM

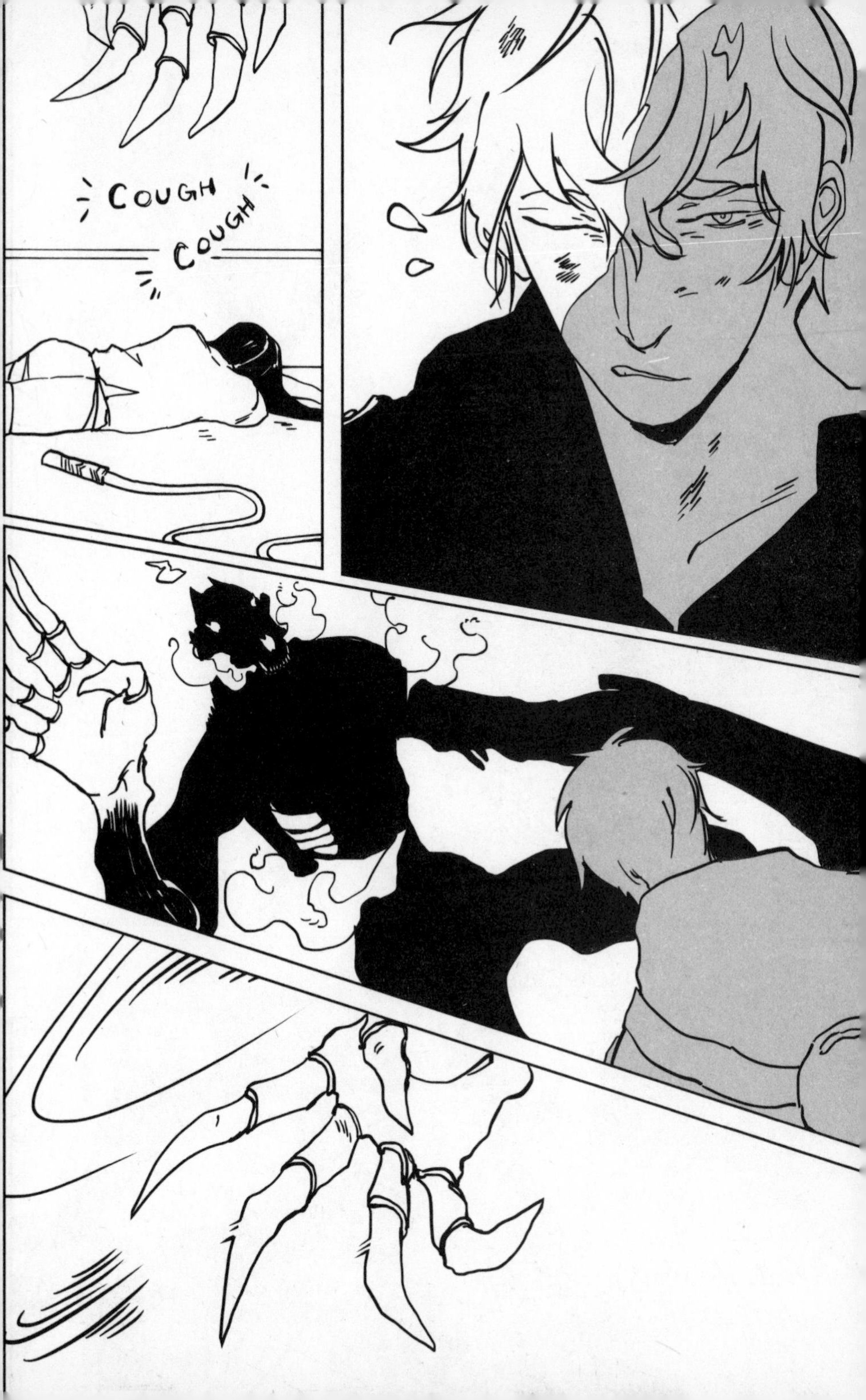
COUGH
COUGH

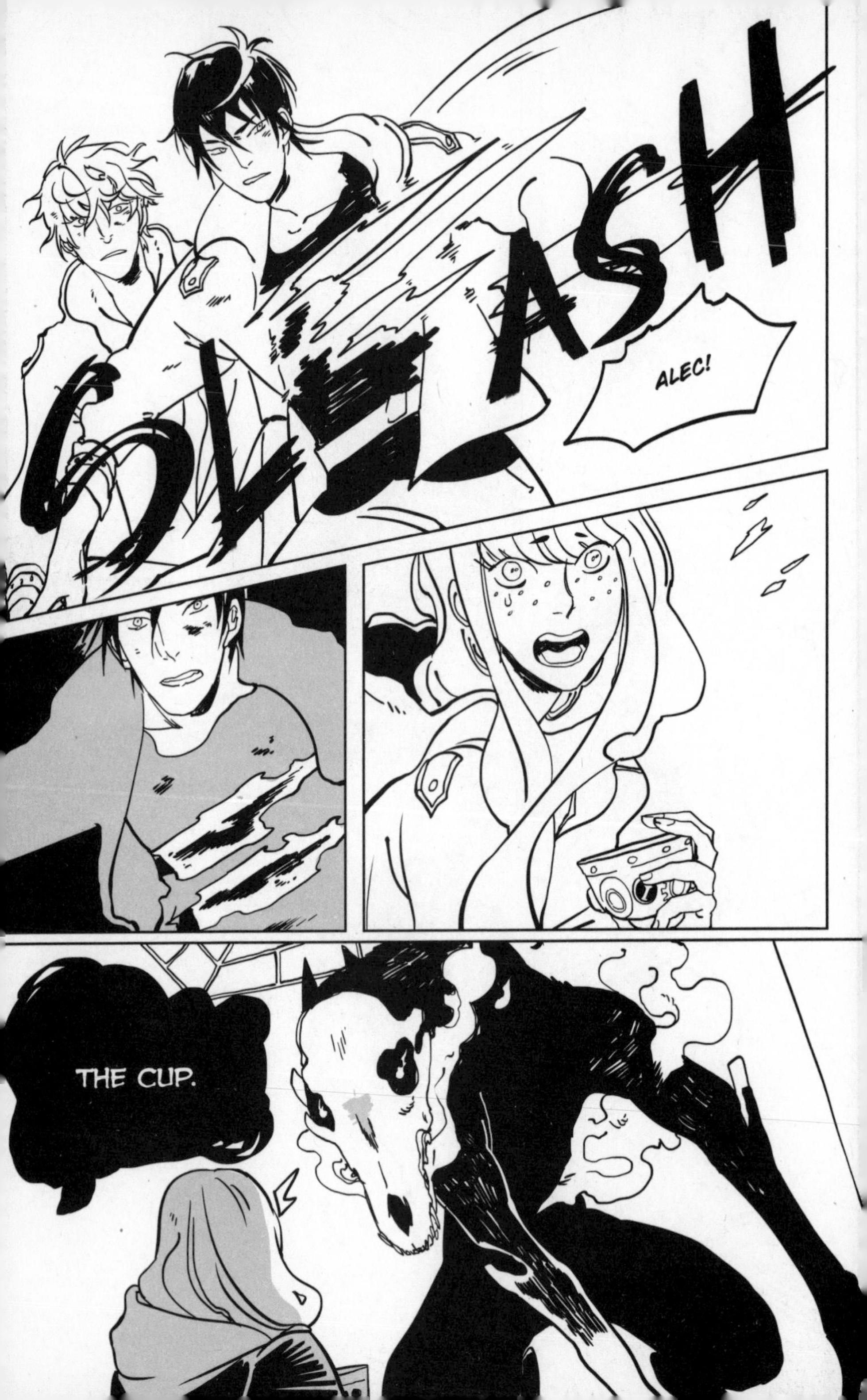
CLASH
ALEC!
THE CUP.

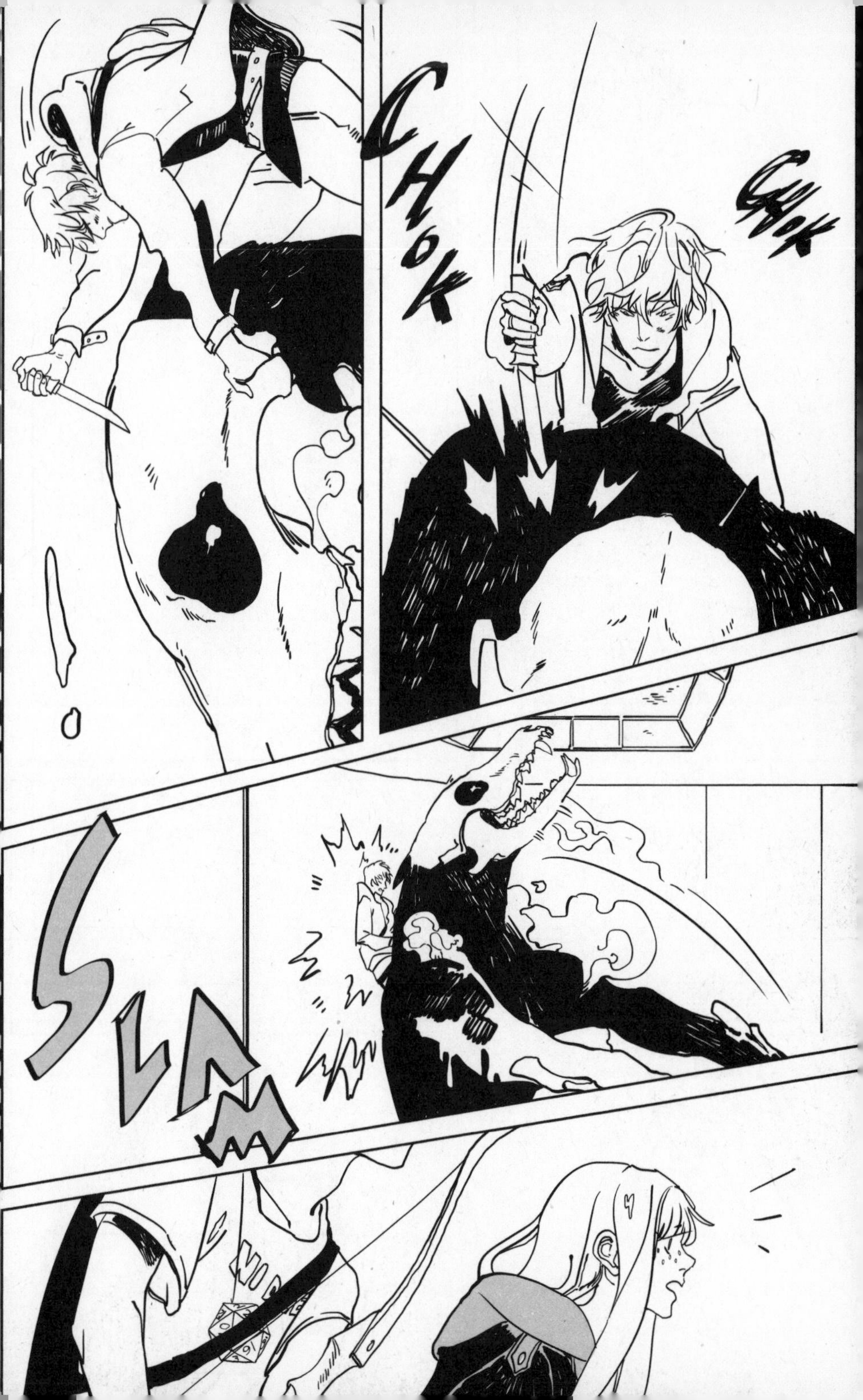
CHOK
CHOK
SLAM

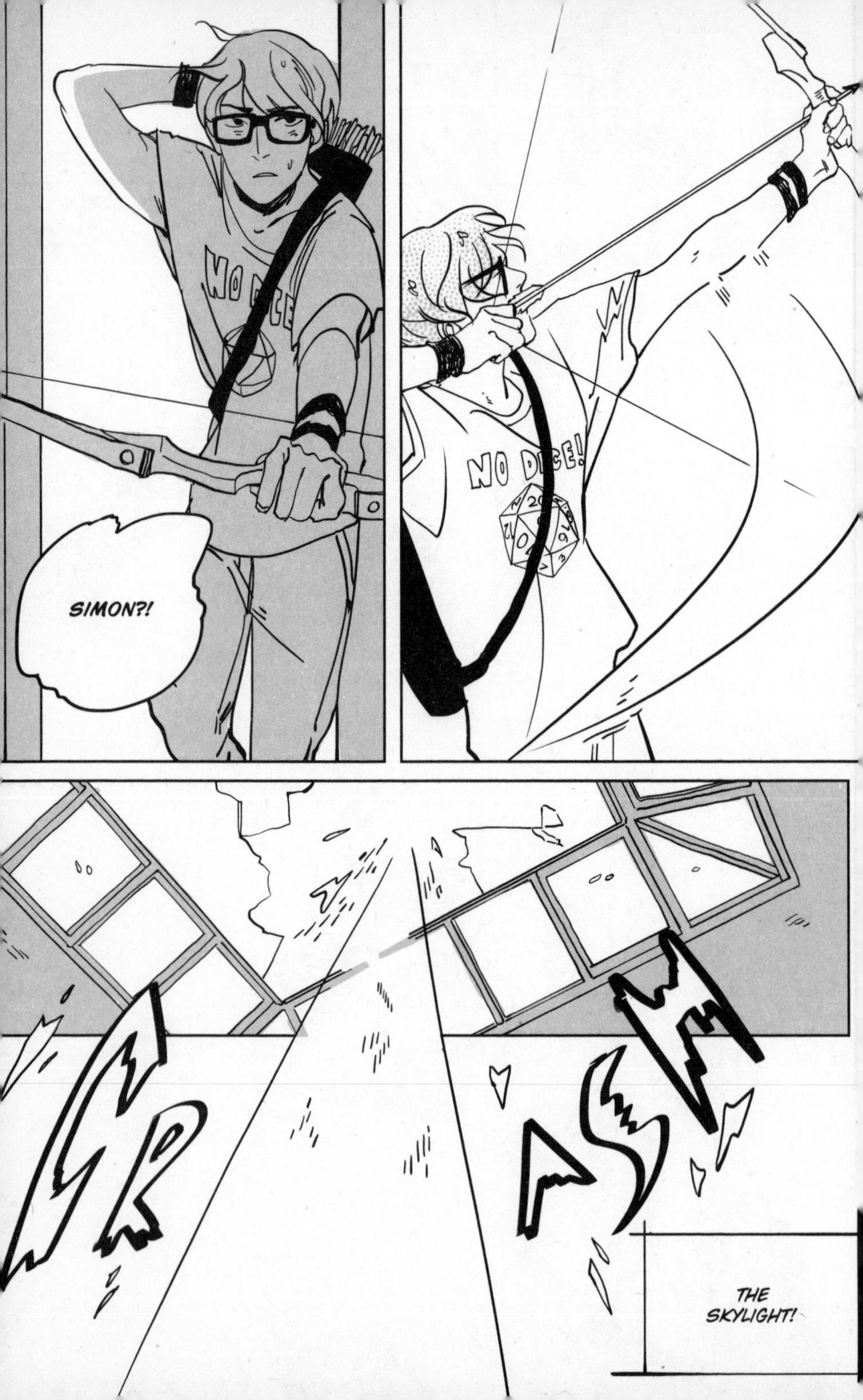
SIMON?!
NO DICE!
CRASH
THE SKYLIGHT!

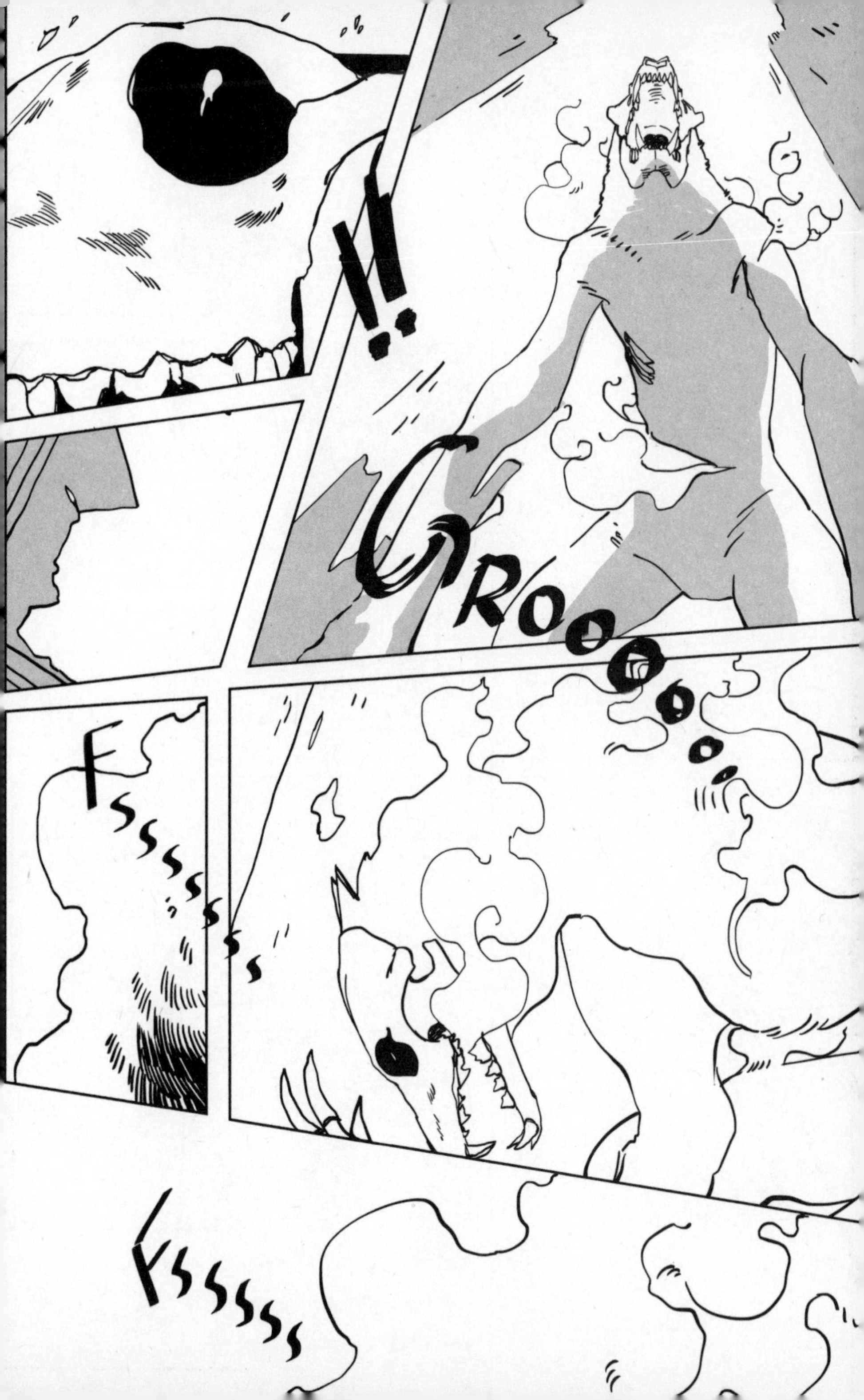
!!
GROOOOOOOO
FSSSSSSS
FSSSSSS

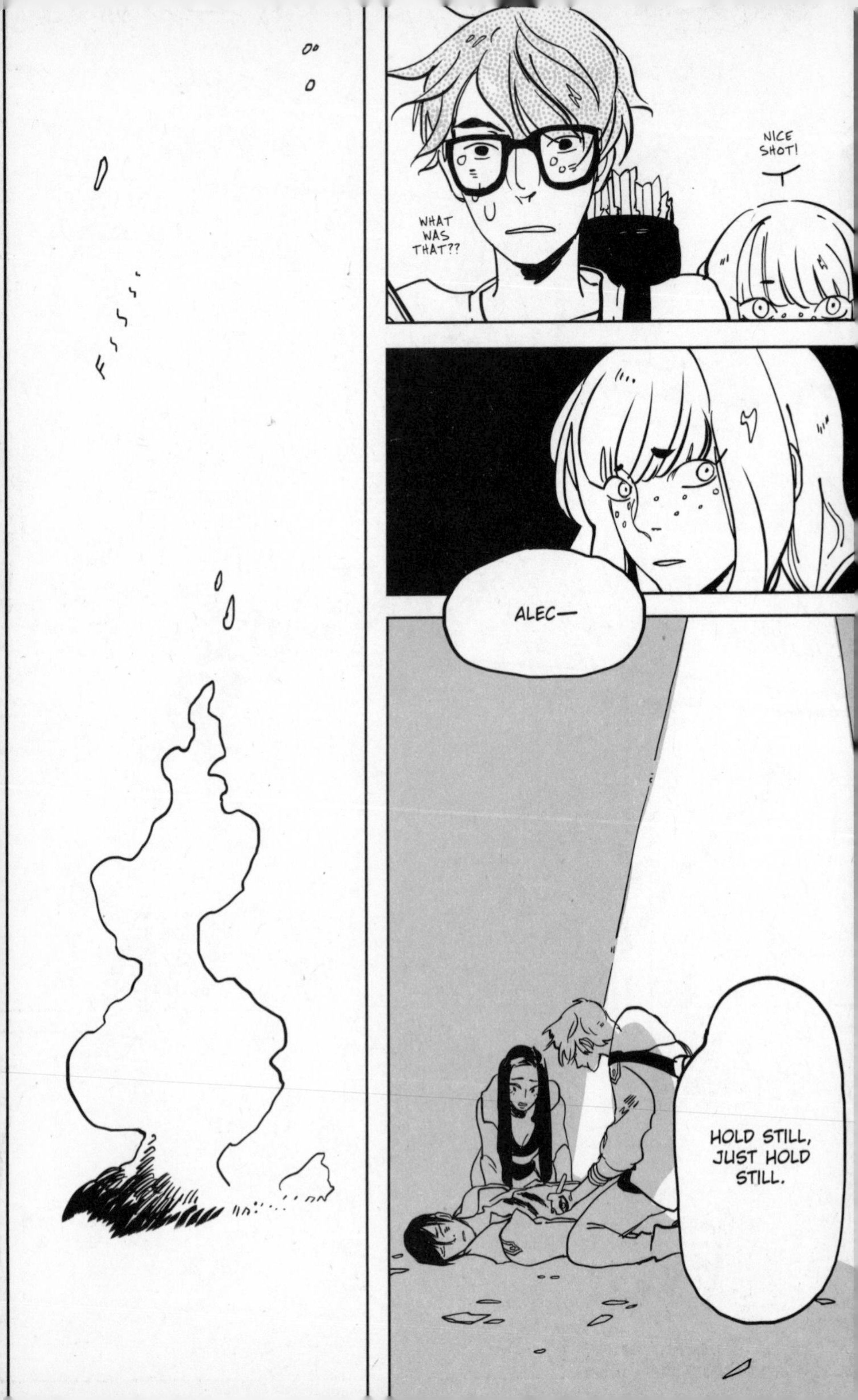
Fsss
WHAT WAS THAT??
NICE SHOT!
ALEC—
HOLD STILL, JUST HOLD STILL.

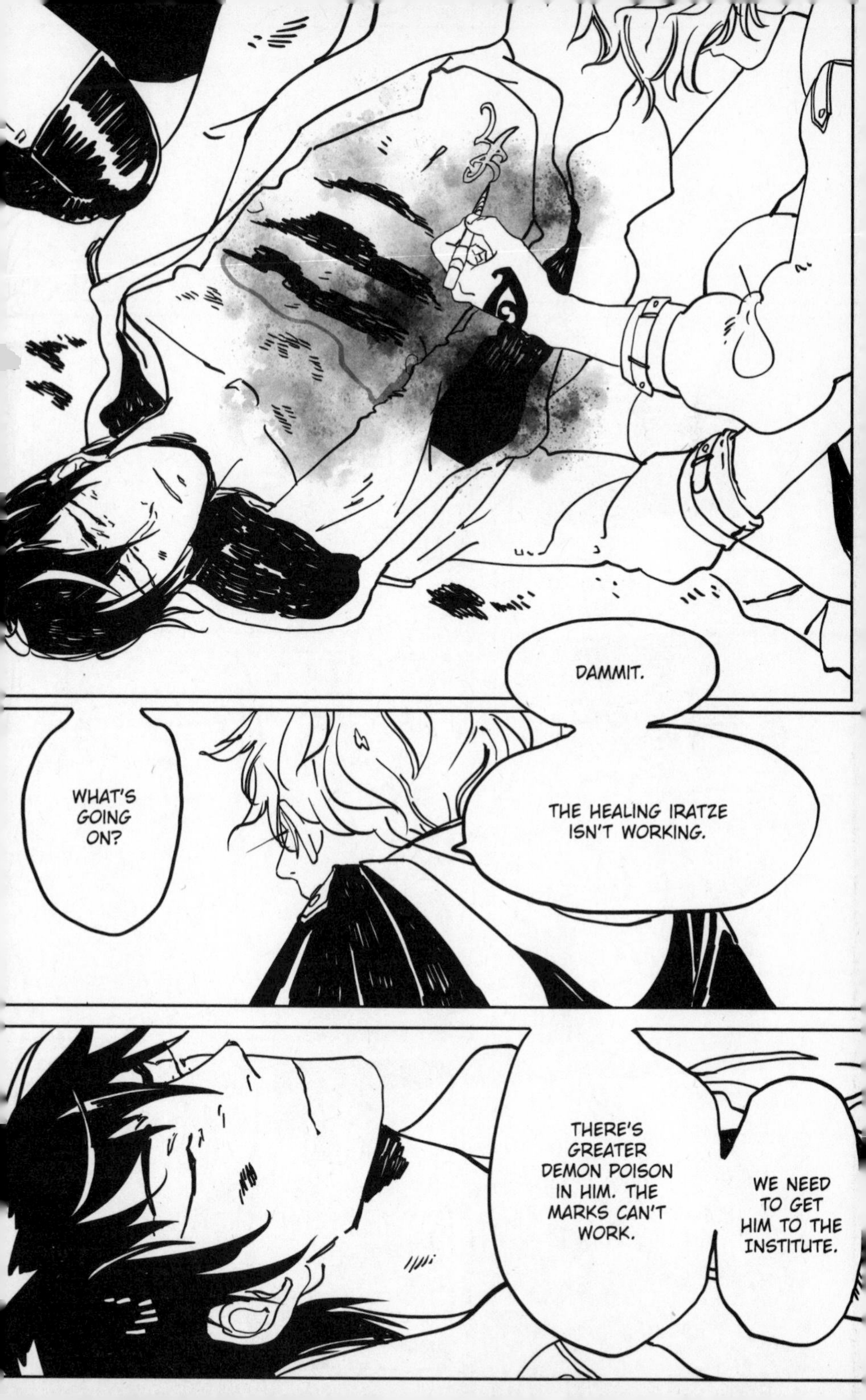
DAMMIT.
WHAT'S GOING ON?
THE HEALING IRATZE ISN'T WORKING.
THERE'S GREATER DEMON POISON IN HIM. THE MARKS CAN'T WORK.
WE NEED TO GET HIM TO THE INSTITUTE.

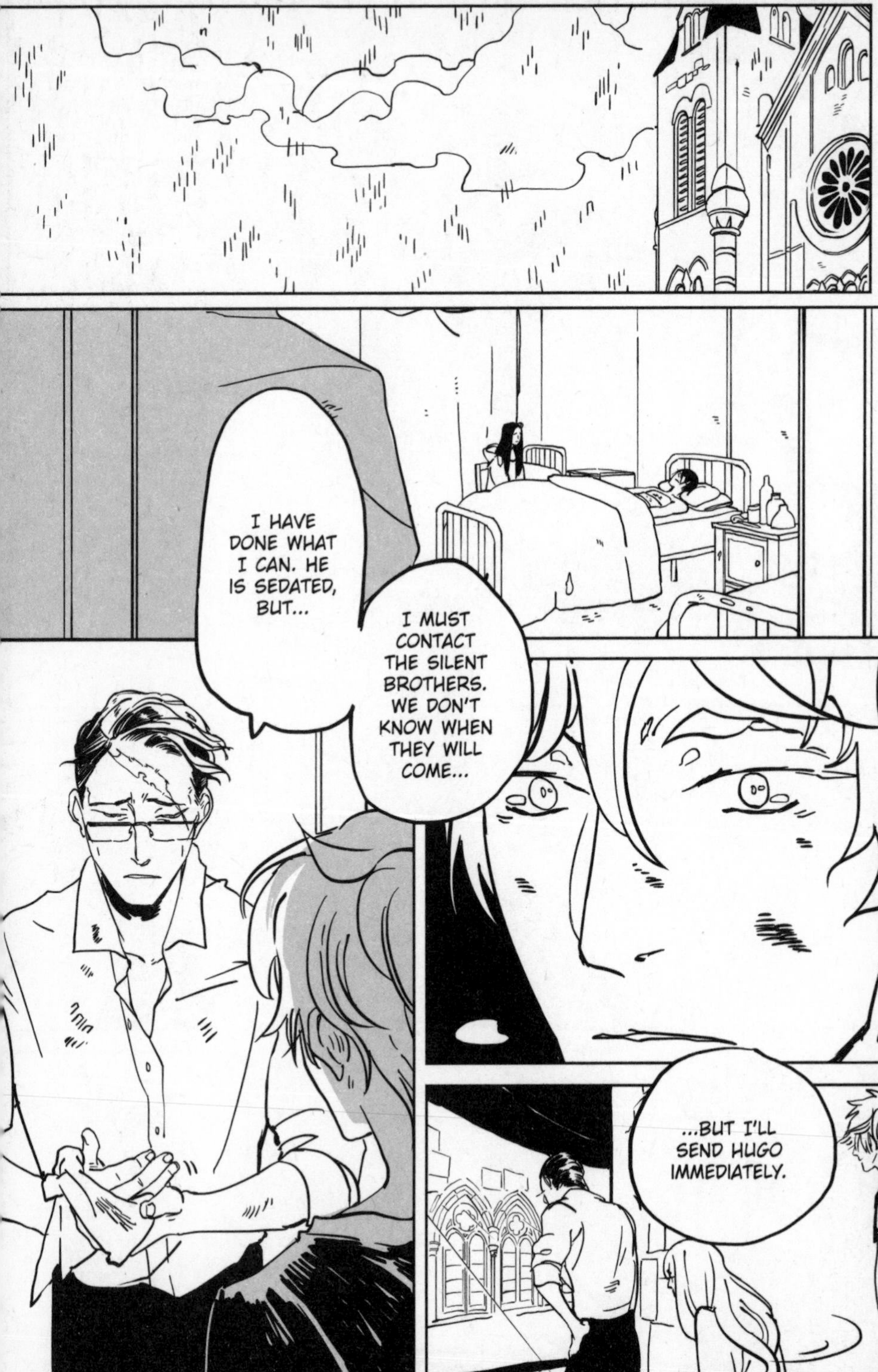
I HAVE DONE WHAT I CAN. HE IS SEDATED, BUT...
I MUST CONTACT THE SILENT BROTHERS. WE DON'T KNOW WHEN THEY WILL COME...
...BUT I'LL SEND HUGO IMMEDIATELY.

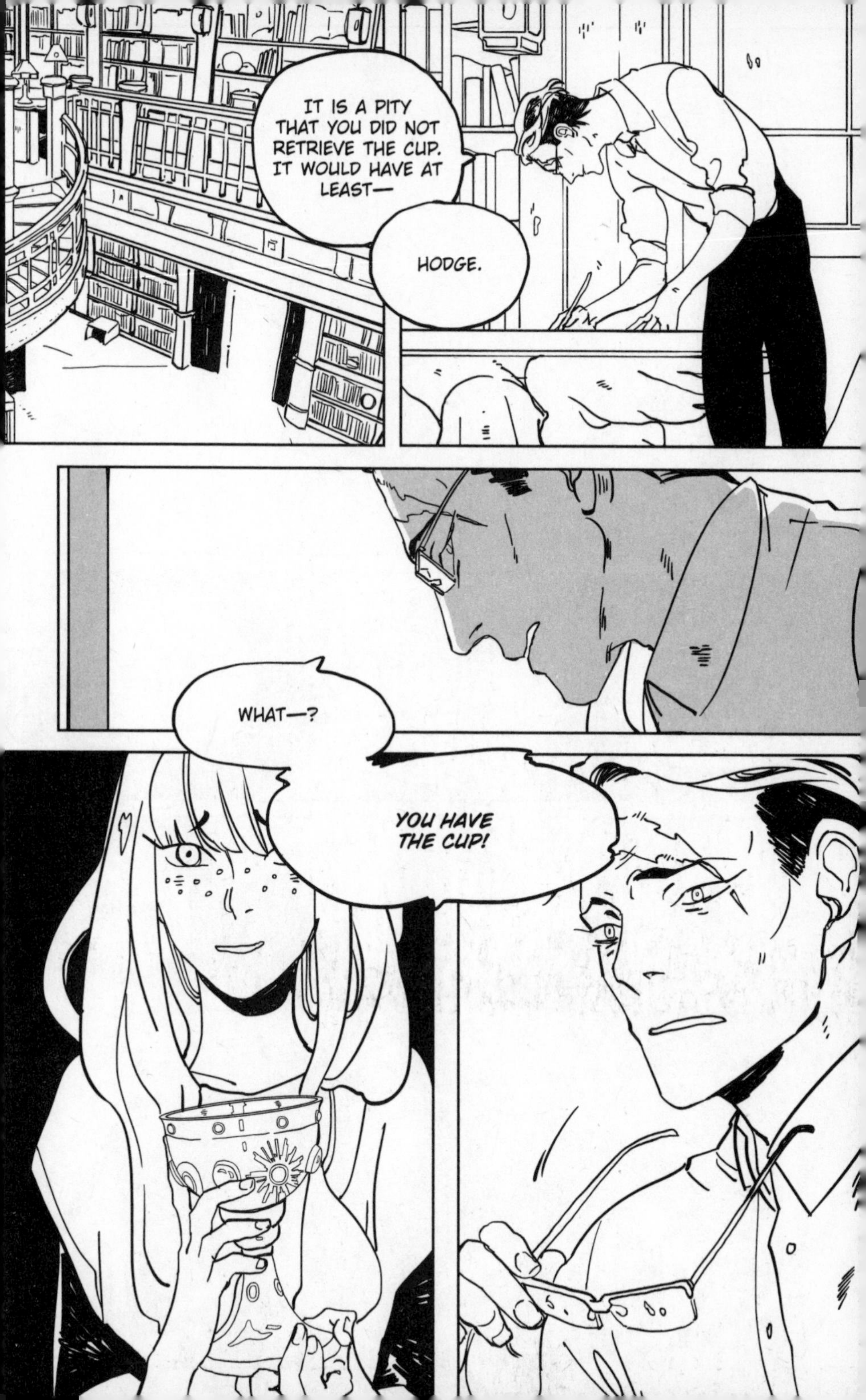
IT IS A PITY THAT YOU DID NOT RETRIEVE THE CUP. IT WOULD HAVE AT LEAST—
HODGE.
WHAT—?
YOU HAVE THE CUP!

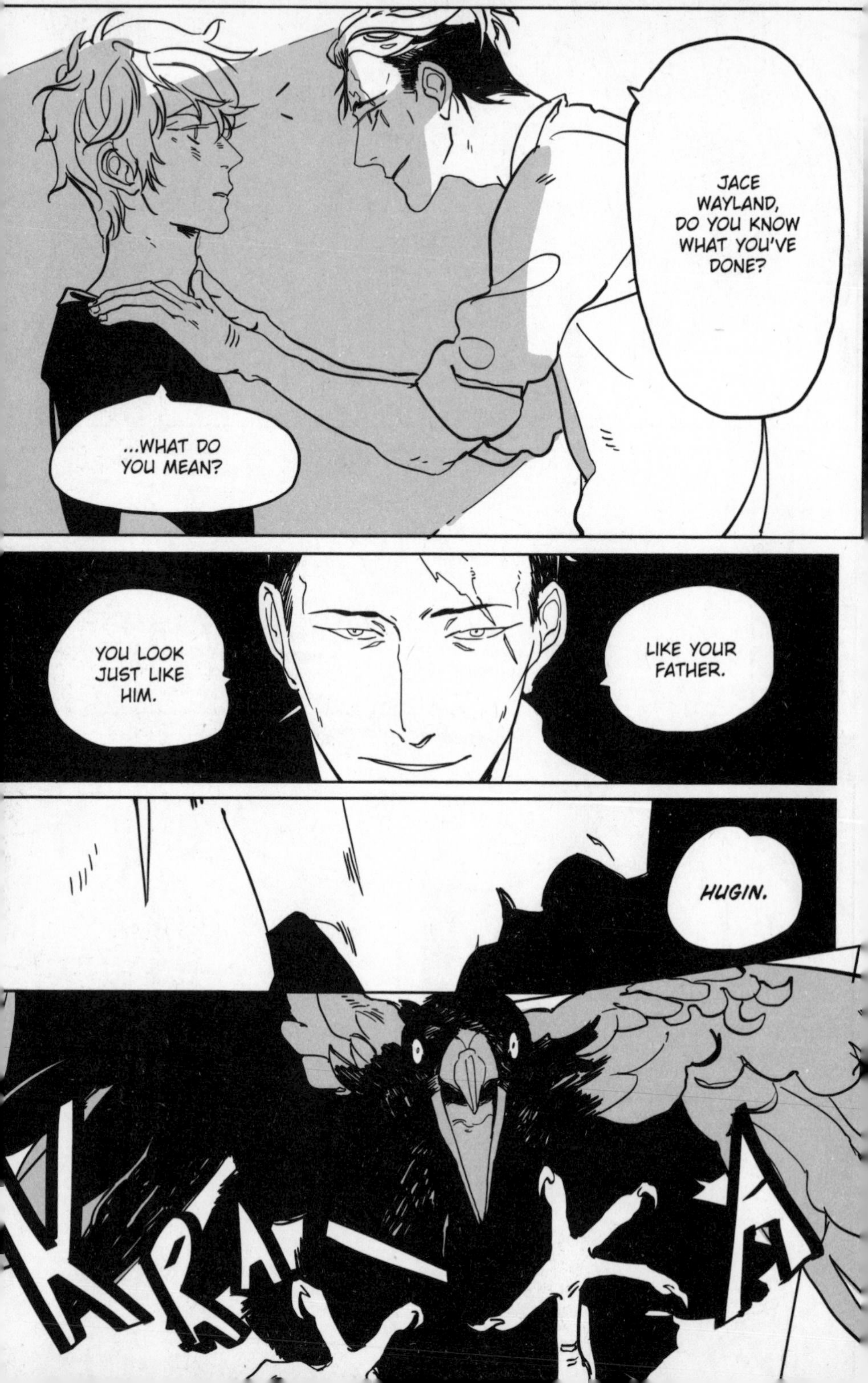
JACE WAYLAND, DO YOU KNOW WHAT YOU'VE DONE?
...WHAT DO YOU MEAN?
YOU LOOK JUST LIKE HIM.
LIKE YOUR FATHER.
HUGIN.
KRA--KA

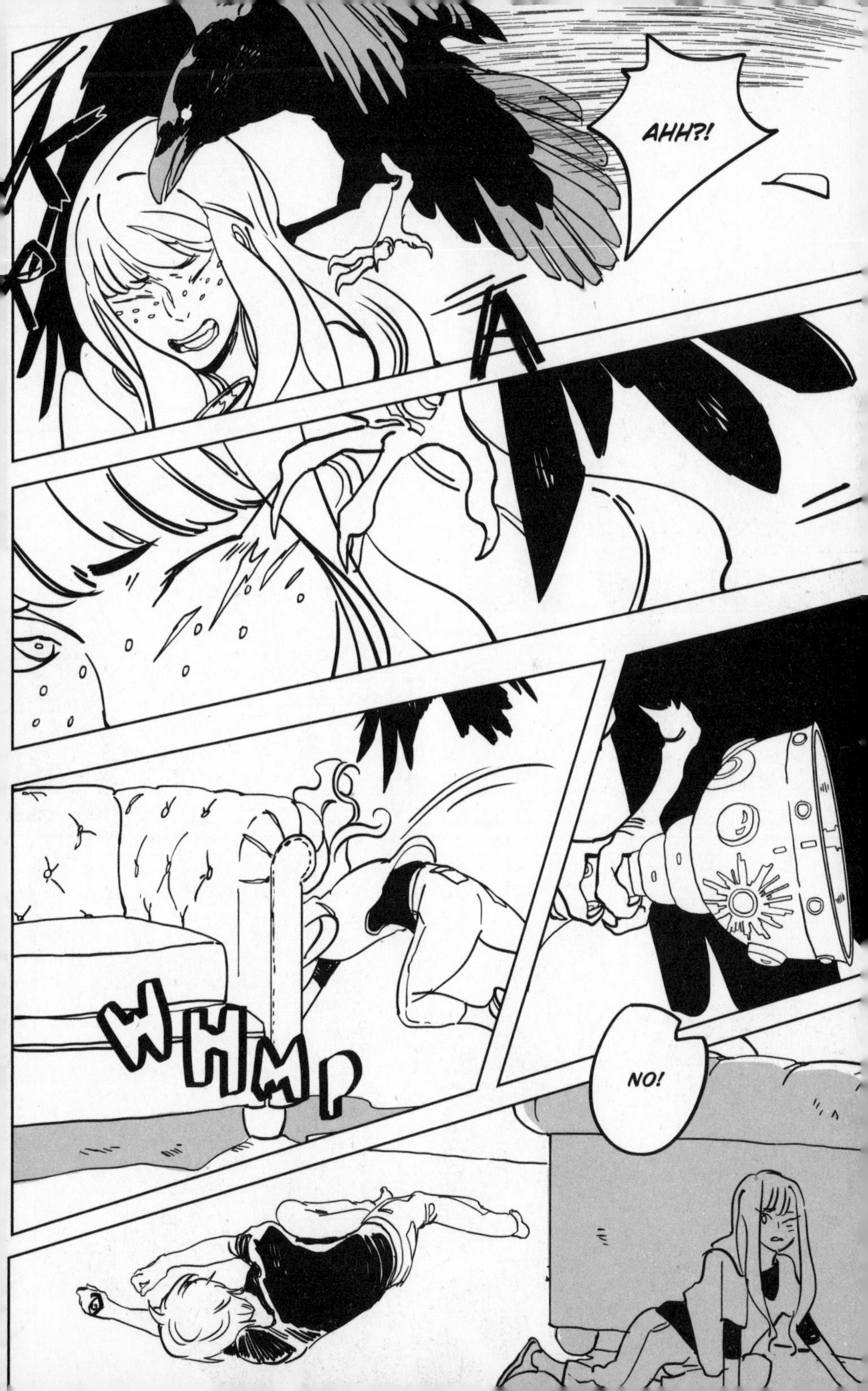
KRRA
AHH?!
WHMP
NO!

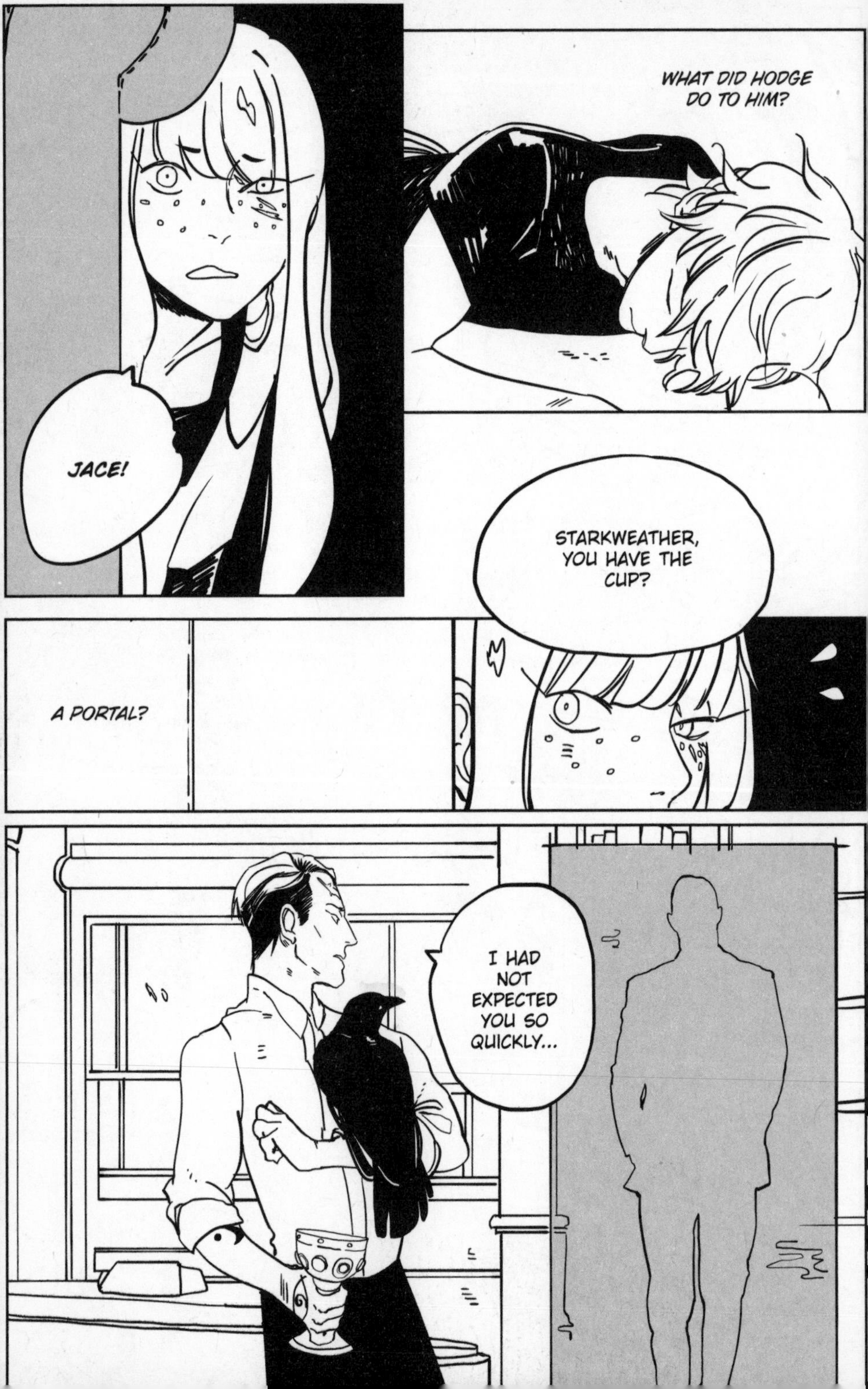
JACE!
WHAT DID HODGE DO TO HIM?
STARKWEATHER, YOU HAVE THE CUP?
A PORTAL?
I HAD NOT EXPECTED YOU SO QUICKLY...

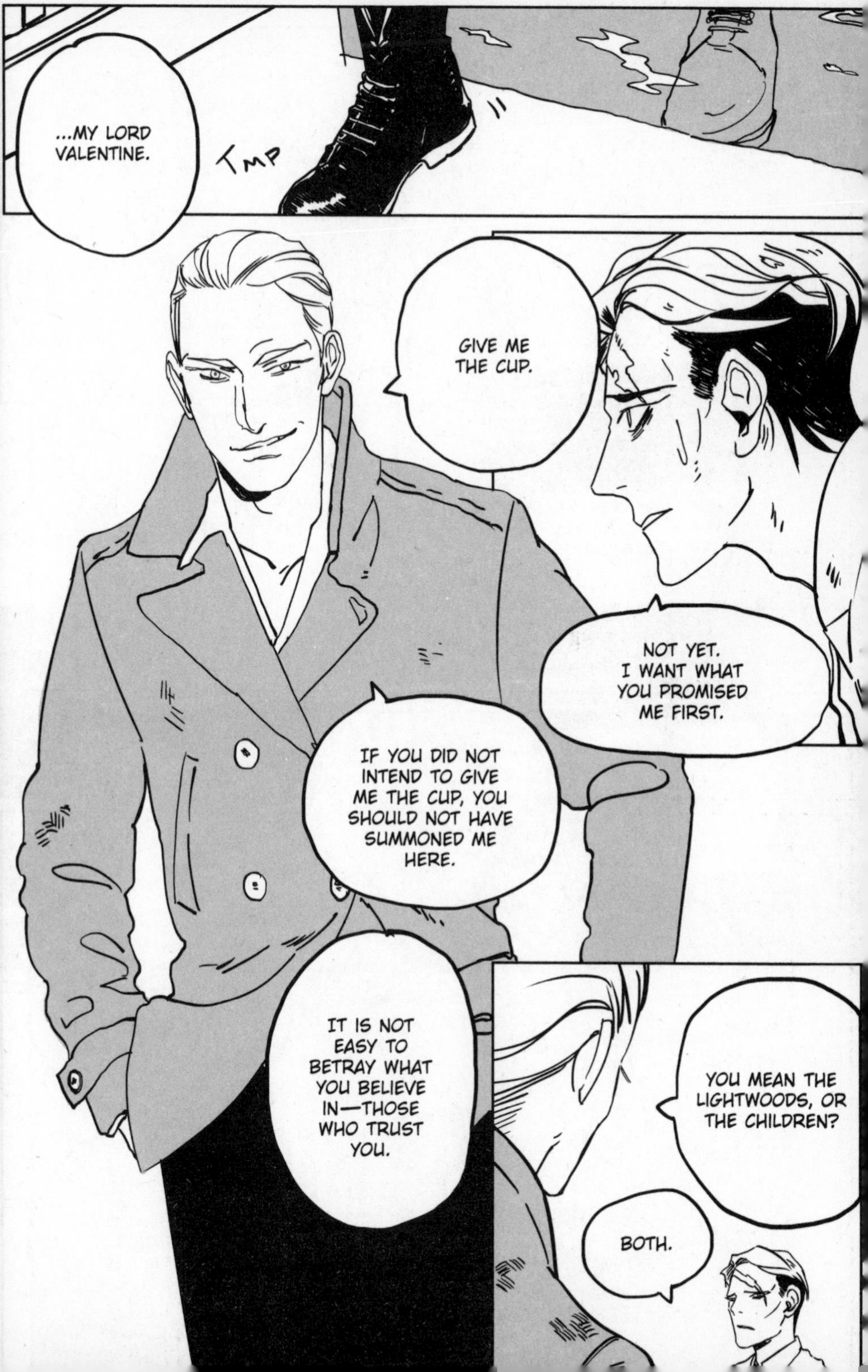
...MY LORD VALENTINE.
TMP
GIVE ME THE CUP.
NOT YET. I WANT WHAT YOU PROMISED ME FIRST.
IF YOU DID NOT INTEND TO GIVE ME THE CUP, YOU SHOULD NOT HAVE SUMMONED ME HERE.
IT IS NOT EASY TO BETRAY WHAT YOU BELIEVE IN—THOSE WHO TRUST YOU.
YOU MEAN THE LIGHTWOODS, OR THE CHILDREN?
BOTH.

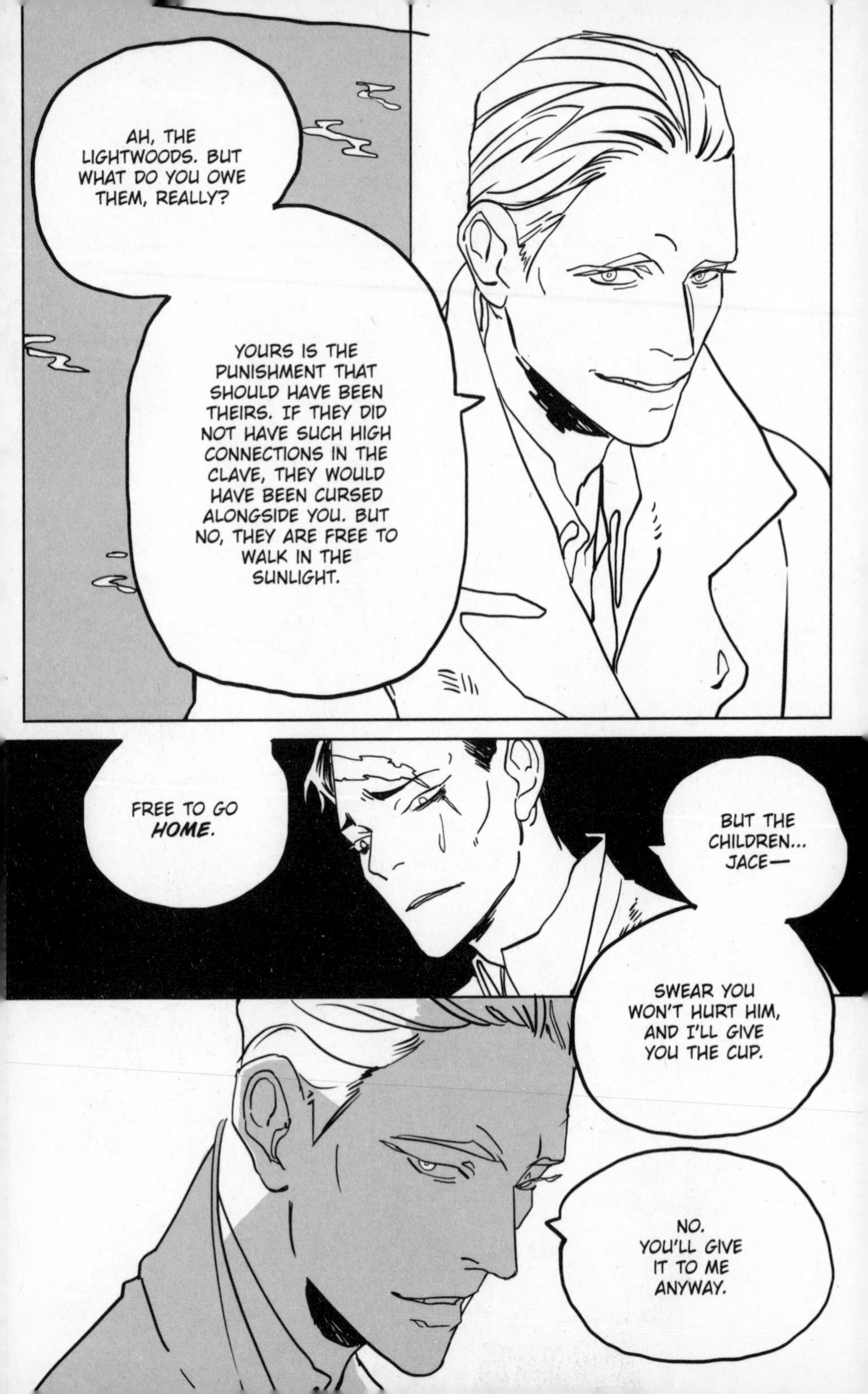
AH, THE LIGHTWOODS. BUT WHAT DO YOU OWE THEM, REALLY?
YOURS IS THE PUNISHMENT THAT SHOULD HAVE BEEN THEIRS. IF THEY DID NOT HAVE SUCH HIGH CONNECTIONS IN THE CLAVE, THEY WOULD HAVE BEEN CURSED ALONGSIDE YOU. BUT NO, THEY ARE FREE TO WALK IN THE SUNLIGHT.
FREE TO GO *HOME*.
BUT THE CHILDREN... JACE—
SWEAR YOU WON'T HURT HIM, AND I'LL GIVE YOU THE CUP.
NO. YOU'LL GIVE IT TO ME ANYWAY.

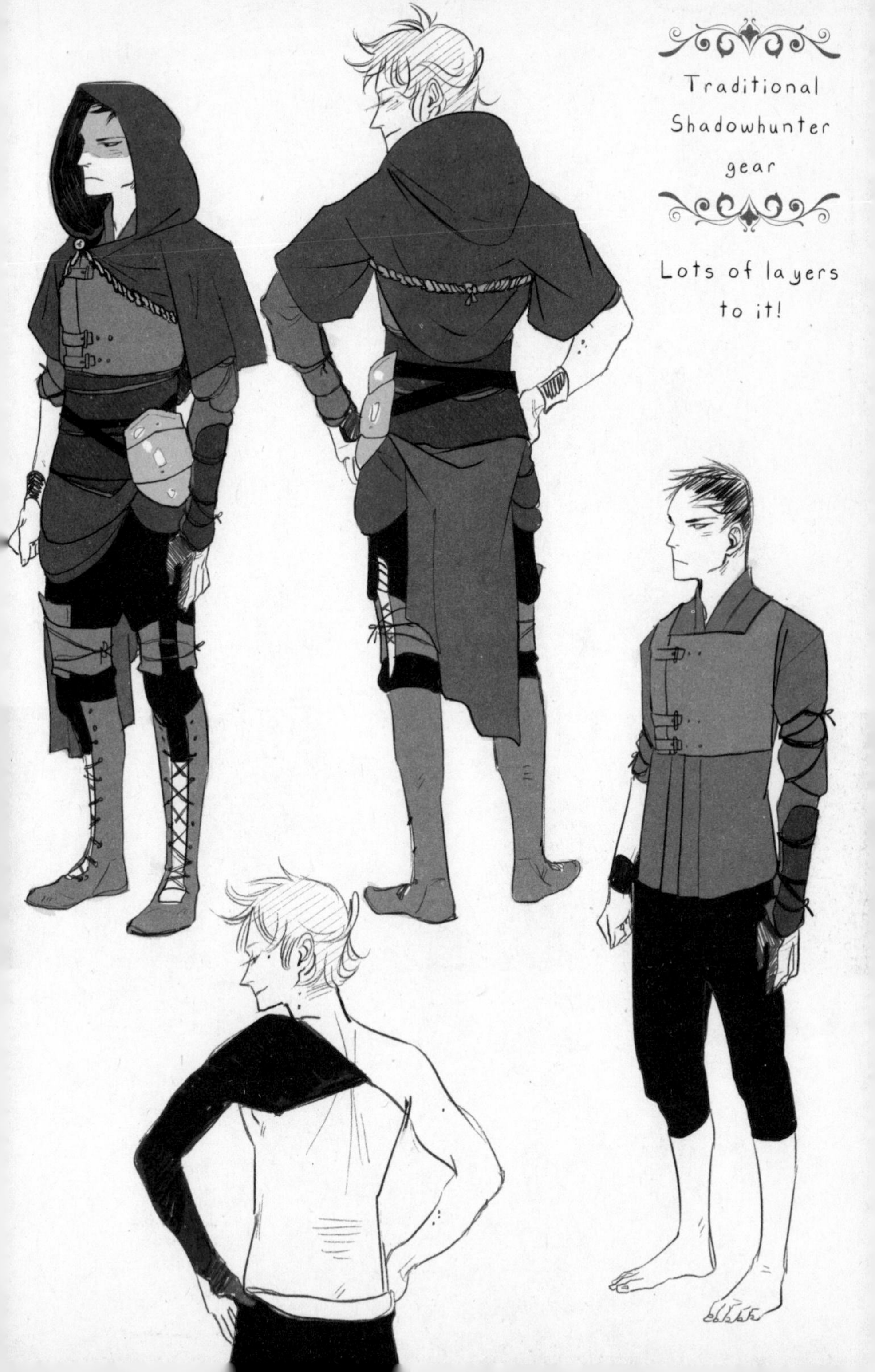
Traditional Shadowhunter gear
Lots of layers to it!

THE MORTAL INSTRUMENTS

THE GRAPHIC NOVEL

Chapter 10

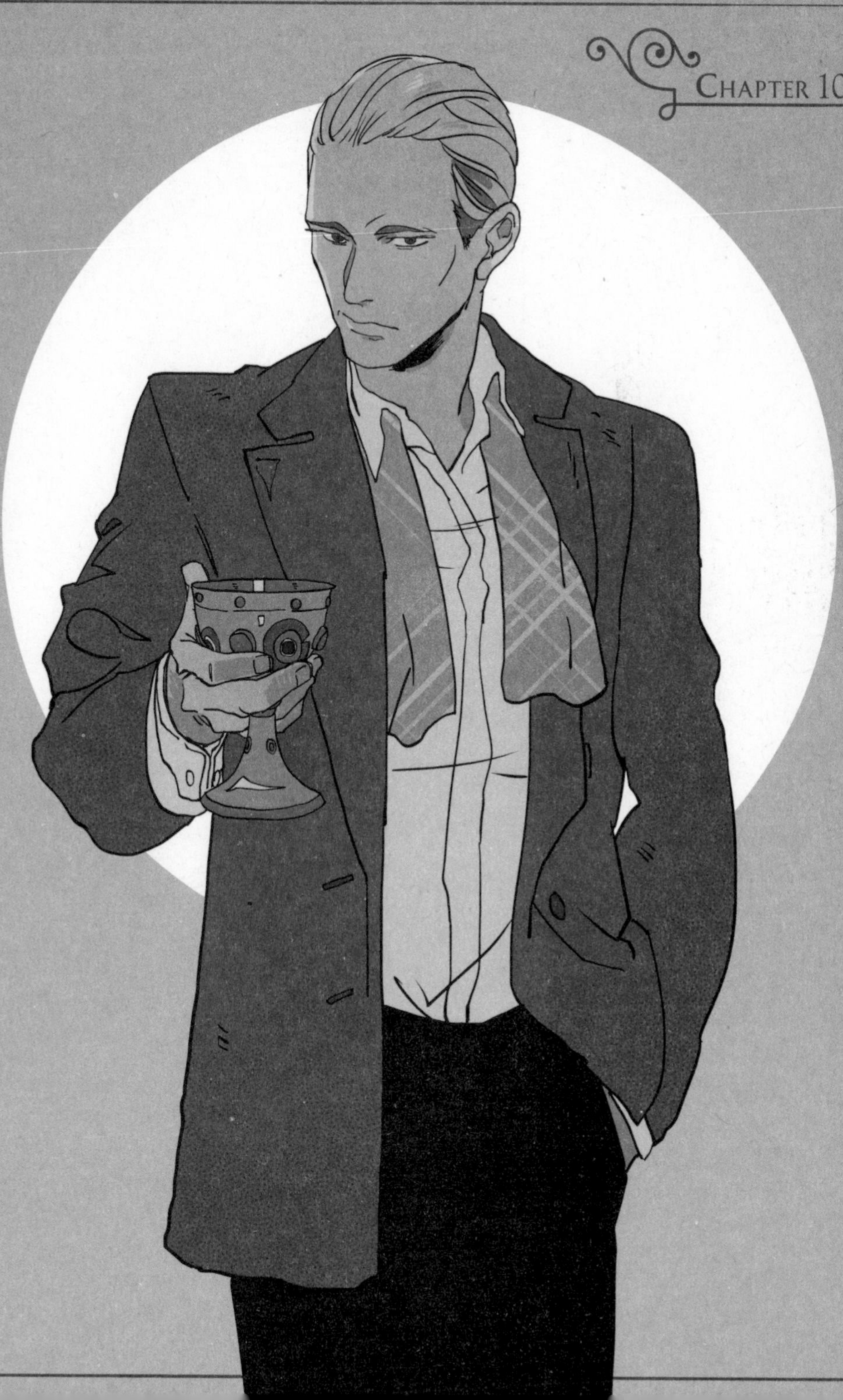

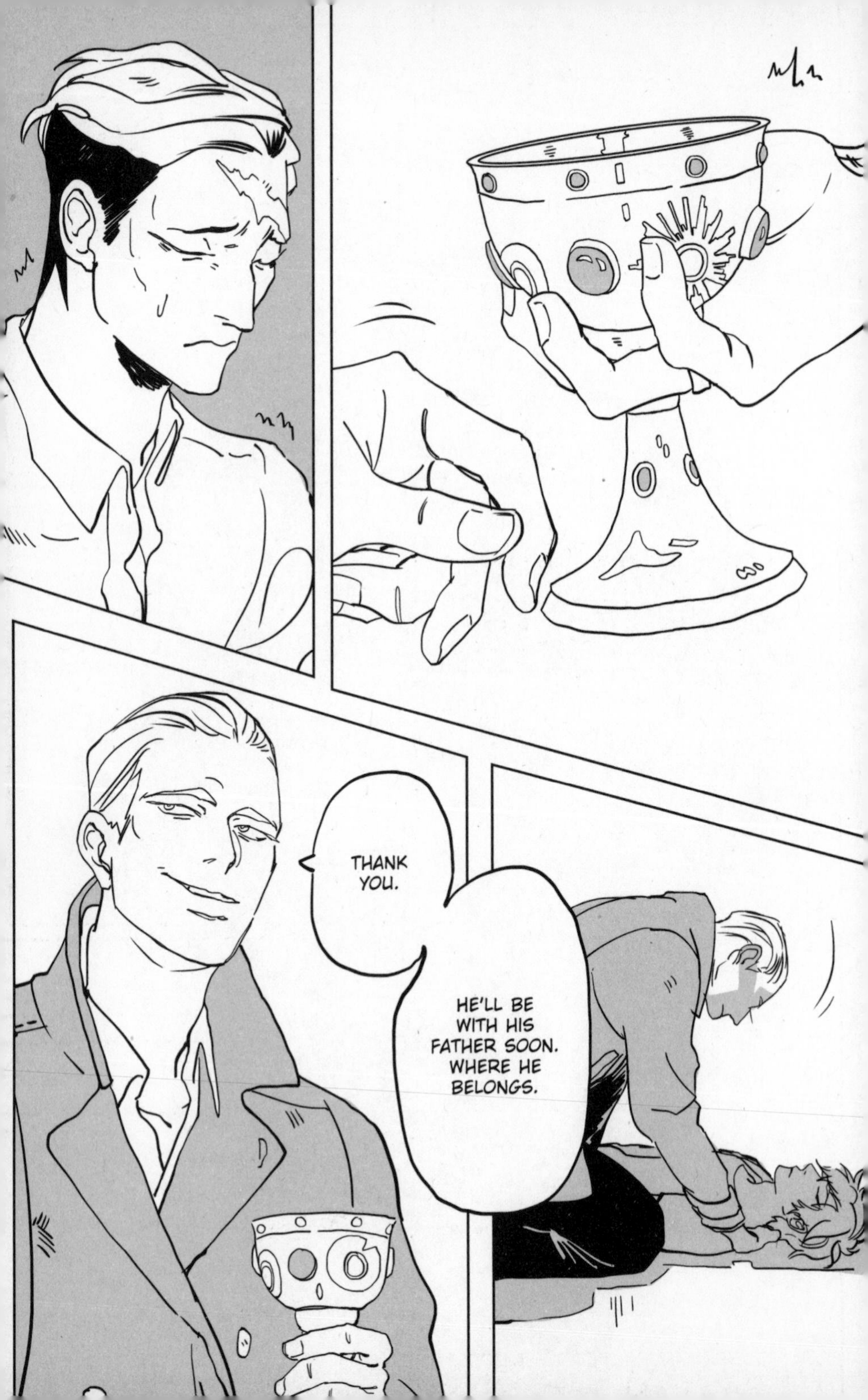
THANK YOU.
HE'LL BE WITH HIS FATHER SOON. WHERE HE BELONGS.

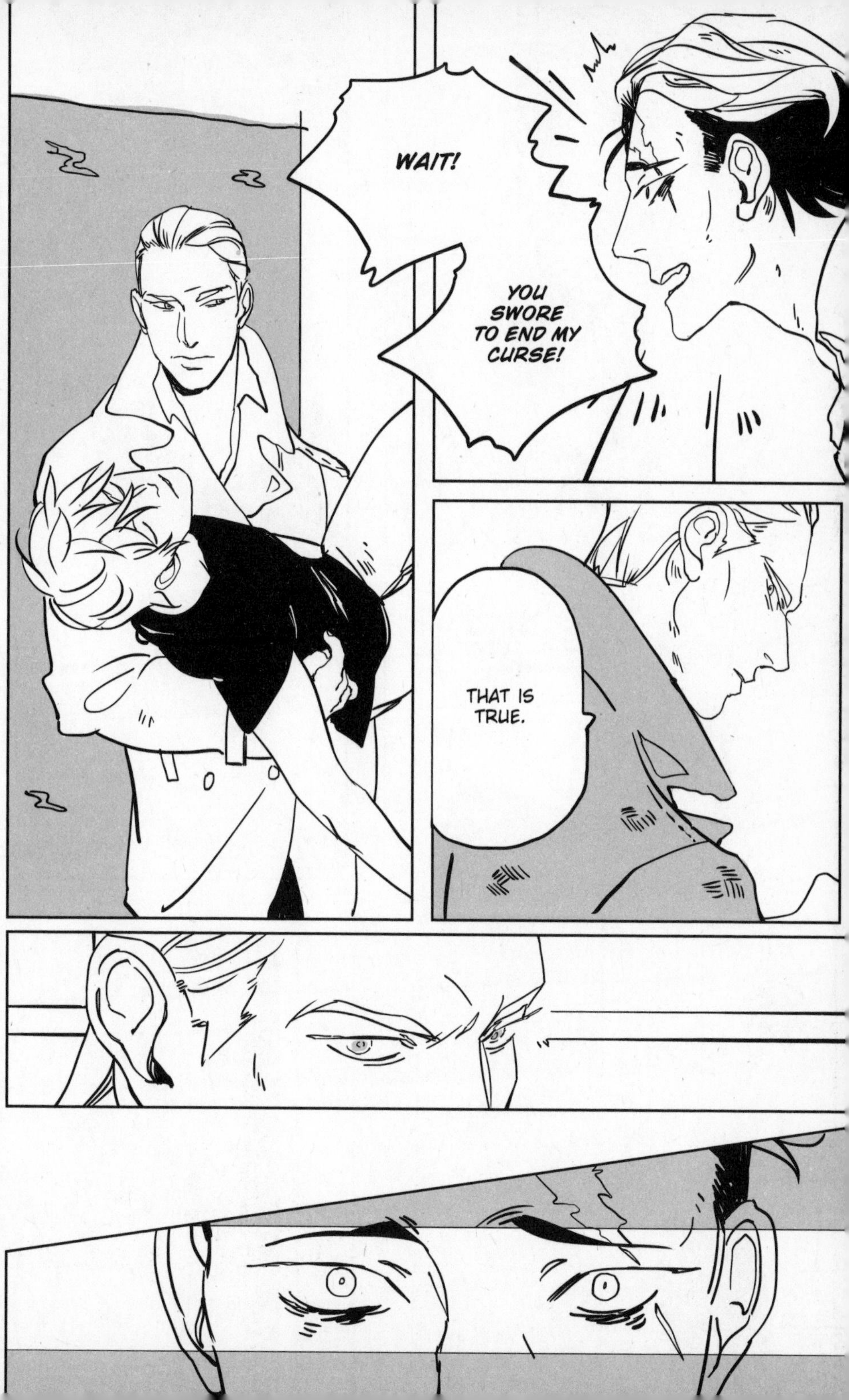
WAIT!
YOU SWORE TO END MY CURSE!
THAT IS TRUE.

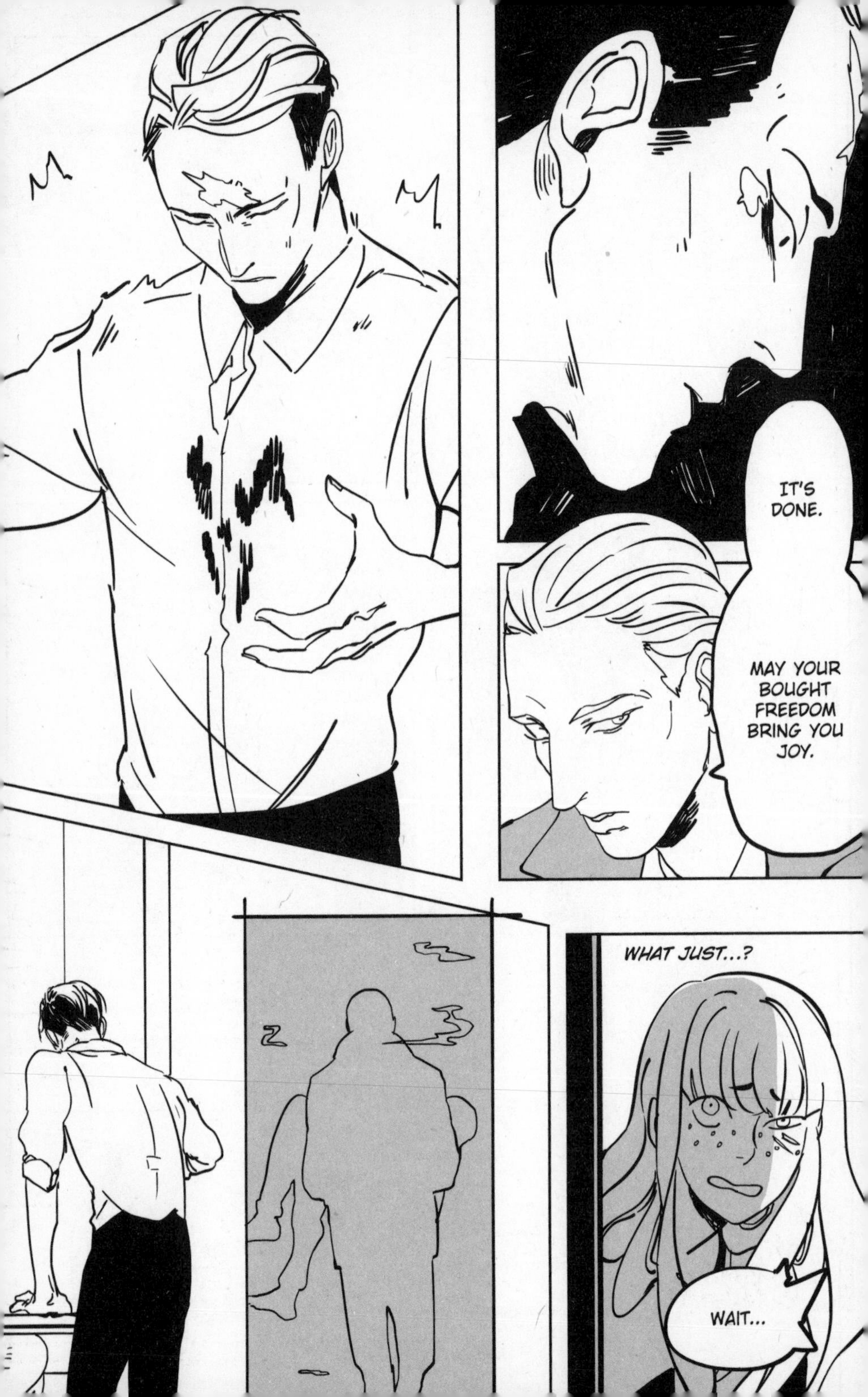
IT'S DONE.
MAY YOUR BOUGHT FREEDOM BRING YOU JOY.
Z
WHAT JUST...?
WAIT...

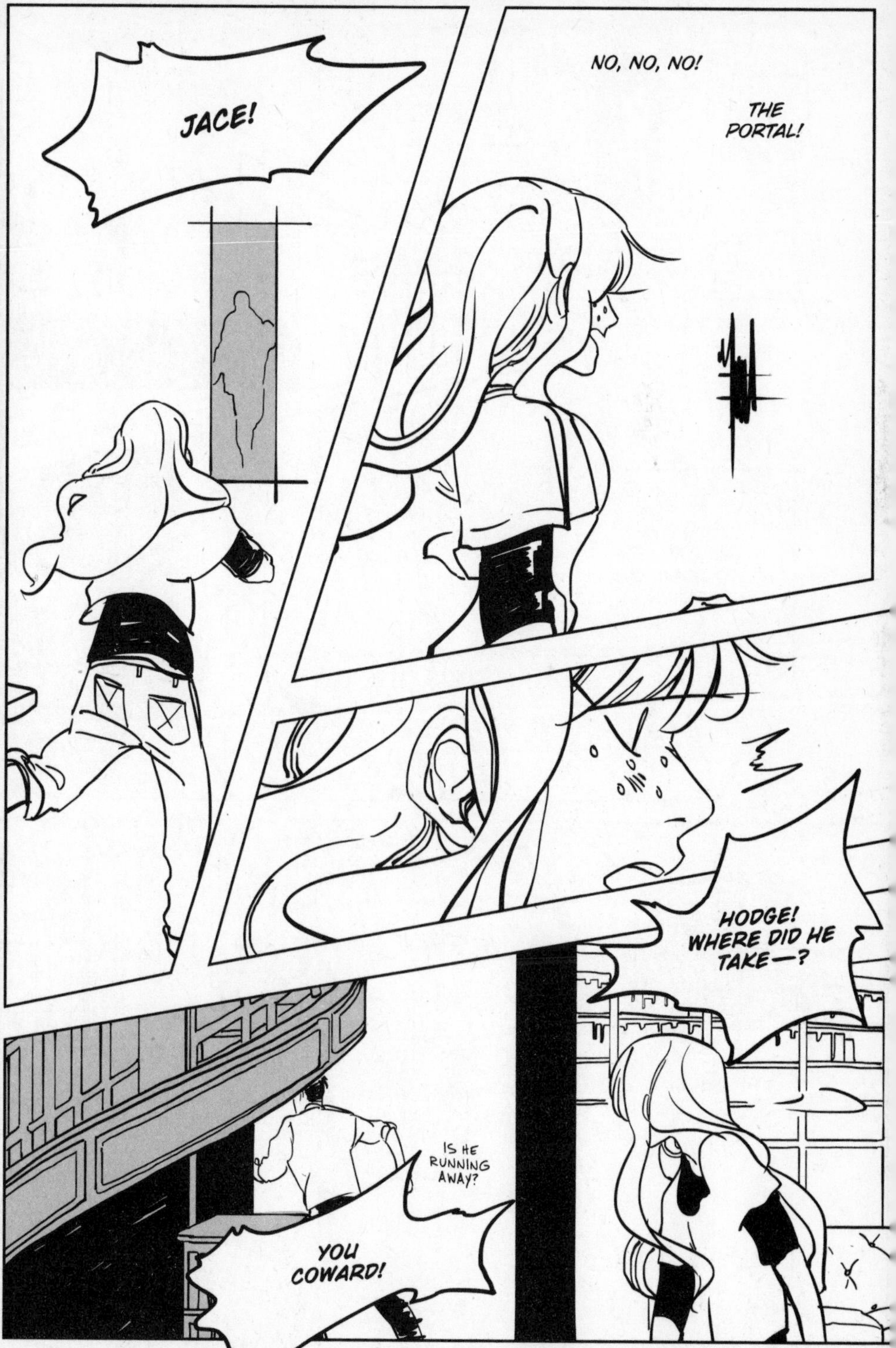
JACE!
NO, NO, NO!
THE PORTAL!
HODGE! WHERE DID HE TAKE—?
IS HE RUNNING AWAY?
YOU COWARD!

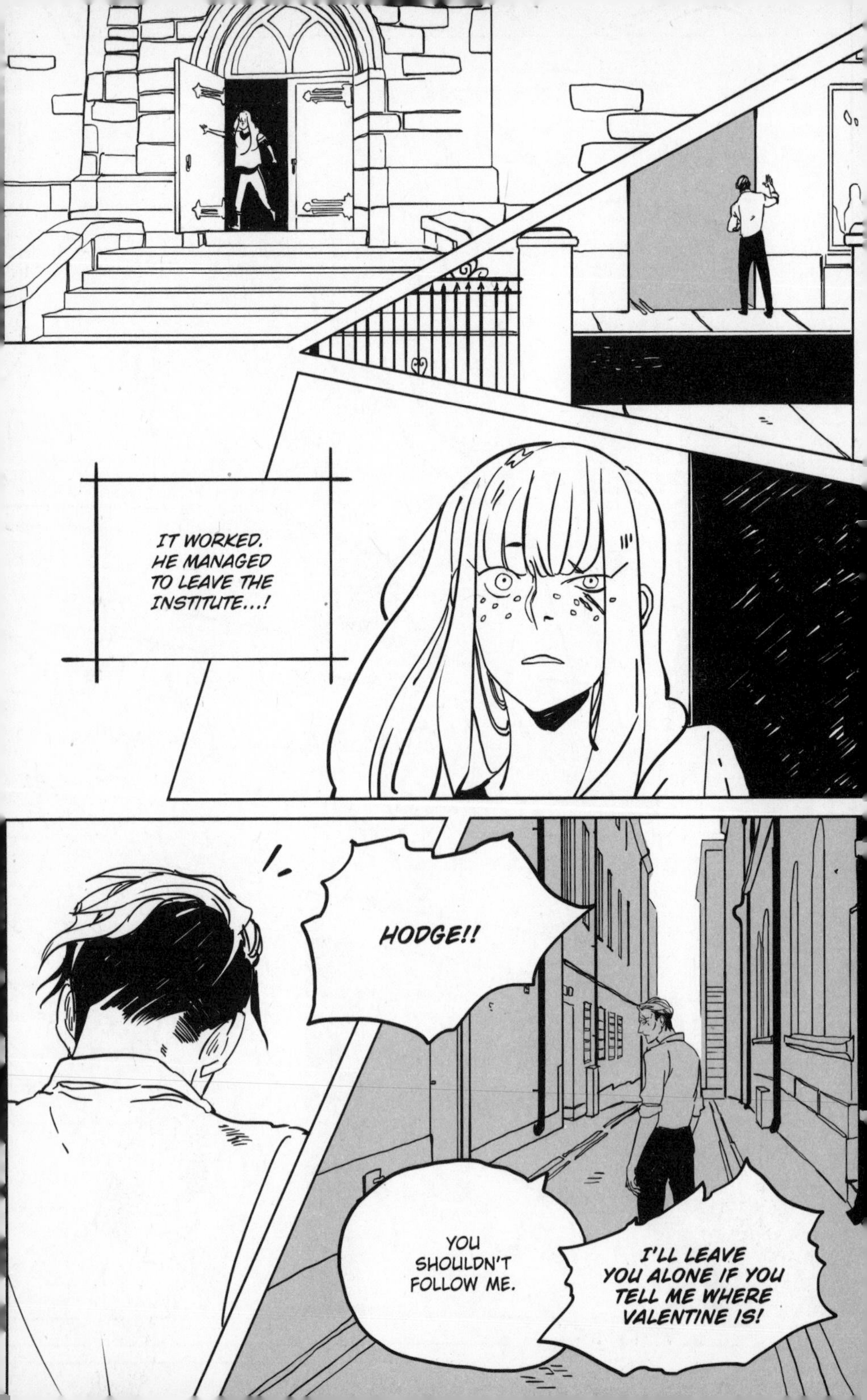
IT WORKED. HE MANAGED TO LEAVE THE INSTITUTE...!
HODGE!!
YOU SHOULDN'T FOLLOW ME.
I'LL LEAVE YOU ALONE IF YOU TELL ME WHERE VALENTINE IS!

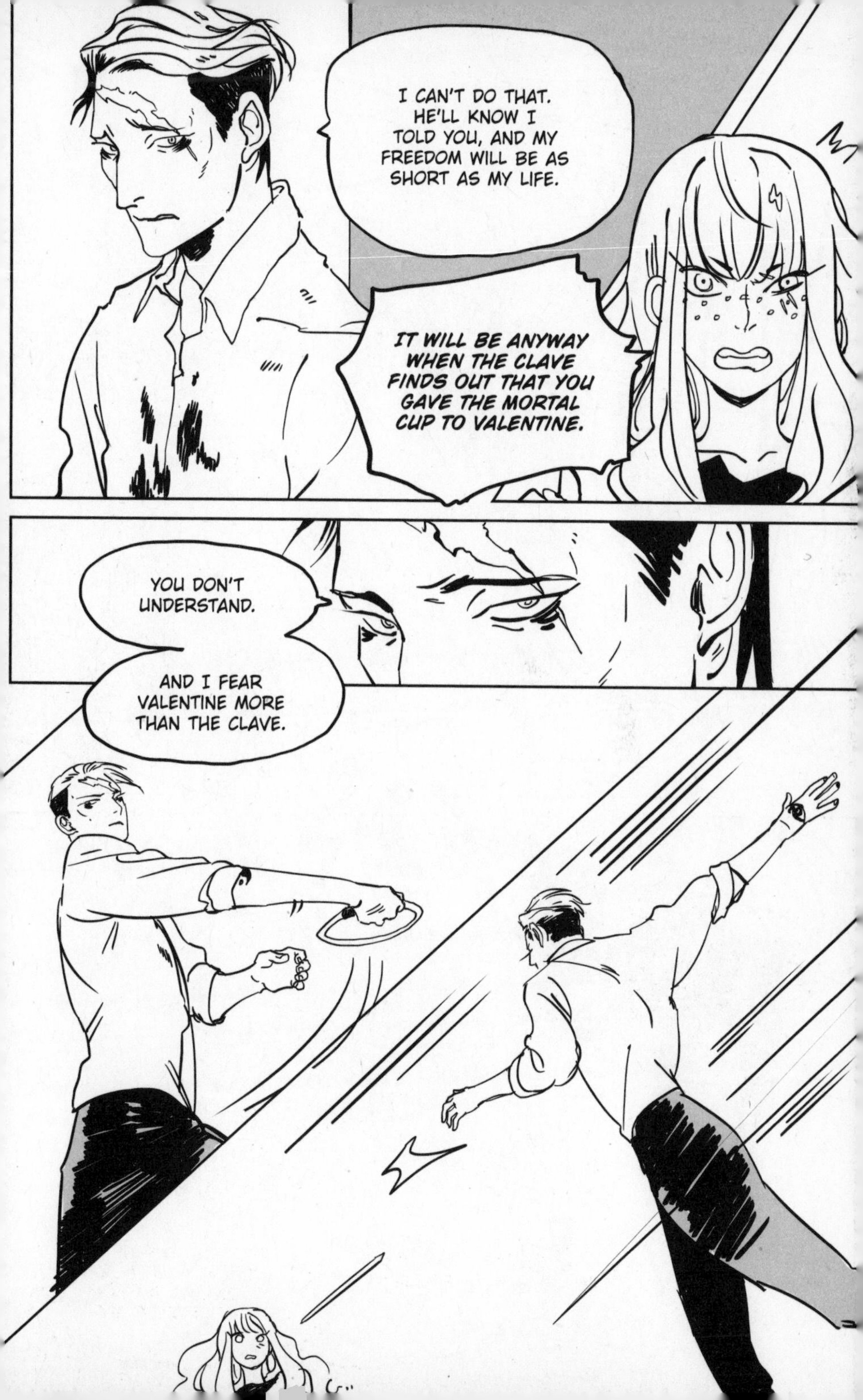
I CAN'T DO THAT. HE'LL KNOW I TOLD YOU, AND MY FREEDOM WILL BE AS SHORT AS MY LIFE.
IT WILL BE ANYWAY WHEN THE CLAVE FINDS OUT THAT YOU GAVE THE MORTAL CUP TO VALENTINE.
YOU DON'T UNDERSTAND.
AND I FEAR VALENTINE MORE THAN THE CLAVE.

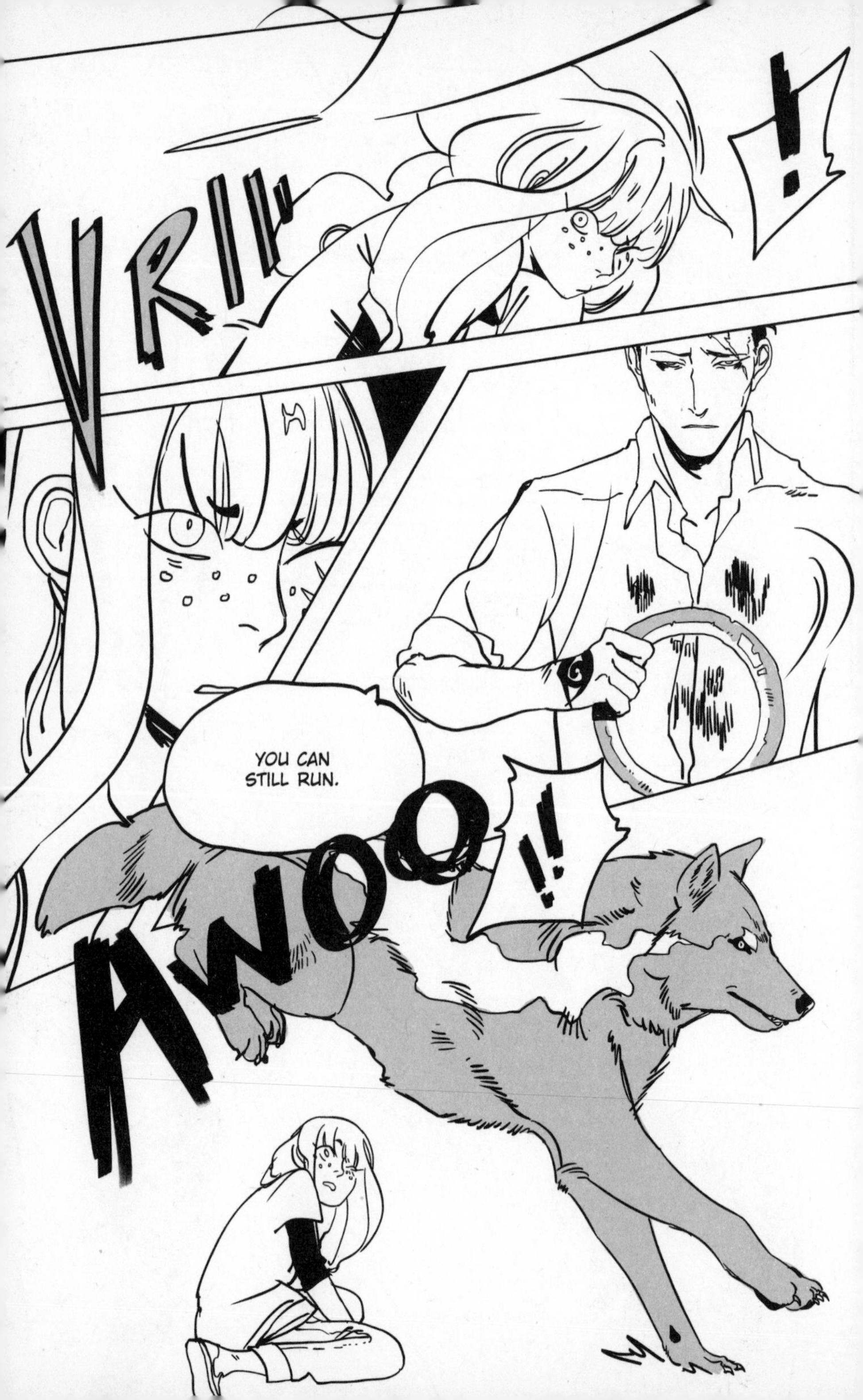
VRII
!
YOU CAN STILL RUN.
AWOO!!

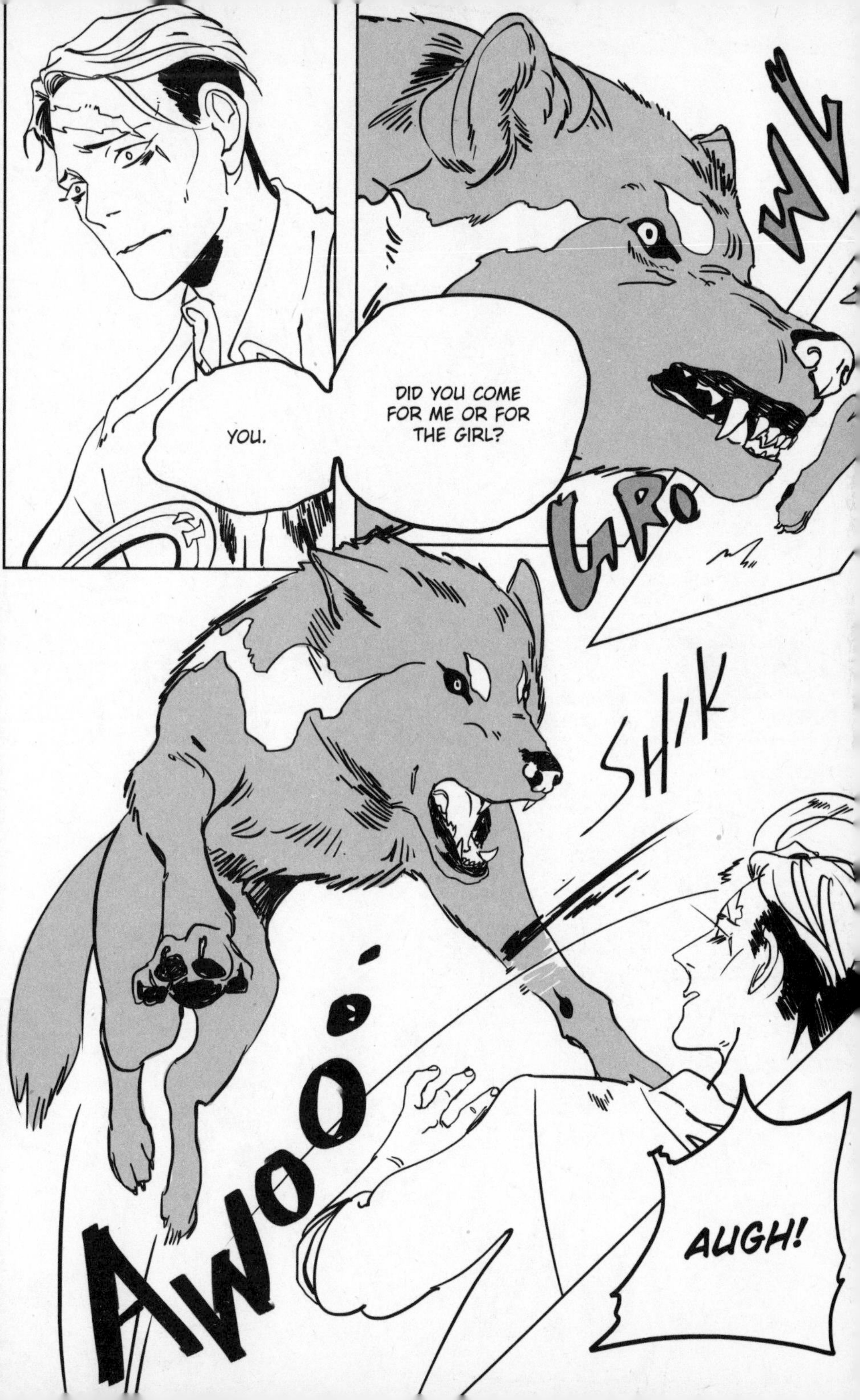
DID YOU COME FOR ME OR FOR THE GIRL?
YOU.
WL
GRO
SHIK
AWOO
AUGH!

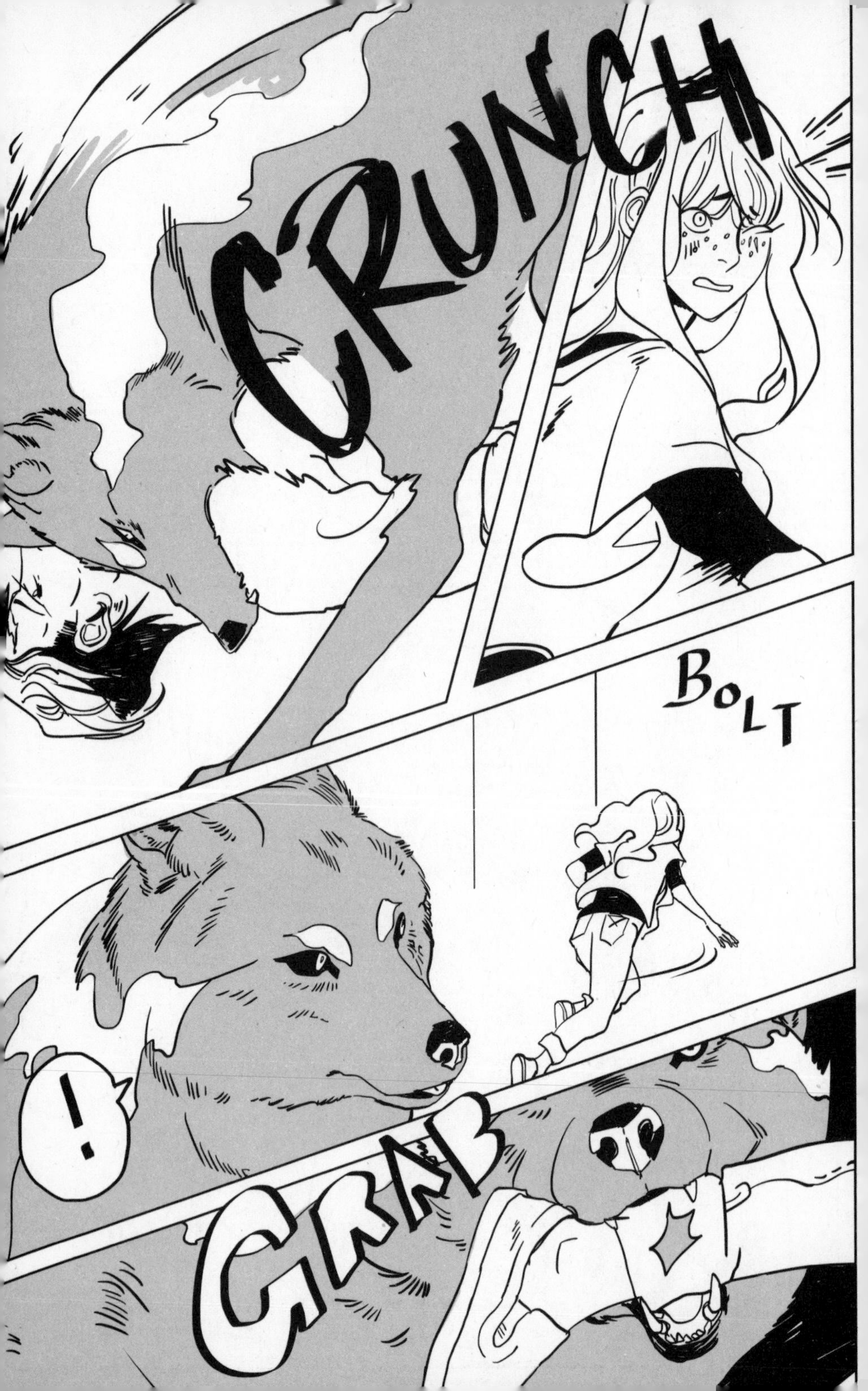
CRUNCH!
BOLT
!
GRAB

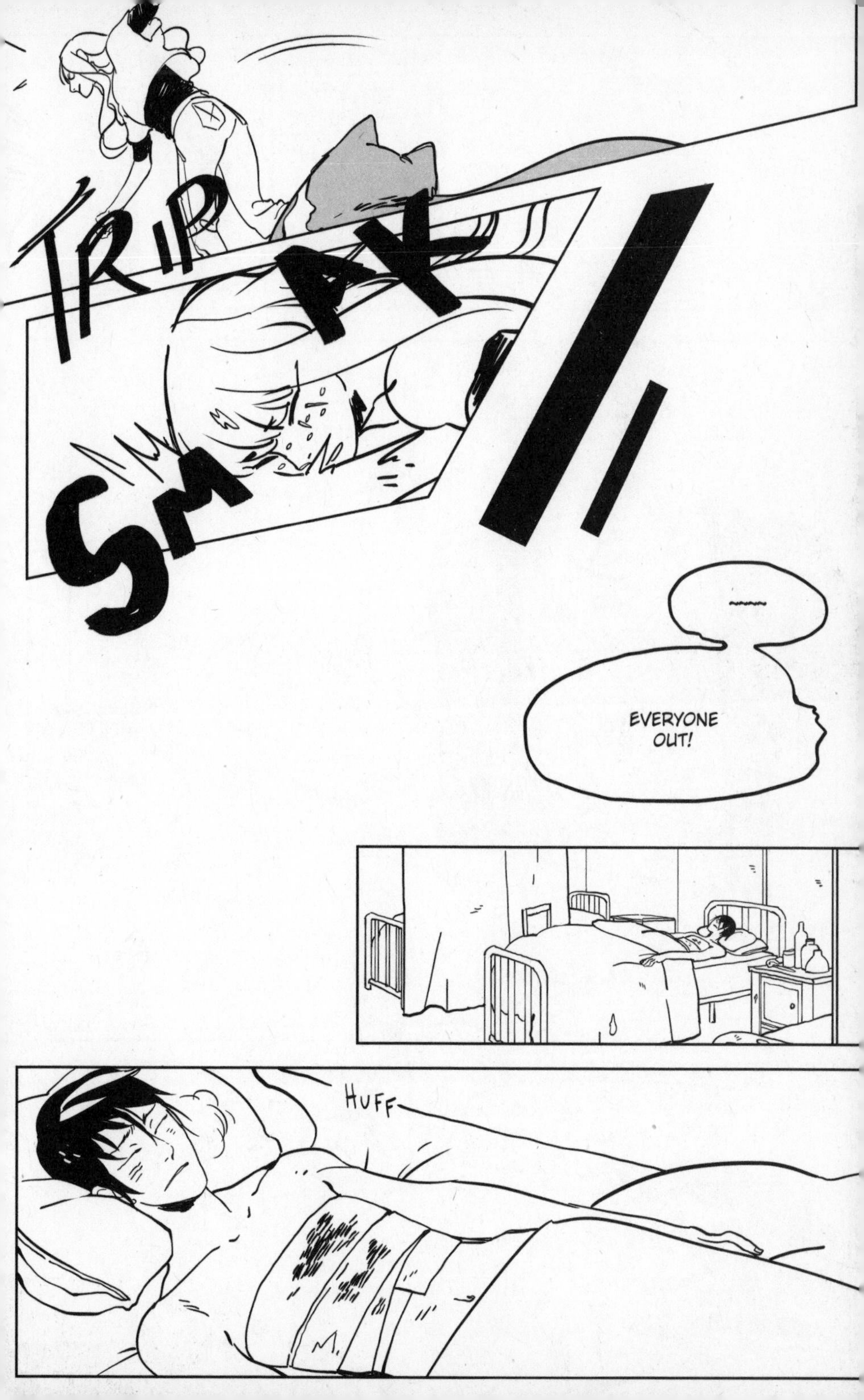
TRIP
SMACK
--
EVERYONE OUT!
HUFF

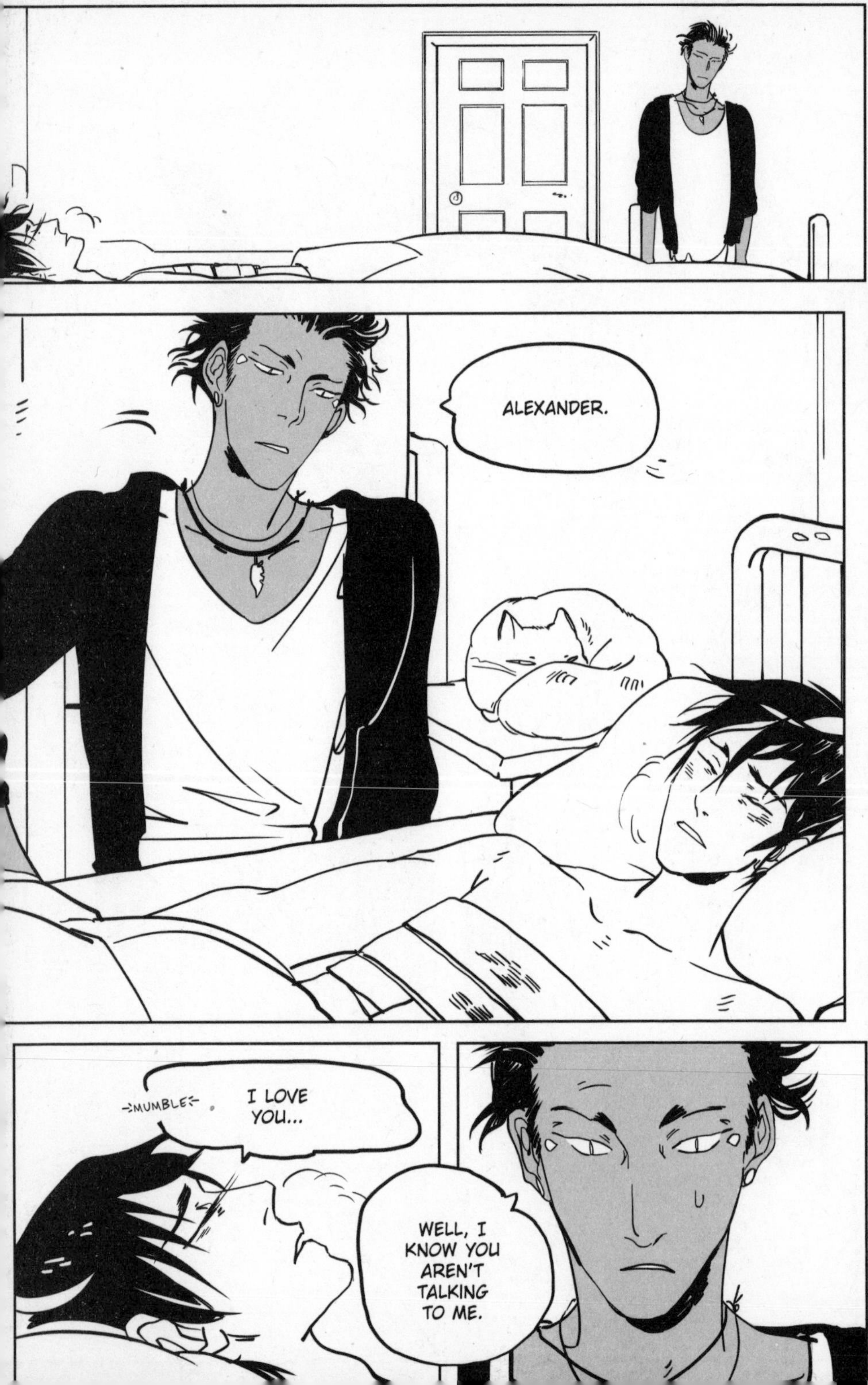
ALEXANDER.
-MUMBLE-
I LOVE YOU...
WELL, I KNOW YOU AREN'T TALKING TO ME.

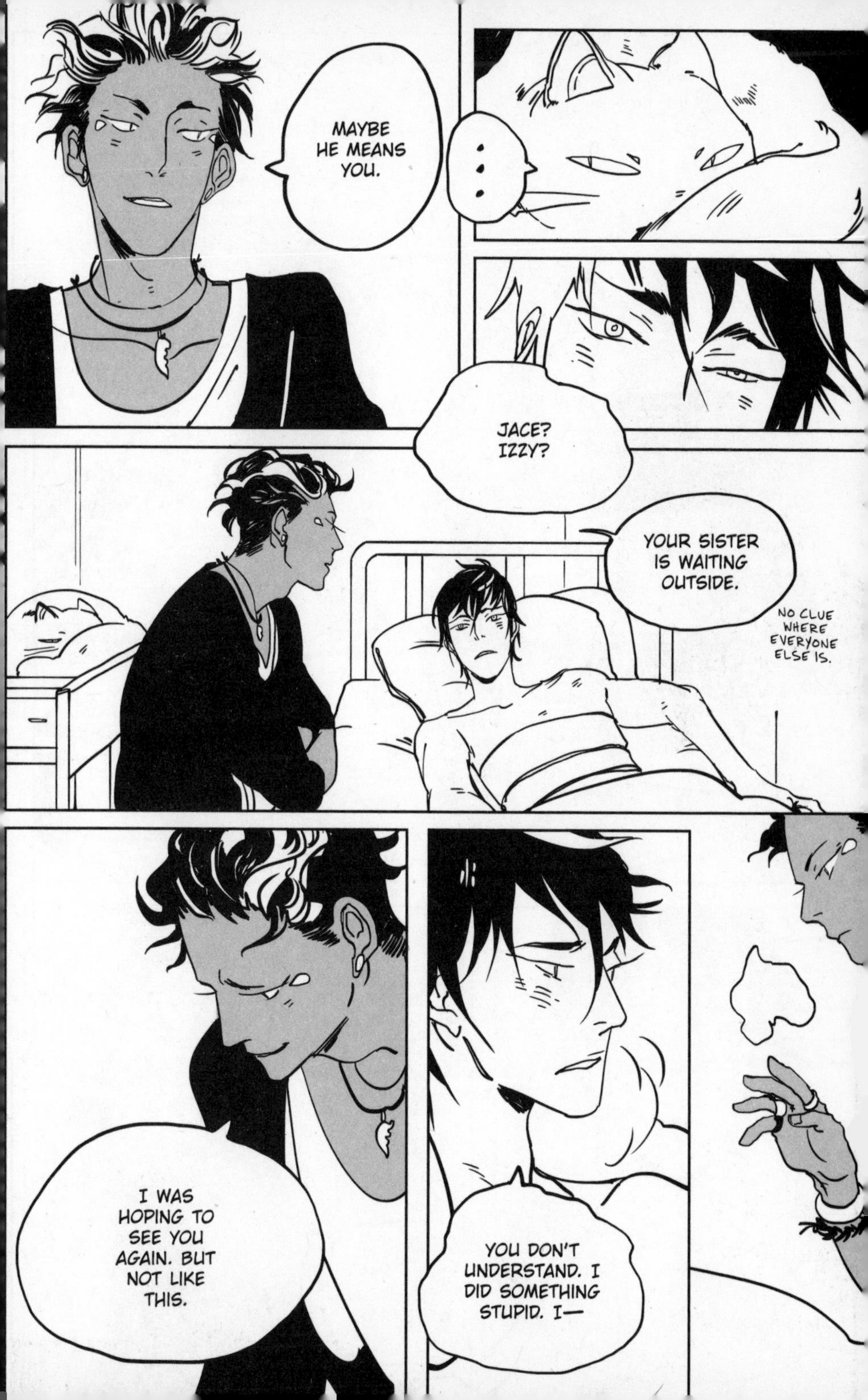
MAYBE HE MEANS YOU.
...
JACE? IZZY?
YOUR SISTER IS WAITING OUTSIDE.
NO CLUE WHERE EVERYONE ELSE IS.
I WAS HOPING TO SEE YOU AGAIN. BUT NOT LIKE THIS.
YOU DON'T UNDERSTAND. I DID SOMETHING STUPID. I—

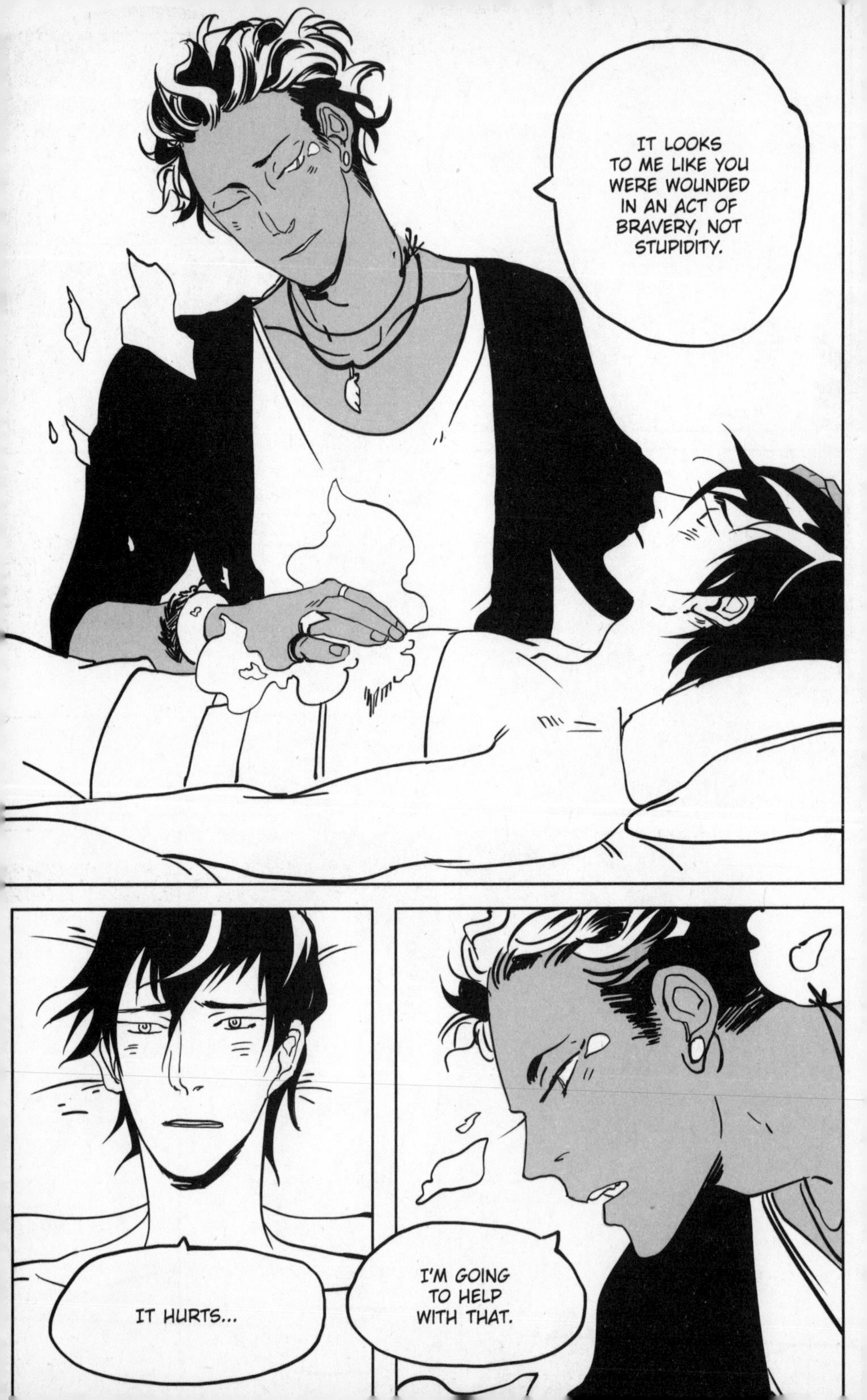
IT LOOKS TO ME LIKE YOU WERE WOUNDED IN AN ACT OF BRAVERY, NOT STUPIDITY.
IT HURTS...
I'M GOING TO HELP WITH THAT.

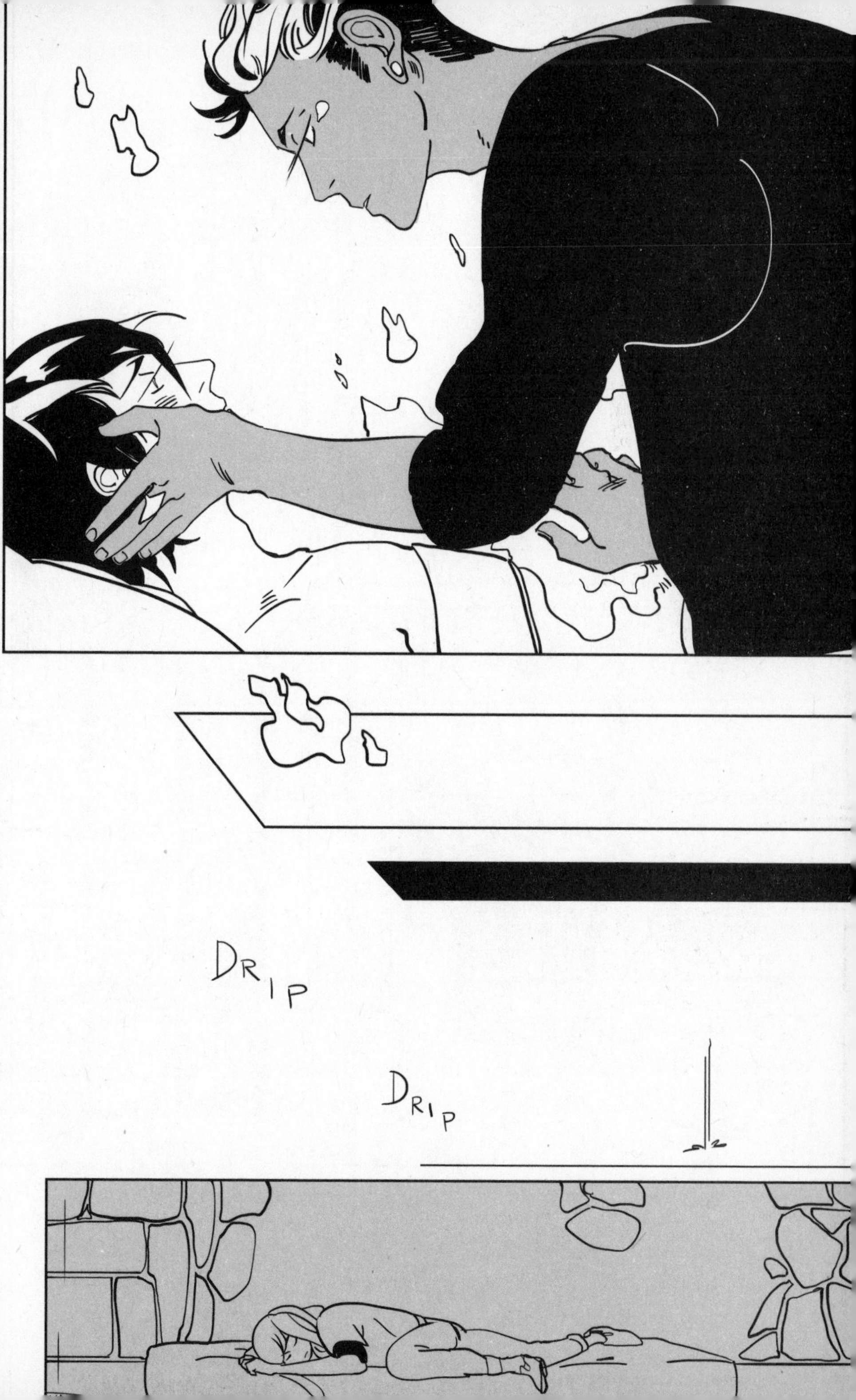
DRIP
DRIP

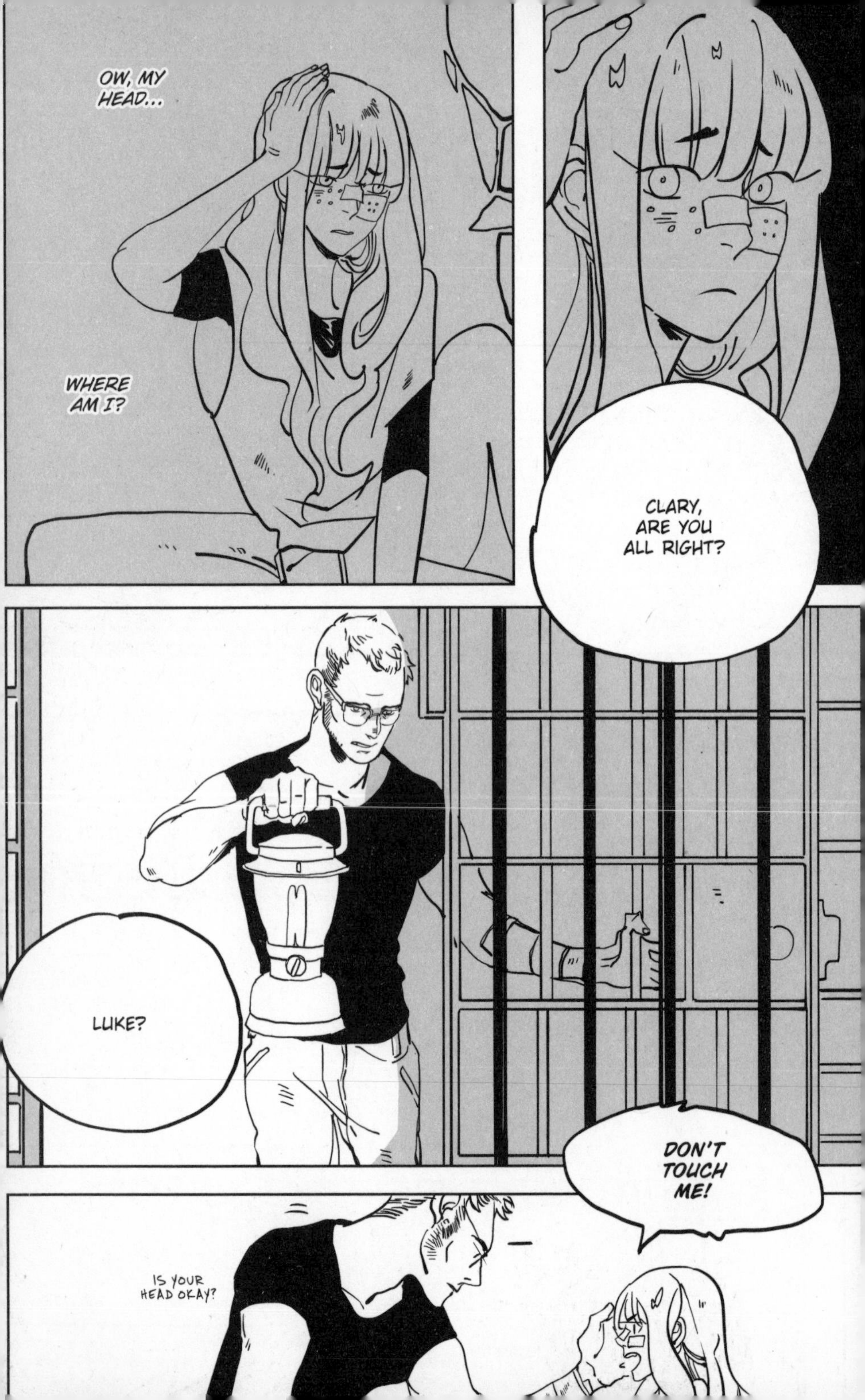
OW, MY HEAD...
WHERE AM I?
CLARY, ARE YOU ALL RIGHT?
LUKE?
DON'T TOUCH ME!
IS YOUR HEAD OKAY?

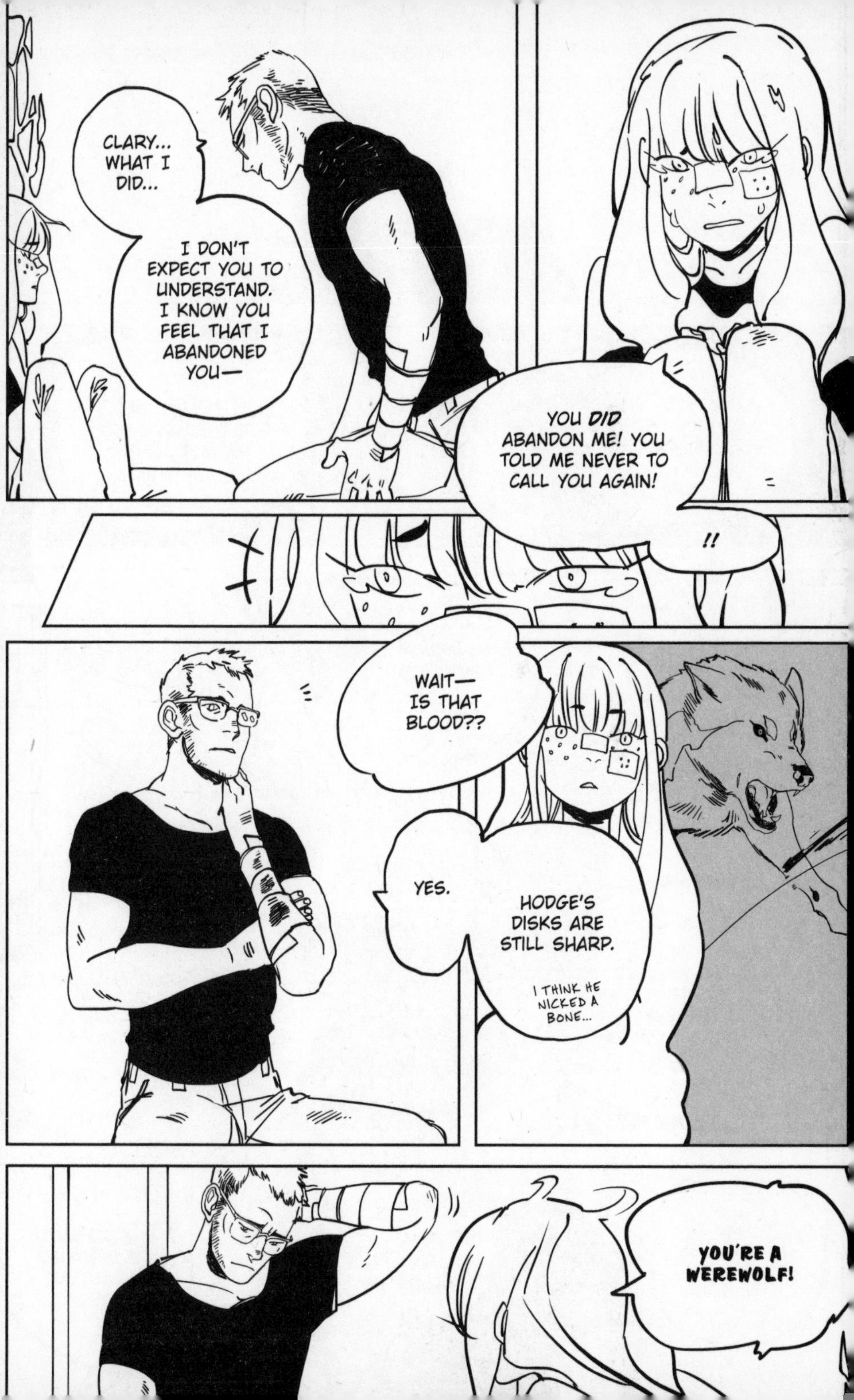

CLARY... WHAT I DID...
I DON'T EXPECT YOU TO UNDERSTAND. I KNOW YOU FEEL THAT I ABANDONED YOU—
YOU *DID* ABANDON ME! YOU TOLD ME NEVER TO CALL YOU AGAIN!
!!
WAIT— IS THAT BLOOD??
YES.
HODGE'S DISKS ARE STILL SHARP.
I THINK HE NICKED A BONE...
YOU'RE A WEREWOLF!

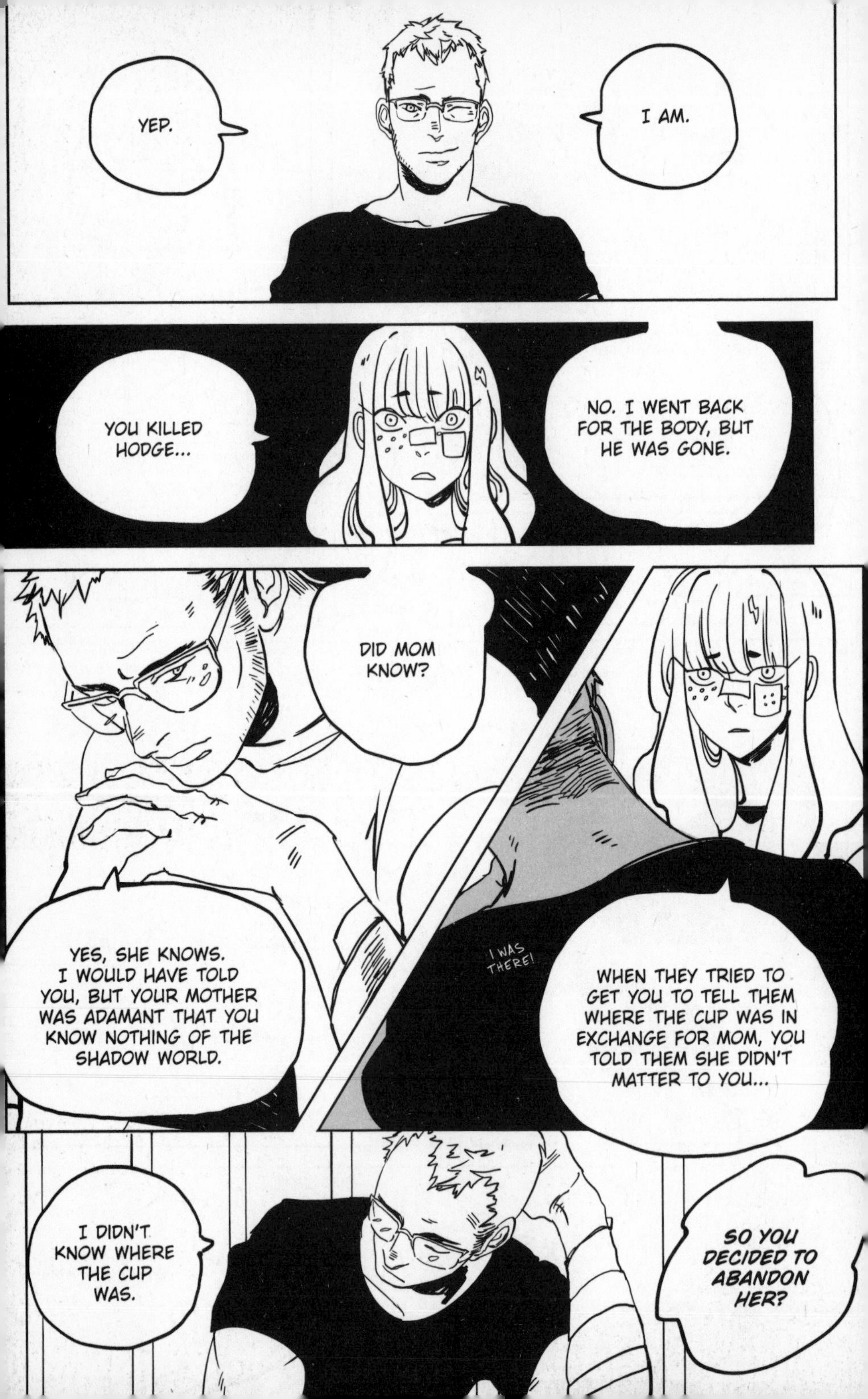
YEP.
I AM.
YOU KILLED HODGE...
NO. I WENT BACK FOR THE BODY, BUT HE WAS GONE.
DID MOM KNOW?
YES, SHE KNOWS. I WOULD HAVE TOLD YOU, BUT YOUR MOTHER WAS ADAMANT THAT YOU KNOW NOTHING OF THE SHADOW WORLD.
I WAS THERE!
WHEN THEY TRIED TO GET YOU TO TELL THEM WHERE THE CUP WAS IN EXCHANGE FOR MOM, YOU TOLD THEM SHE DIDN'T MATTER TO YOU...
I DIDN'T KNOW WHERE THE CUP WAS.
SO YOU DECIDED TO ABANDON HER?

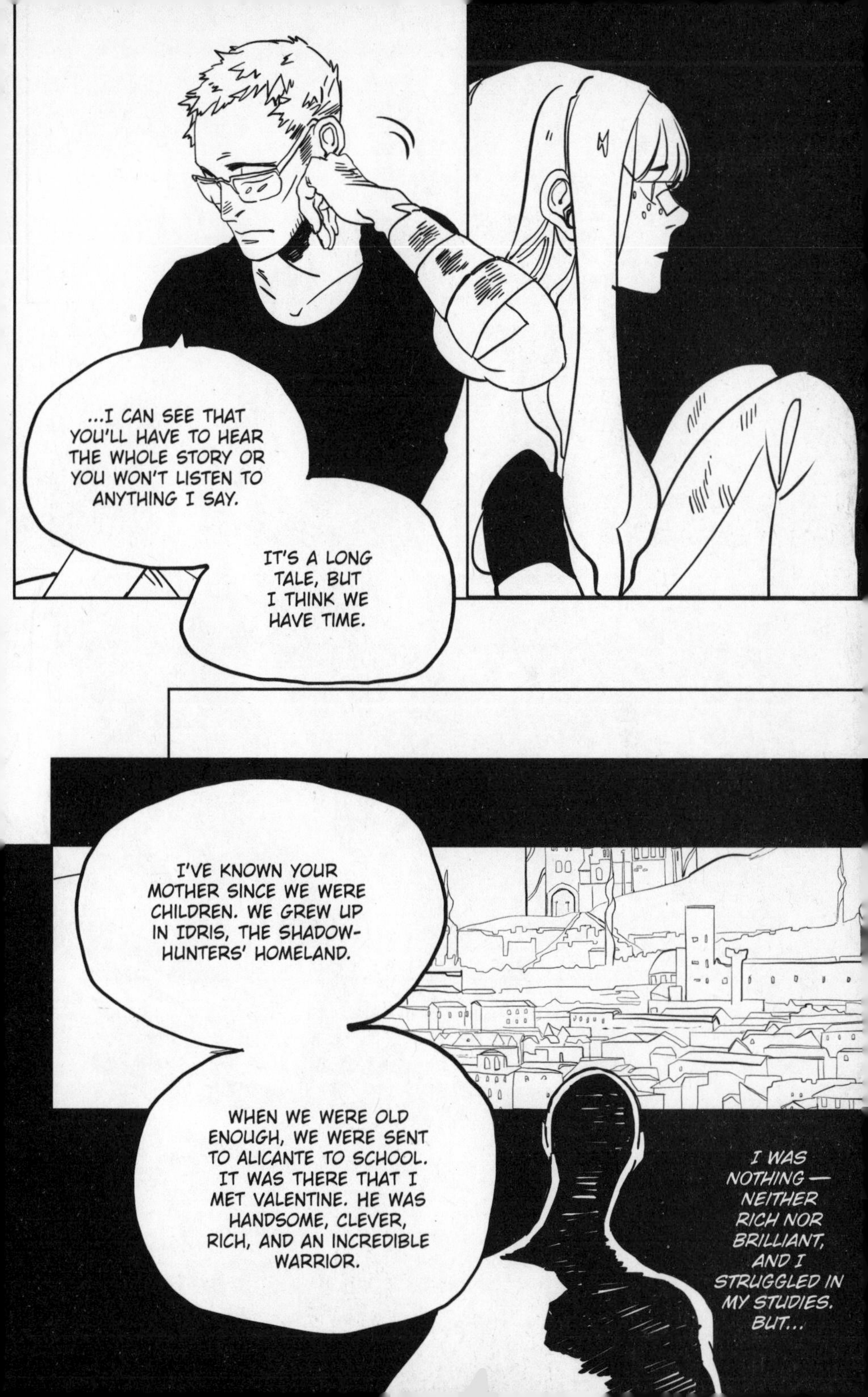
...I CAN SEE THAT YOU'LL HAVE TO HEAR THE WHOLE STORY OR YOU WON'T LISTEN TO ANYTHING I SAY.
IT'S A LONG TALE, BUT I THINK WE HAVE TIME.
I'VE KNOWN YOUR MOTHER SINCE WE WERE CHILDREN. WE GREW UP IN IDRIS, THE SHADOW-HUNTERS' HOMELAND.
WHEN WE WERE OLD ENOUGH, WE WERE SENT TO ALICANTE TO SCHOOL. IT WAS THERE THAT I MET VALENTINE. HE WAS HANDSOME, CLEVER, RICH, AND AN INCREDIBLE WARRIOR.
I WAS NOTHING—NEITHER RICH NOR BRILLIANT, AND I STRUGGLED IN MY STUDIES. BUT...

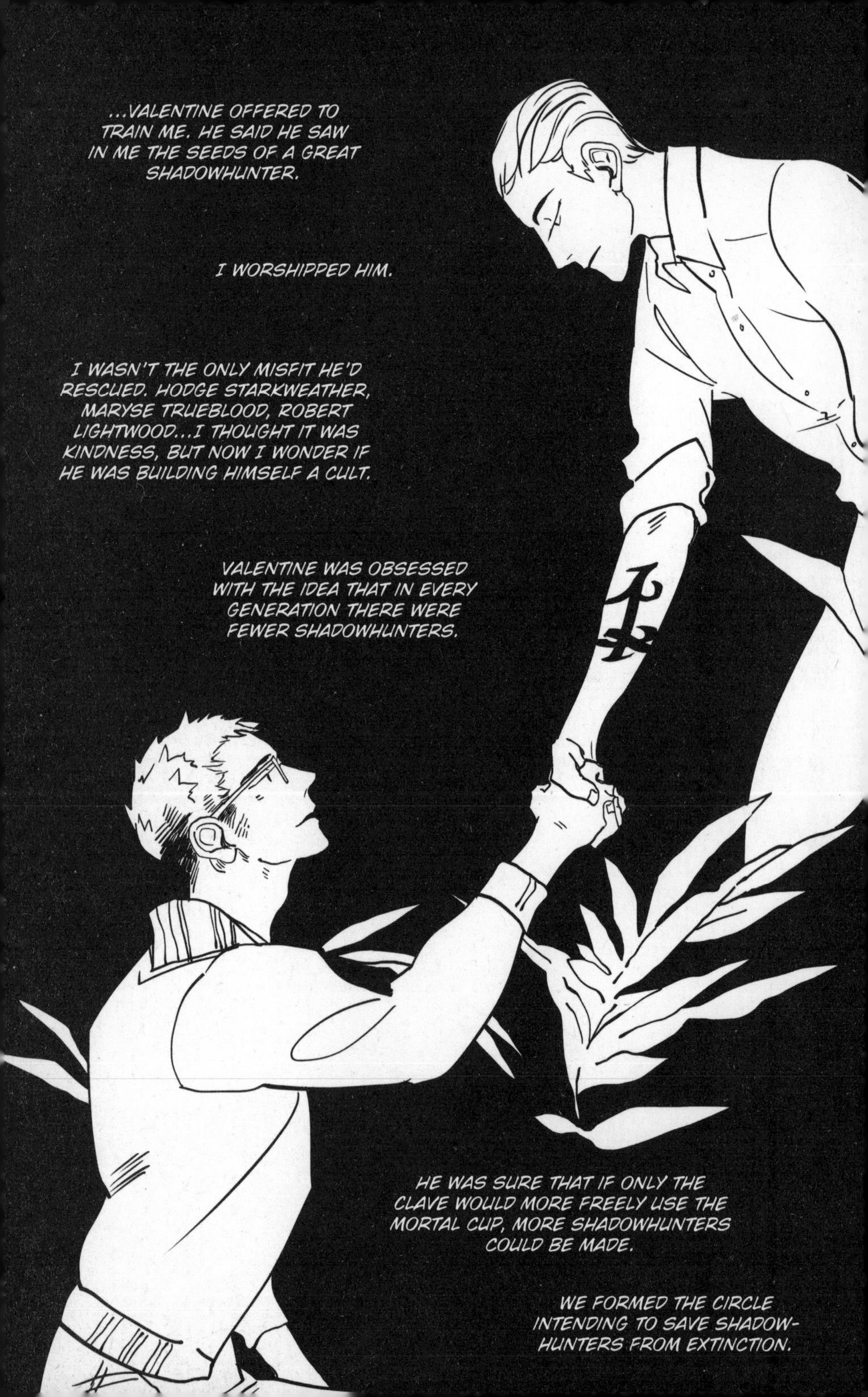
...VALENTINE OFFERED TO TRAIN ME. HE SAID HE SAW IN ME THE SEEDS OF A GREAT SHADOWHUNTER.
I WORSHIPPED HIM.
I WASN'T THE ONLY MISFIT HE'D RESCUED. HODGE STARKWEATHER, MARYSE TRUEBLOOD, ROBERT LIGHTWOOD...I THOUGHT IT WAS KINDNESS, BUT NOW I WONDER IF HE WAS BUILDING HIMSELF A CULT.
VALENTINE WAS OBSESSED WITH THE IDEA THAT IN EVERY GENERATION THERE WERE FEWER SHADOWHUNTERS.
HE WAS SURE THAT IF ONLY THE CLAVE WOULD MORE FREELY USE THE MORTAL CUP, MORE SHADOWHUNTERS COULD BE MADE.
WE FORMED THE CIRCLE INTENDING TO SAVE SHADOW-HUNTERS FROM EXTINCTION.

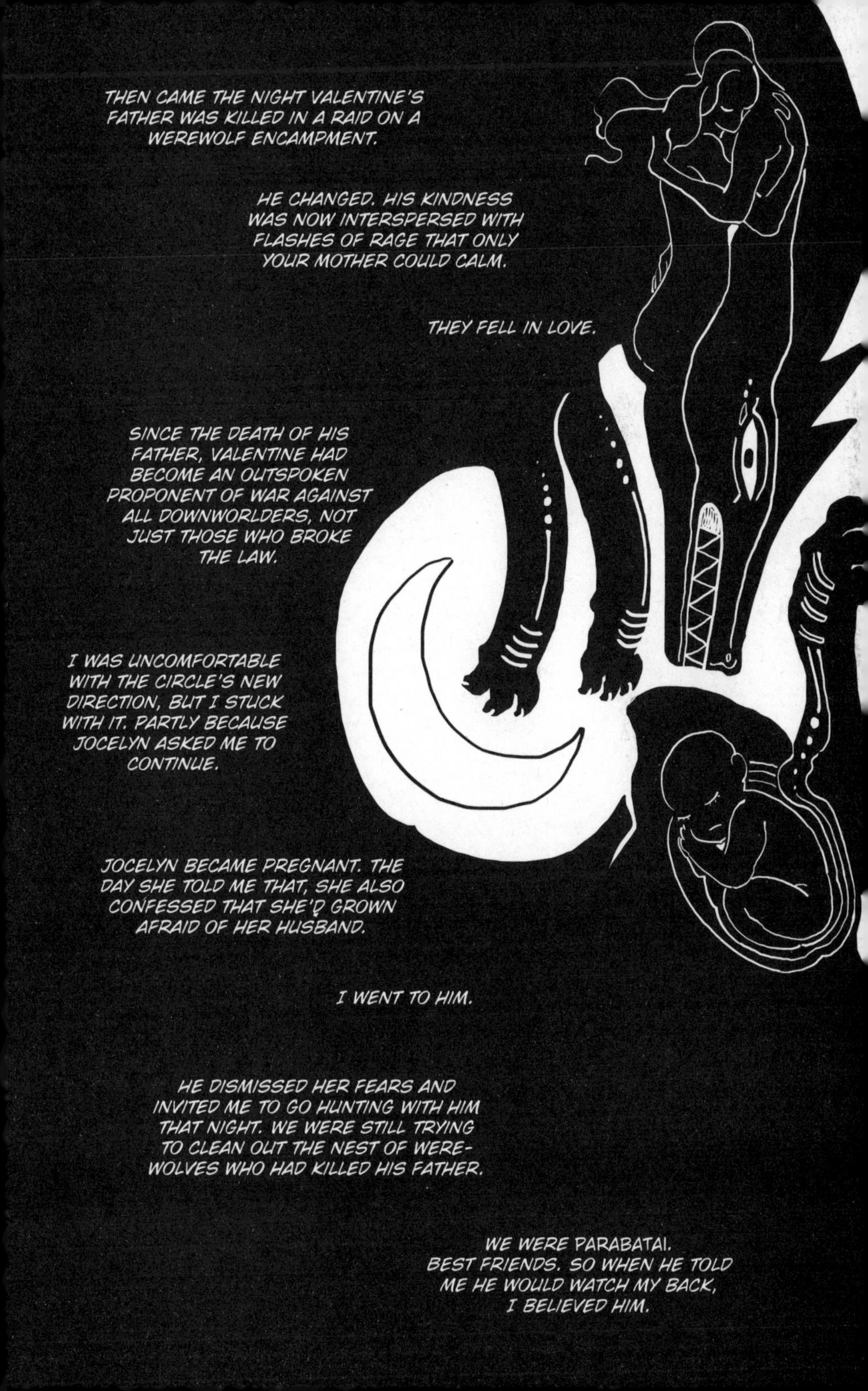
THEN CAME THE NIGHT VALENTINE'S FATHER WAS KILLED IN A RAID ON A WEREWOLF ENCAMPMENT.
HE CHANGED. HIS KINDNESS WAS NOW INTERSPERSED WITH FLASHES OF RAGE THAT ONLY YOUR MOTHER COULD CALM.
THEY FELL IN LOVE.
SINCE THE DEATH OF HIS FATHER, VALENTINE HAD BECOME AN OUTSPOKEN PROPONENT OF WAR AGAINST ALL DOWNWORLDERS, NOT JUST THOSE WHO BROKE THE LAW.
I WAS UNCOMFORTABLE WITH THE CIRCLE'S NEW DIRECTION, BUT I STUCK WITH IT. PARTLY BECAUSE JOCELYN ASKED ME TO CONTINUE.
JOCELYN BECAME PREGNANT. THE DAY SHE TOLD ME THAT, SHE ALSO CONFESSED THAT SHE'D GROWN AFRAID OF HER HUSBAND.
I WENT TO HIM.
HE DISMISSED HER FEARS AND INVITED ME TO GO HUNTING WITH HIM THAT NIGHT. WE WERE STILL TRYING TO CLEAN OUT THE NEST OF WERE-WOLVES WHO HAD KILLED HIS FATHER.
WE WERE PARABATAI. BEST FRIENDS. SO WHEN HE TOLD ME HE WOULD WATCH MY BACK, I BELIEVED HIM.

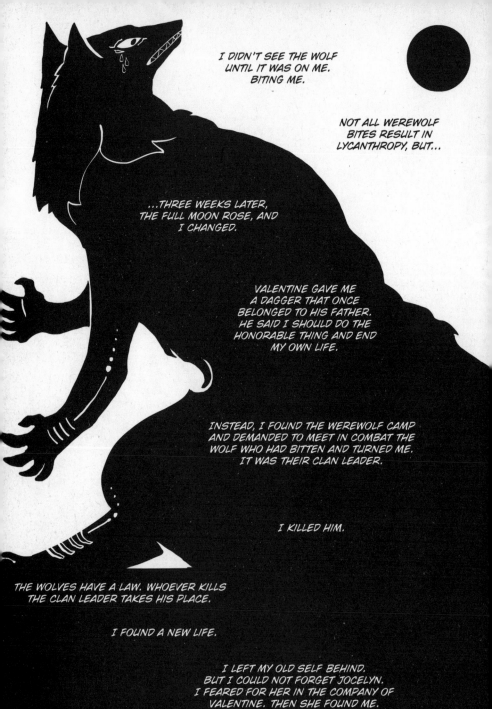

I DIDN'T SEE THE WOLF
UNTIL IT WAS ON ME.
BITING ME.

NOT ALL WEREWOLF
BITES RESULT IN
LYCANTHROPY, BUT...

...THREE WEEKS LATER,
THE FULL MOON ROSE, AND
I CHANGED.

VALENTINE GAVE ME
A DAGGER THAT ONCE
BELONGED TO HIS FATHER.
HE SAID I SHOULD DO THE
HONORABLE THING AND END
MY OWN LIFE.

INSTEAD, I FOUND THE WEREWOLF CAMP
AND DEMANDED TO MEET IN COMBAT THE
WOLF WHO HAD BITTEN AND TURNED ME.
IT WAS THEIR CLAN LEADER.

I KILLED HIM.

THE WOLVES HAVE A LAW. WHOEVER KILLS
THE CLAN LEADER TAKES HIS PLACE.

I FOUND A NEW LIFE.

I LEFT MY OLD SELF BEHIND.
BUT I COULD NOT FORGET JOCELYN.
I FEARED FOR HER IN THE COMPANY OF
VALENTINE. THEN SHE FOUND ME.

VALENTINE HAD TOLD THE CIRCLE
I'D KILLED MYSELF, BUT SHE HAD
NOT BELIEVED IT.

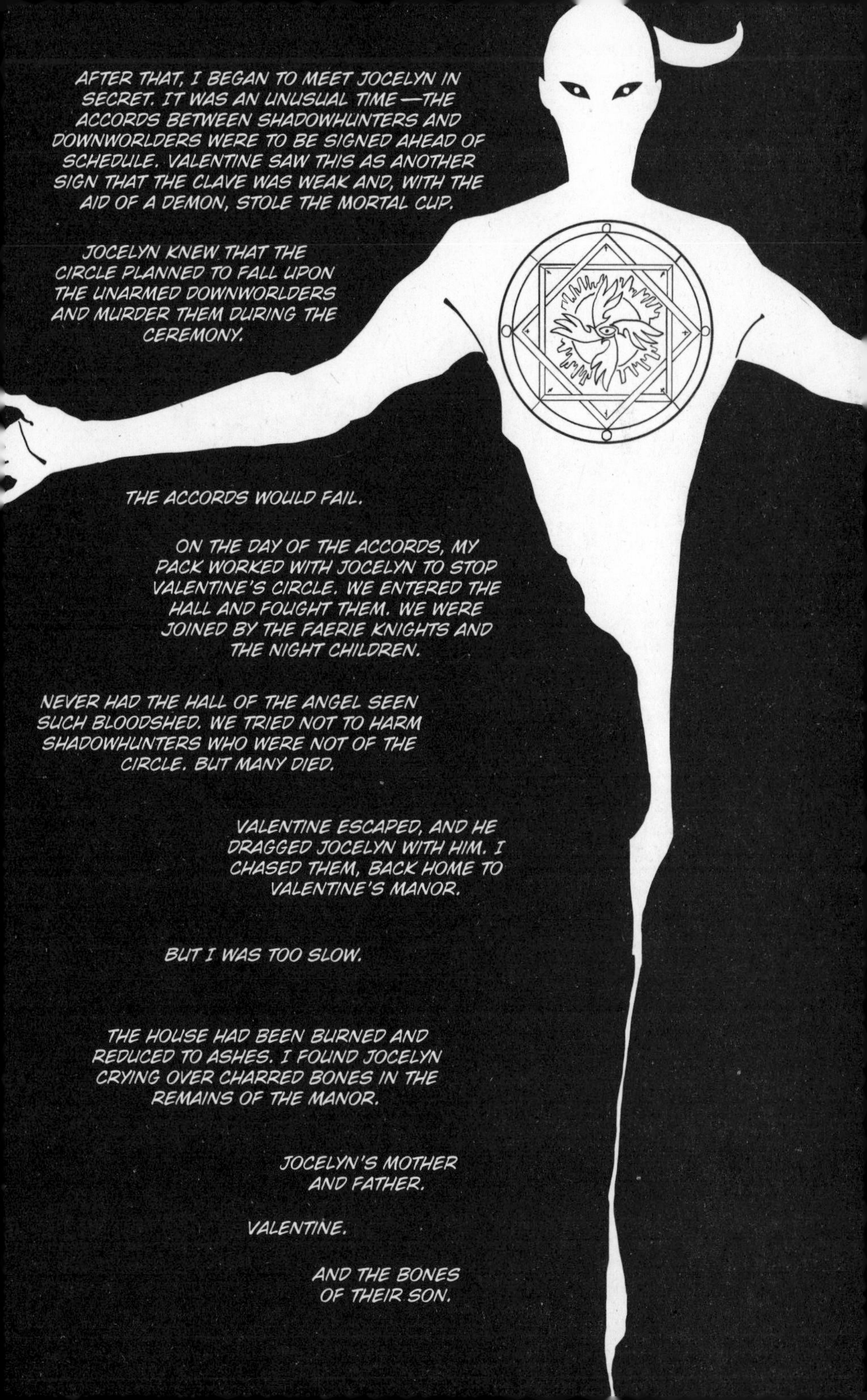
AFTER THAT, I BEGAN TO MEET JOCELYN IN SECRET. IT WAS AN UNUSUAL TIME—THE ACCORDS BETWEEN SHADOWHUNTERS AND DOWNWORLDERS WERE TO BE SIGNED AHEAD OF SCHEDULE. VALENTINE SAW THIS AS ANOTHER SIGN THAT THE CLAVE WAS WEAK AND, WITH THE AID OF A DEMON, STOLE THE MORTAL CUP.
JOCELYN KNEW THAT THE CIRCLE PLANNED TO FALL UPON THE UNARMED DOWNWORLDERS AND MURDER THEM DURING THE CEREMONY.
THE ACCORDS WOULD FAIL.
ON THE DAY OF THE ACCORDS, MY PACK WORKED WITH JOCELYN TO STOP VALENTINE'S CIRCLE. WE ENTERED THE HALL AND FOUGHT THEM. WE WERE JOINED BY THE FAERIE KNIGHTS AND THE NIGHT CHILDREN.
NEVER HAD THE HALL OF THE ANGEL SEEN SUCH BLOODSHED. WE TRIED NOT TO HARM SHADOWHUNTERS WHO WERE NOT OF THE CIRCLE. BUT MANY DIED.
VALENTINE ESCAPED, AND HE DRAGGED JOCELYN WITH HIM. I CHASED THEM, BACK HOME TO VALENTINE'S MANOR.
BUT I WAS TOO SLOW.
THE HOUSE HAD BEEN BURNED AND REDUCED TO ASHES. I FOUND JOCELYN CRYING OVER CHARRED BONES IN THE REMAINS OF THE MANOR.
JOCELYN'S MOTHER AND FATHER.
VALENTINE.
AND THE BONES OF THEIR SON.

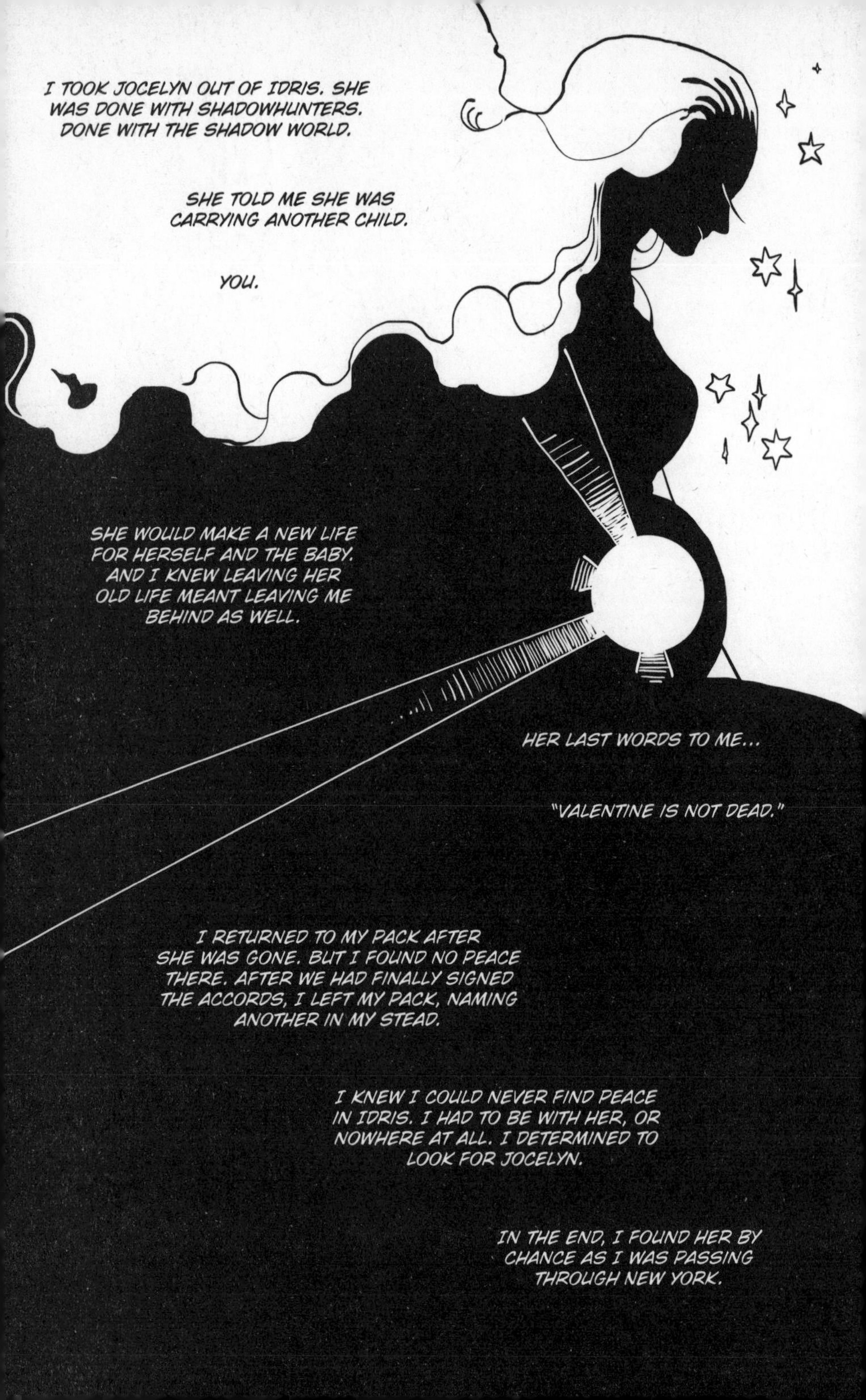
I TOOK JOCELYN OUT OF IDRIS. SHE WAS DONE WITH SHADOWHUNTERS. DONE WITH THE SHADOW WORLD.
SHE TOLD ME SHE WAS CARRYING ANOTHER CHILD.
YOU.
SHE WOULD MAKE A NEW LIFE FOR HERSELF AND THE BABY. AND I KNEW LEAVING HER OLD LIFE MEANT LEAVING ME BEHIND AS WELL.
HER LAST WORDS TO ME...
"VALENTINE IS NOT DEAD."
I RETURNED TO MY PACK AFTER SHE WAS GONE. BUT I FOUND NO PEACE THERE. AFTER WE HAD FINALLY SIGNED THE ACCORDS, I LEFT MY PACK, NAMING ANOTHER IN MY STEAD.
I KNEW I COULD NEVER FIND PEACE IN IDRIS. I HAD TO BE WITH HER, OR NOWHERE AT ALL. I DETERMINED TO LOOK FOR JOCELYN.
IN THE END, I FOUND HER BY CHANCE AS I WAS PASSING THROUGH NEW YORK.

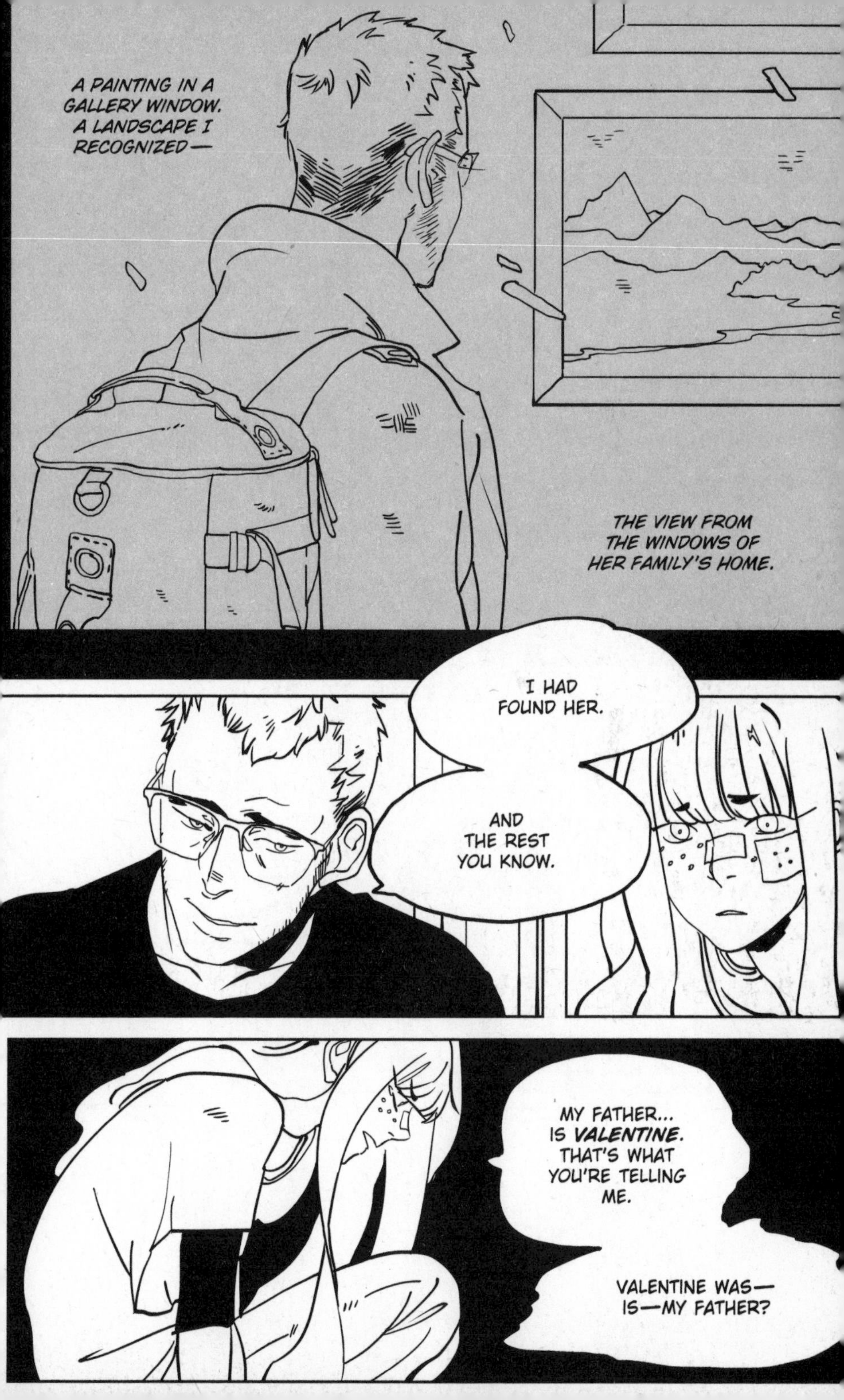
A PAINTING IN A GALLERY WINDOW. A LANDSCAPE I RECOGNIZED—
THE VIEW FROM THE WINDOWS OF HER FAMILY'S HOME.
I HAD FOUND HER.
AND THE REST YOU KNOW.
MY FATHER... IS VALENTINE. THAT'S WHAT YOU'RE TELLING ME.
VALENTINE WAS—IS—MY FATHER?

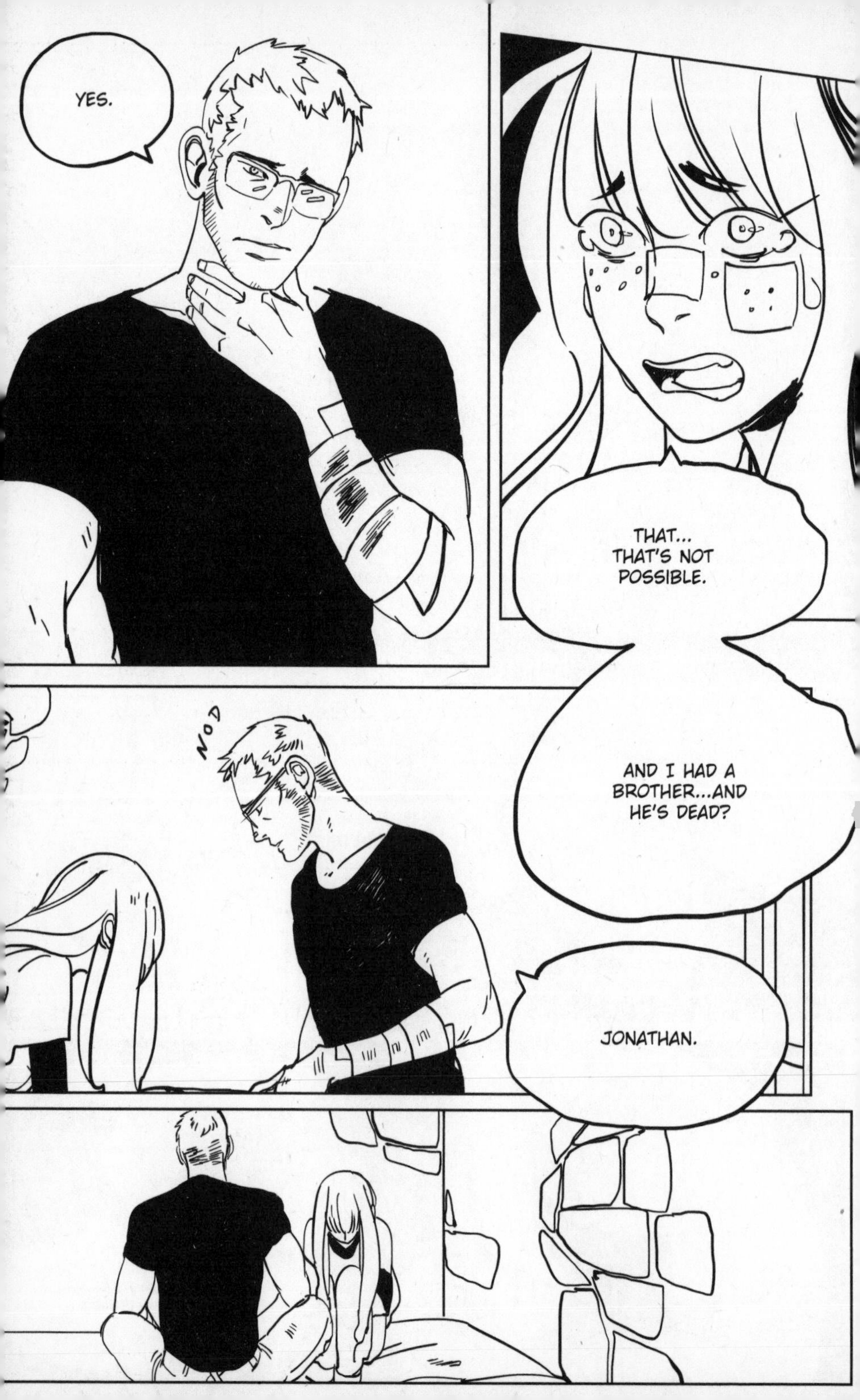
YES.
THAT... THAT'S NOT POSSIBLE.
NOD
AND I HAD A BROTHER...AND HE'S DEAD?
JONATHAN.

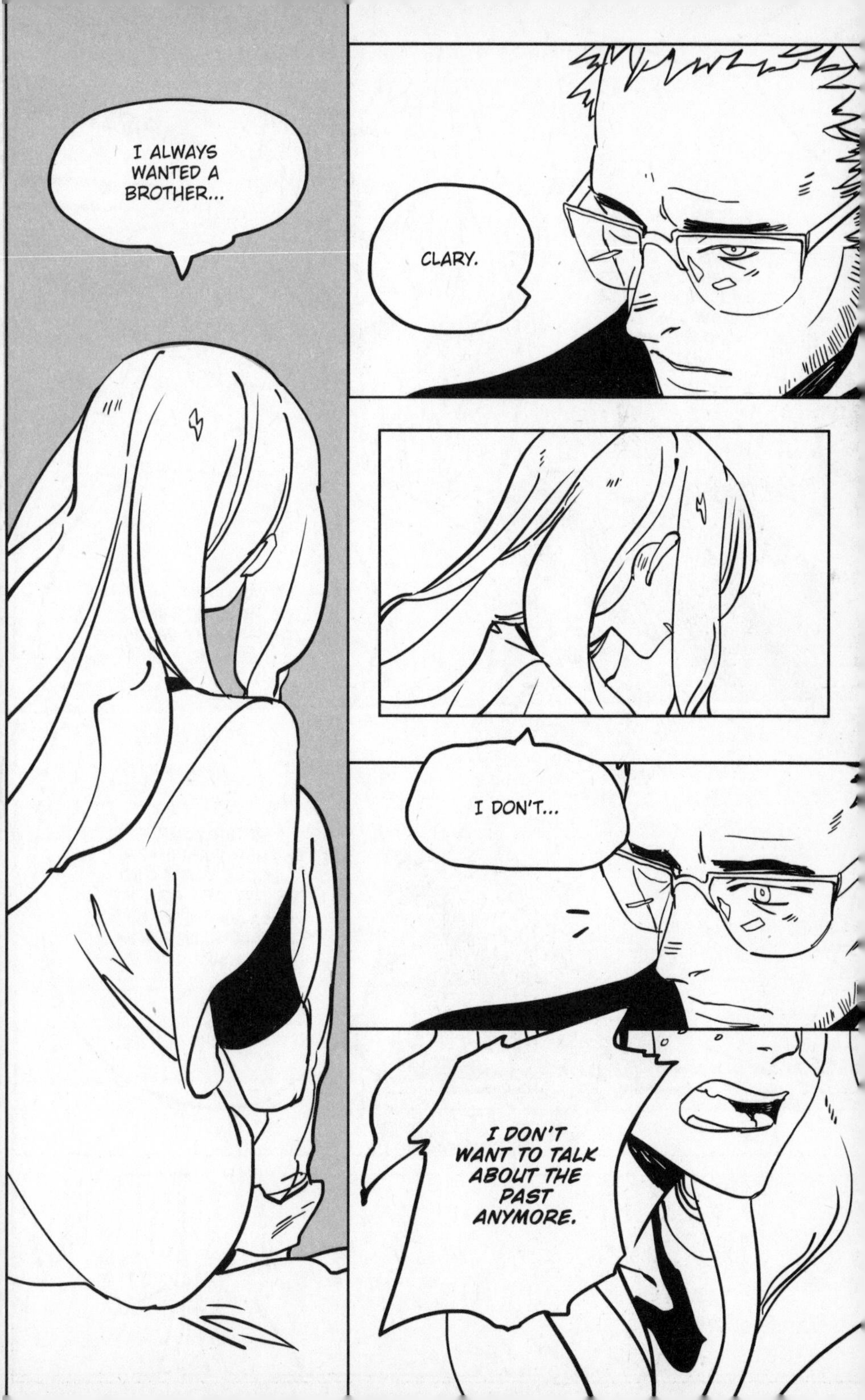
I ALWAYS WANTED A BROTHER...
CLARY.
I DON'T...
I DON'T WANT TO TALK ABOUT THE PAST ANYMORE.

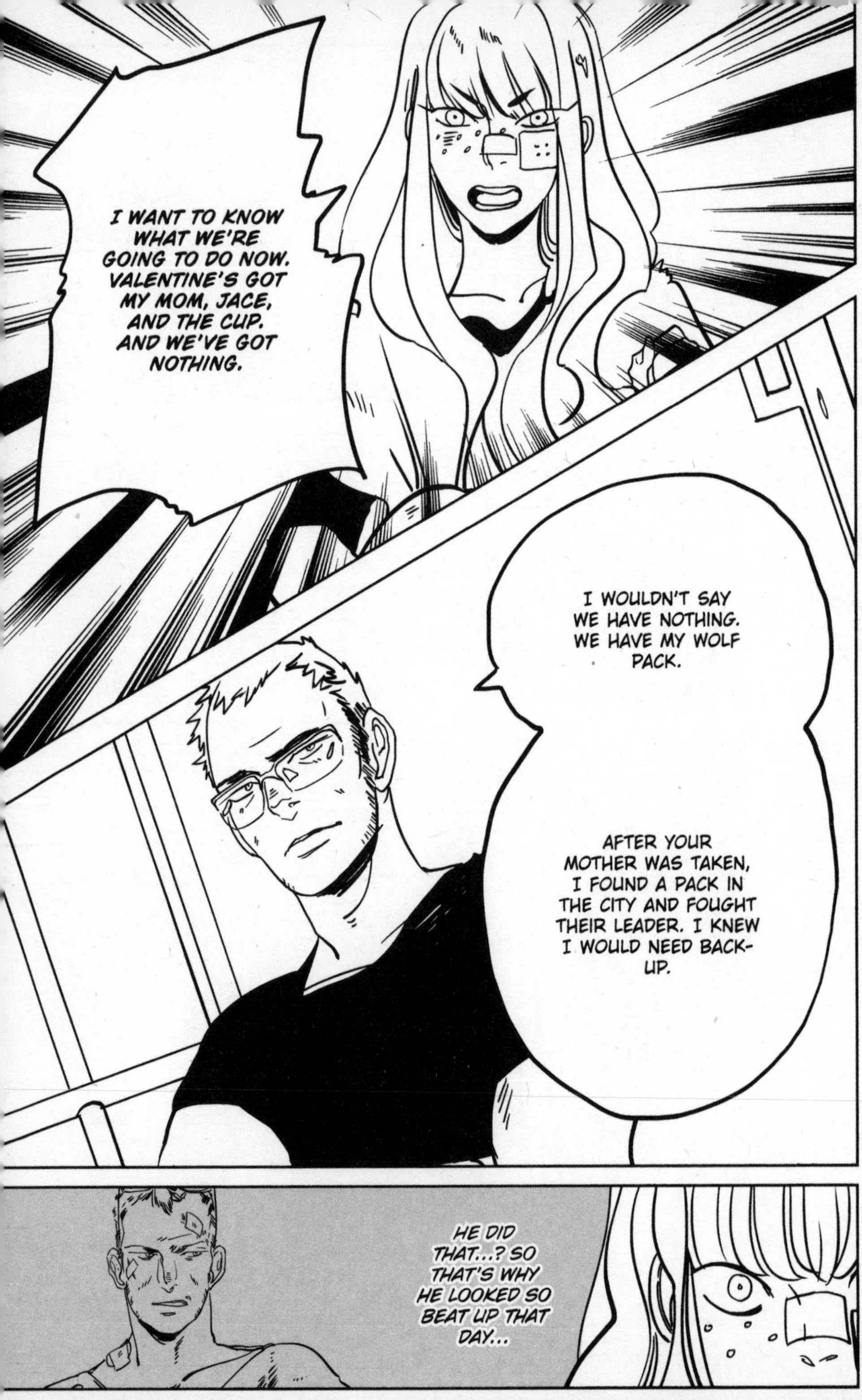
I WANT TO KNOW WHAT WE'RE GOING TO DO NOW. VALENTINE'S GOT MY MOM, JACE, AND THE CUP. AND WE'VE GOT NOTHING.
I WOULDN'T SAY WE HAVE NOTHING. WE HAVE MY WOLF PACK.
AFTER YOUR MOTHER WAS TAKEN, I FOUND A PACK IN THE CITY AND FOUGHT THEIR LEADER. I KNEW I WOULD NEED BACK-UP.
HE DID THAT...? SO THAT'S WHY HE LOOKED SO BEAT UP THAT DAY...

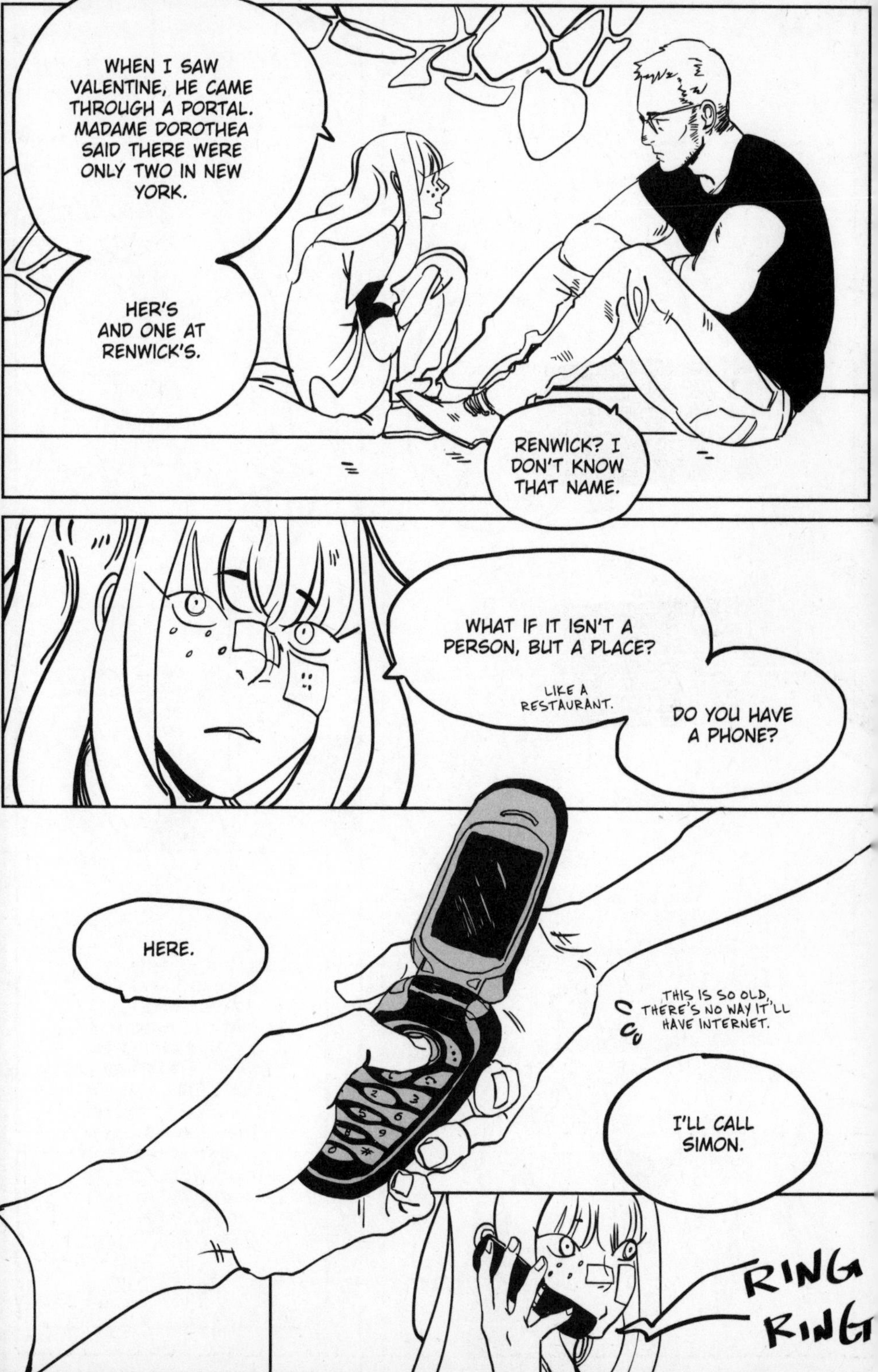
WHEN I SAW VALENTINE, HE CAME THROUGH A PORTAL. MADAME DOROTHEA SAID THERE WERE ONLY TWO IN NEW YORK.
HER'S AND ONE AT RENWICK'S.
RENWICK? I DON'T KNOW THAT NAME.
WHAT IF IT ISN'T A PERSON, BUT A PLACE?
LIKE A RESTAURANT.
DO YOU HAVE A PHONE?
HERE.
THIS IS SO OLD, THERE'S NO WAY IT'LL HAVE INTERNET.
I'LL CALL SIMON.
RING RING

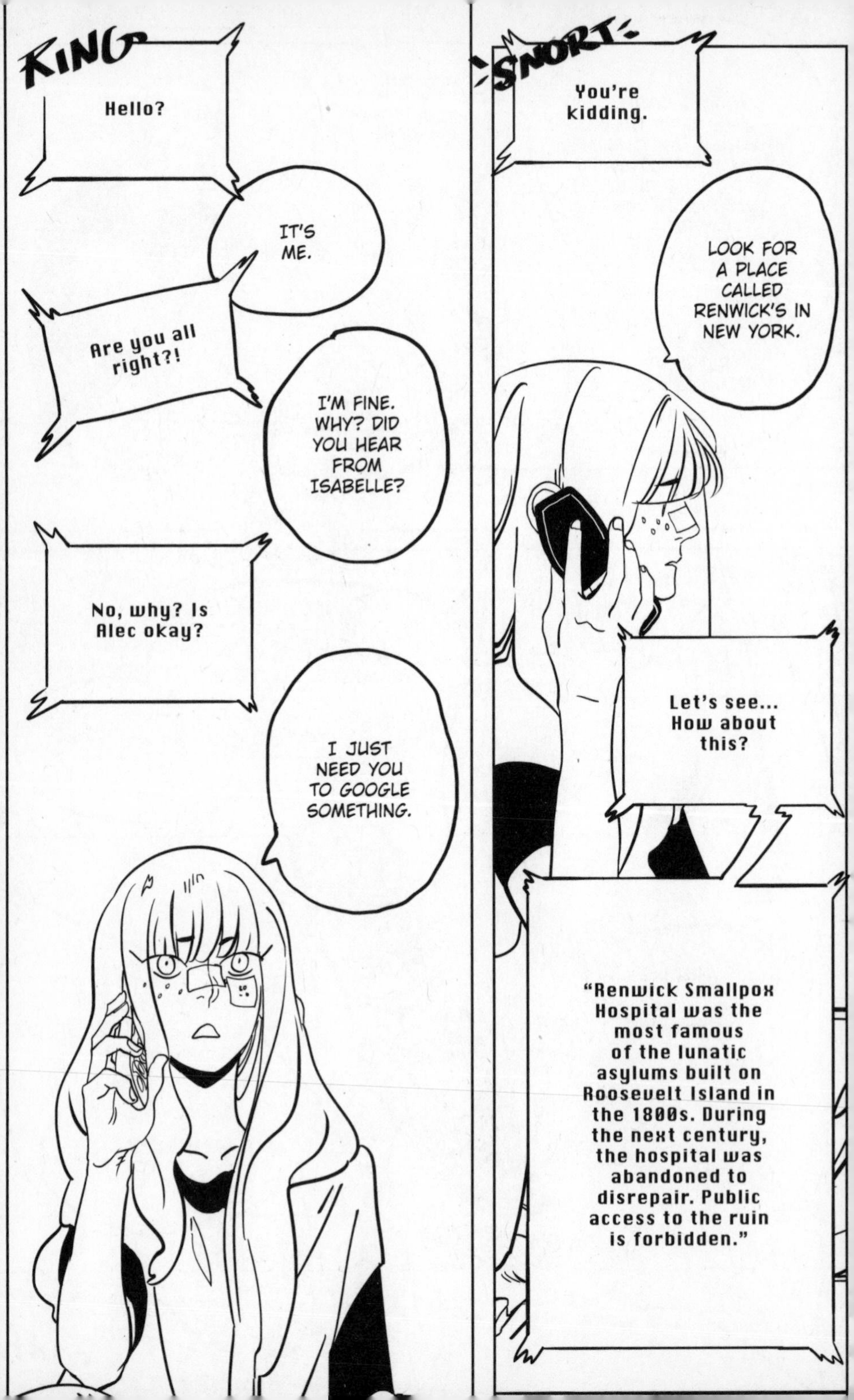
KING
Hello?
IT'S ME.
Are you all right?!
I'M FINE. WHY? DID YOU HEAR FROM ISABELLE?
No, why? Is Alec okay?
I JUST NEED YOU TO GOOGLE SOMETHING.
SNORT
You're kidding.
LOOK FOR A PLACE CALLED RENWICK'S IN NEW YORK.
Let's see... How about this?
"Renwick Smallpox Hospital was the most famous of the lunatic asylums built on Roosevelt Island in the 1800s. During the next century, the hospital was abandoned to disrepair. Public access to the ruin is forbidden."

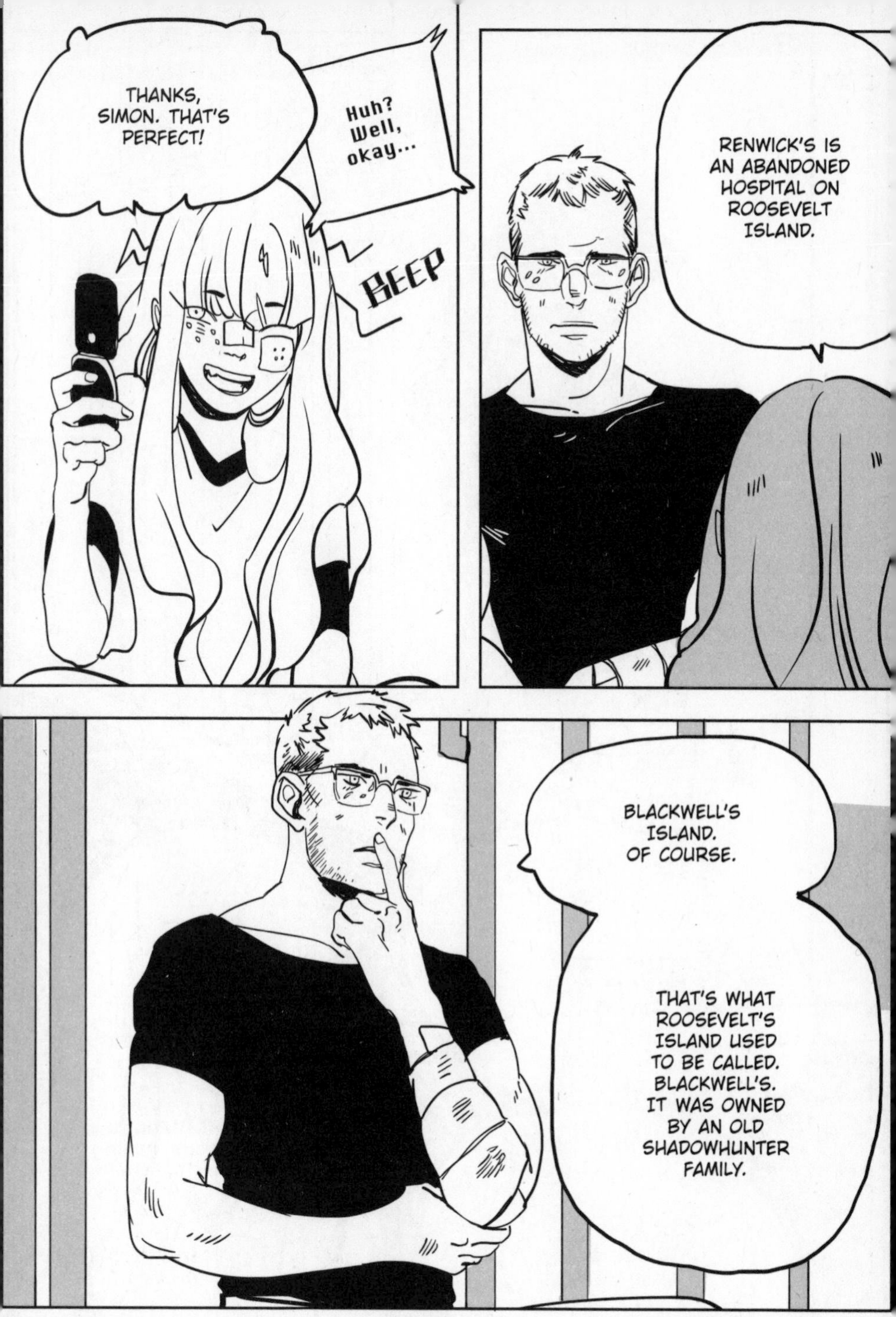
THANKS, SIMON. THAT'S PERFECT!
Huh? Well, okay...
BEEP
RENWICK'S IS AN ABANDONED HOSPITAL ON ROOSEVELT ISLAND.
BLACKWELL'S ISLAND. OF COURSE.
THAT'S WHAT ROOSEVELT'S ISLAND USED TO BE CALLED. BLACKWELL'S. IT WAS OWNED BY AN OLD SHADOWHUNTER FAMILY.

AND BLACKWELL IS ONE OF VALENTINE'S LACKEYS, COINCIDENTALLY.

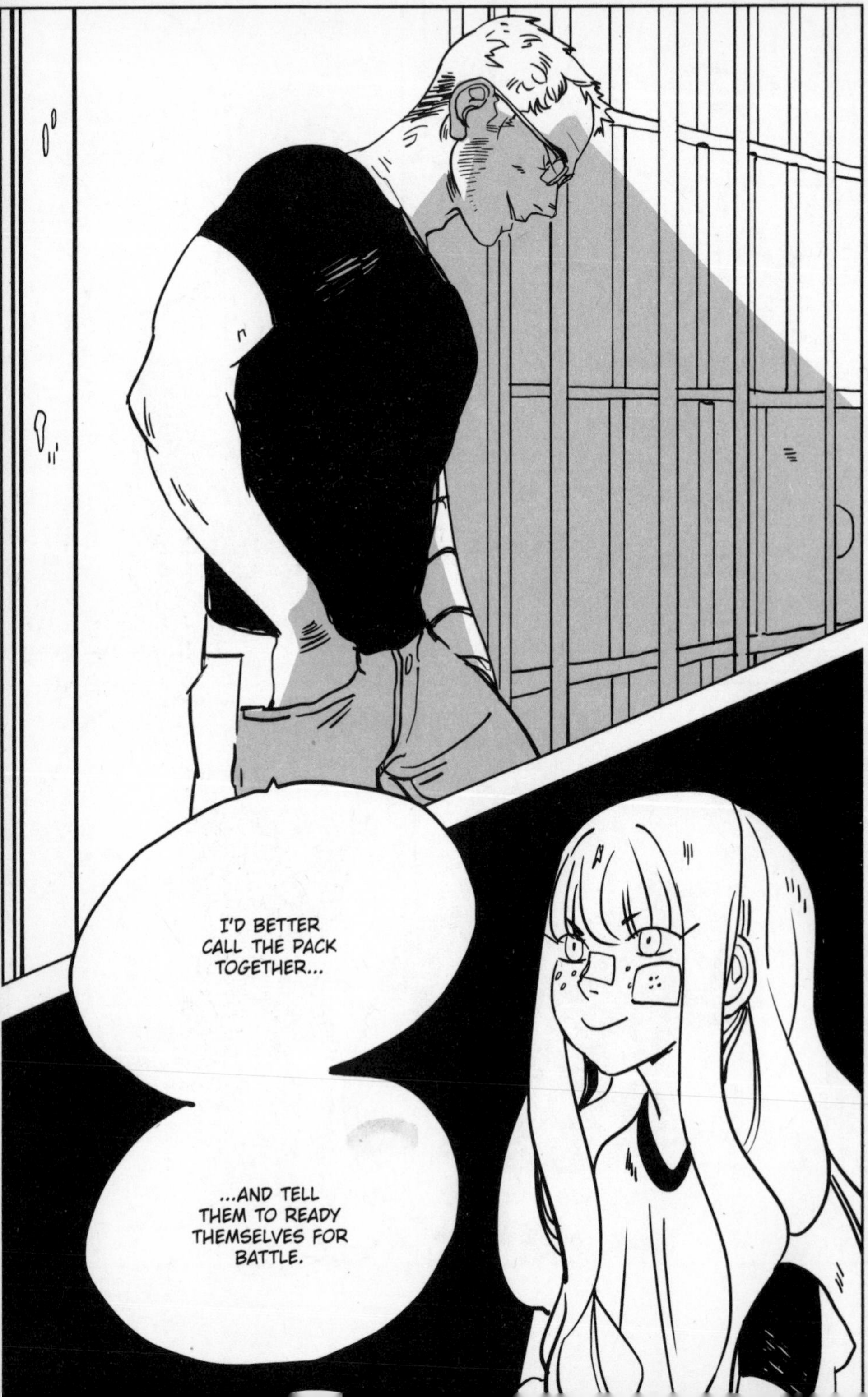
I'D BETTER CALL THE PACK TOGETHER...
...AND TELL THEM TO READY THEMSELVES FOR BATTLE.

Training gear
for Shadowhunters
training in
the Institute!

THE MORTAL INSTRUMENTS

THE GRAPHIC NOVEL

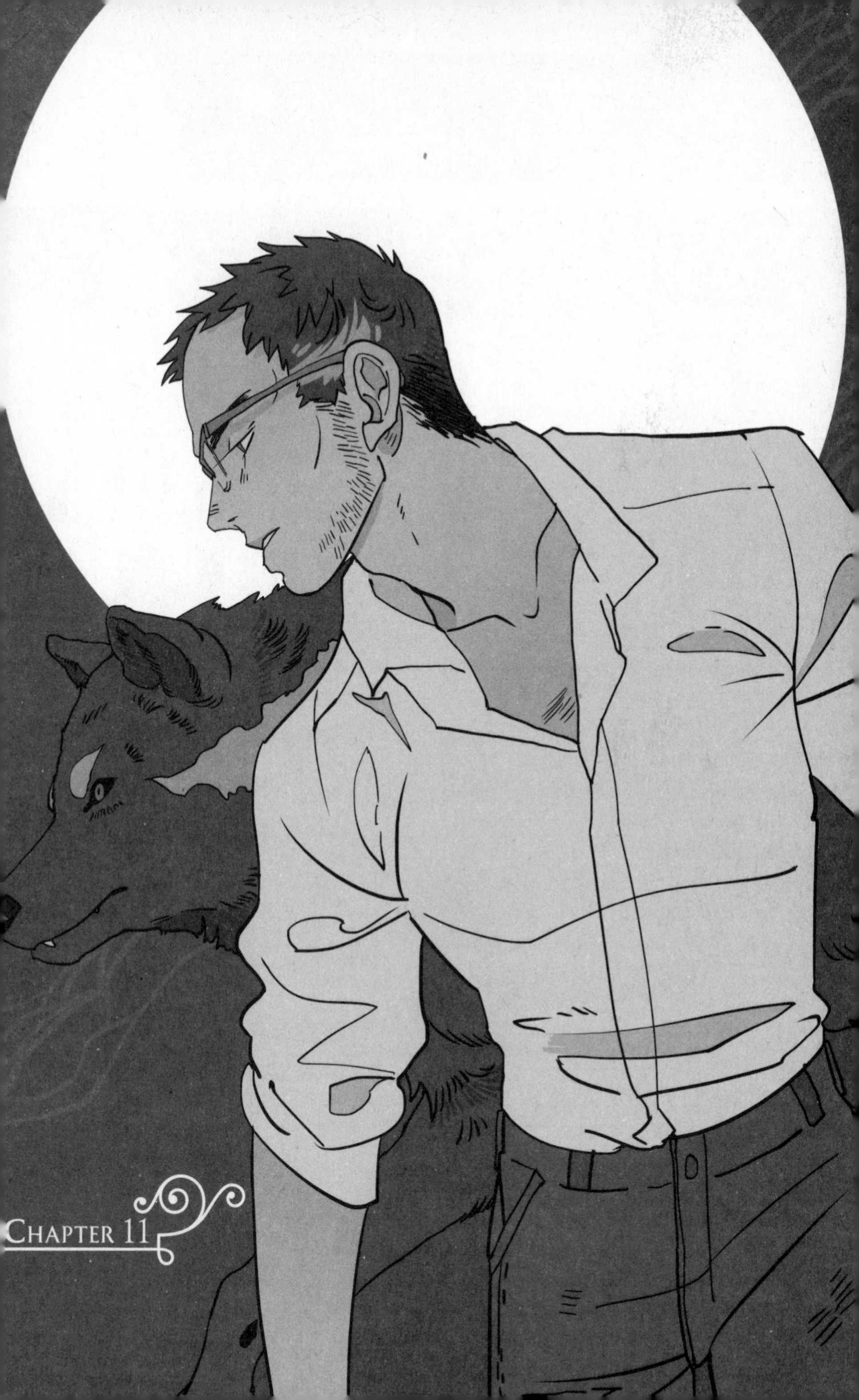

Chapter 11

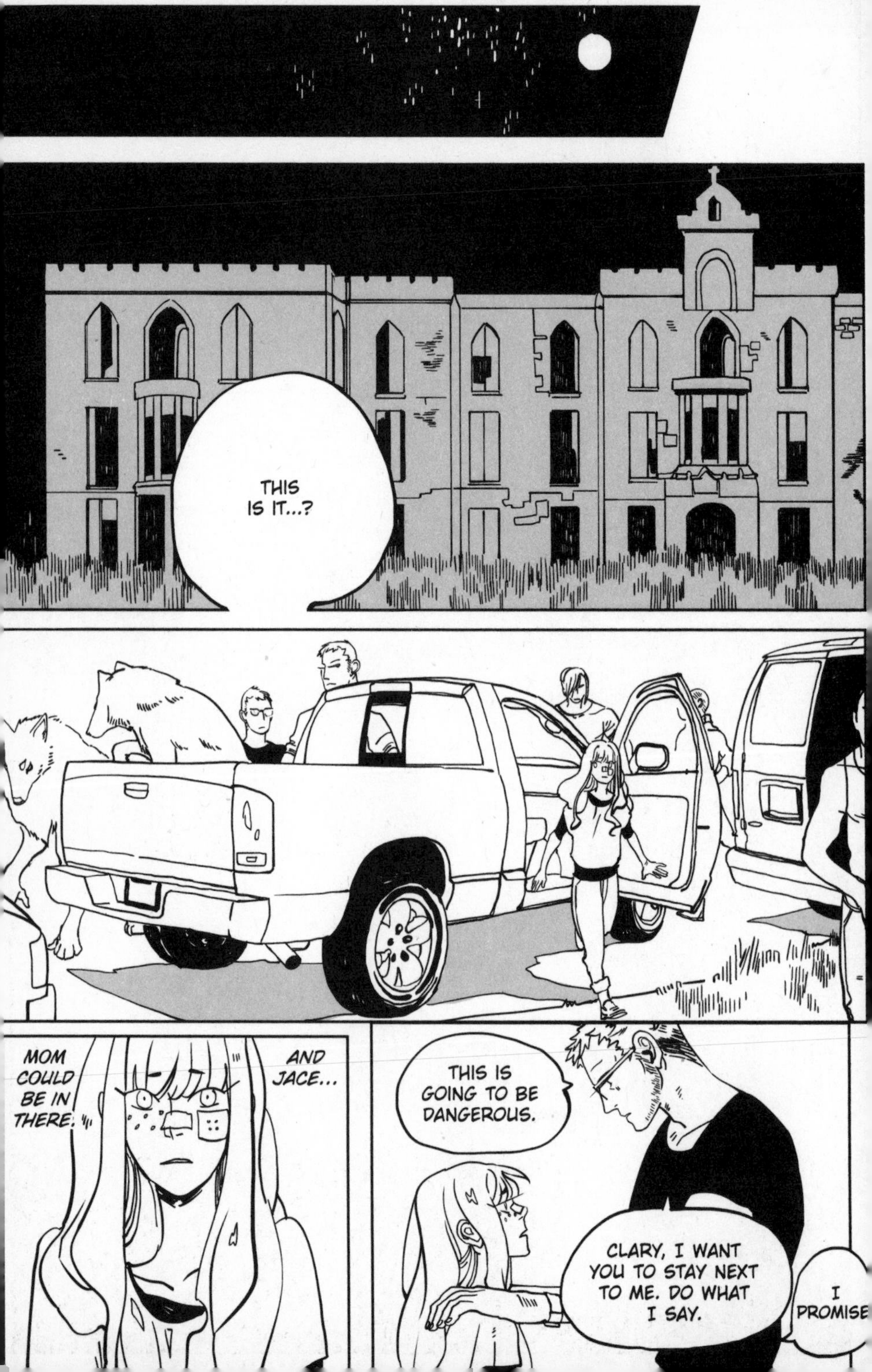
THIS IS IT...?
MOM COULD BE IN THERE.
AND JACE...
THIS IS GOING TO BE DANGEROUS.
CLARY, I WANT YOU TO STAY NEXT TO ME. DO WHAT I SAY.
I PROMISE

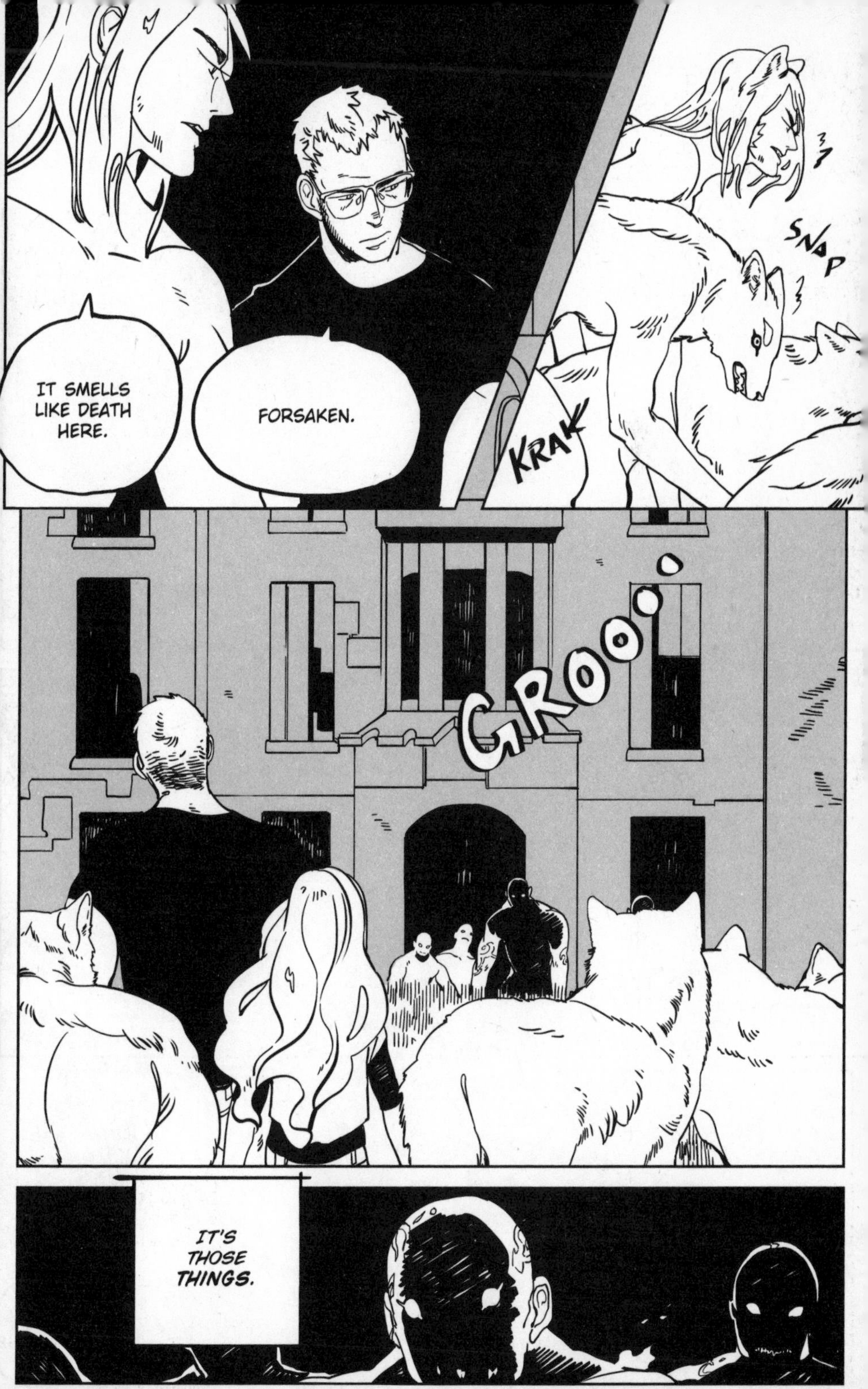
IT SMELLS LIKE DEATH HERE.
FORSAKEN.
KRAK
SNAP
GROOOO
IT'S THOSE THINGS.

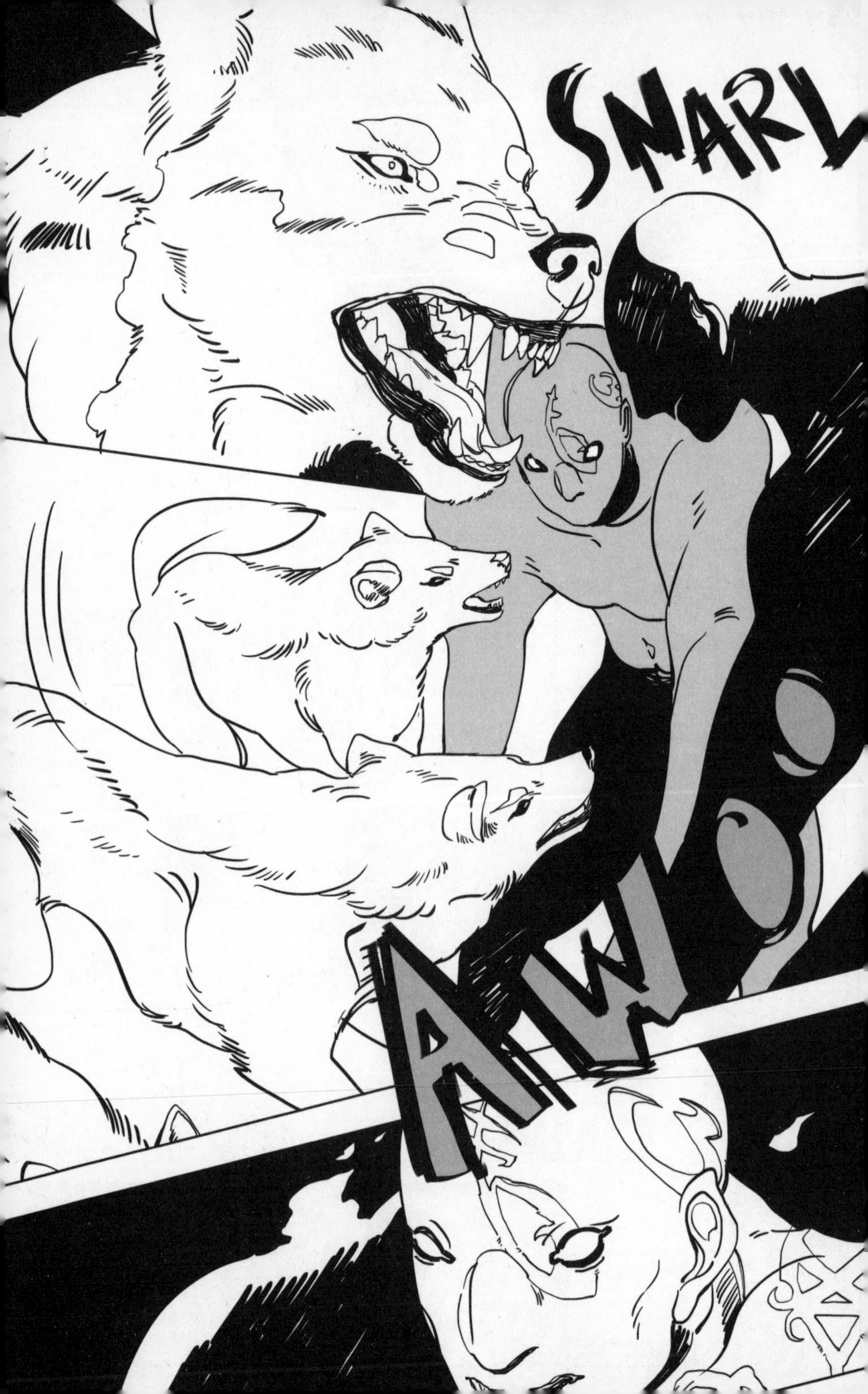
SNARL
AWOOO

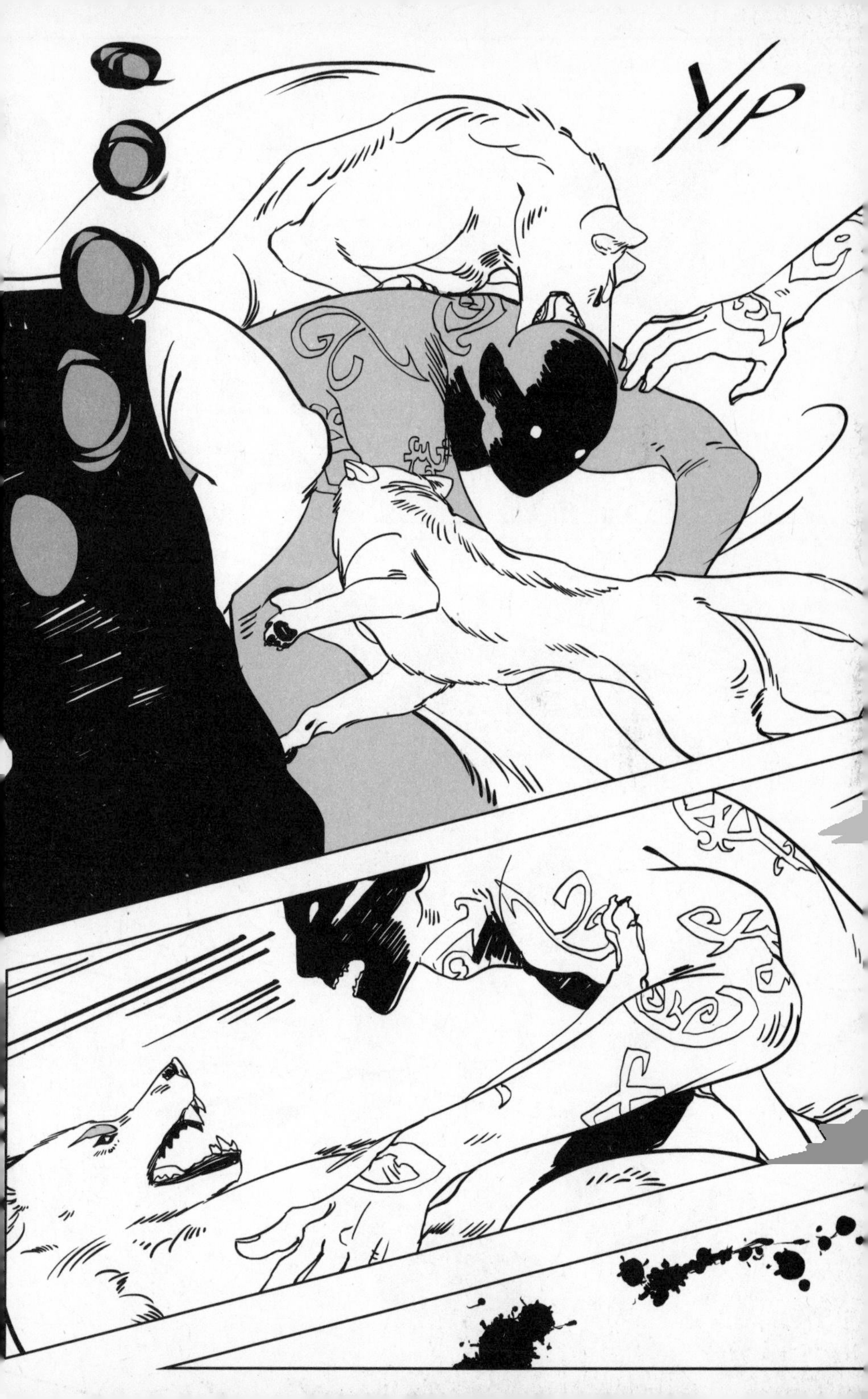
YIP

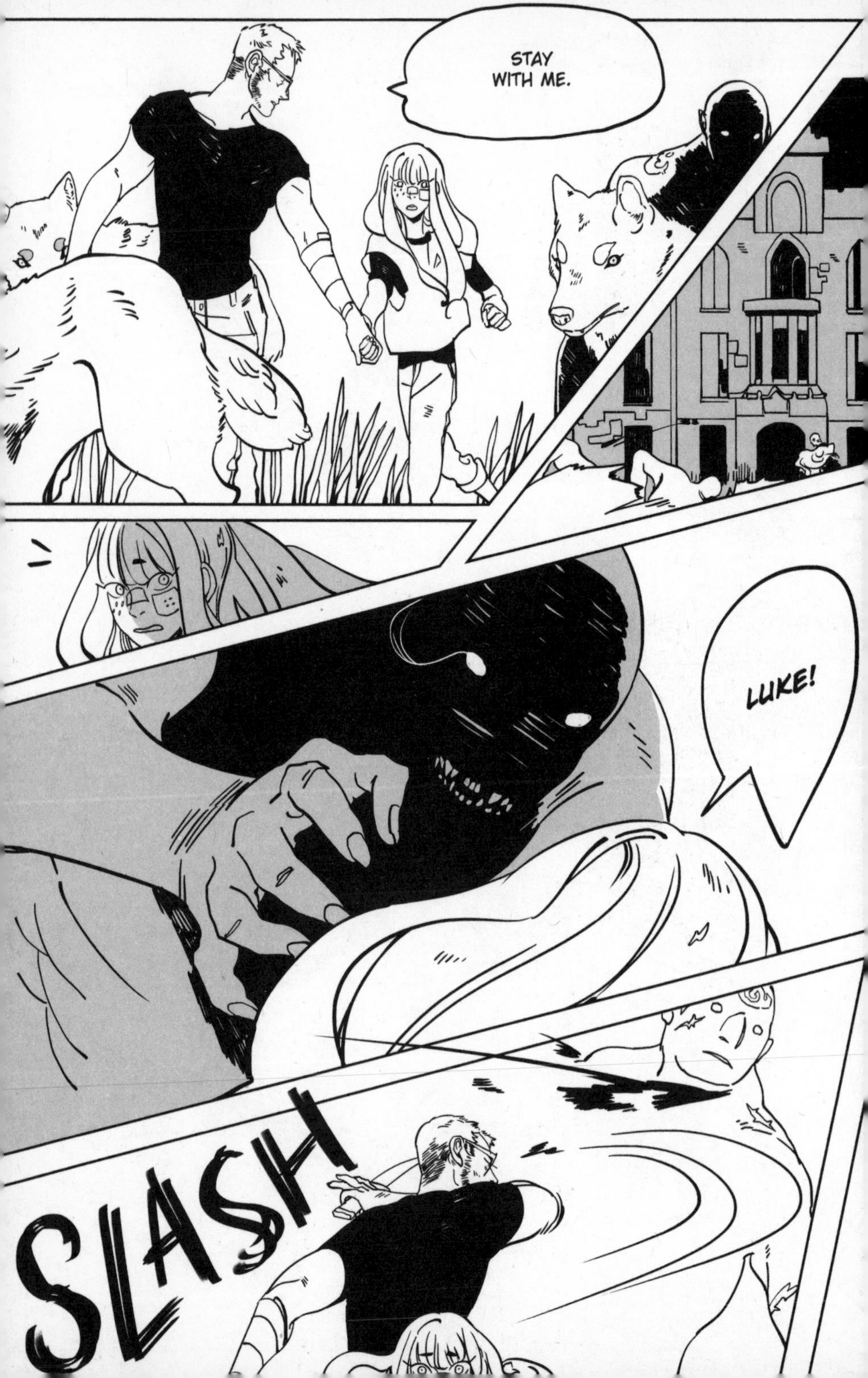
STAY WITH ME.
LUKE!
SLASH

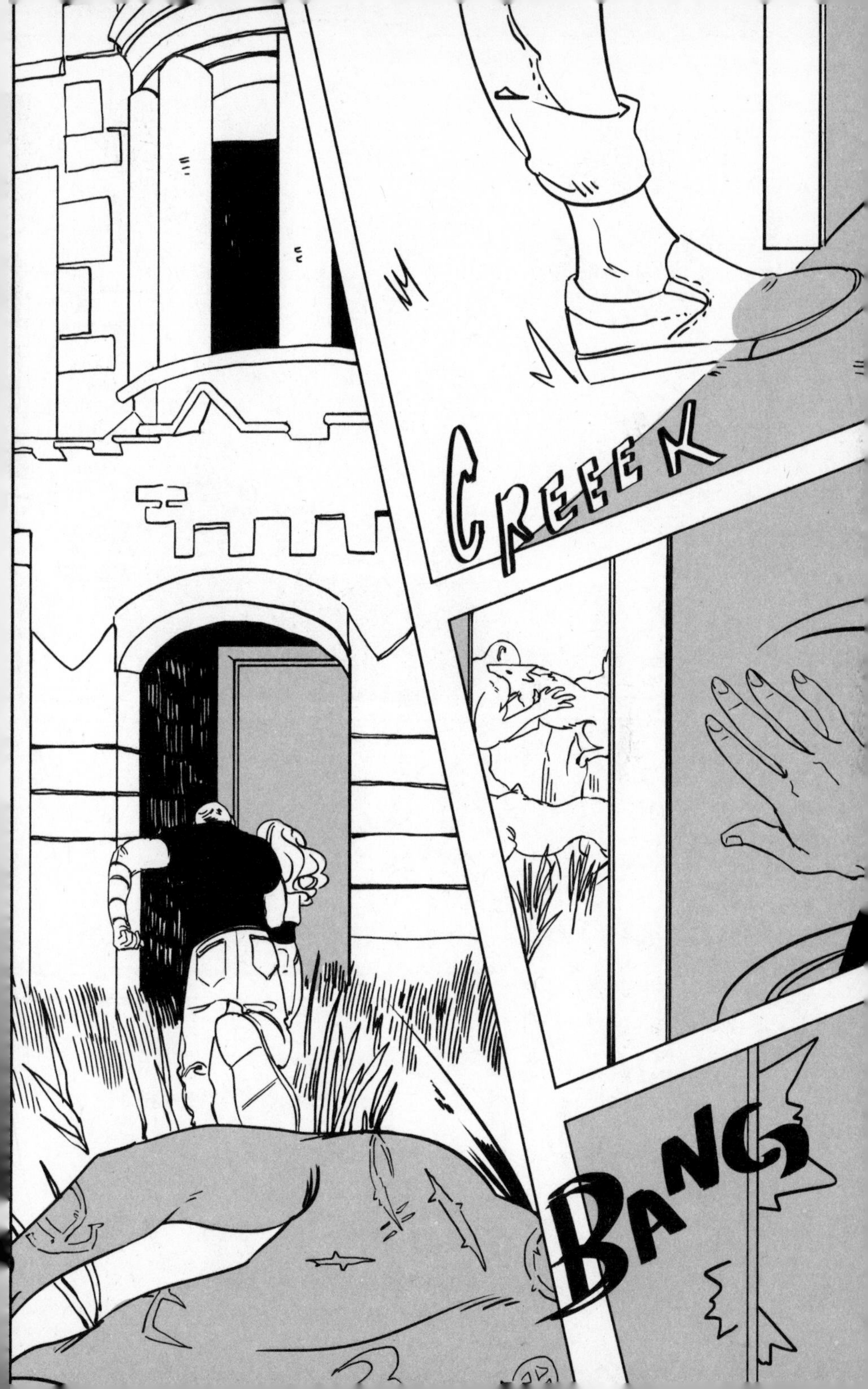
CREEEK
BANG

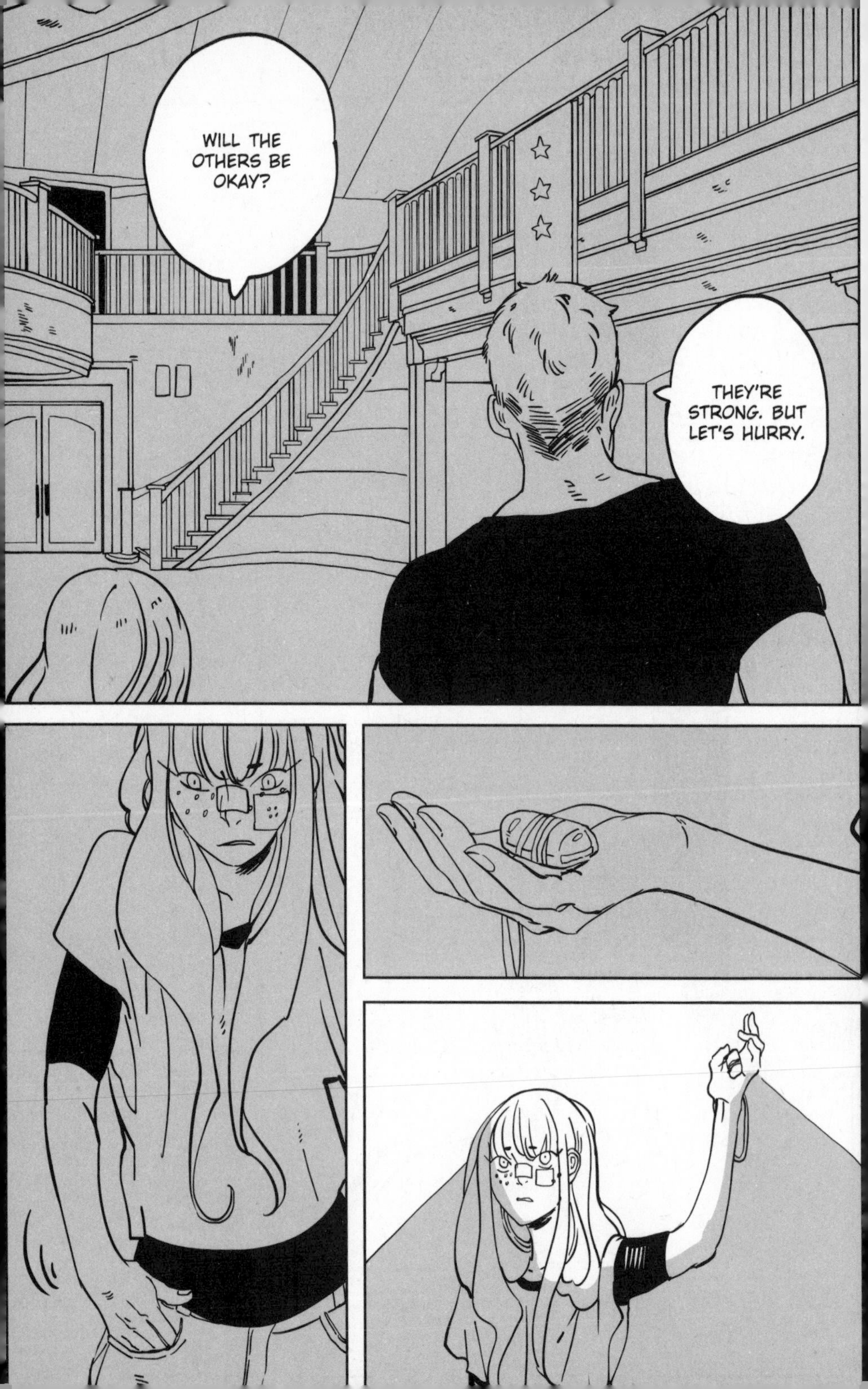
WILL THE OTHERS BE OKAY?
THEY'RE STRONG. BUT LET'S HURRY.

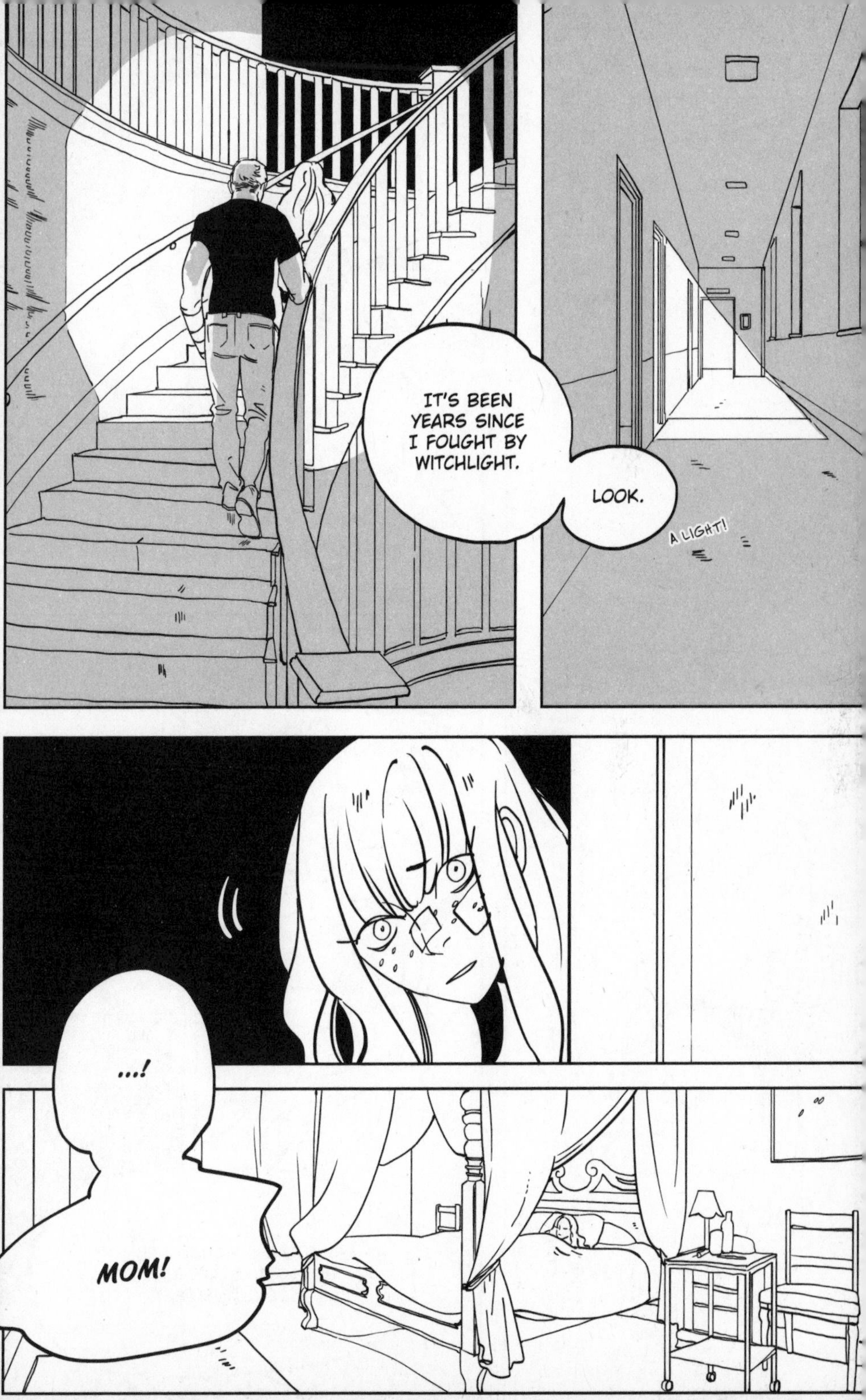
IT'S BEEN YEARS SINCE I FOUGHT BY WITCHLIGHT.
LOOK.
A LIGHT!
...!
MOM!

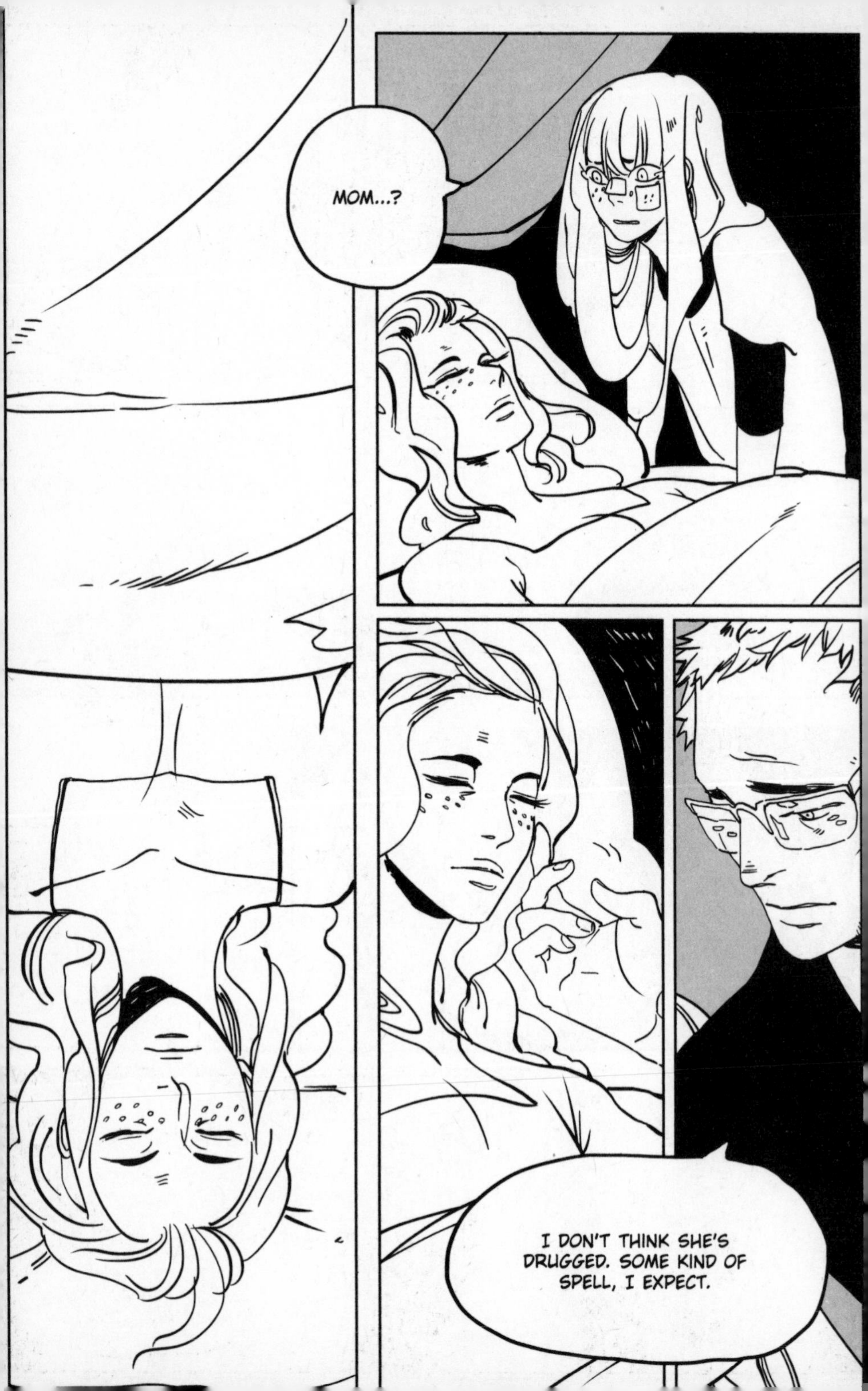
MOM...?
I DON'T THINK SHE'S DRUGGED. SOME KIND OF SPELL, I EXPECT.

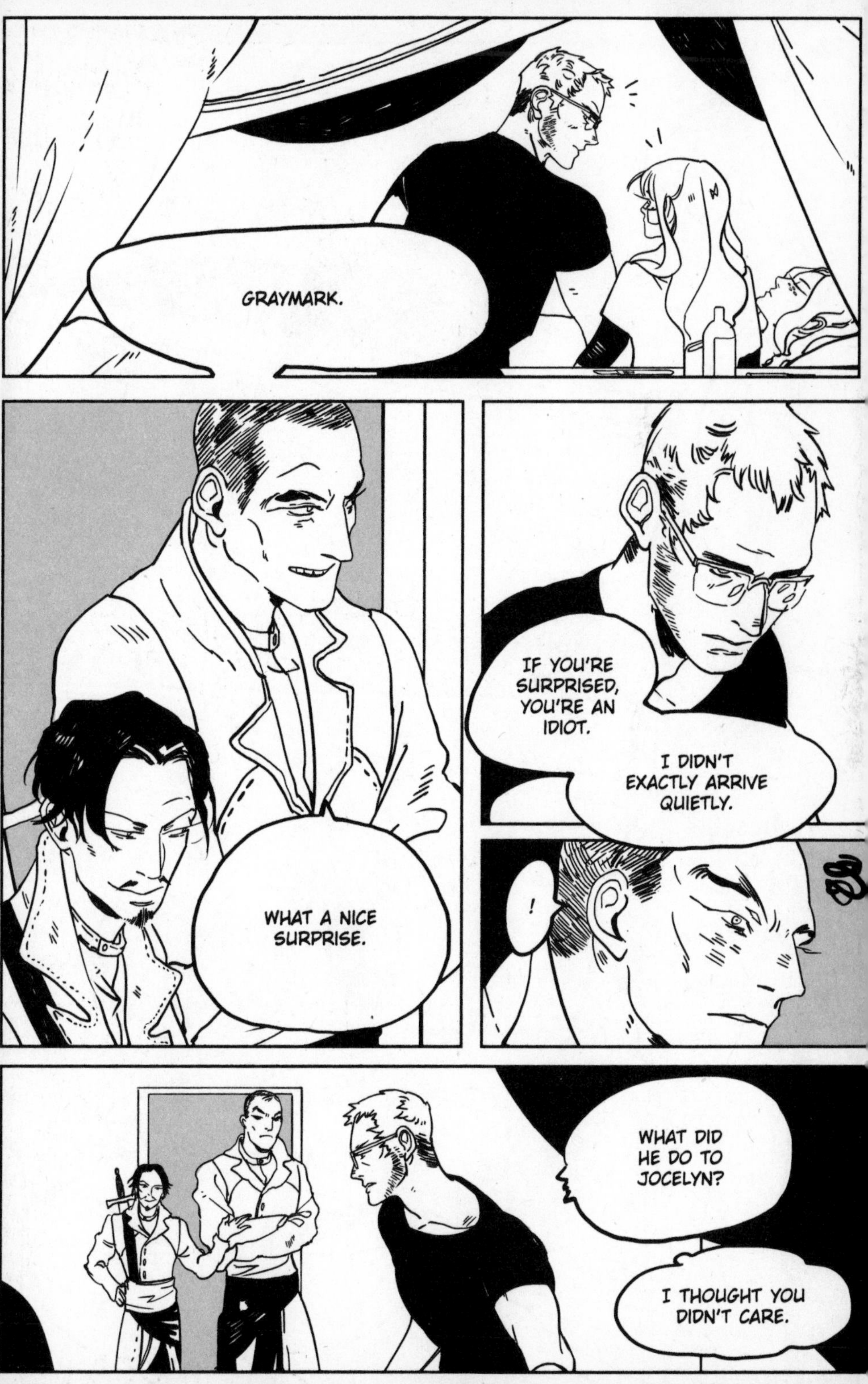
GRAYMARK.
WHAT A NICE SURPRISE.
IF YOU'RE SURPRISED, YOU'RE AN IDIOT.
I DIDN'T EXACTLY ARRIVE QUIETLY.
WHAT DID HE DO TO JOCELYN?
I THOUGHT YOU DIDN'T CARE.

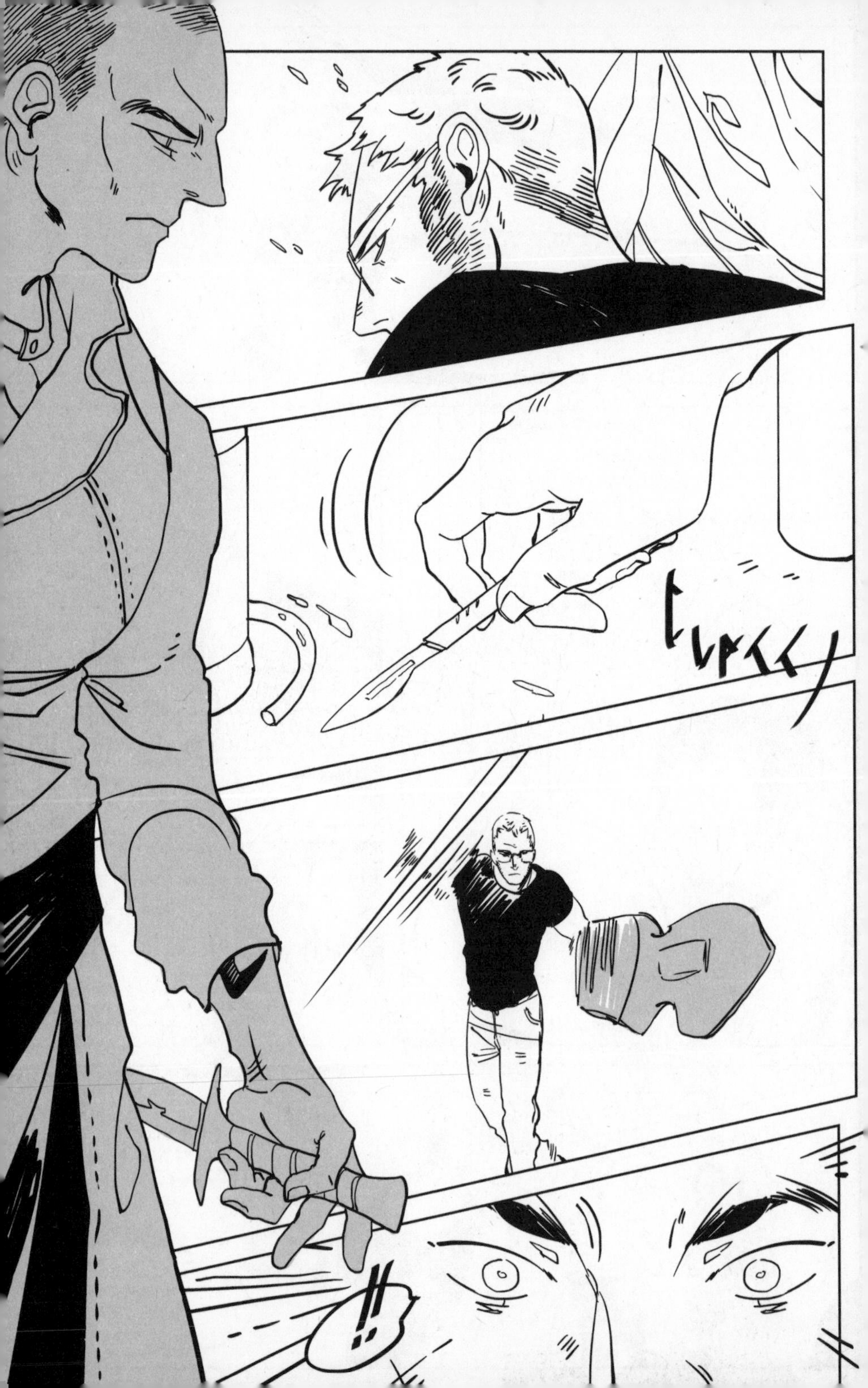
!!

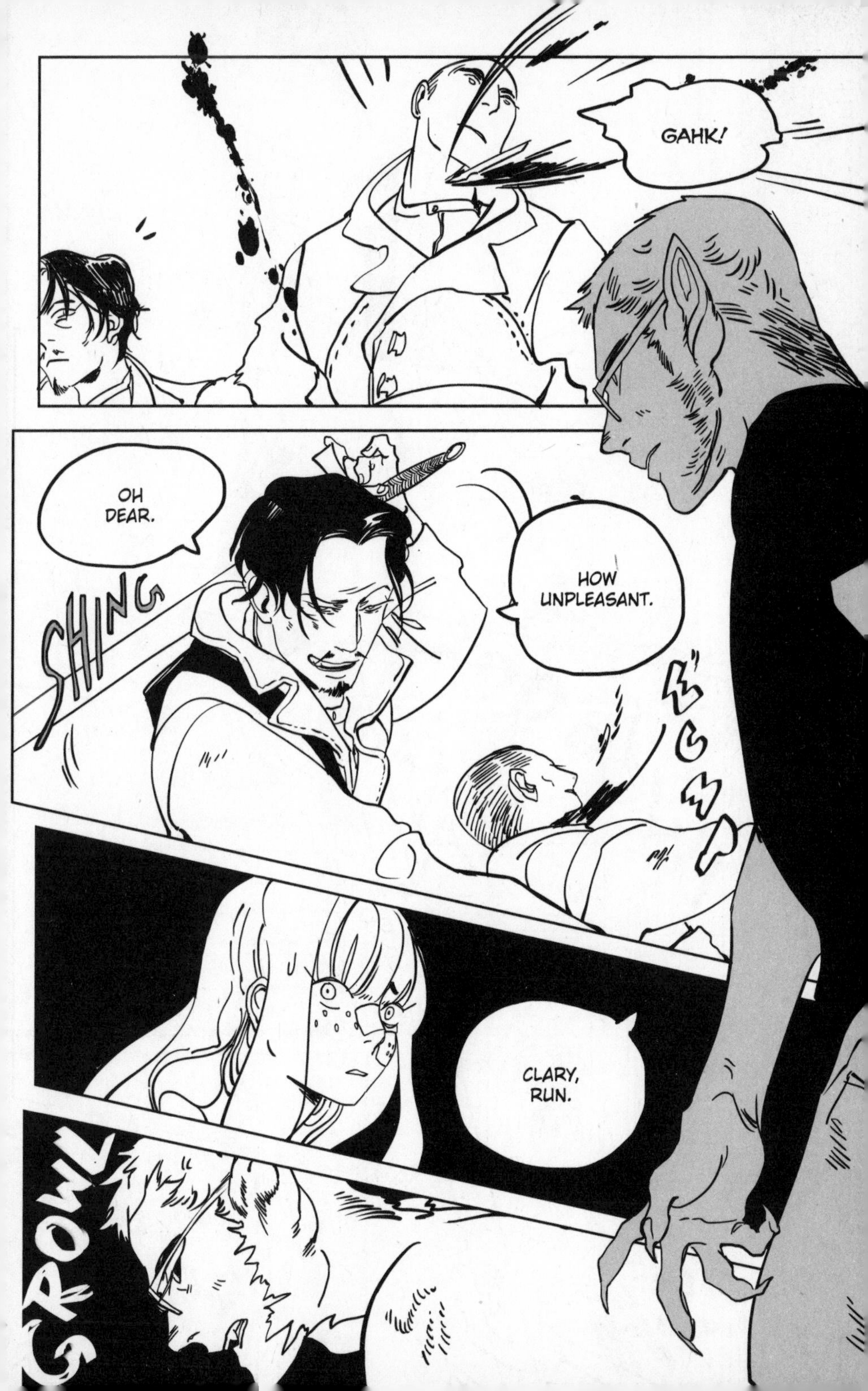
GAHK!
OH DEAR.
SHING
HOW UNPLEASANT.
CLARY, RUN.
GROWL

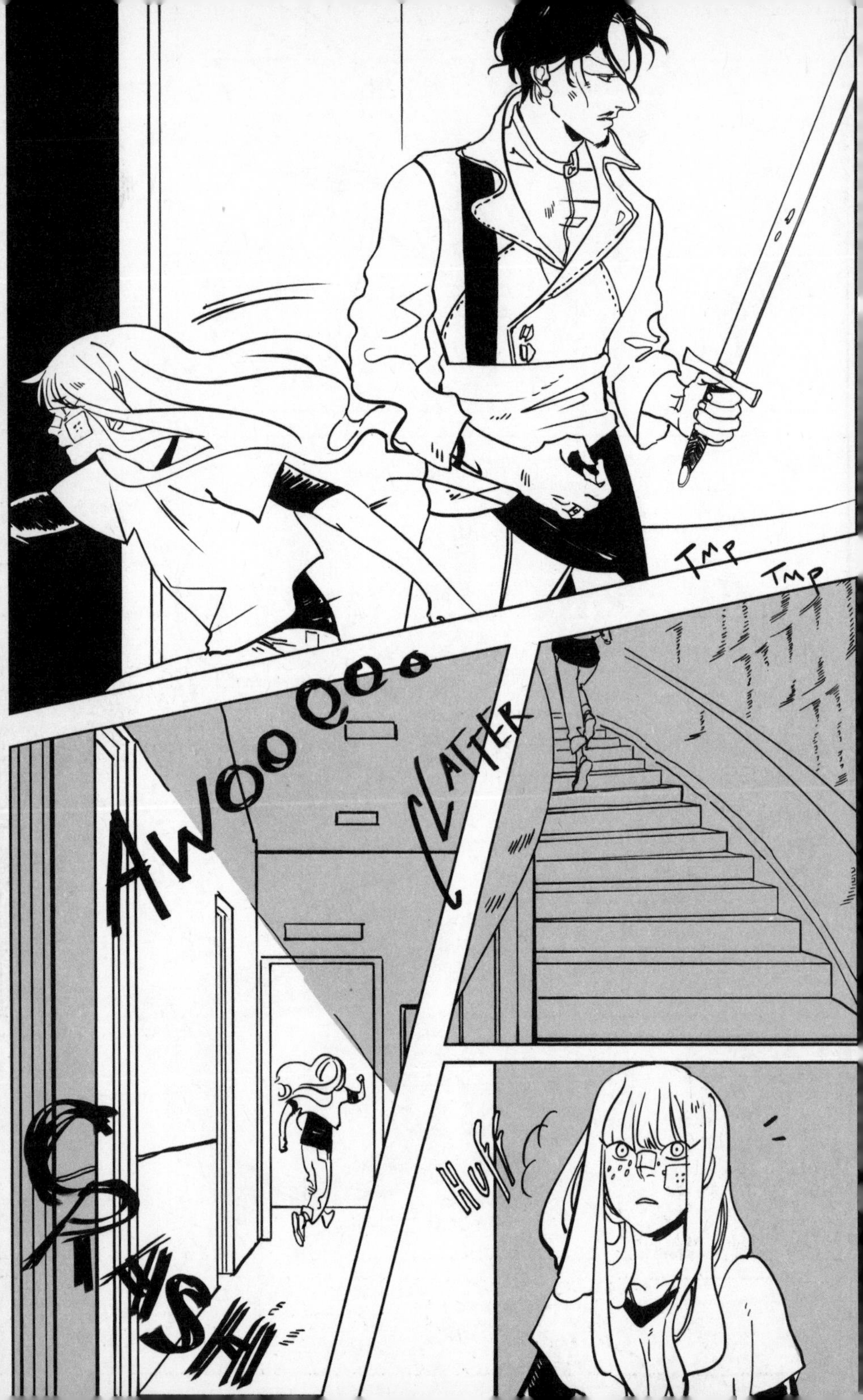

TMP
TMP
AWOOOOOo
CLATTER
CRASH
HUFF

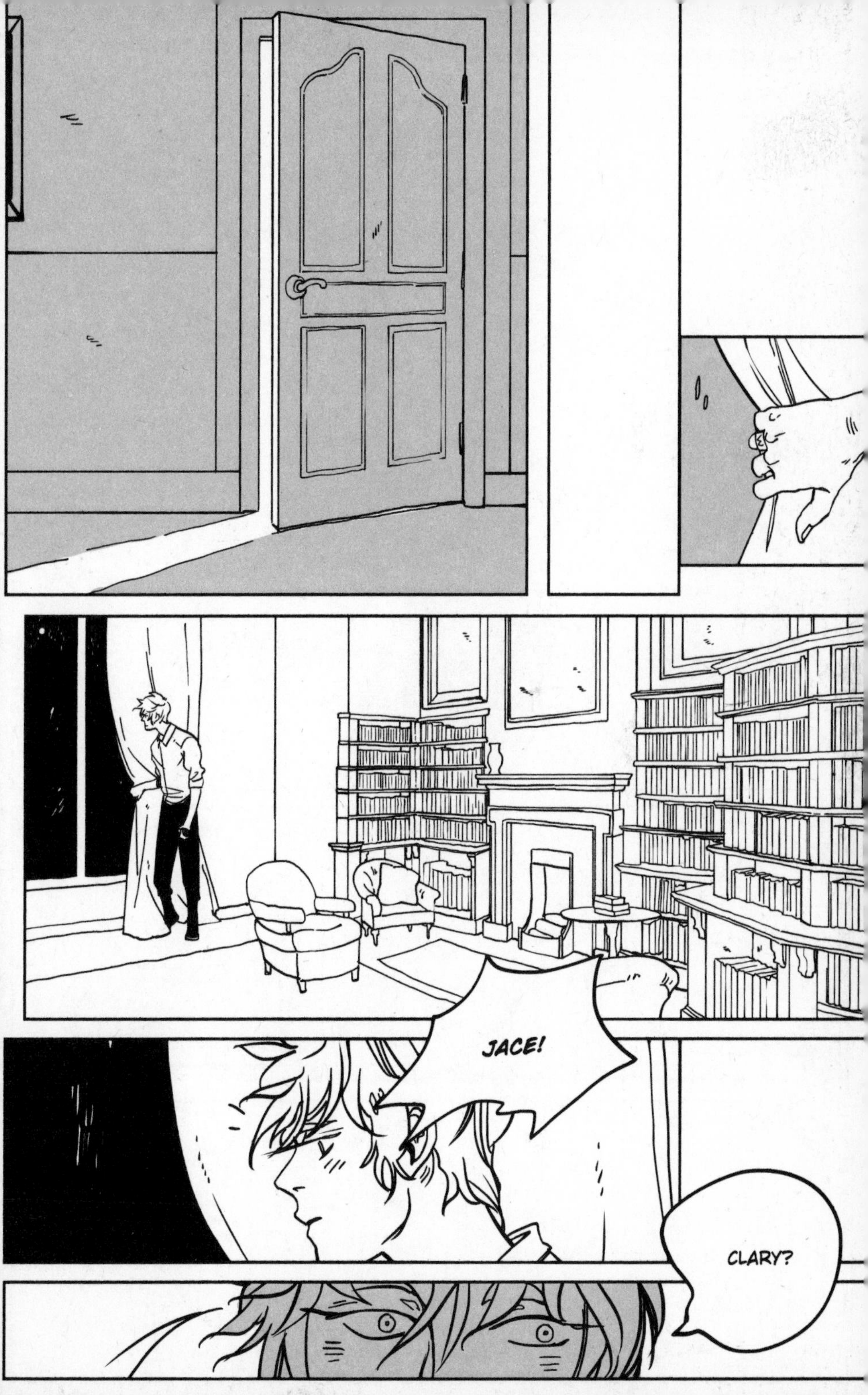
JACE!
CLARY?

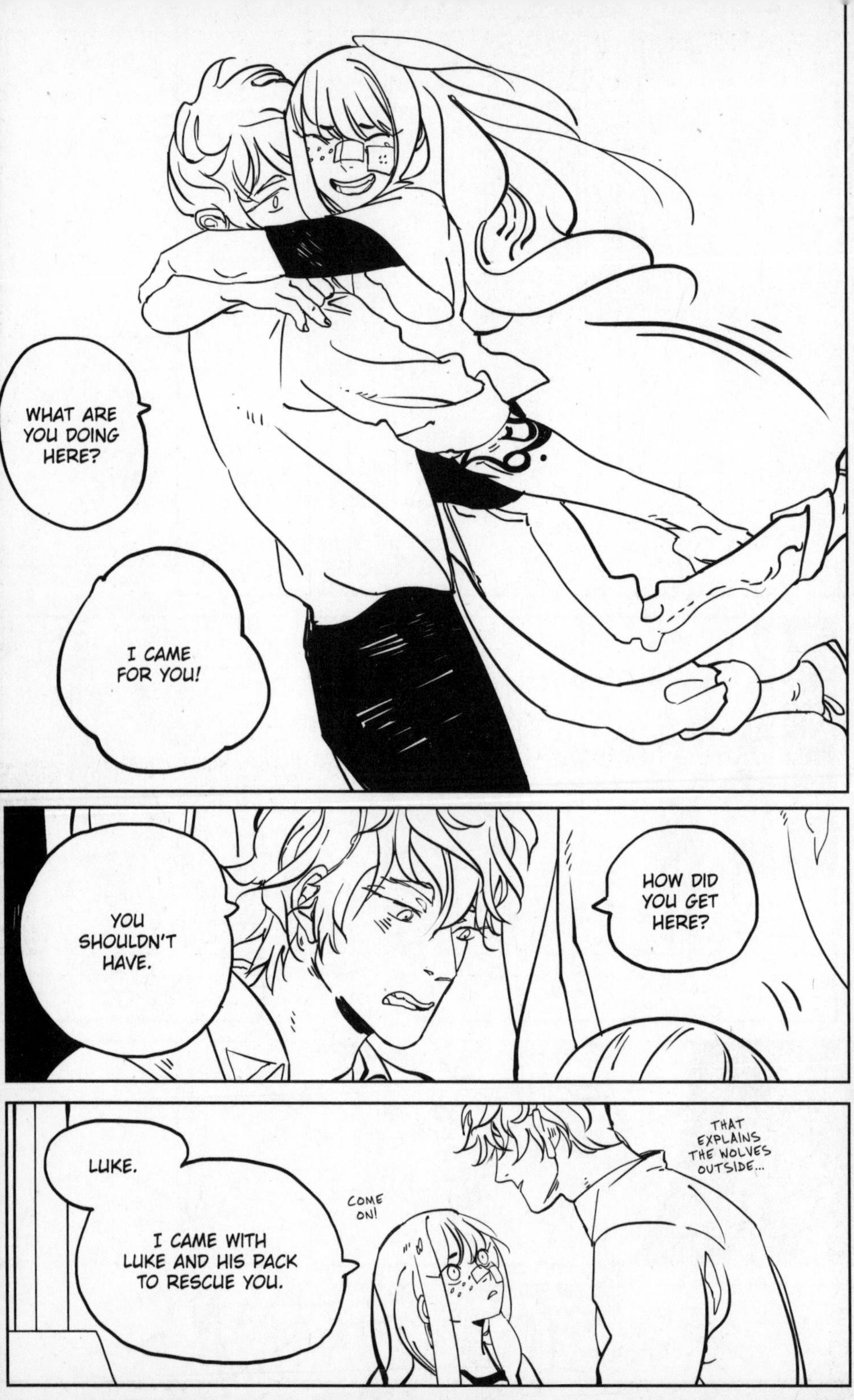
WHAT ARE YOU DOING HERE?
I CAME FOR YOU!
YOU SHOULDN'T HAVE.
HOW DID YOU GET HERE?
LUKE.
I CAME WITH LUKE AND HIS PACK TO RESCUE YOU.
COME ON!
THAT EXPLAINS THE WOLVES OUTSIDE...

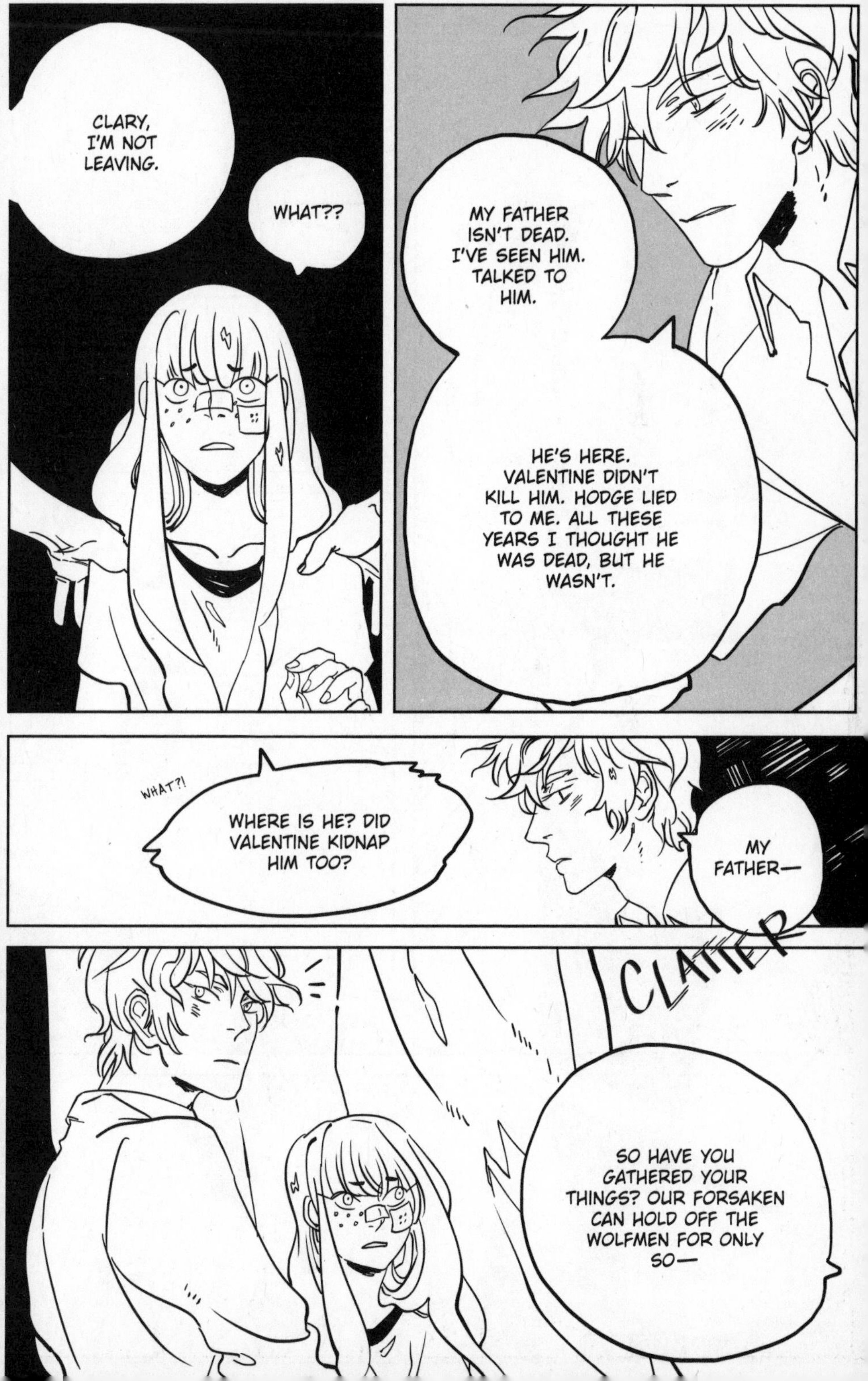
CLARY, I'M NOT LEAVING.
WHAT??
MY FATHER ISN'T DEAD. I'VE SEEN HIM. TALKED TO HIM.
HE'S HERE. VALENTINE DIDN'T KILL HIM. HODGE LIED TO ME. ALL THESE YEARS I THOUGHT HE WAS DEAD, BUT HE WASN'T.
WHAT?!
WHERE IS HE? DID VALENTINE KIDNAP HIM TOO?
MY FATHER—
CLATTER
SO HAVE YOU GATHERED YOUR THINGS? OUR FORSAKEN CAN HOLD OFF THE WOLFMEN FOR ONLY SO—

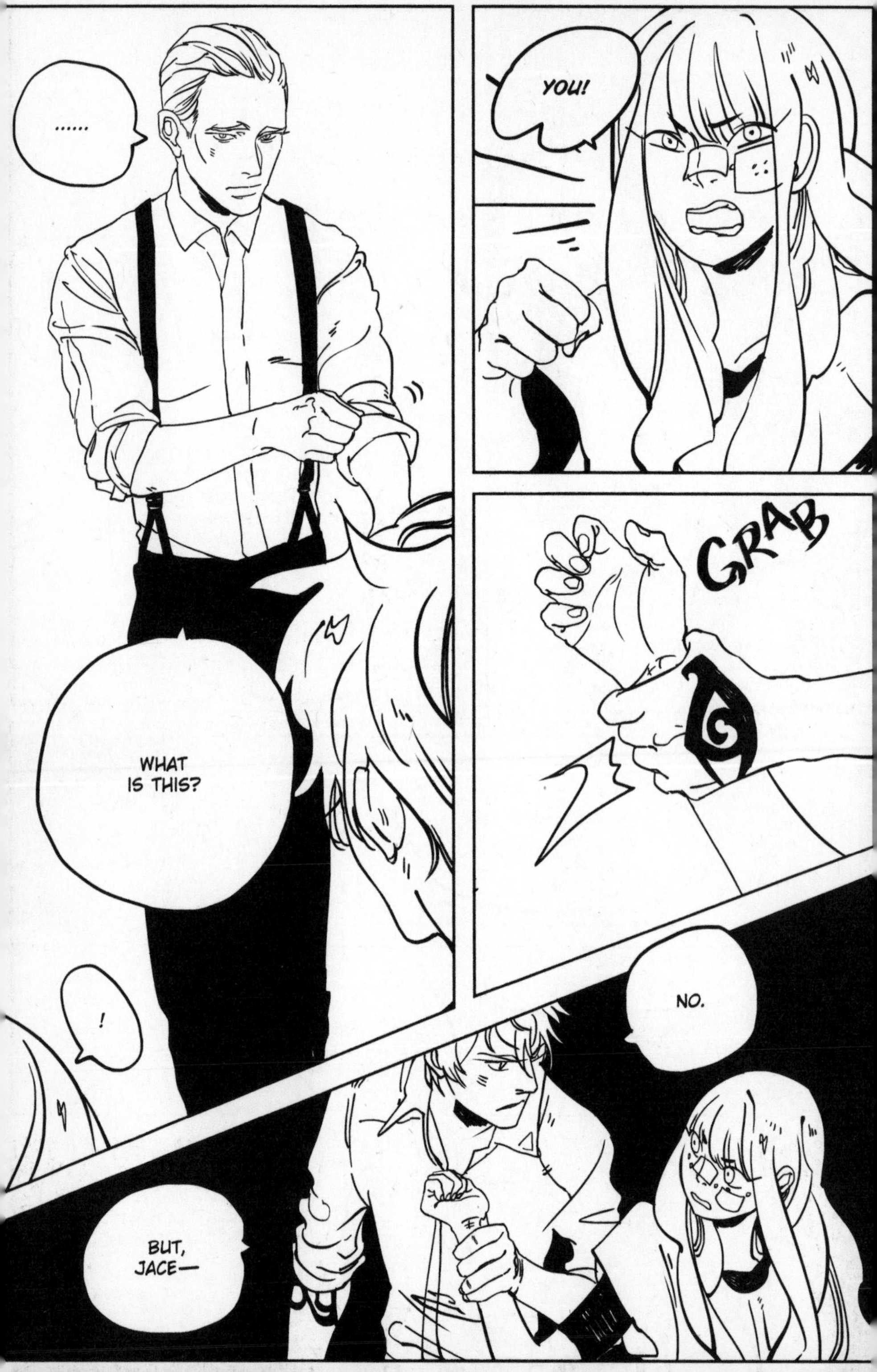
......
YOU!
WHAT IS THIS?
GRAB
!
NO.
BUT, JACE—

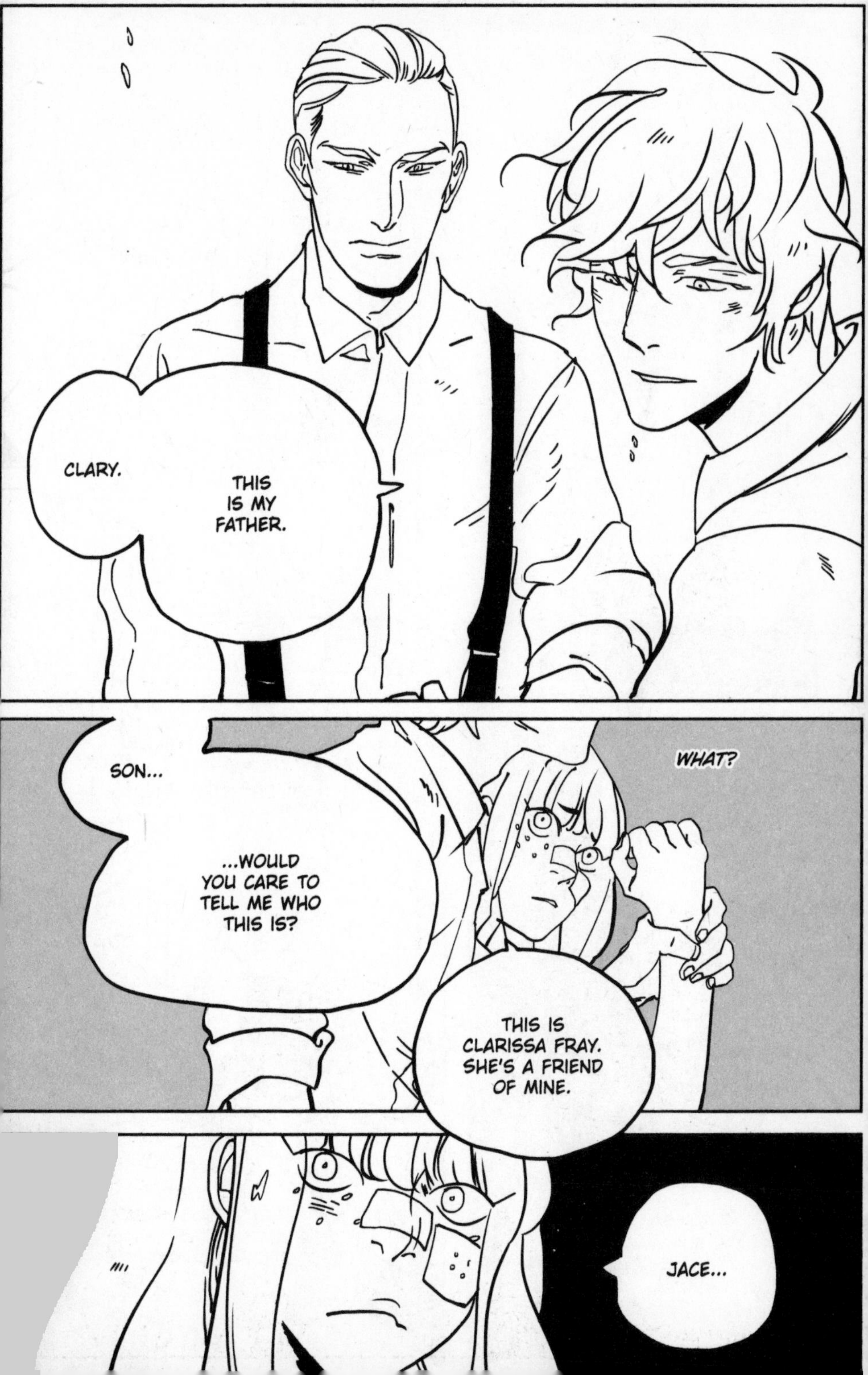
CLARY.
THIS IS MY FATHER.
SON...
...WOULD YOU CARE TO TELL ME WHO THIS IS?
WHAT?
THIS IS CLARISSA FRAY. SHE'S A FRIEND OF MINE.
JACE...

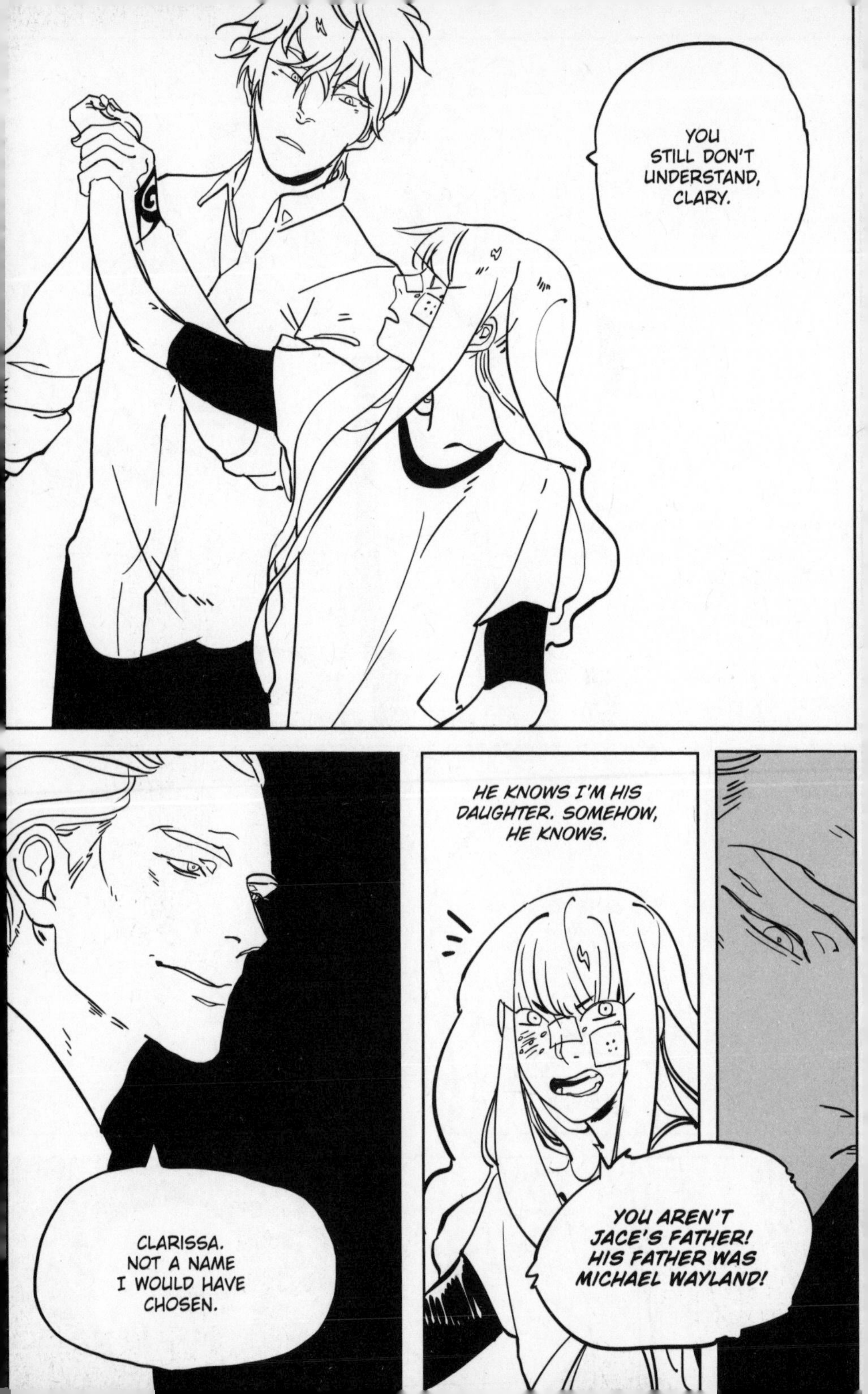
YOU STILL DON'T UNDERSTAND, CLARY.
CLARISSA. NOT A NAME I WOULD HAVE CHOSEN.
HE KNOWS I'M HIS DAUGHTER. SOMEHOW, HE KNOWS.
YOU AREN'T JACE'S FATHER! HIS FATHER WAS MICHAEL WAYLAND!

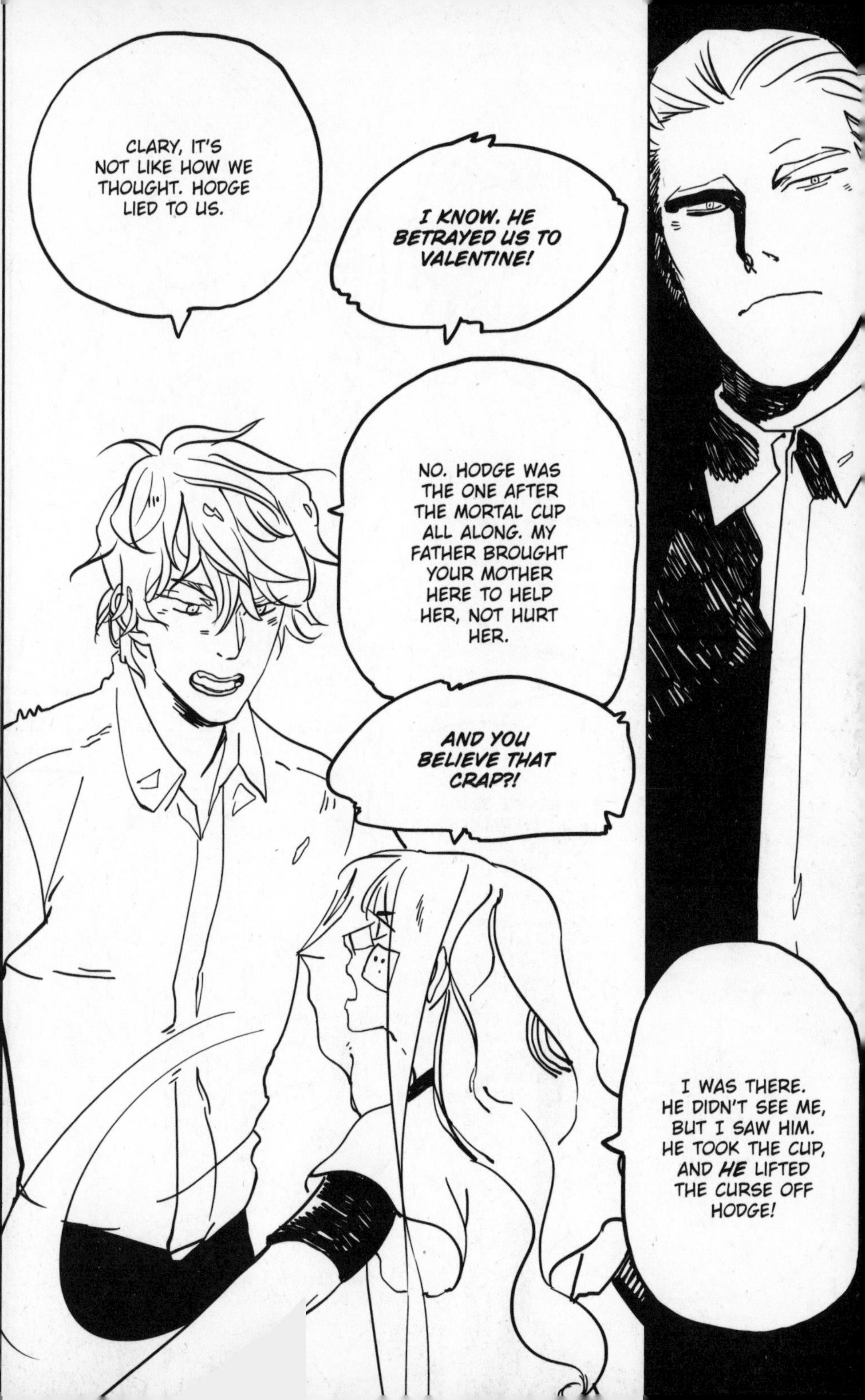
CLARY, IT'S NOT LIKE HOW WE THOUGHT. HODGE LIED TO US.
I KNOW. HE BETRAYED US TO VALENTINE!
NO. HODGE WAS THE ONE AFTER THE MORTAL CUP ALL ALONG. MY FATHER BROUGHT YOUR MOTHER HERE TO HELP HER, NOT HURT HER.
AND YOU BELIEVE THAT CRAP?!
I WAS THERE. HE DIDN'T SEE ME, BUT I SAW HIM. HE TOOK THE CUP, AND *HE* LIFTED THE CURSE OFF HODGE!

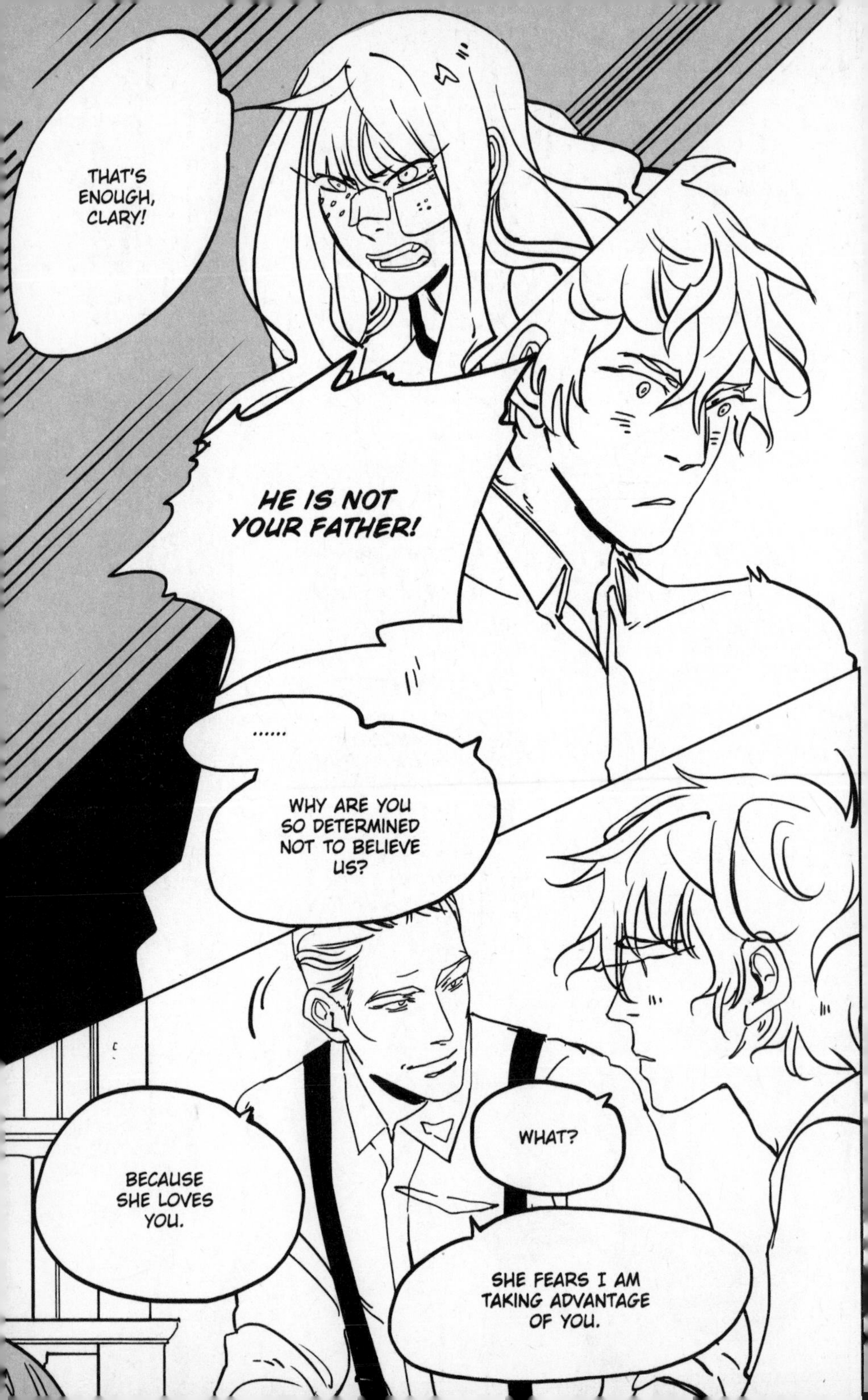
THAT'S ENOUGH, CLARY!
HE IS NOT YOUR FATHER!
......
WHY ARE YOU SO DETERMINED NOT TO BELIEVE US?
WHAT?
BECAUSE SHE LOVES YOU.
SHE FEARS I AM TAKING ADVANTAGE OF YOU.

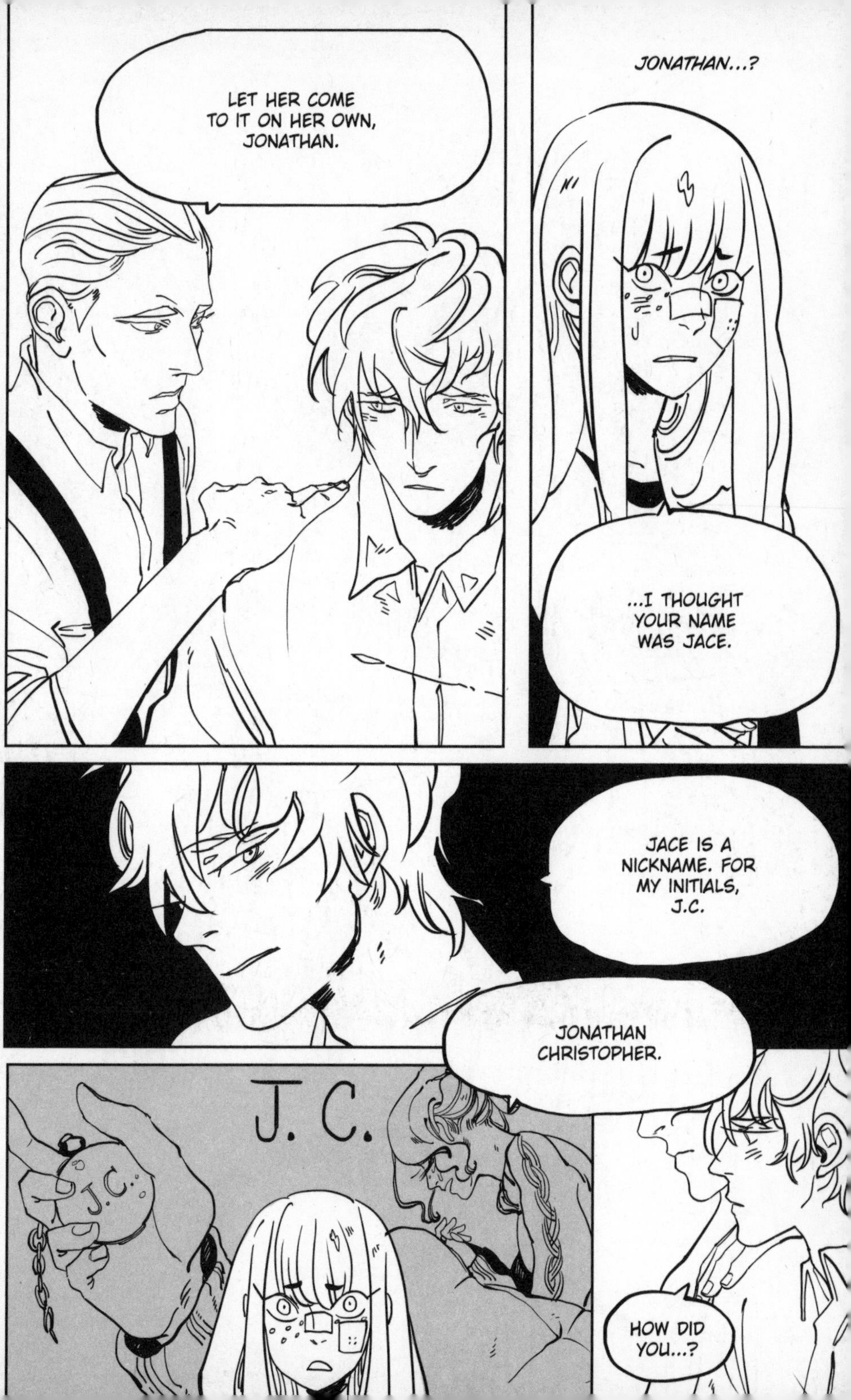
LET HER COME TO IT ON HER OWN, JONATHAN.
JONATHAN...?
...I THOUGHT YOUR NAME WAS JACE.
JACE IS A NICKNAME. FOR MY INITIALS, J.C.
JONATHAN CHRISTOPHER.
J. C.
J.C.
HOW DID YOU...?

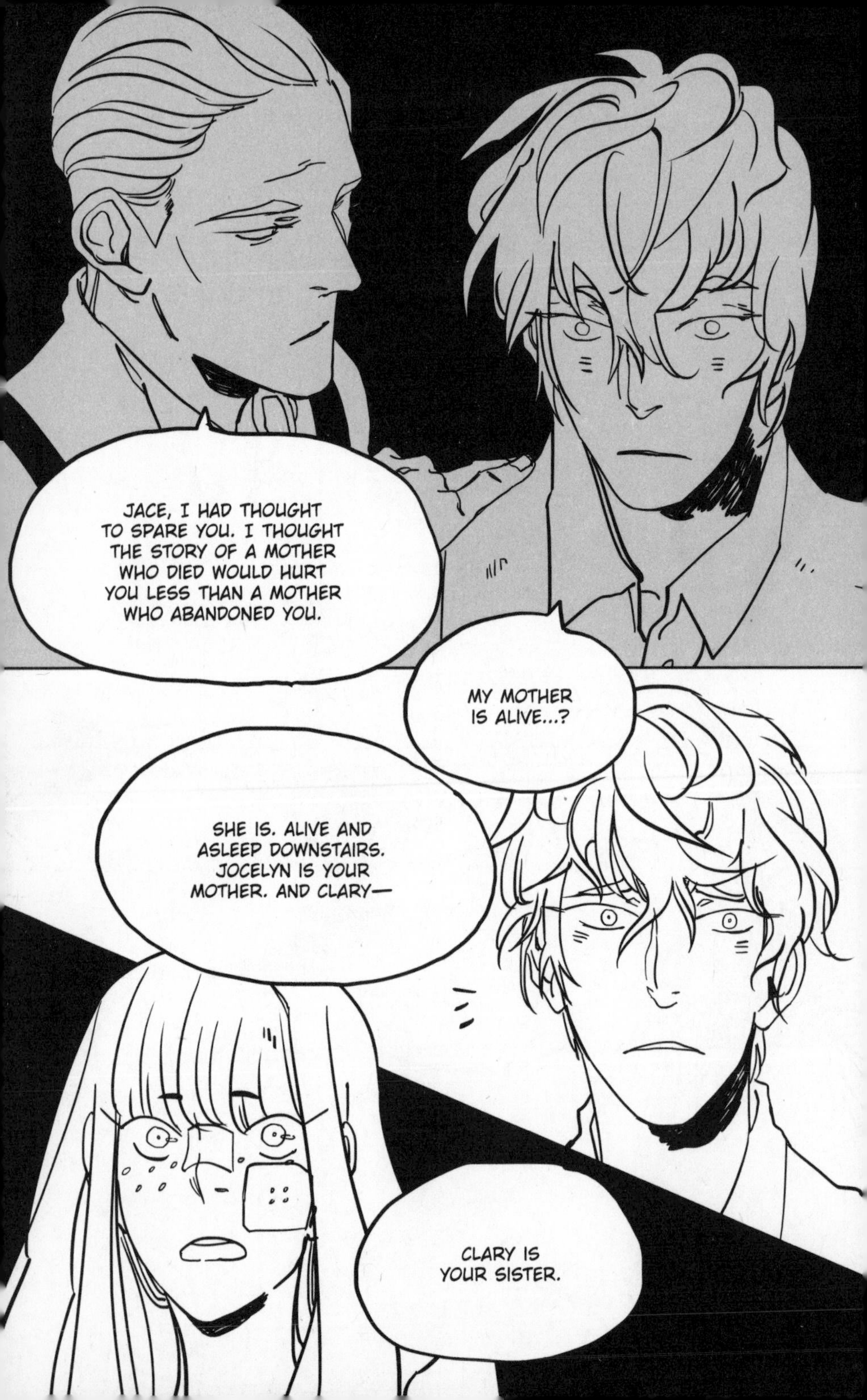
JACE, I HAD THOUGHT TO SPARE YOU. I THOUGHT THE STORY OF A MOTHER WHO DIED WOULD HURT YOU LESS THAN A MOTHER WHO ABANDONED YOU.
MY MOTHER IS ALIVE...?
SHE IS. ALIVE AND ASLEEP DOWNSTAIRS. JOCELYN IS YOUR MOTHER. AND CLARY—
CLARY IS YOUR SISTER.

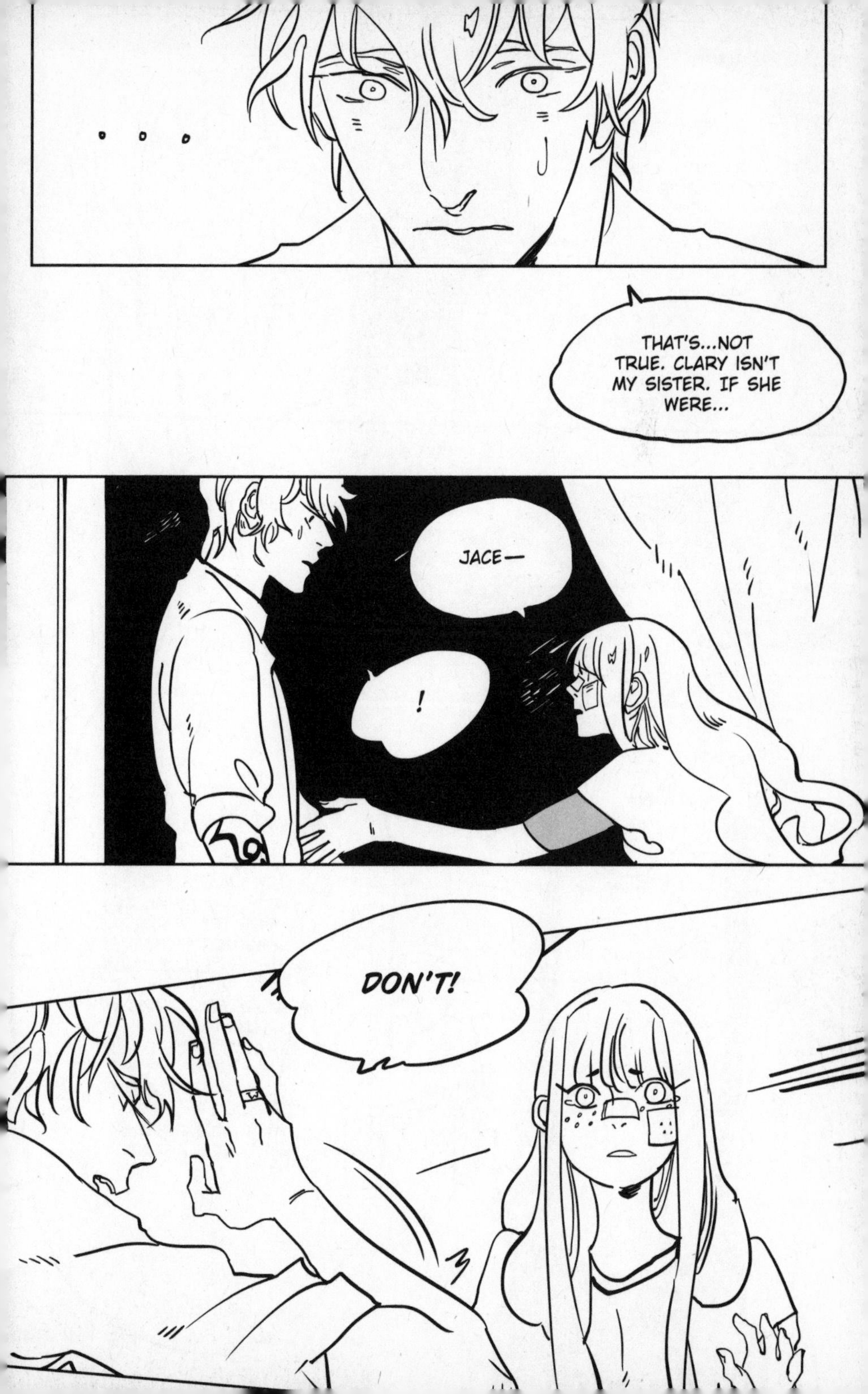
...
THAT'S...NOT TRUE. CLARY ISN'T MY SISTER. IF SHE WERE...
JACE—
!
DON'T!

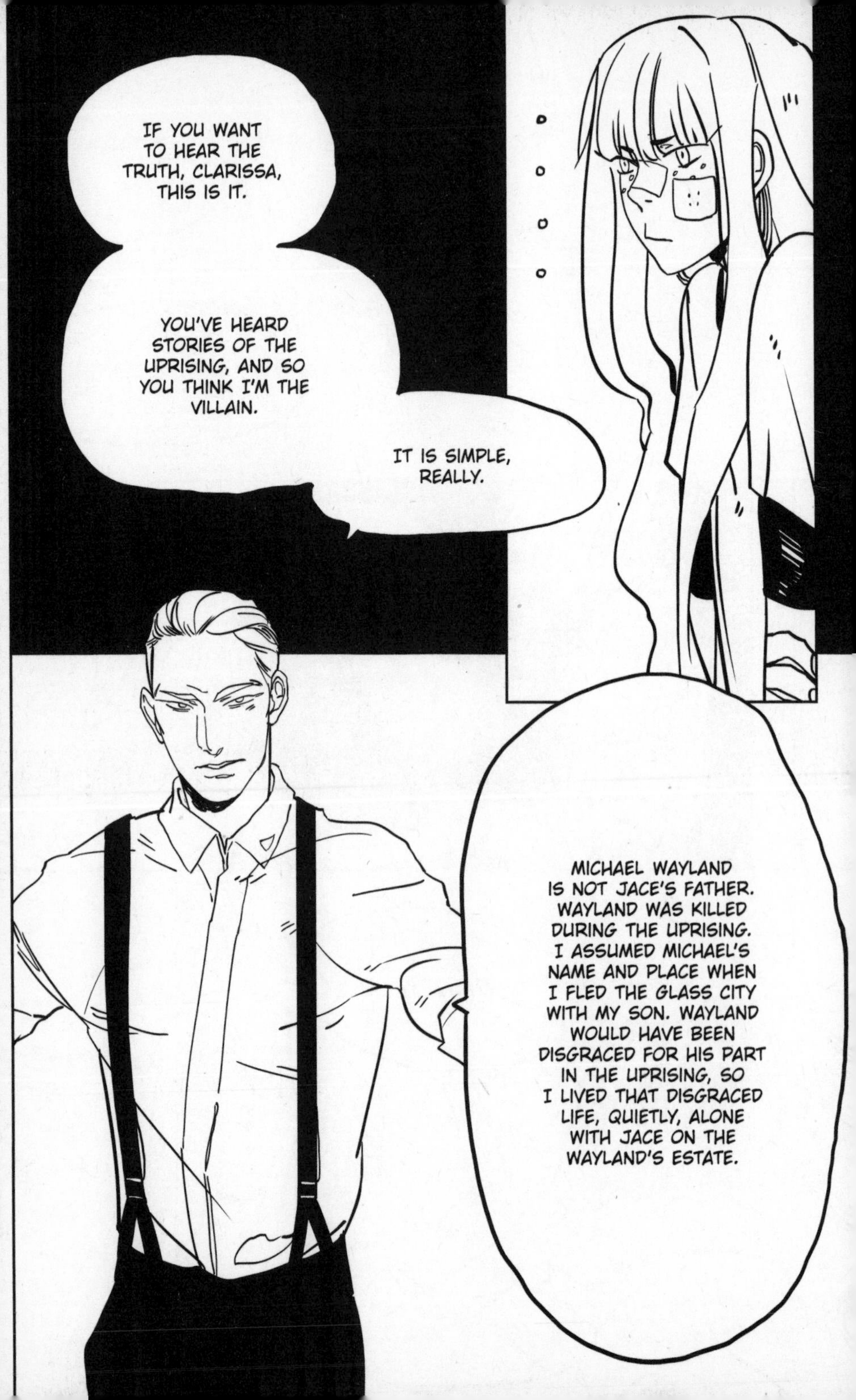
IF YOU WANT TO HEAR THE TRUTH, CLARISSA, THIS IS IT.
YOU'VE HEARD STORIES OF THE UPRISING, AND SO YOU THINK I'M THE VILLAIN.
IT IS SIMPLE, REALLY.
...
MICHAEL WAYLAND IS NOT JACE'S FATHER. WAYLAND WAS KILLED DURING THE UPRISING. I ASSUMED MICHAEL'S NAME AND PLACE WHEN I FLED THE GLASS CITY WITH MY SON. WAYLAND WOULD HAVE BEEN DISGRACED FOR HIS PART IN THE UPRISING, SO I LIVED THAT DISGRACED LIFE, QUIETLY, ALONE WITH JACE ON THE WAYLAND'S ESTATE.

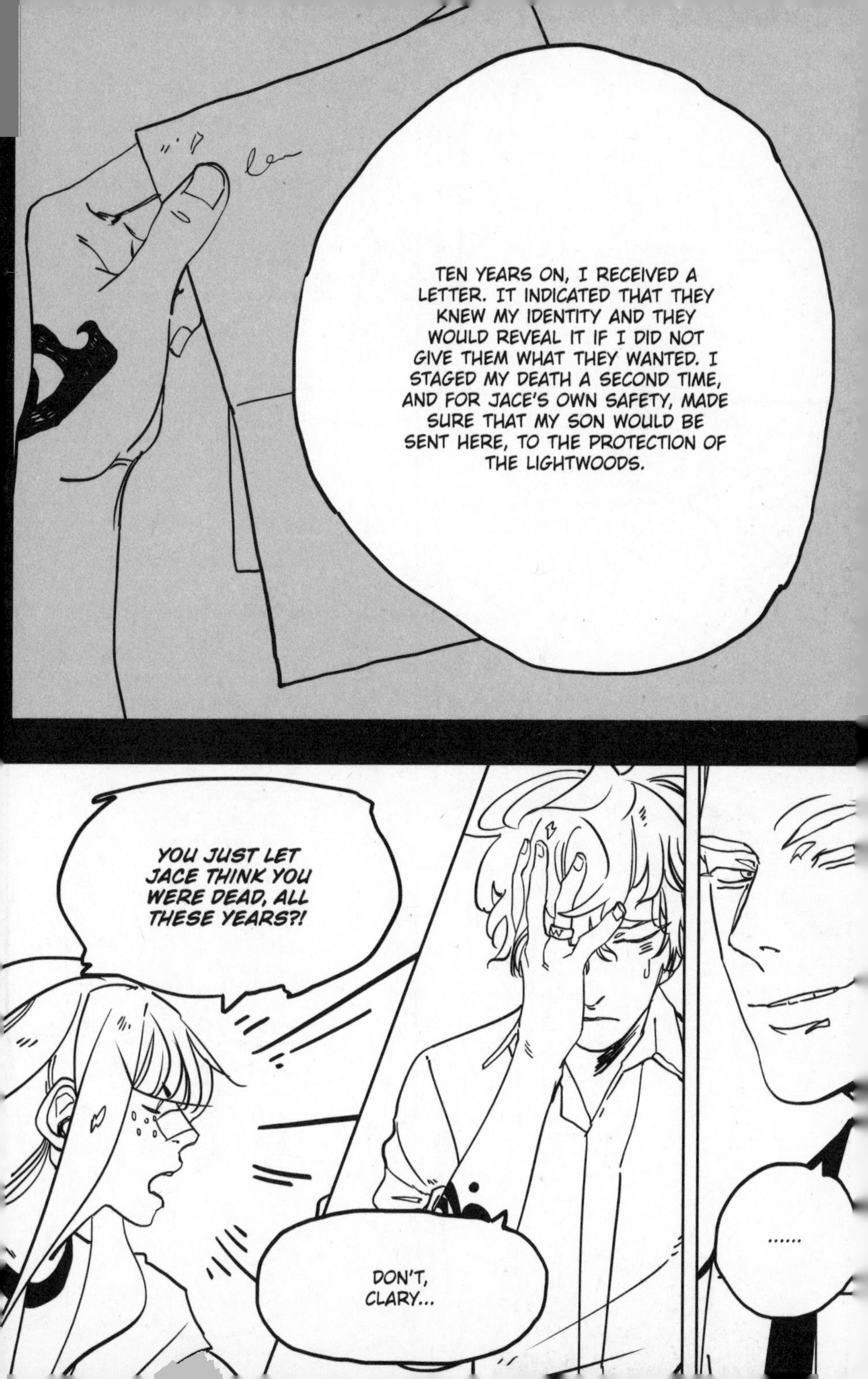
TEN YEARS ON, I RECEIVED A LETTER. IT INDICATED THAT THEY KNEW MY IDENTITY AND THEY WOULD REVEAL IT IF I DID NOT GIVE THEM WHAT THEY WANTED. I STAGED MY DEATH A SECOND TIME, AND FOR JACE'S OWN SAFETY, MADE SURE THAT MY SON WOULD BE SENT HERE, TO THE PROTECTION OF THE LIGHTWOODS.
YOU JUST LET JACE THINK YOU WERE DEAD, ALL THESE YEARS?!
DON'T, CLARY...
......

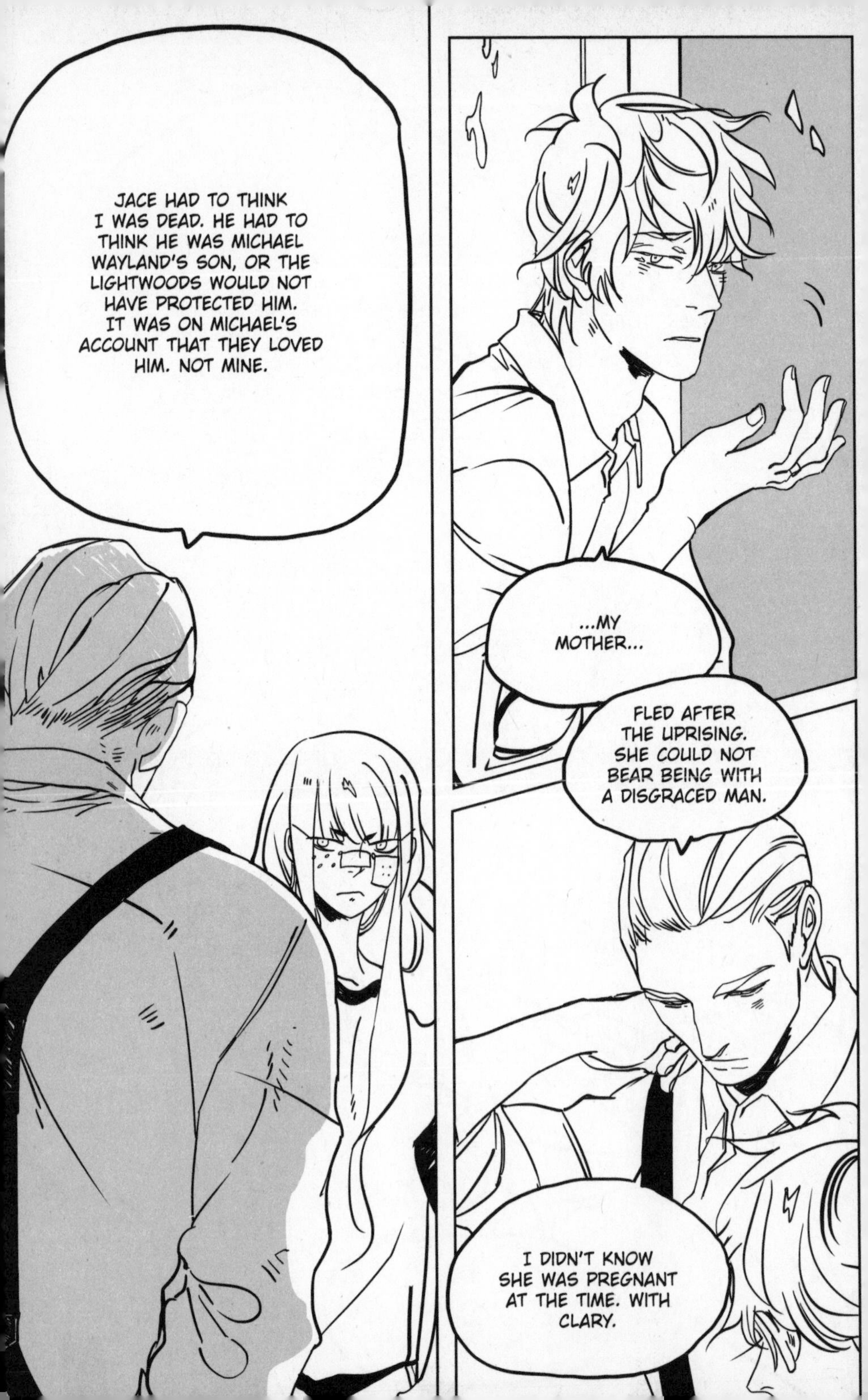
JACE HAD TO THINK I WAS DEAD. HE HAD TO THINK HE WAS MICHAEL WAYLAND'S SON, OR THE LIGHTWOODS WOULD NOT HAVE PROTECTED HIM. IT WAS ON MICHAEL'S ACCOUNT THAT THEY LOVED HIM. NOT MINE.
...MY MOTHER...
FLED AFTER THE UPRISING. SHE COULD NOT BEAR BEING WITH A DISGRACED MAN.
I DIDN'T KNOW SHE WAS PREGNANT AT THE TIME. WITH CLARY.

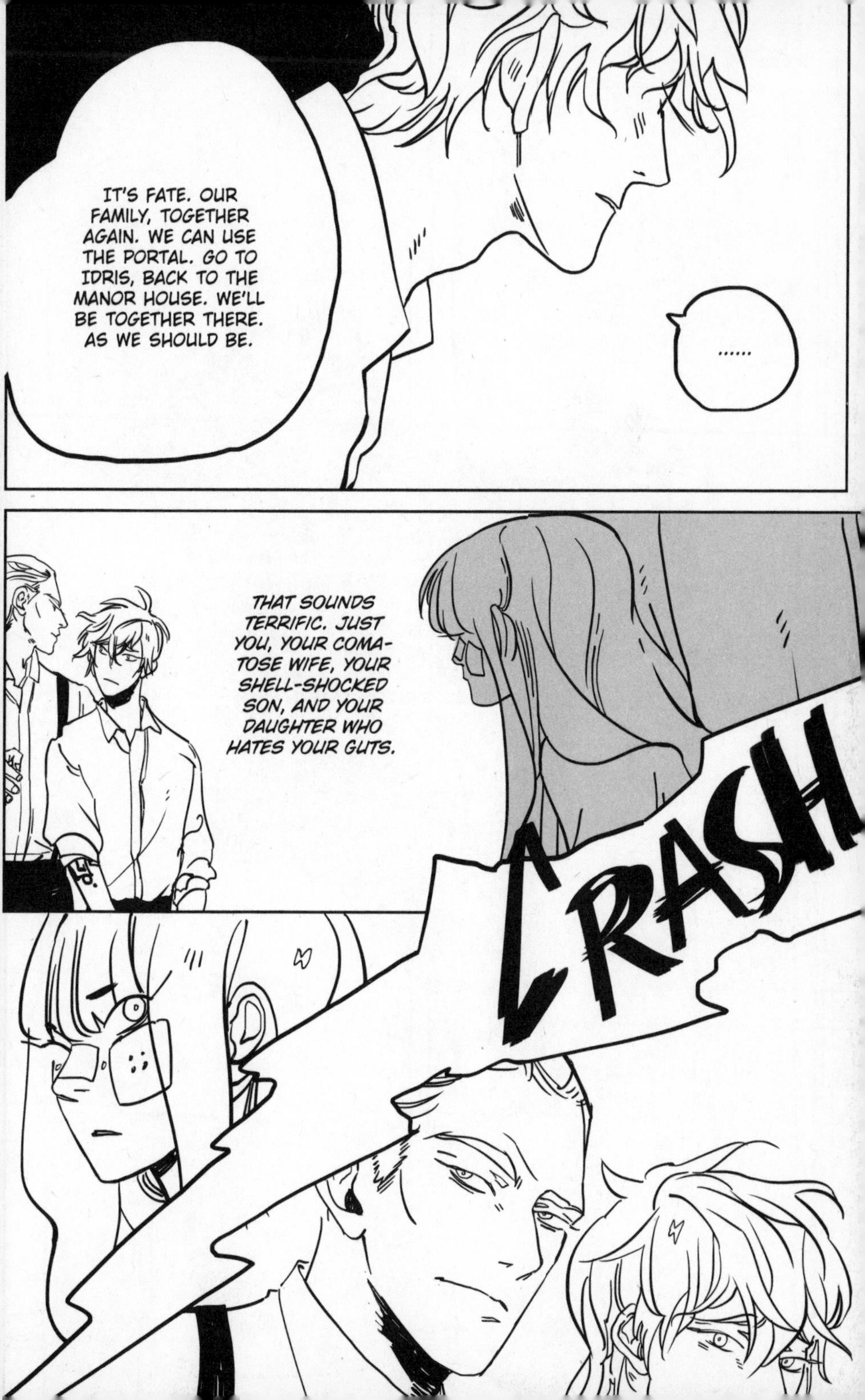
IT'S FATE. OUR FAMILY, TOGETHER AGAIN. WE CAN USE THE PORTAL. GO TO IDRIS, BACK TO THE MANOR HOUSE. WE'LL BE TOGETHER THERE. AS WE SHOULD BE.
......
THAT SOUNDS TERRIFIC. JUST YOU, YOUR COMATOSE WIFE, YOUR SHELL-SHOCKED SON, AND YOUR DAUGHTER WHO HATES YOUR GUTS.
CRASH

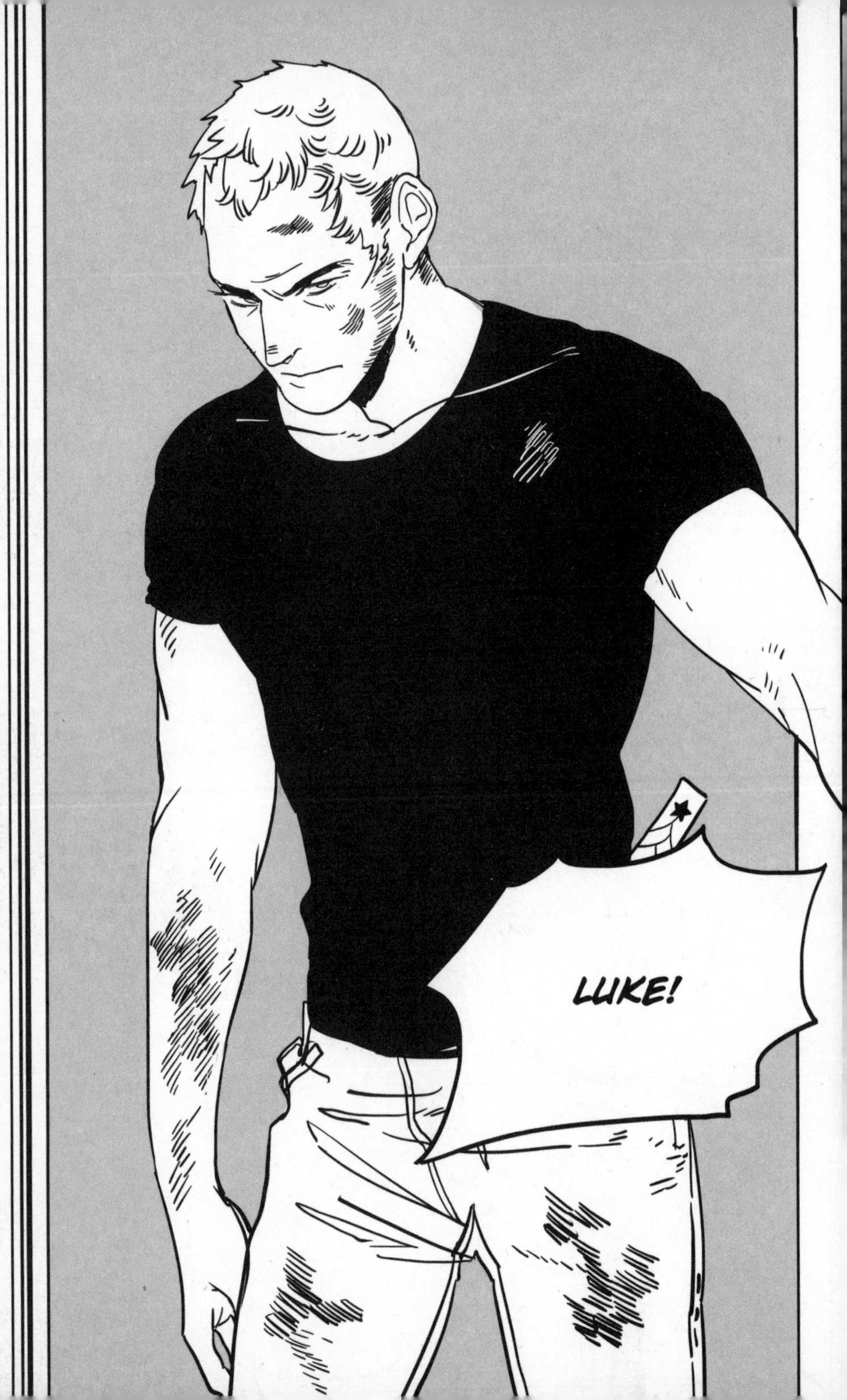
LUKE!

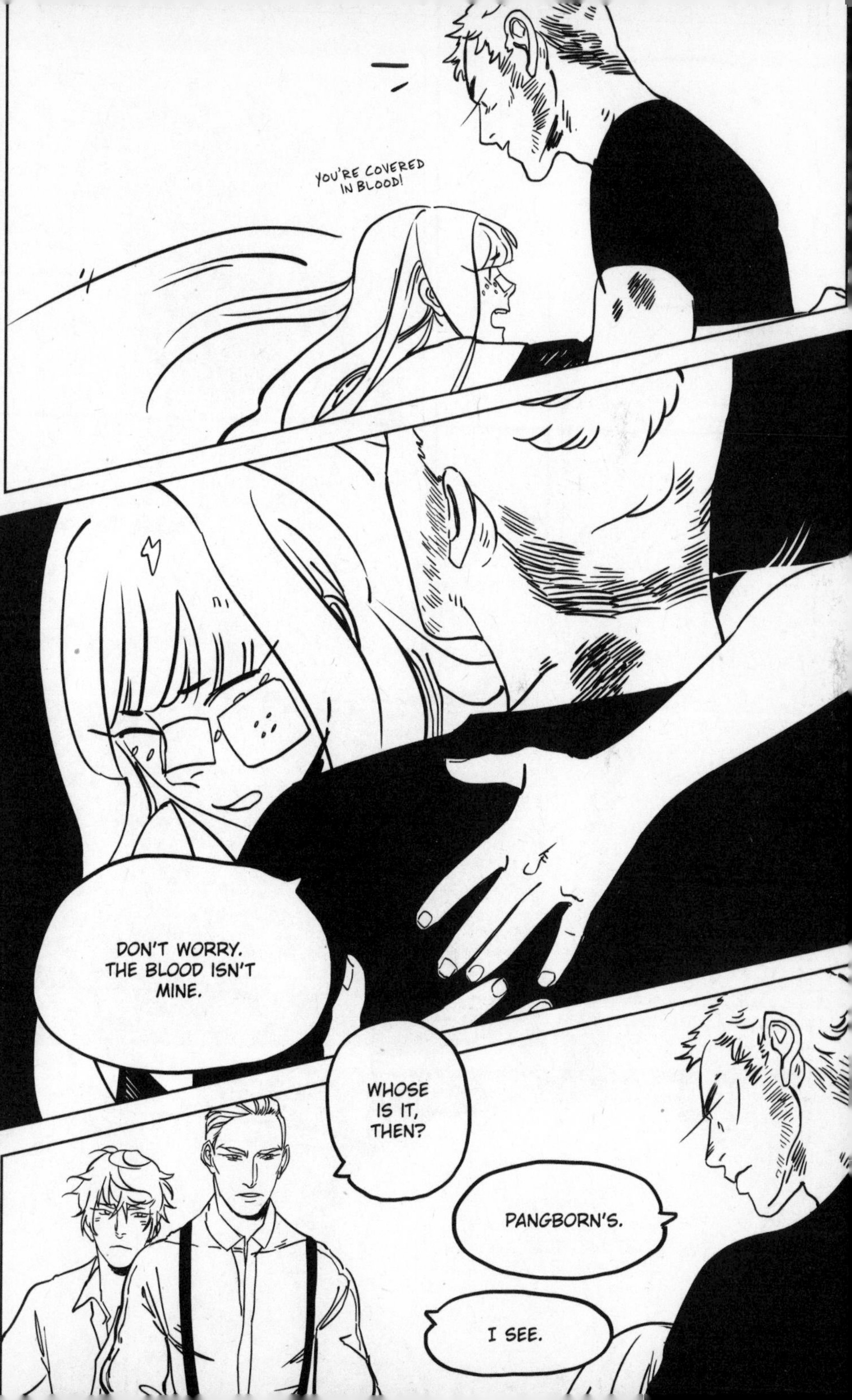
YOU'RE COVERED IN BLOOD!
DON'T WORRY. THE BLOOD ISN'T MINE.
WHOSE IS IT, THEN?
PANGBORN'S.
I SEE.

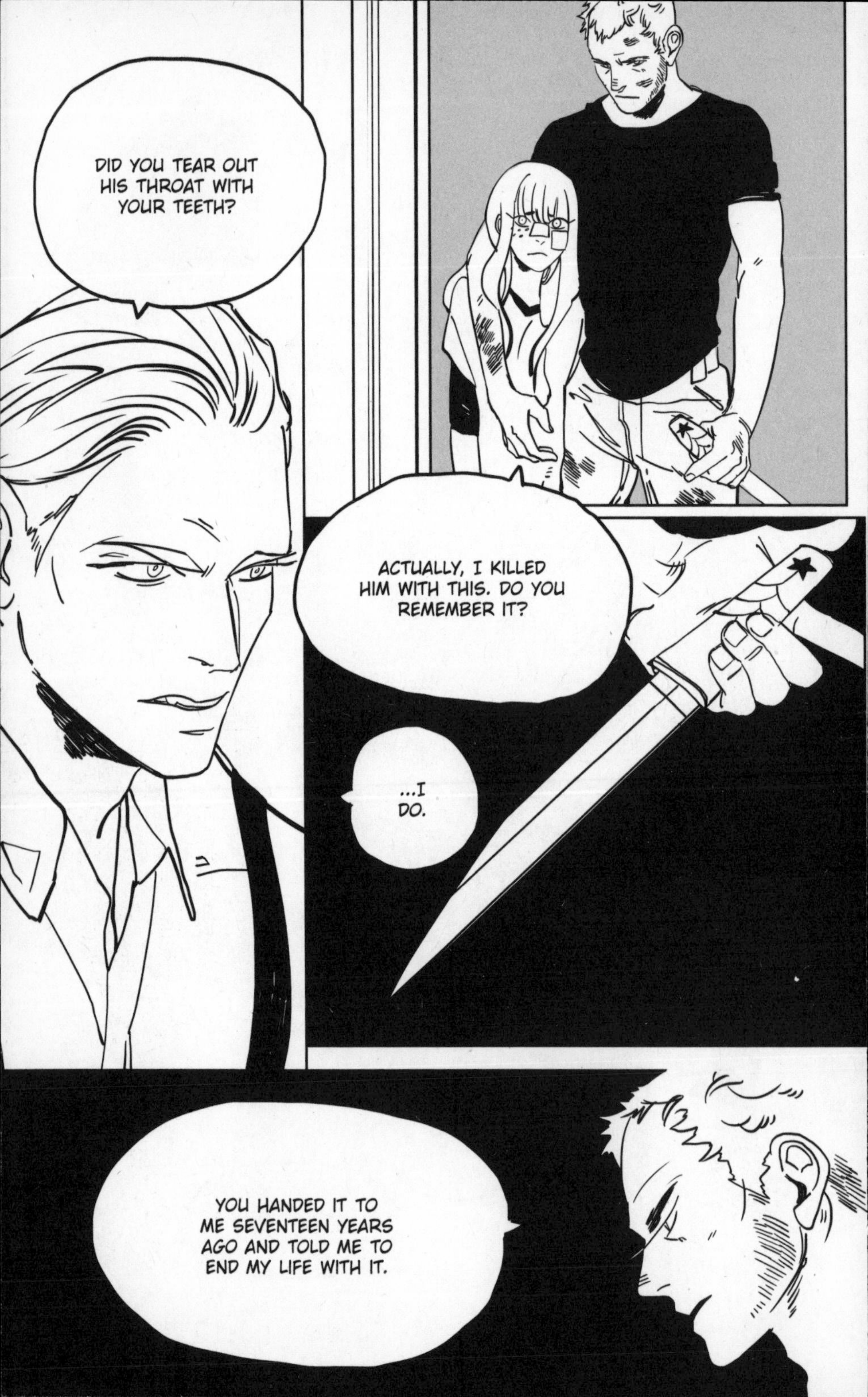
DID YOU TEAR OUT HIS THROAT WITH YOUR TEETH?
ACTUALLY, I KILLED HIM WITH THIS. DO YOU REMEMBER IT?
...I DO.
YOU HANDED IT TO ME SEVENTEEN YEARS AGO AND TOLD ME TO END MY LIFE WITH IT.

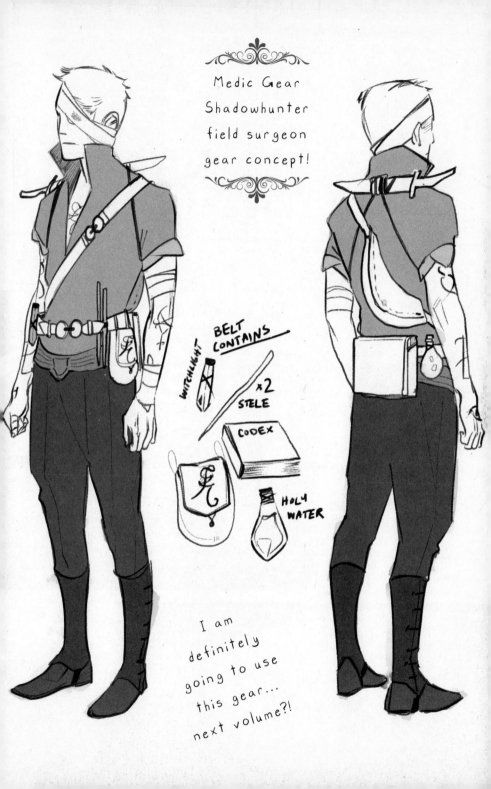

Medic Gear
Shadowhunter
field surgeon
gear concept!

BELT CONTAINS

WITCHLIGHT

×2 STELE

CODEX

HOLY WATER

I am
definitely
going to use
this gear...
next volume?!

THE MORTAL INSTRUMENTS

THE GRAPHIC NOVEL

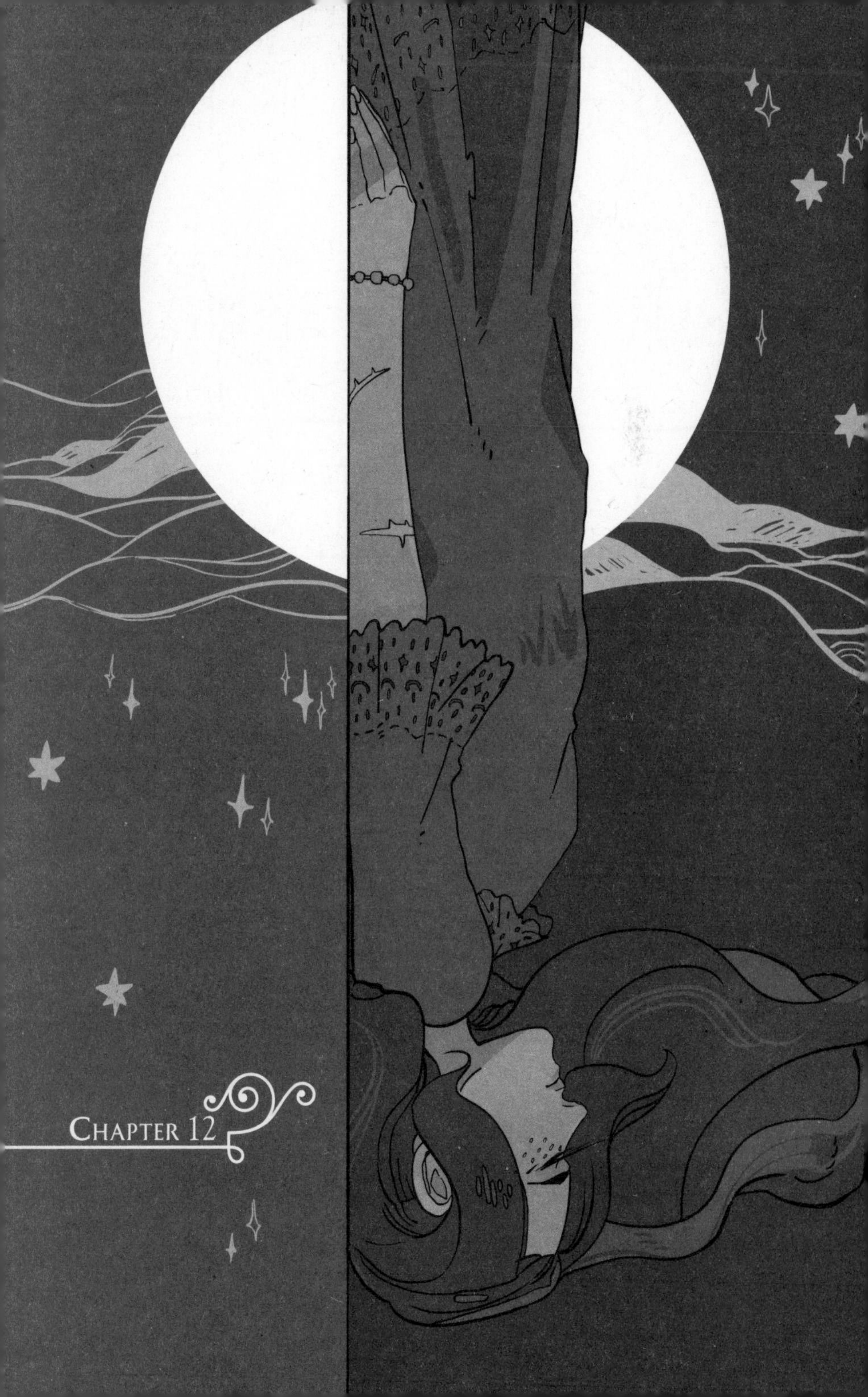

Chapter 12

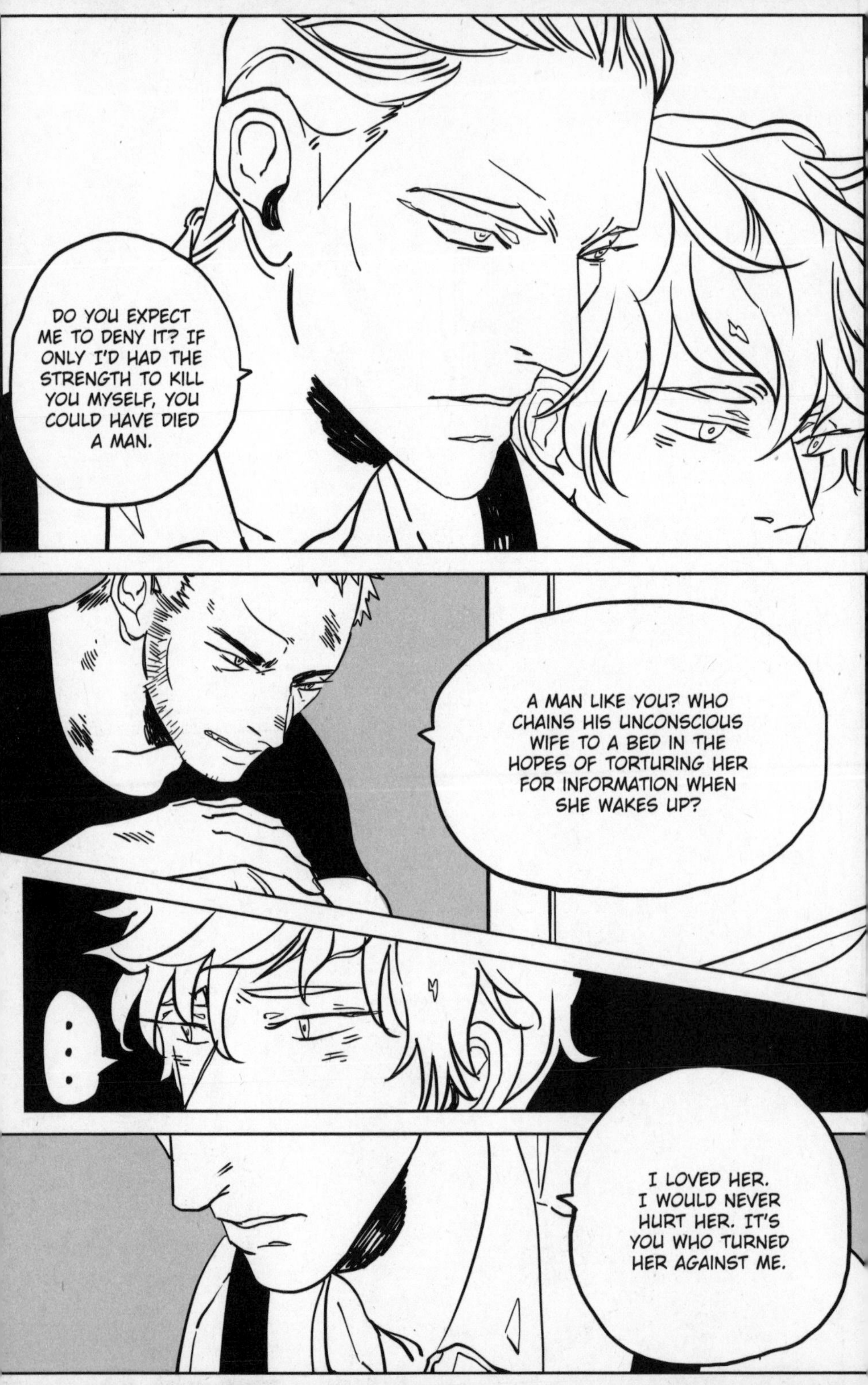
DO YOU EXPECT ME TO DENY IT? IF ONLY I'D HAD THE STRENGTH TO KILL YOU MYSELF, YOU COULD HAVE DIED A MAN.
A MAN LIKE YOU? WHO CHAINS HIS UNCONSCIOUS WIFE TO A BED IN THE HOPES OF TORTURING HER FOR INFORMATION WHEN SHE WAKES UP?
...
I LOVED HER. I WOULD NEVER HURT HER. IT'S YOU WHO TURNED HER AGAINST ME.

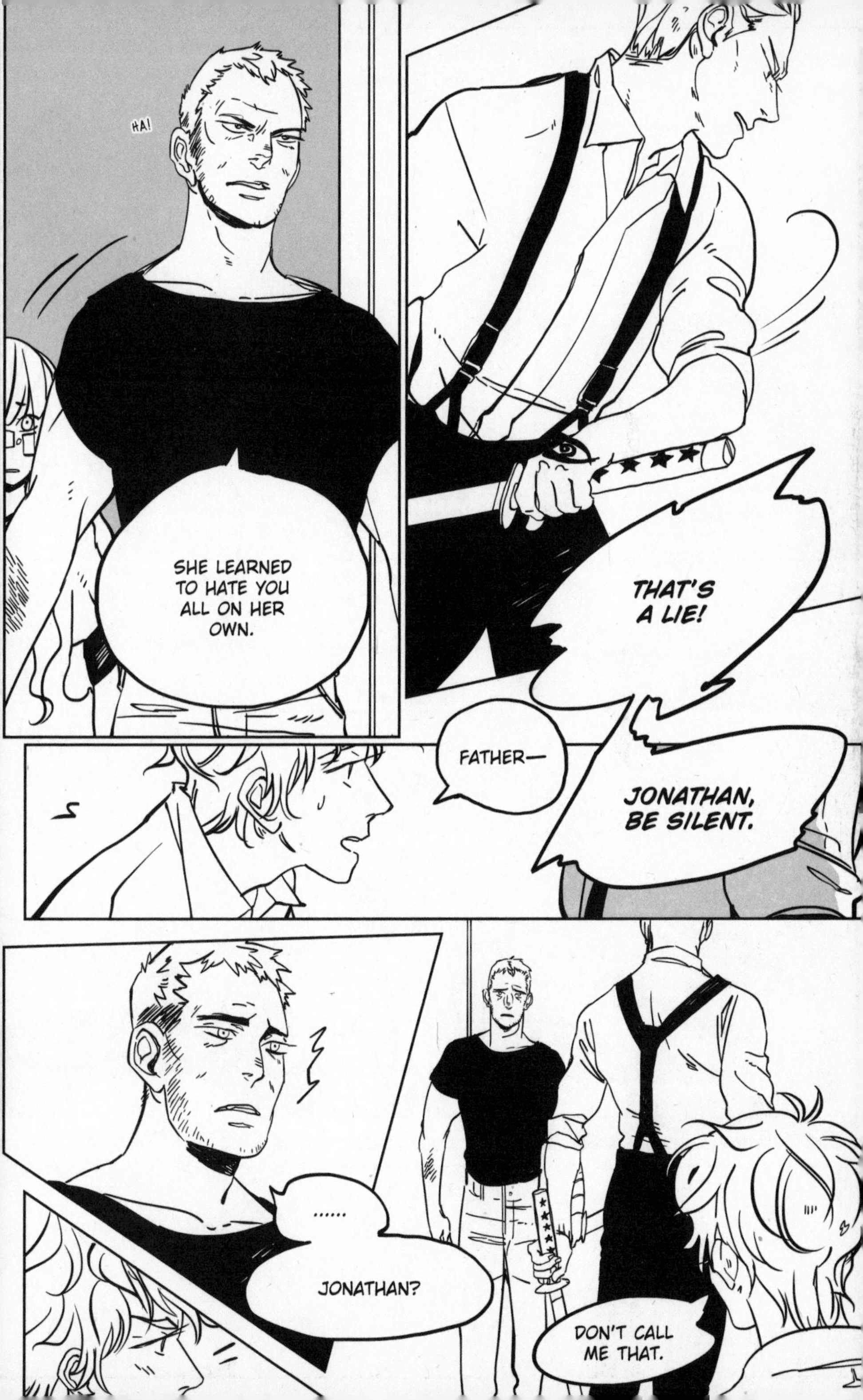
HA!
SHE LEARNED TO HATE YOU ALL ON HER OWN.
THAT'S A LIE!
FATHER—
JONATHAN, BE SILENT.
......
JONATHAN?
DON'T CALL ME THAT.

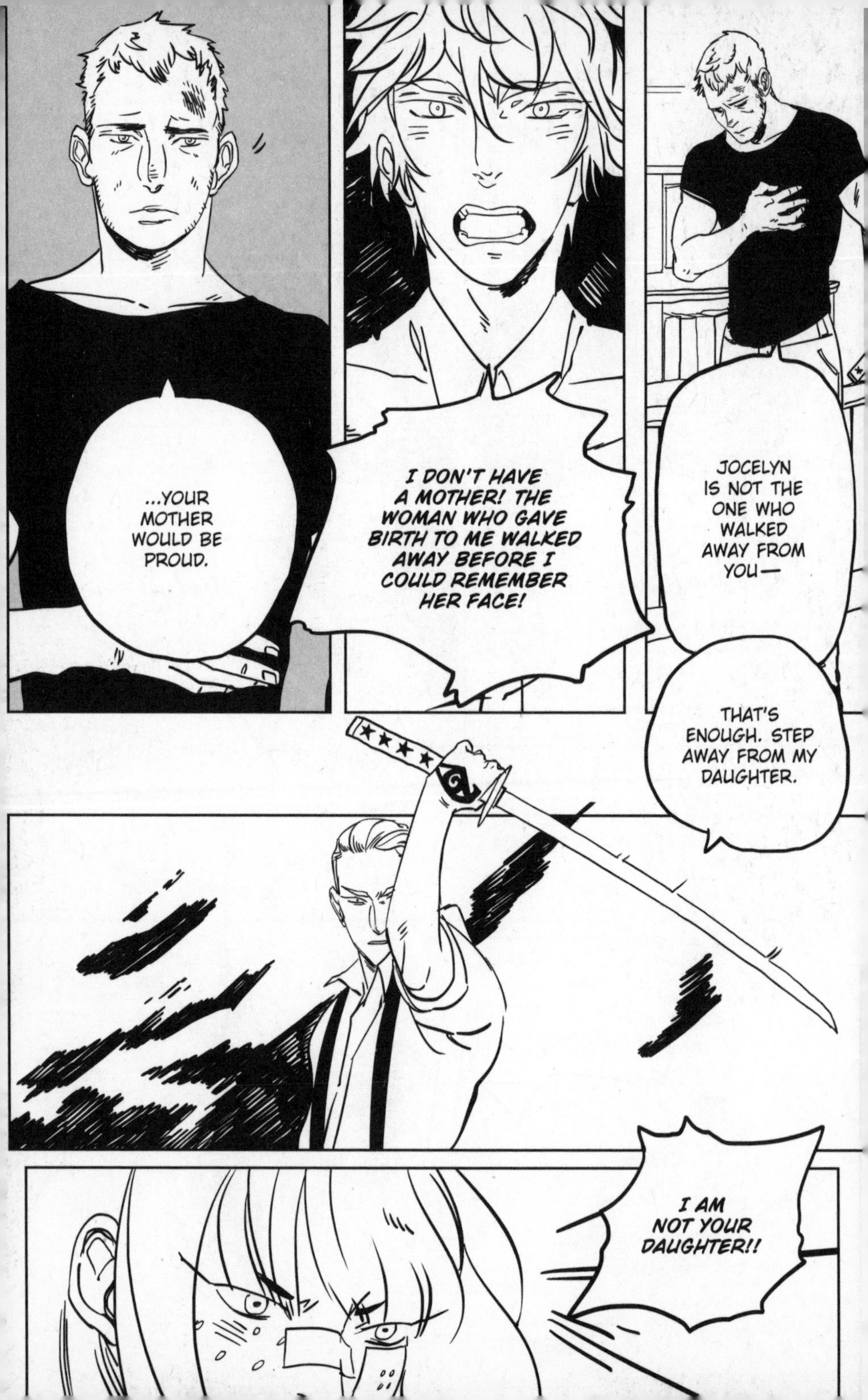
...YOUR MOTHER WOULD BE PROUD.
I DON'T HAVE A MOTHER! THE WOMAN WHO GAVE BIRTH TO ME WALKED AWAY BEFORE I COULD REMEMBER HER FACE!
JOCELYN IS NOT THE ONE WHO WALKED AWAY FROM YOU—
THAT'S ENOUGH. STEP AWAY FROM MY DAUGHTER.
I AM NOT YOUR DAUGHTER!!

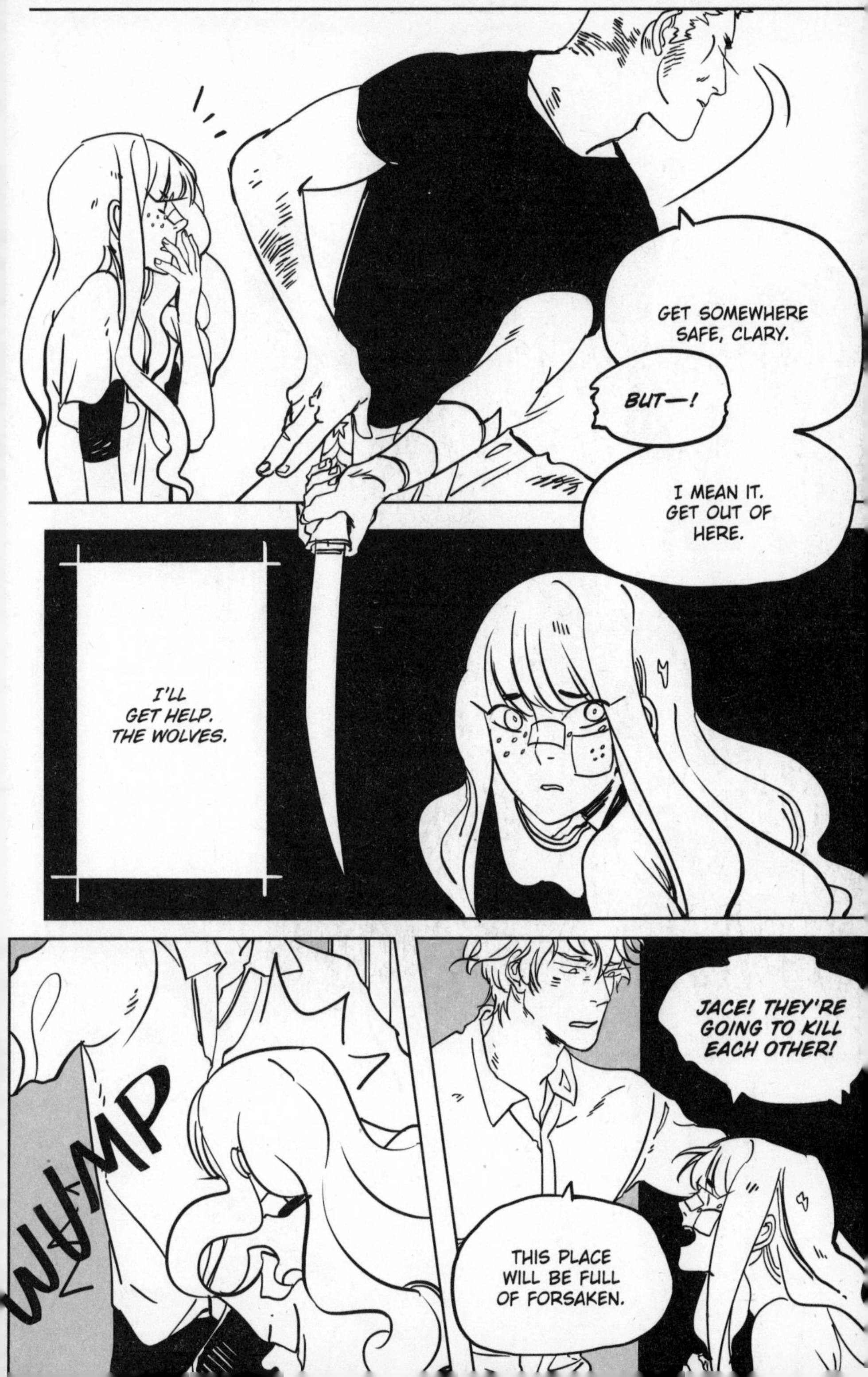
GET SOMEWHERE SAFE, CLARY.
BUT—!
I MEAN IT. GET OUT OF HERE.
I'LL GET HELP. THE WOLVES.
WHMP
JACE! THEY'RE GOING TO KILL EACH OTHER!
THIS PLACE WILL BE FULL OF FORSAKEN.

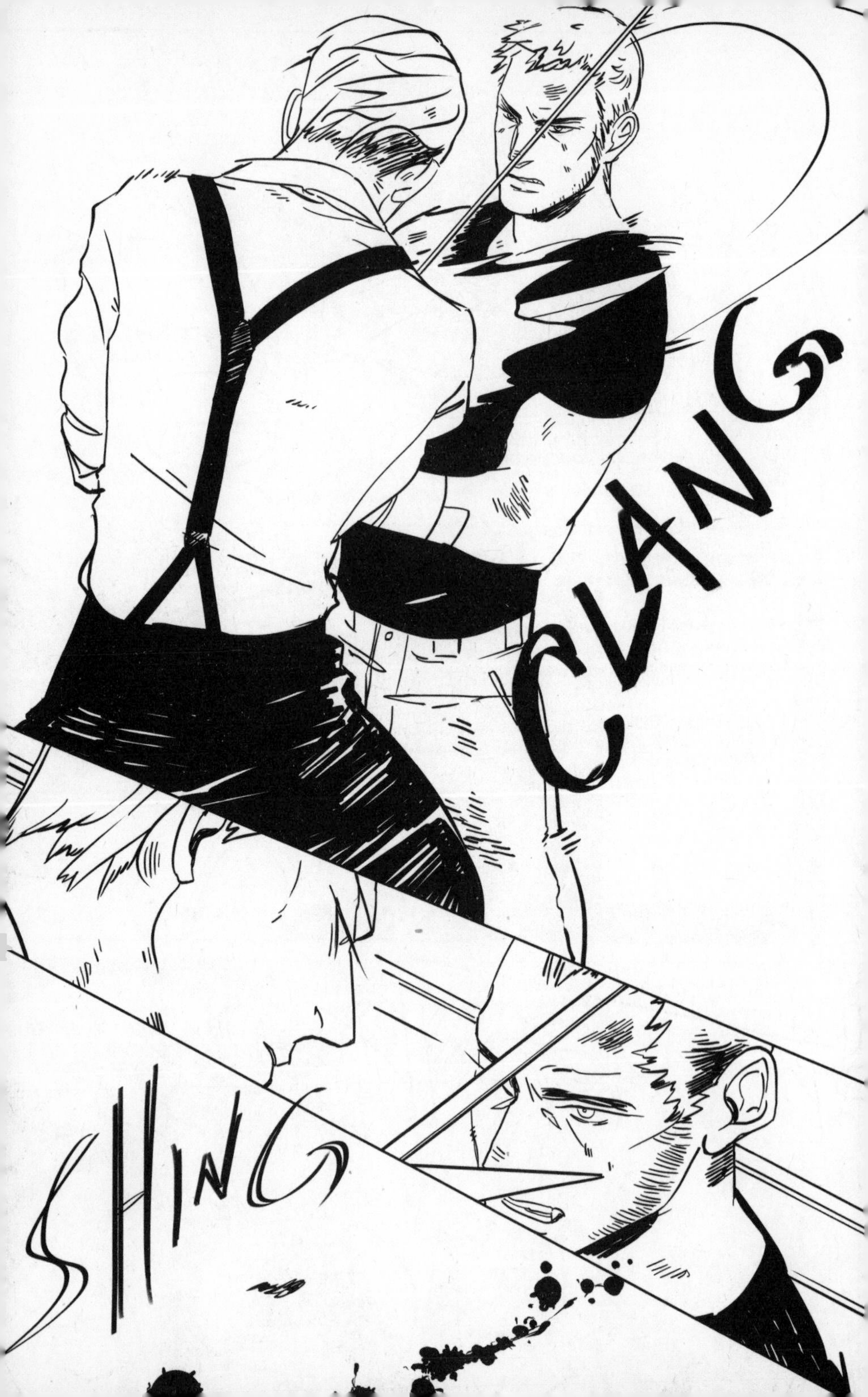
CLANG
SHING

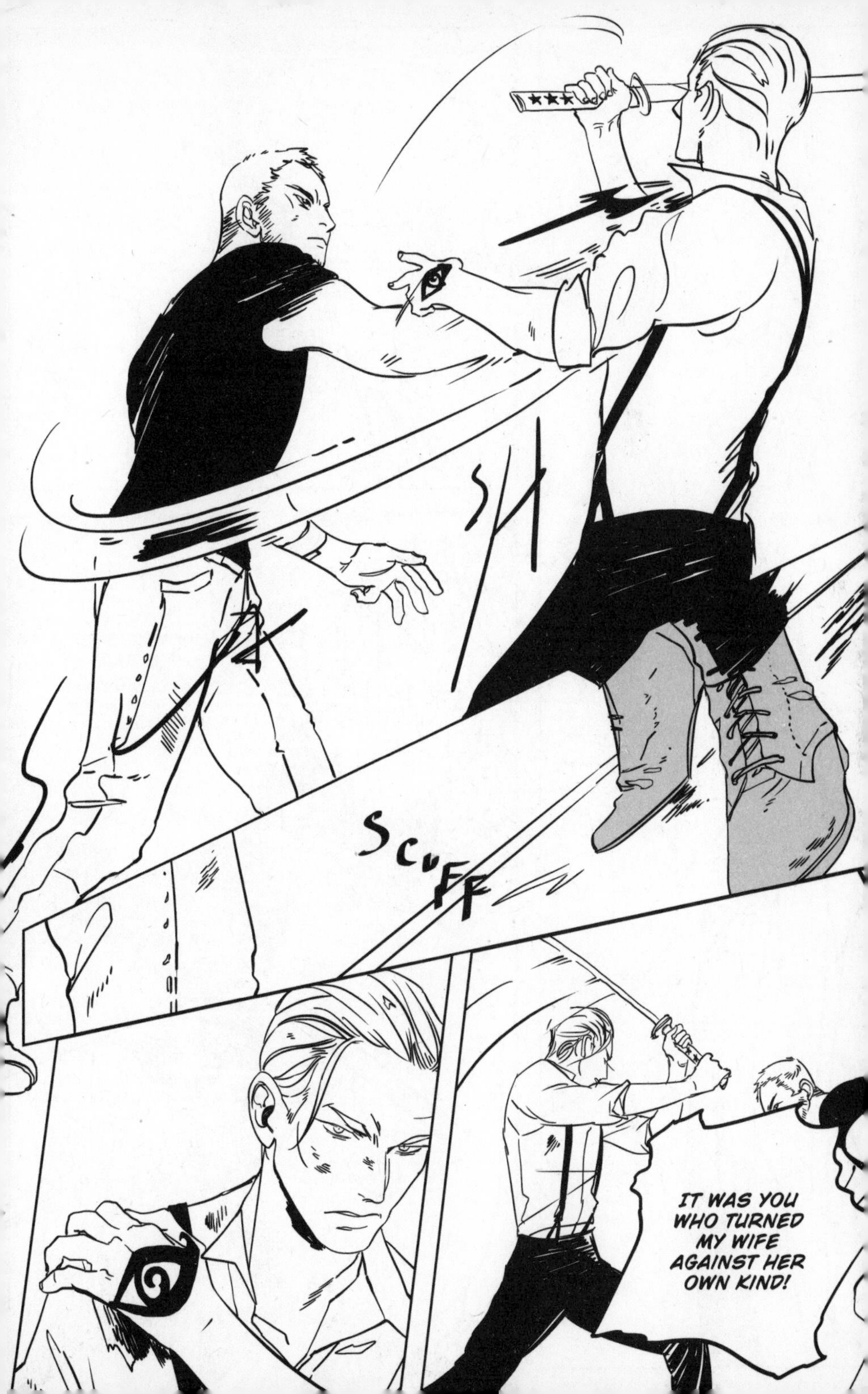
SH
SCUFF
IT WAS YOU WHO TURNED MY WIFE AGAINST HER OWN KIND!

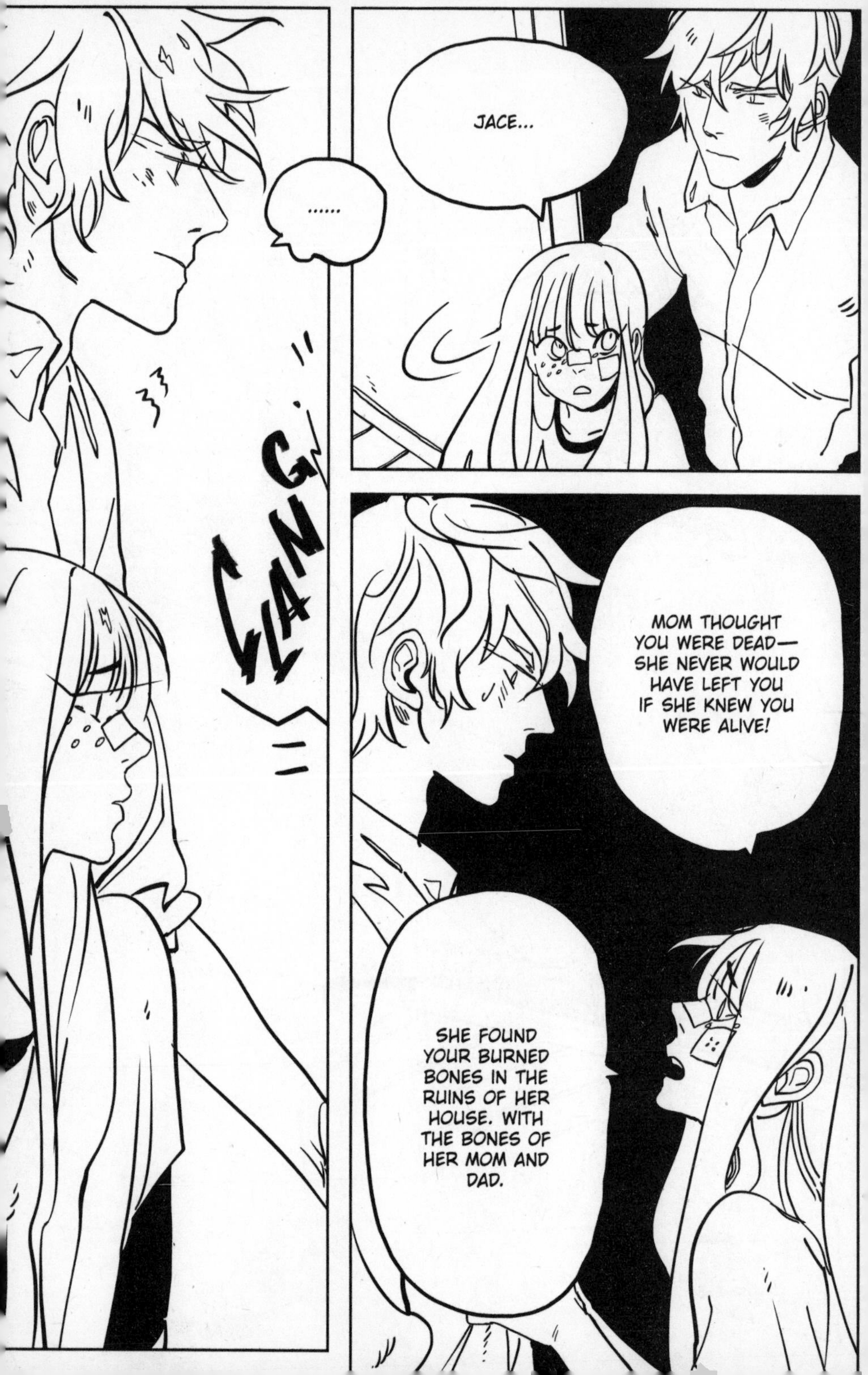
......
CLANG
JACE...
MOM THOUGHT YOU WERE DEAD— SHE NEVER WOULD HAVE LEFT YOU IF SHE KNEW YOU WERE ALIVE!
SHE FOUND YOUR BURNED BONES IN THE RUINS OF HER HOUSE. WITH THE BONES OF HER MOM AND DAD.

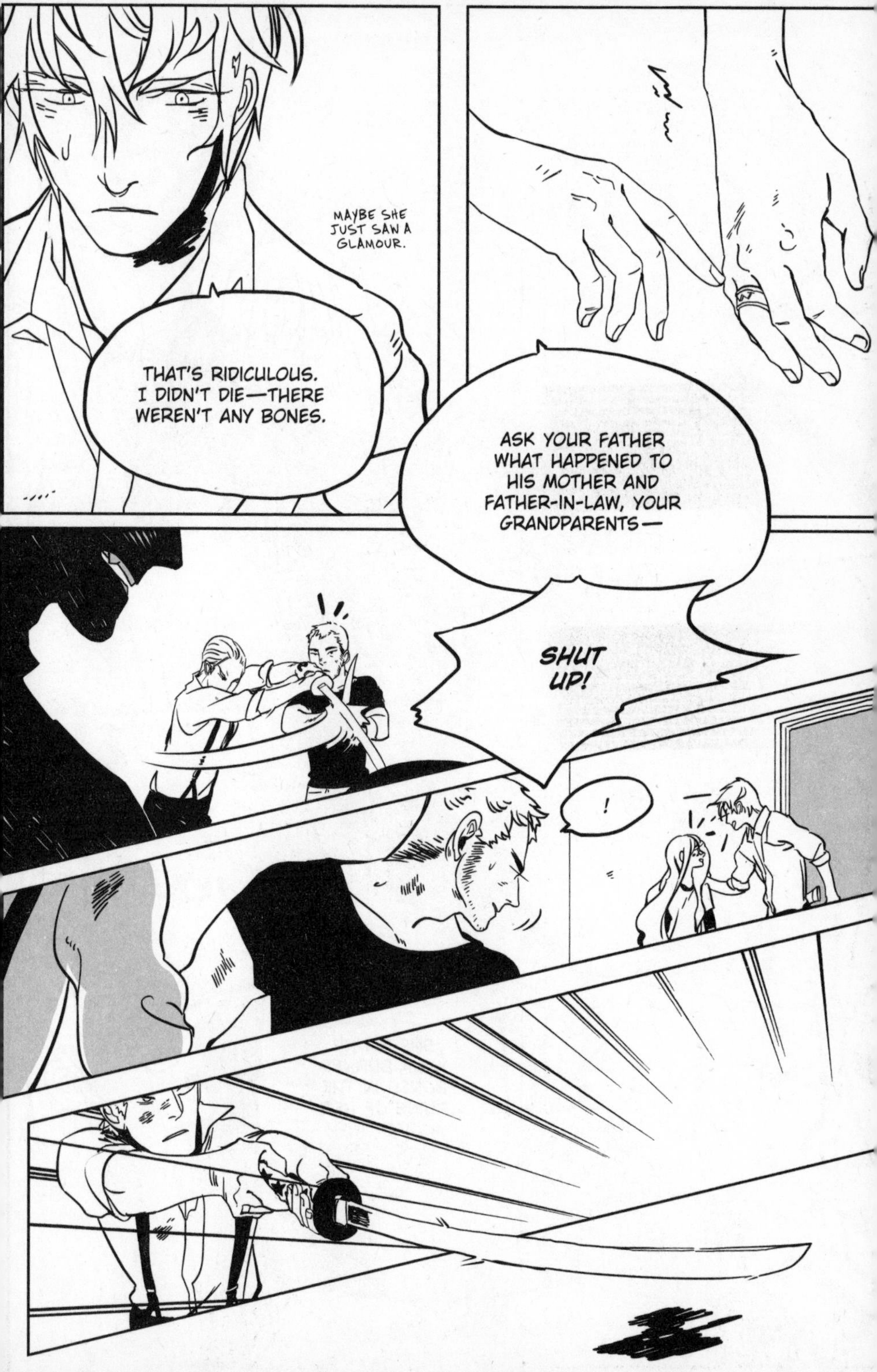
MAYBE SHE JUST SAW A GLAMOUR.
THAT'S RIDICULOUS. I DIDN'T DIE—THERE WEREN'T ANY BONES.
ASK YOUR FATHER WHAT HAPPENED TO HIS MOTHER AND FATHER-IN-LAW, YOUR GRANDPARENTS—
SHUT UP!
!

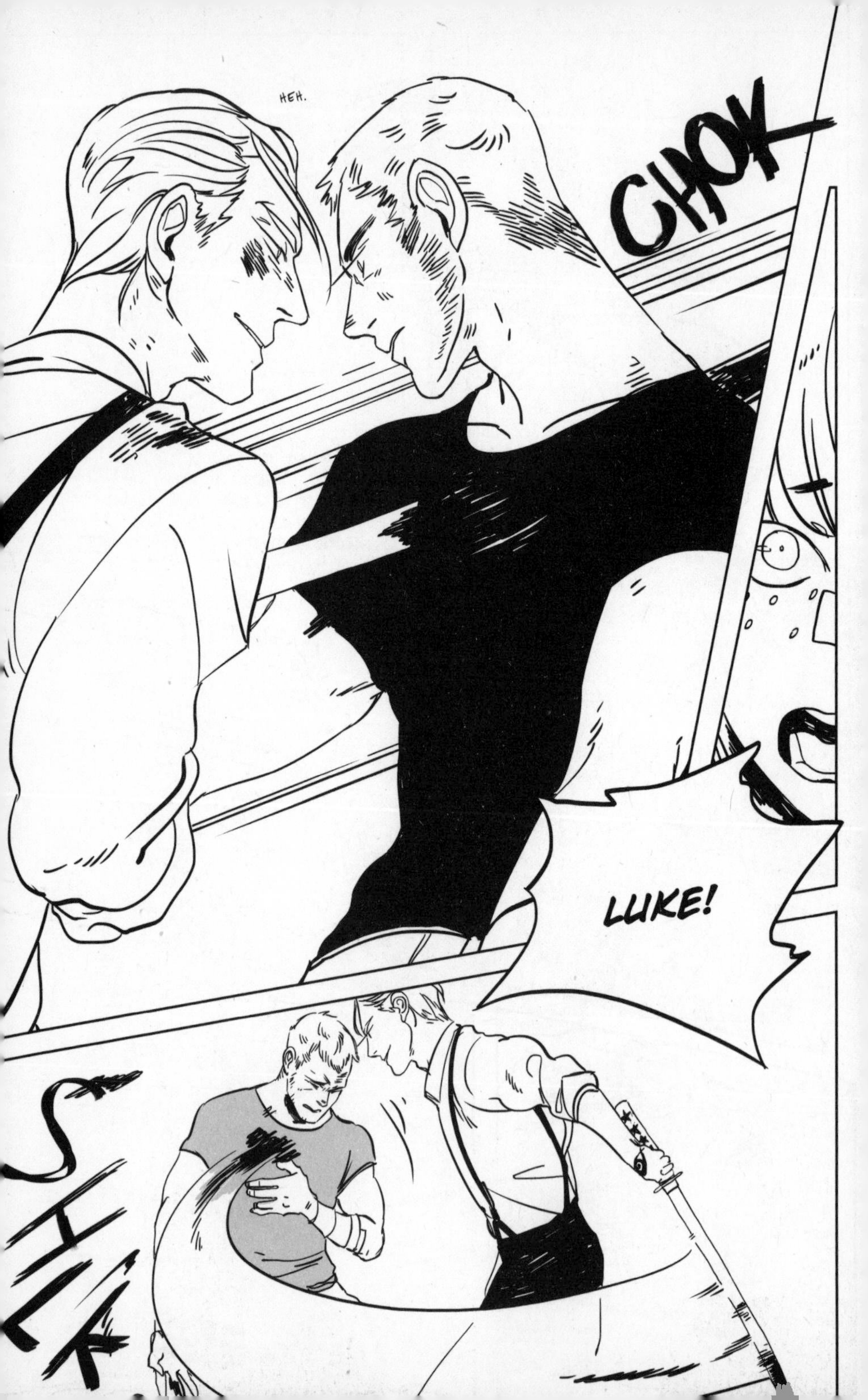
HEH.
CHOK
LUKE!
SHLK

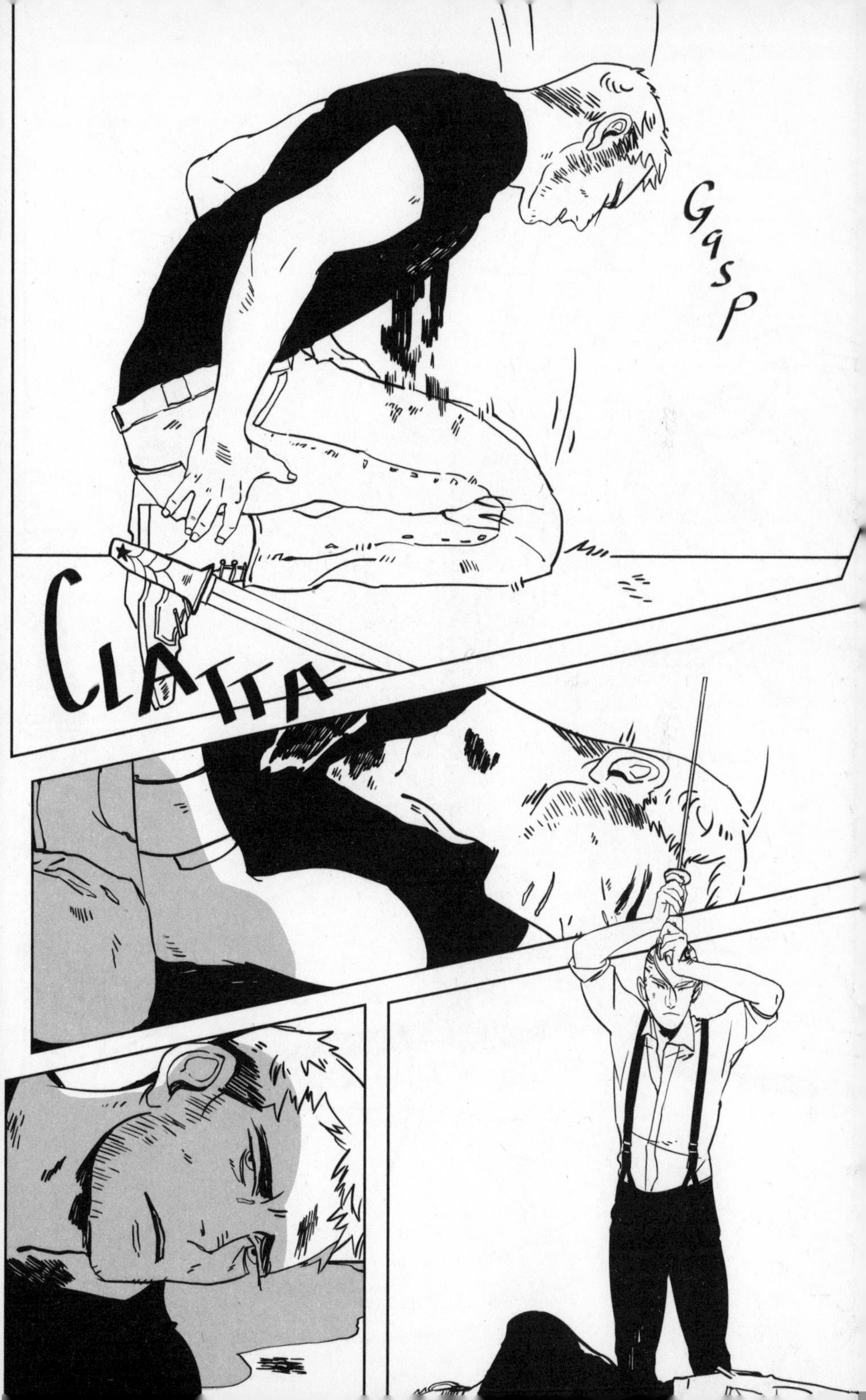
Gasp
CLATTA

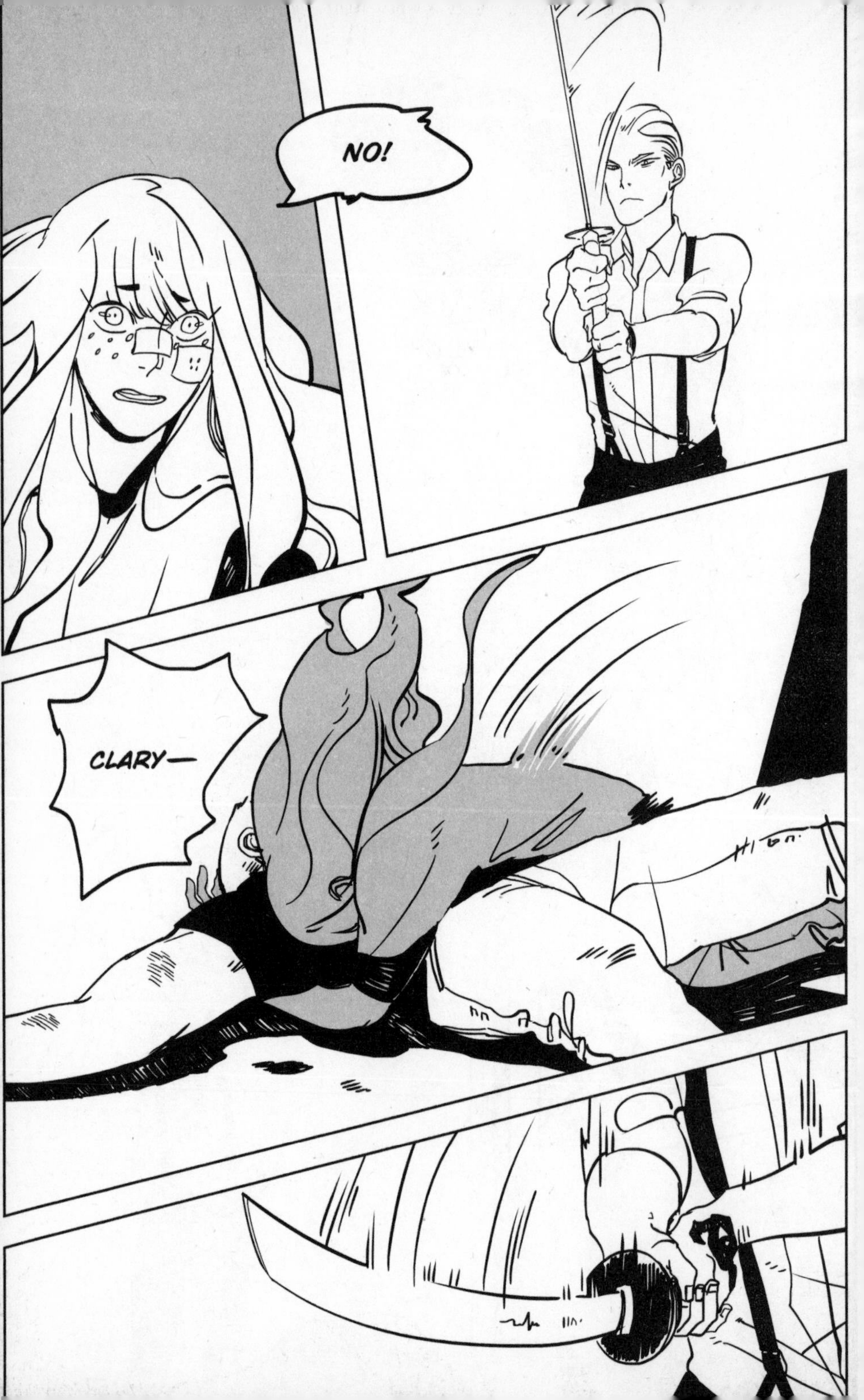
NO!
CLARY—

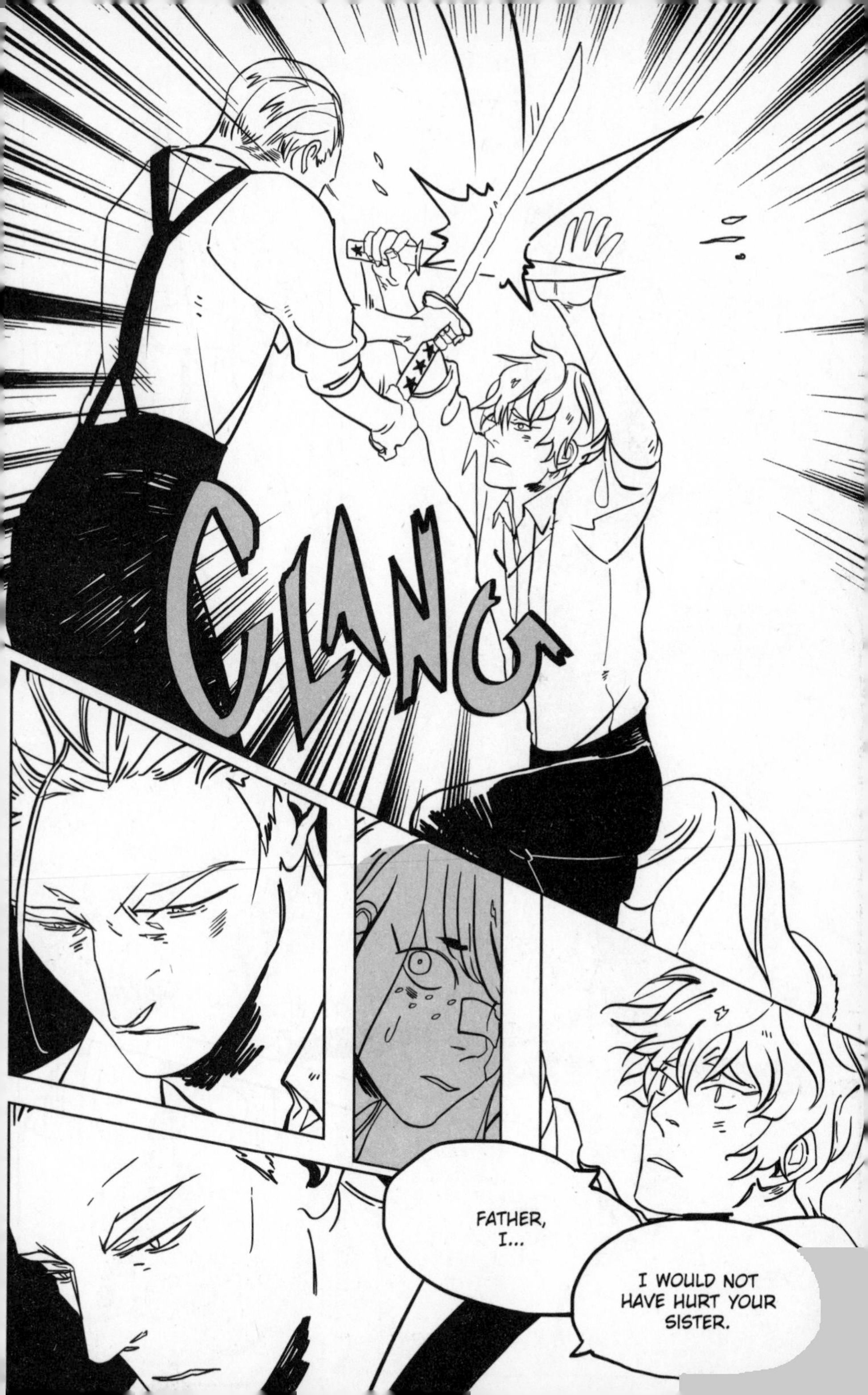
CLANG
FATHER, I...
I WOULD NOT HAVE HURT YOUR SISTER.

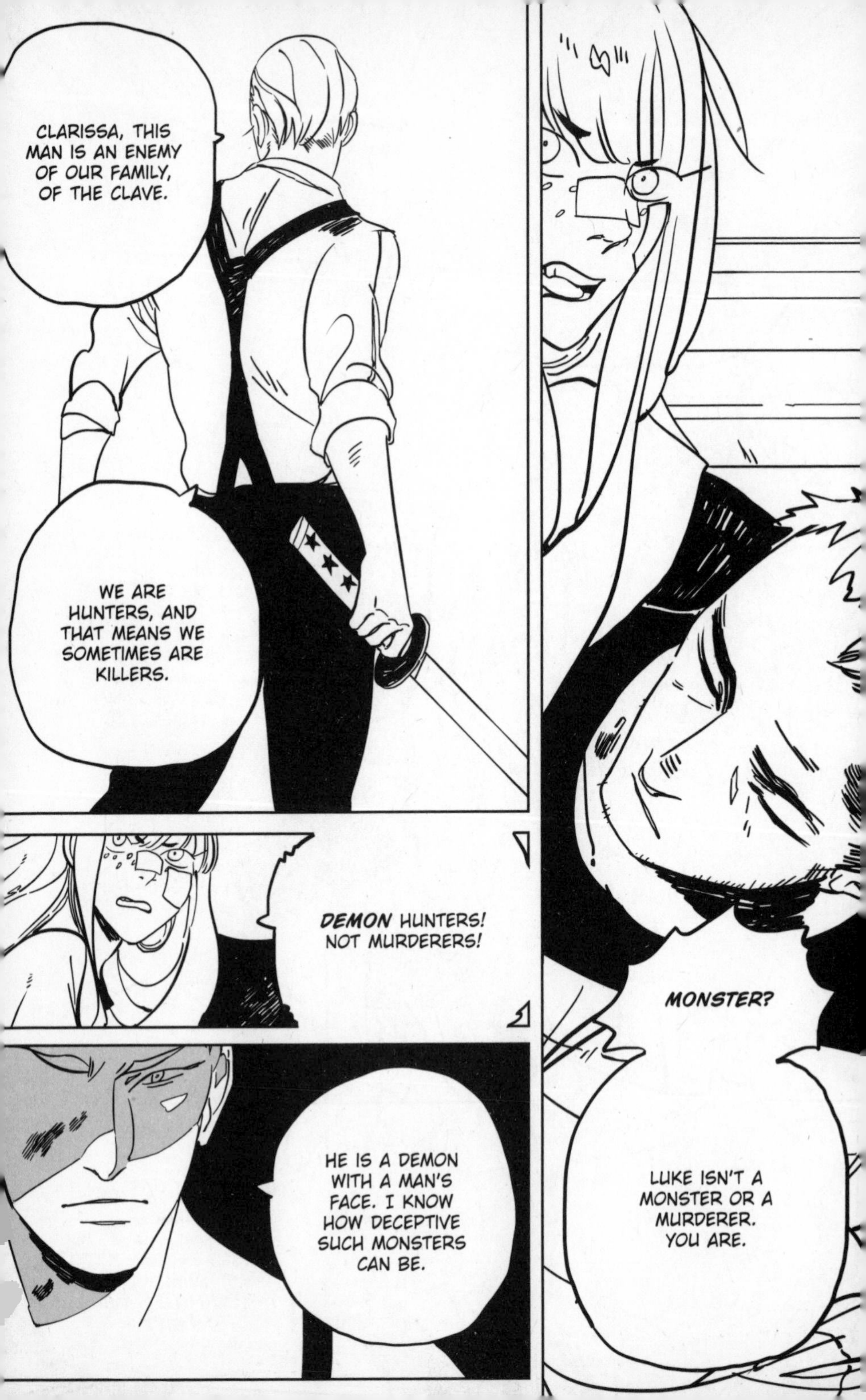
CLARISSA, THIS MAN IS AN ENEMY OF OUR FAMILY, OF THE CLAVE.
WE ARE HUNTERS, AND THAT MEANS WE SOMETIMES ARE KILLERS.
DEMON HUNTERS! NOT MURDERERS!
HE IS A DEMON WITH A MAN'S FACE. I KNOW HOW DECEPTIVE SUCH MONSTERS CAN BE.
MONSTER?
LUKE ISN'T A MONSTER OR A MURDERER. YOU ARE.

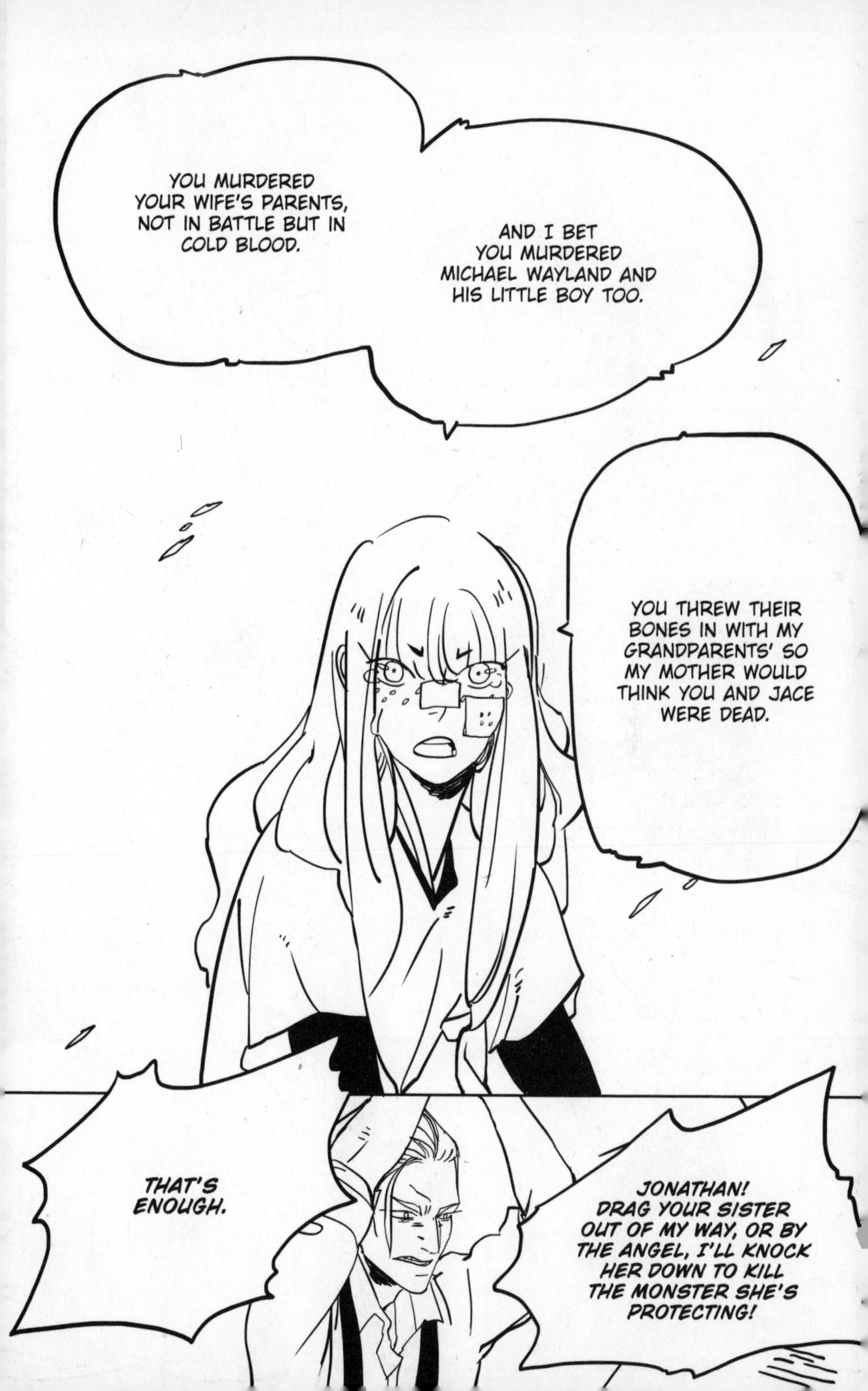
YOU MURDERED YOUR WIFE'S PARENTS, NOT IN BATTLE BUT IN COLD BLOOD.
AND I BET YOU MURDERED MICHAEL WAYLAND AND HIS LITTLE BOY TOO.
YOU THREW THEIR BONES IN WITH MY GRANDPARENTS' SO MY MOTHER WOULD THINK YOU AND JACE WERE DEAD.
THAT'S ENOUGH.
JONATHAN! DRAG YOUR SISTER OUT OF MY WAY, OR BY THE ANGEL, I'LL KNOCK HER DOWN TO KILL THE MONSTER SHE'S PROTECTING!

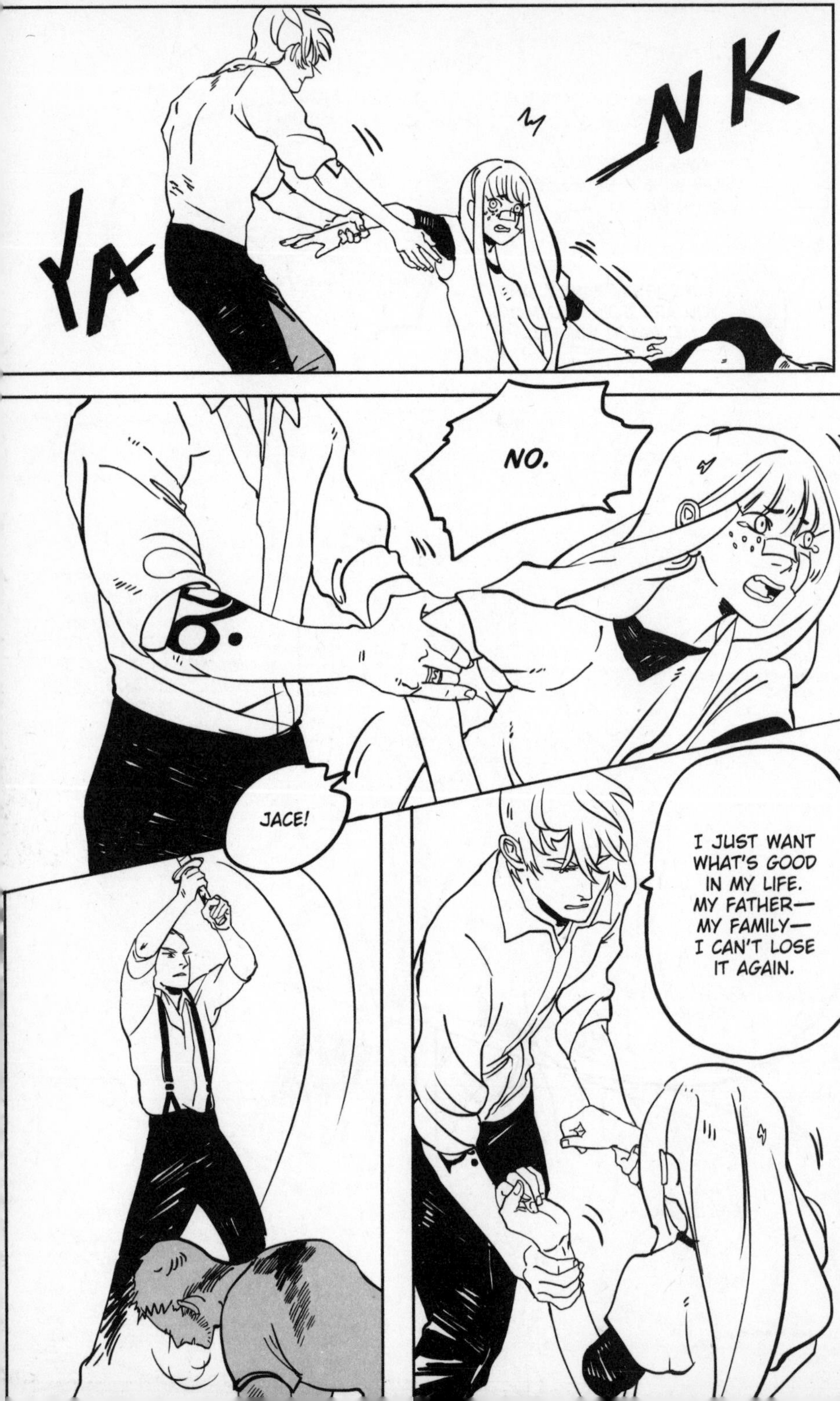
YA
NK
NO.
JACE!
I JUST WANT WHAT'S GOOD IN MY LIFE. MY FATHER— MY FAMILY— I CAN'T LOSE IT AGAIN.

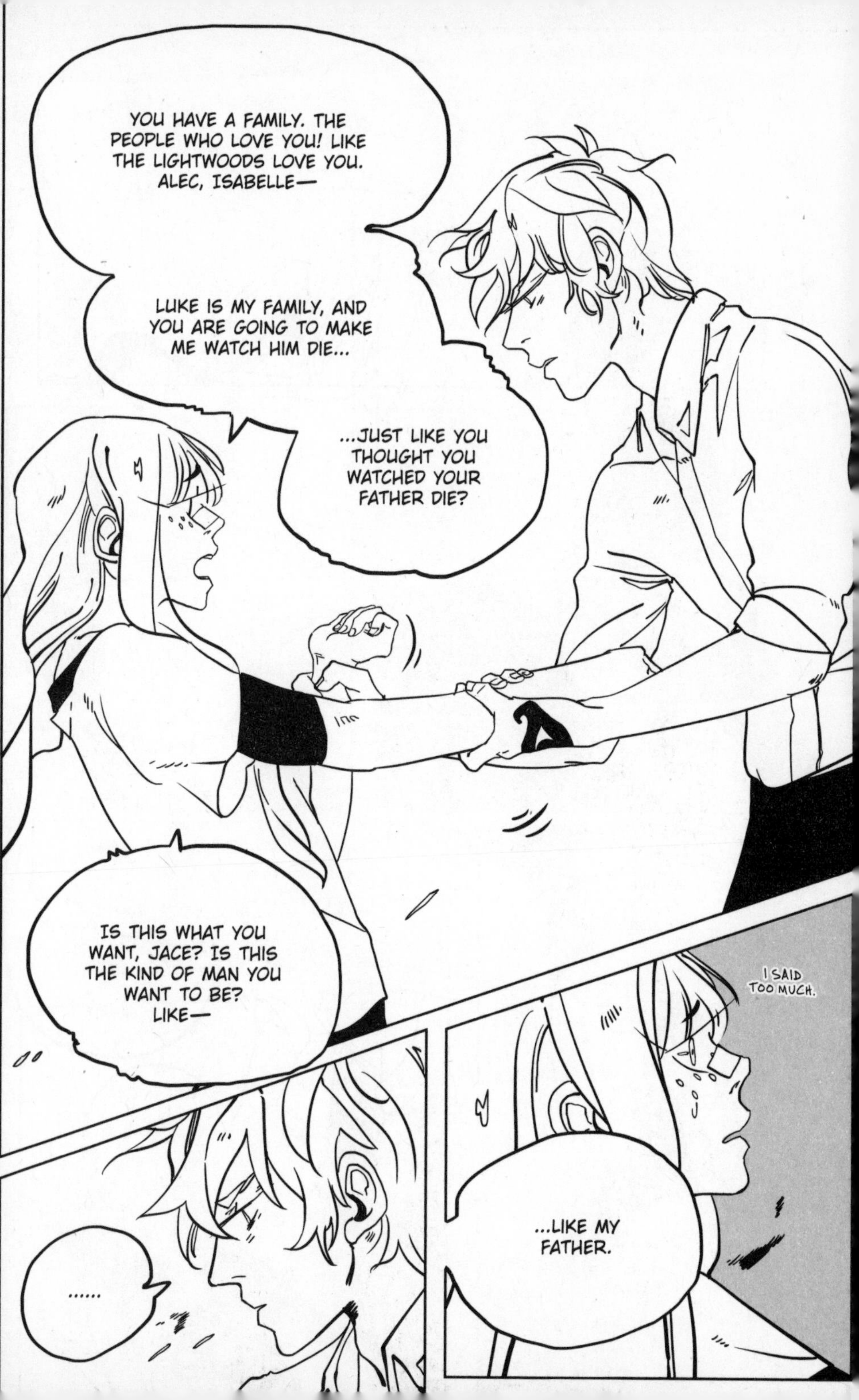
YOU HAVE A FAMILY. THE PEOPLE WHO LOVE YOU! LIKE THE LIGHTWOODS LOVE YOU. ALEC, ISABELLE—
LUKE IS MY FAMILY, AND YOU ARE GOING TO MAKE ME WATCH HIM DIE...
...JUST LIKE YOU THOUGHT YOU WATCHED YOUR FATHER DIE?
IS THIS WHAT YOU WANT, JACE? IS THIS THE KIND OF MAN YOU WANT TO BE? LIKE—
I SAID TOO MUCH.
......
...LIKE MY FATHER.

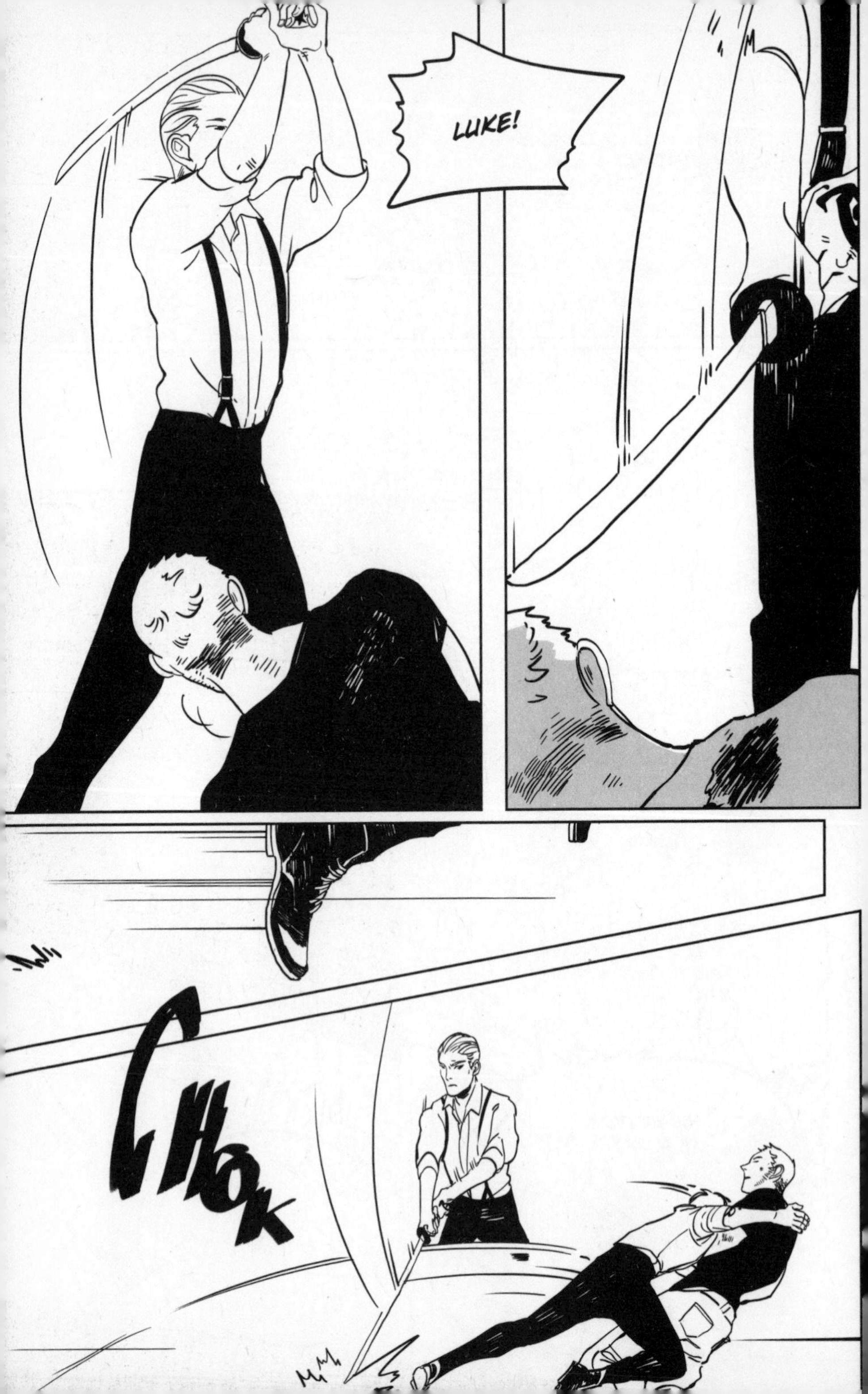
LUKE!
CHOK

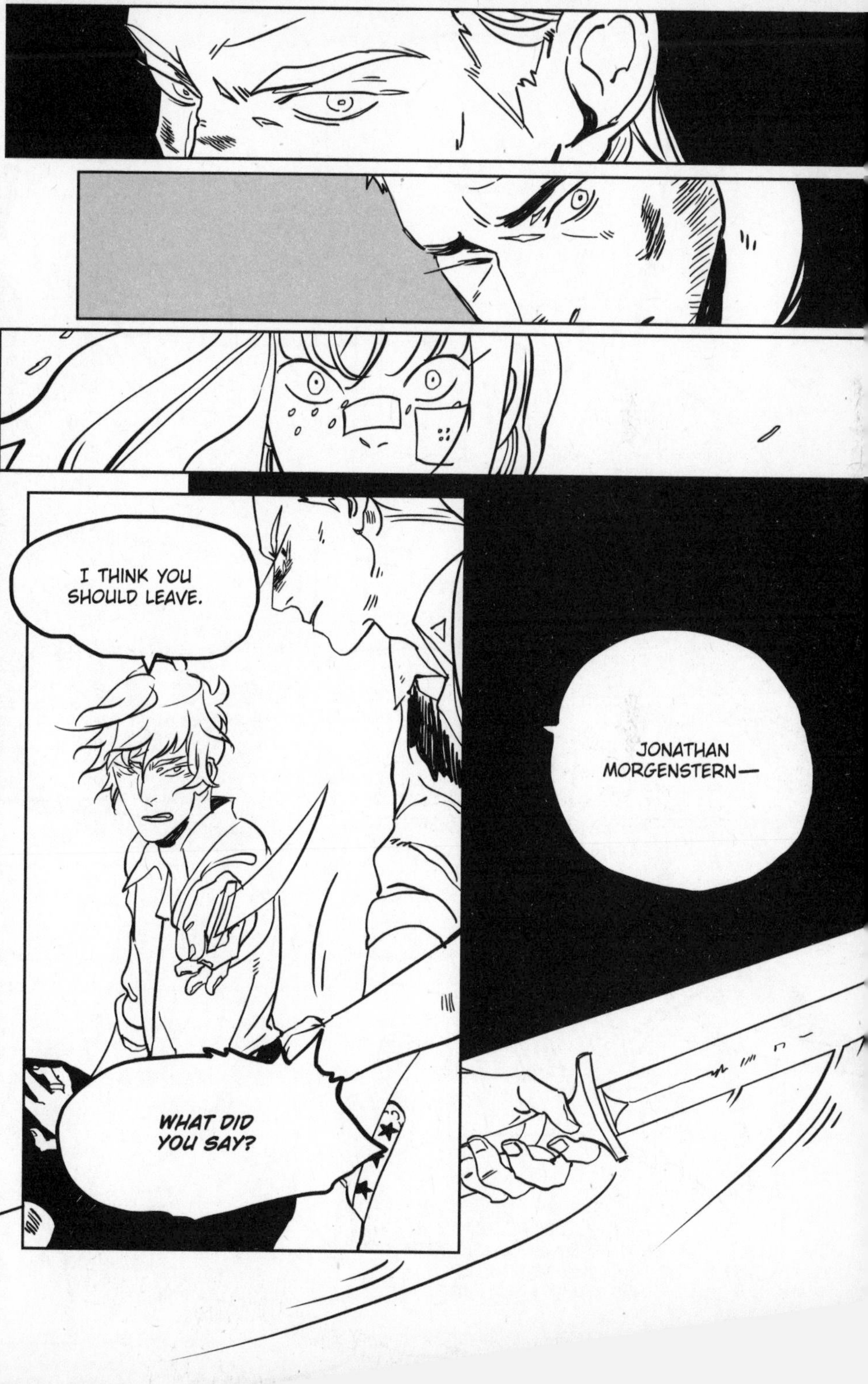
I THINK YOU SHOULD LEAVE.
JONATHAN MORGENSTERN—
WHAT DID YOU SAY?

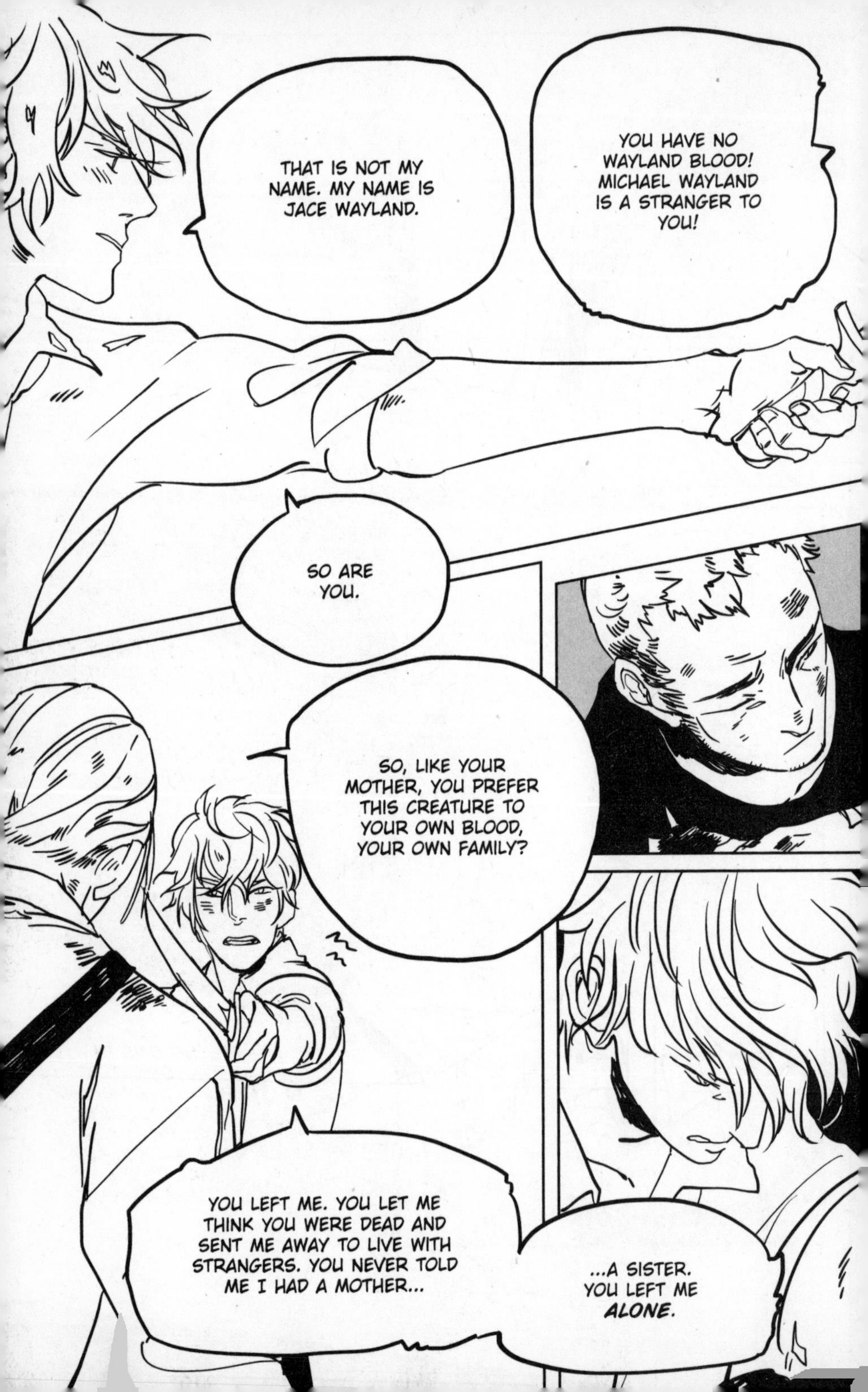
THAT IS NOT MY NAME. MY NAME IS JACE WAYLAND.
YOU HAVE NO WAYLAND BLOOD! MICHAEL WAYLAND IS A STRANGER TO YOU!
SO ARE YOU.
SO, LIKE YOUR MOTHER, YOU PREFER THIS CREATURE TO YOUR OWN BLOOD, YOUR OWN FAMILY?
YOU LEFT ME. YOU LET ME THINK YOU WERE DEAD AND SENT ME AWAY TO LIVE WITH STRANGERS. YOU NEVER TOLD ME I HAD A MOTHER...
...A SISTER. YOU LEFT ME *ALONE*.

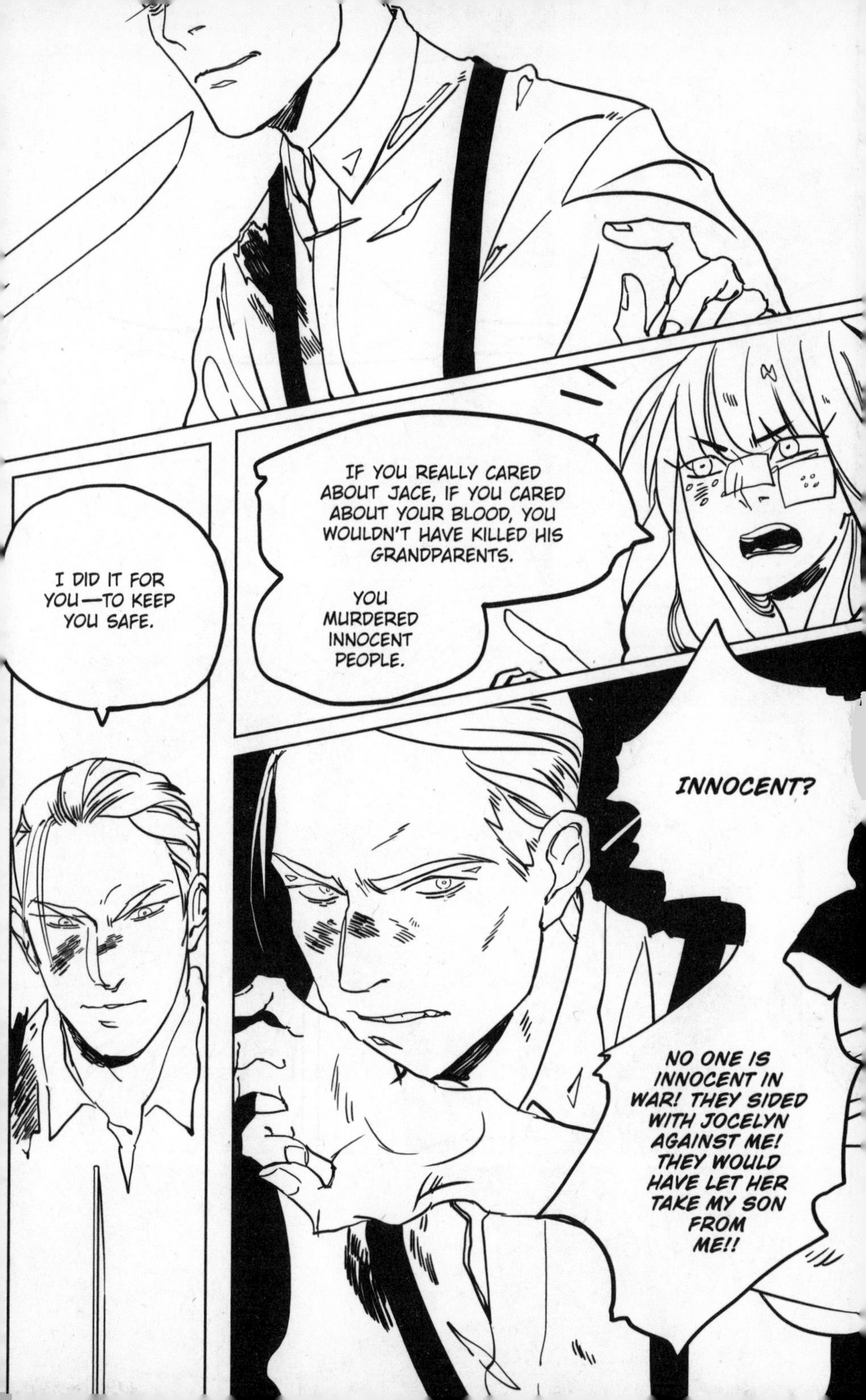
IF YOU REALLY CARED ABOUT JACE, IF YOU CARED ABOUT YOUR BLOOD, YOU WOULDN'T HAVE KILLED HIS GRANDPARENTS.
YOU MURDERED INNOCENT PEOPLE.
I DID IT FOR YOU—TO KEEP YOU SAFE.
INNOCENT?
NO ONE IS INNOCENT IN WAR! THEY SIDED WITH JOCELYN AGAINST ME! THEY WOULD HAVE LET HER TAKE MY SON FROM ME!!

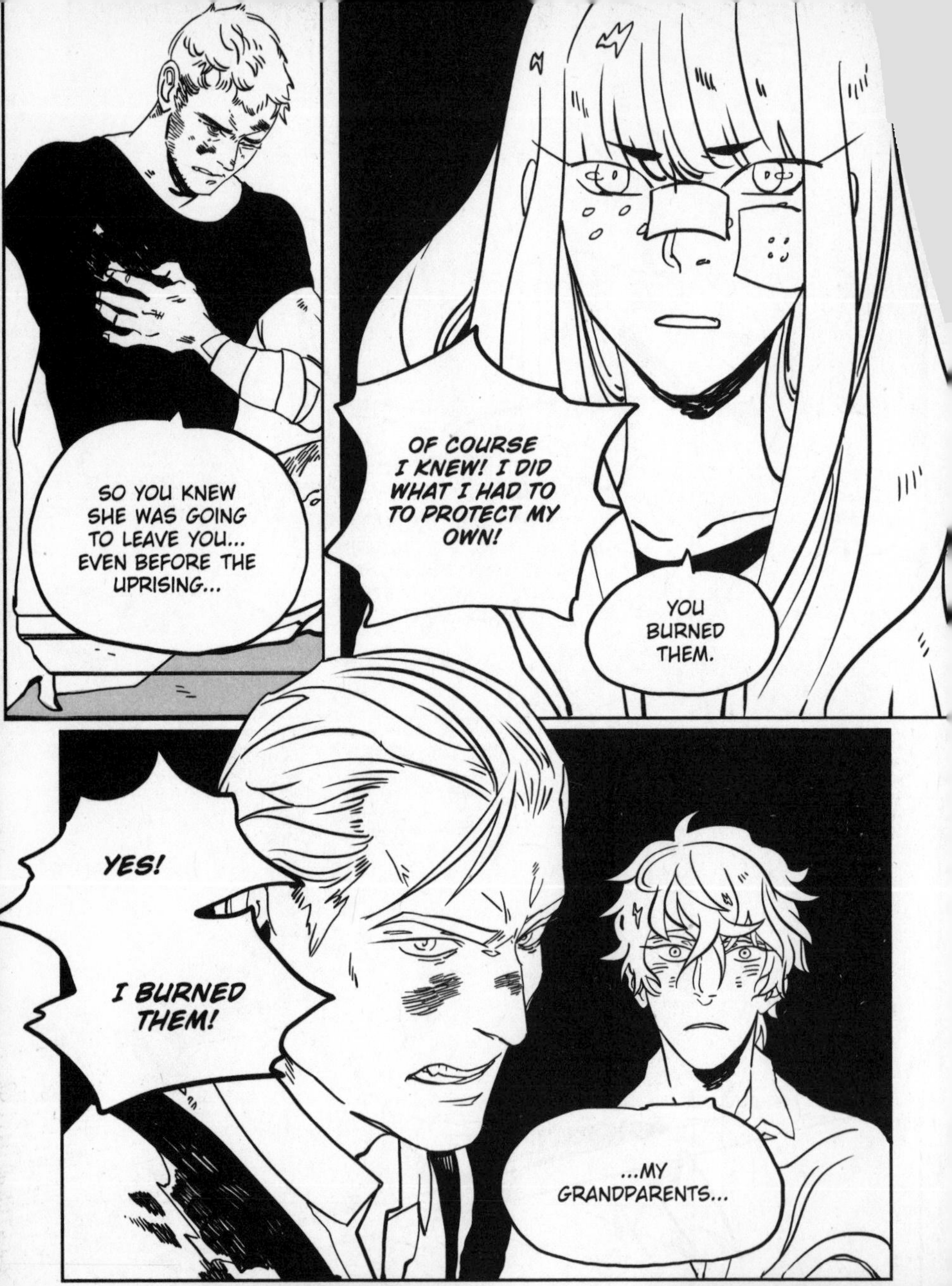
SO YOU KNEW SHE WAS GOING TO LEAVE YOU... EVEN BEFORE THE UPRISING...
OF COURSE I KNEW! I DID WHAT I HAD TO TO PROTECT MY OWN!
YOU BURNED THEM.
YES!
I BURNED THEM!
...MY GRANDPARENTS...

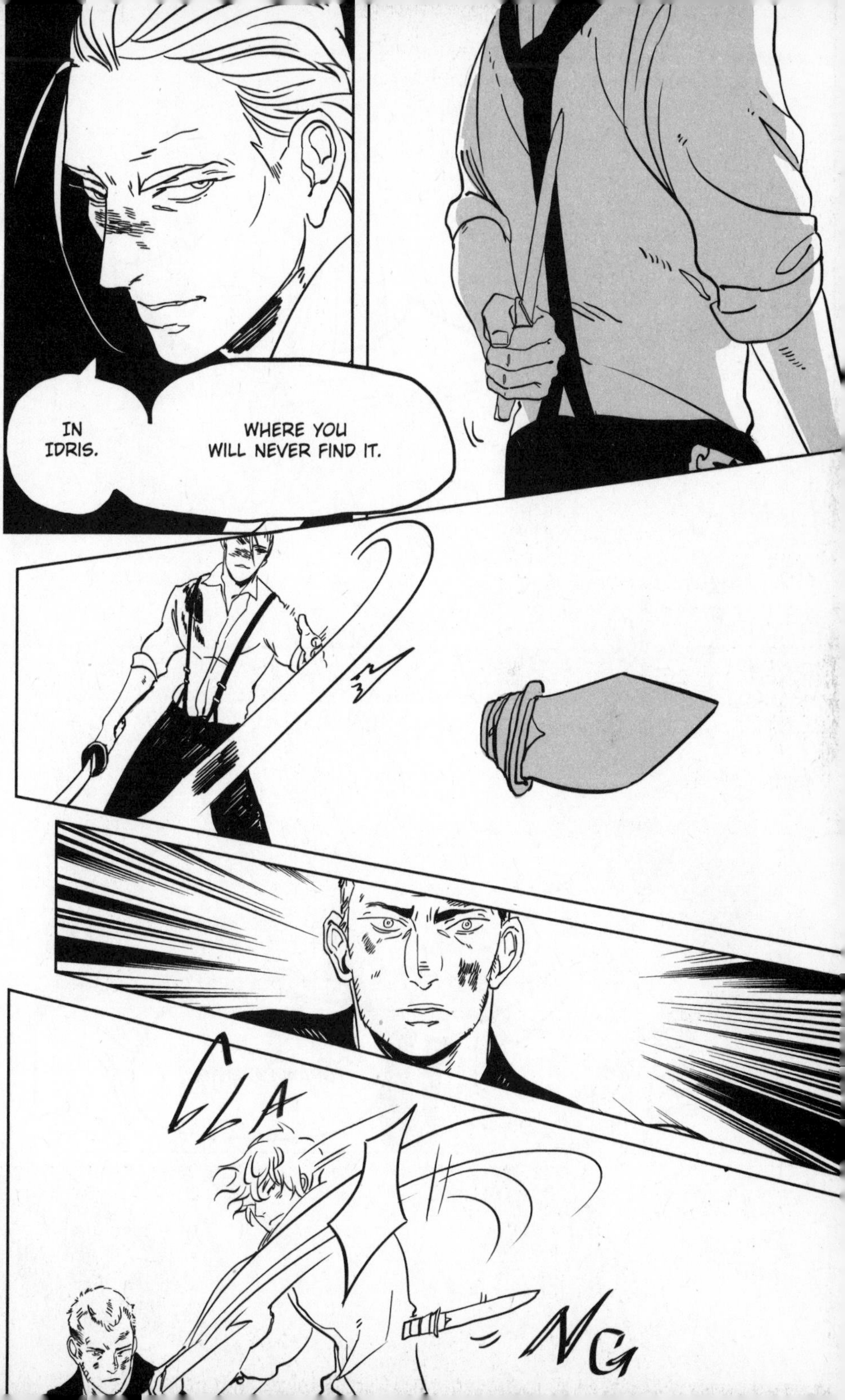
IN IDRIS.
WHERE YOU WILL NEVER FIND IT.
CLANG

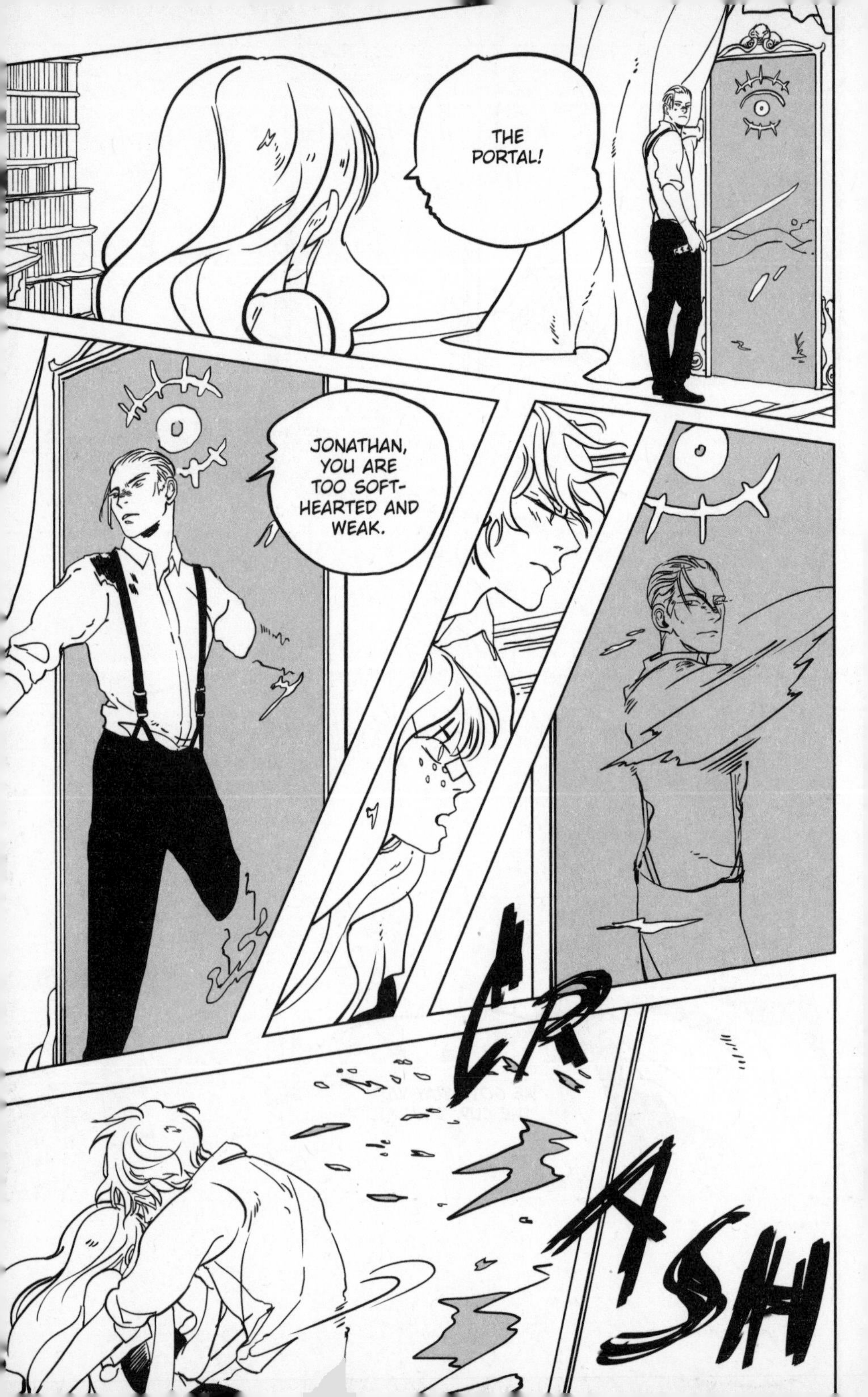
THE PORTAL!
JONATHAN, YOU ARE TOO SOFT-HEARTED AND WEAK.
CRASH

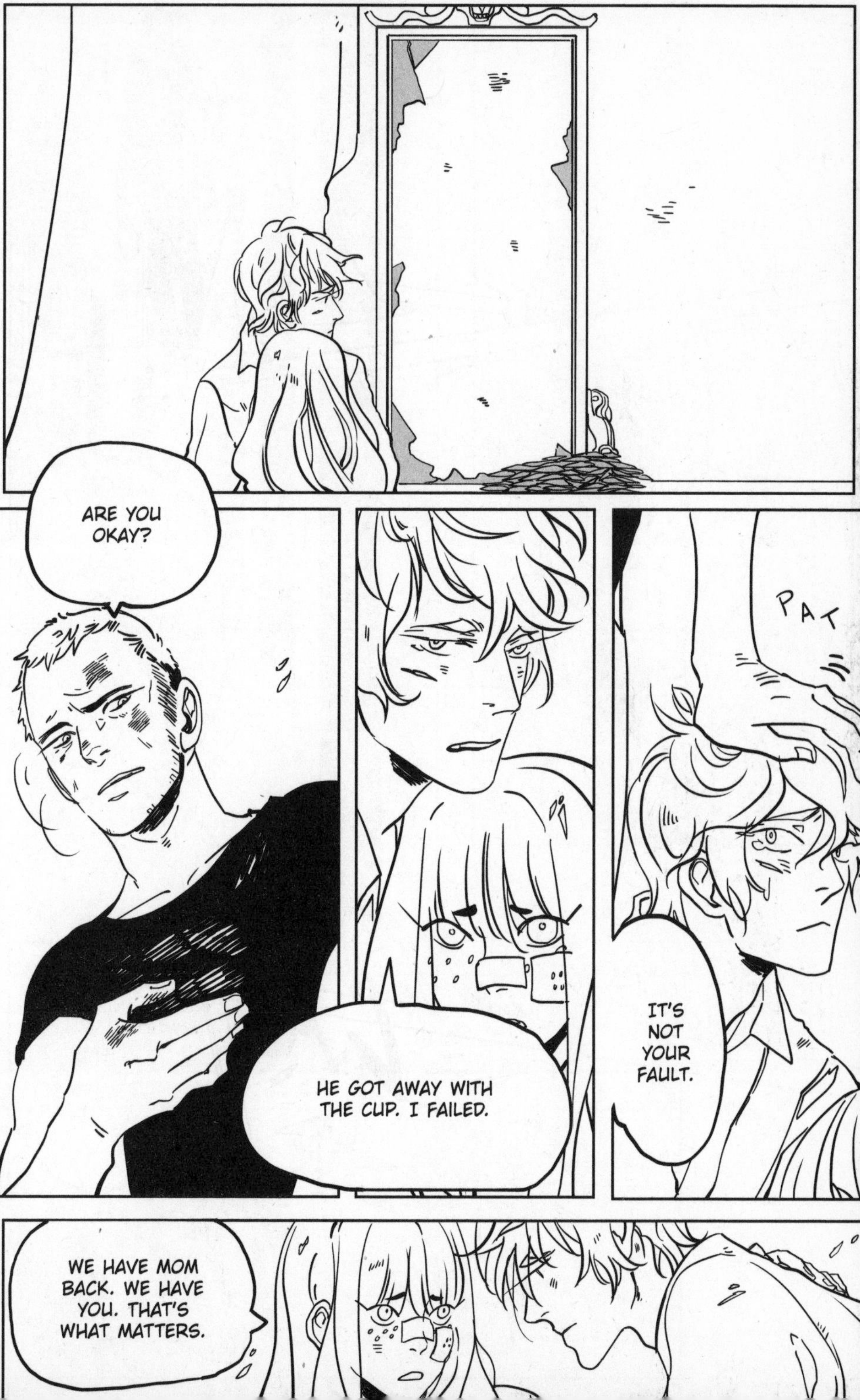
ARE YOU OKAY?
HE GOT AWAY WITH THE CUP. I FAILED.
PAT
IT'S NOT YOUR FAULT.
WE HAVE MOM BACK. WE HAVE YOU. THAT'S WHAT MATTERS.

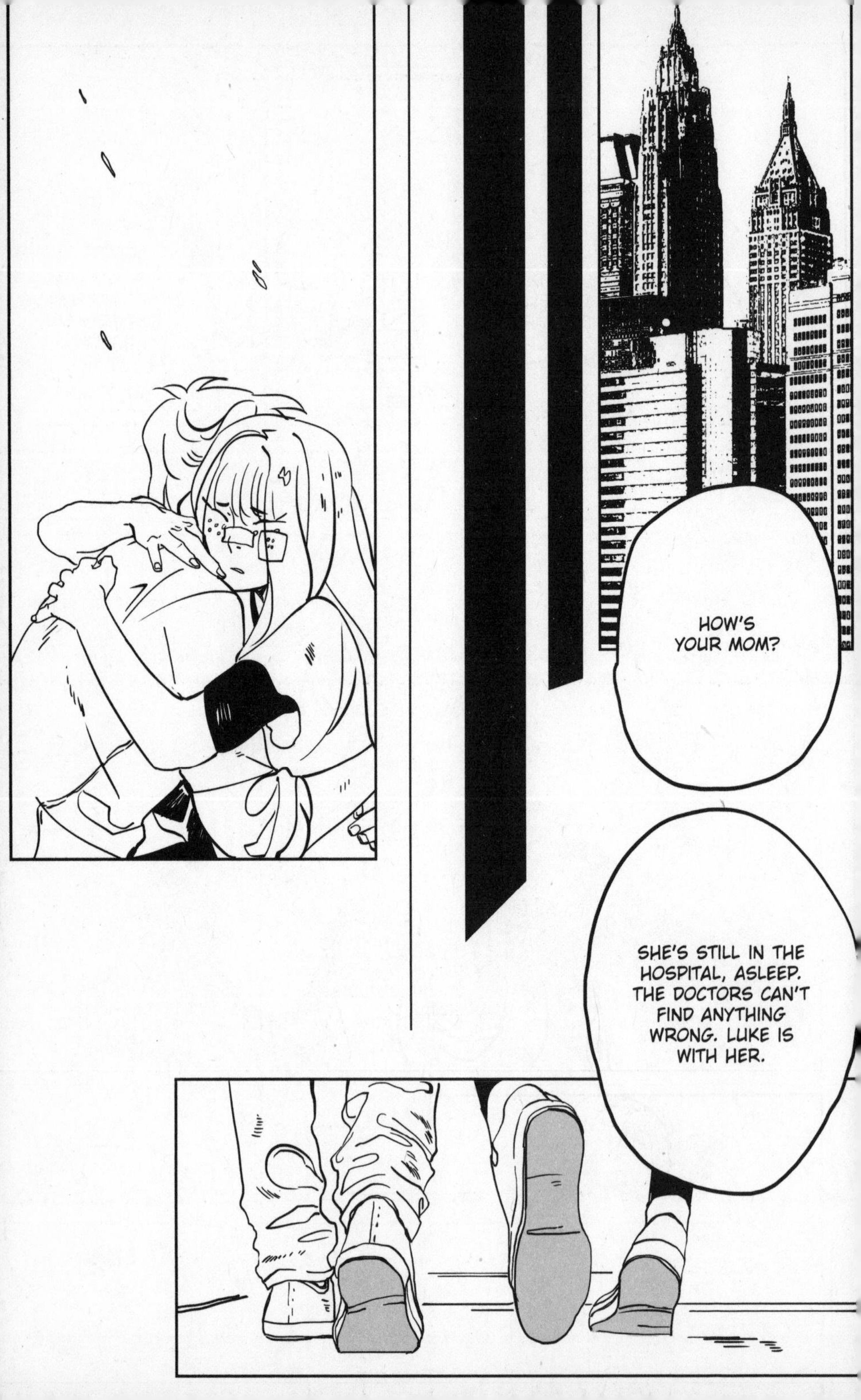
HOW'S YOUR MOM?
SHE'S STILL IN THE HOSPITAL, ASLEEP. THE DOCTORS CAN'T FIND ANYTHING WRONG. LUKE IS WITH HER.

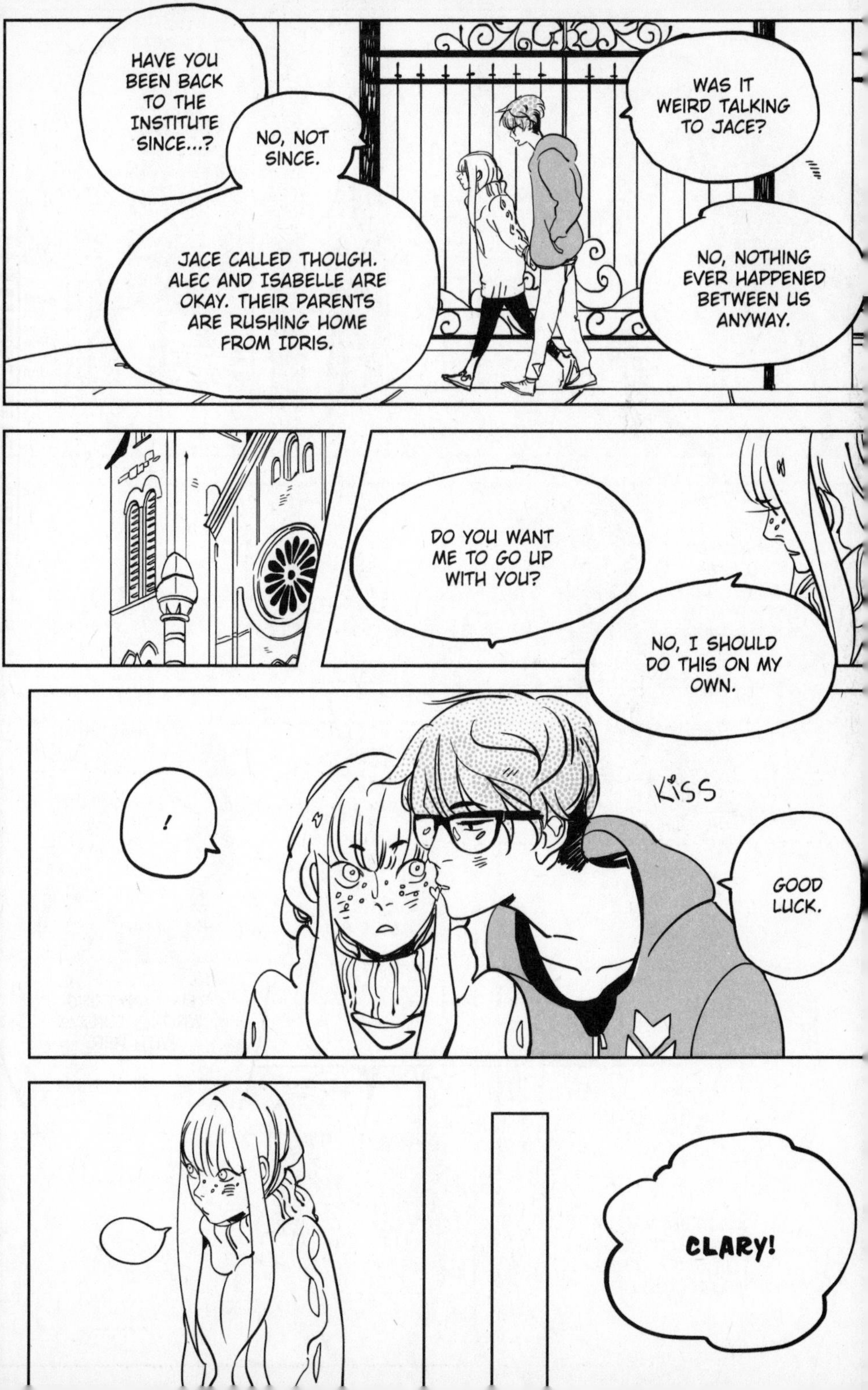
HAVE YOU BEEN BACK TO THE INSTITUTE SINCE...?
NO, NOT SINCE.
JACE CALLED THOUGH. ALEC AND ISABELLE ARE OKAY. THEIR PARENTS ARE RUSHING HOME FROM IDRIS.
WAS IT WEIRD TALKING TO JACE?
NO, NOTHING EVER HAPPENED BETWEEN US ANYWAY.
DO YOU WANT ME TO GO UP WITH YOU?
NO, I SHOULD DO THIS ON MY OWN.
!
KISS
GOOD LUCK.
CLARY!

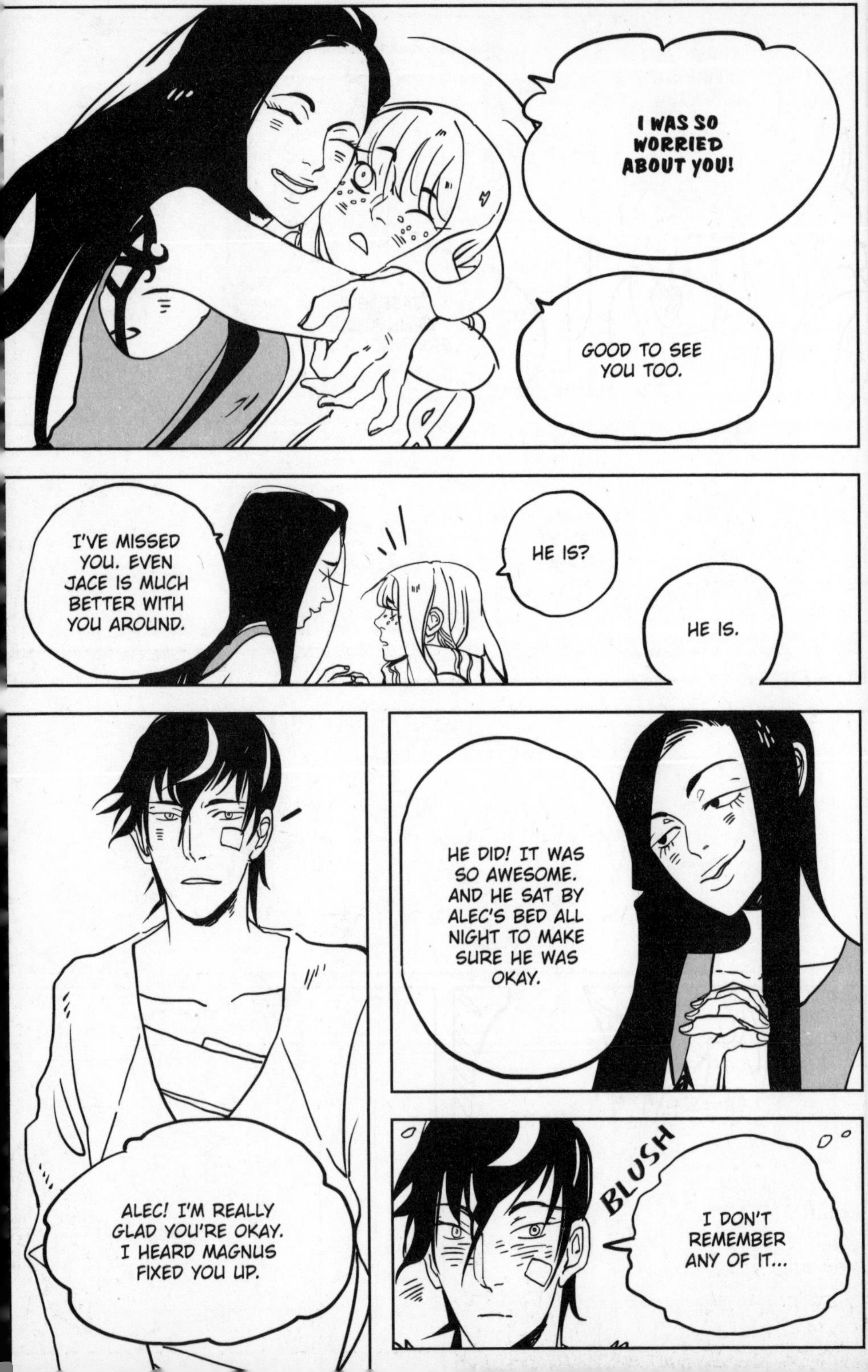
I WAS SO WORRIED ABOUT YOU!
GOOD TO SEE YOU TOO.
I'VE MISSED YOU. EVEN JACE IS MUCH BETTER WITH YOU AROUND.
HE IS?
HE IS.
ALEC! I'M REALLY GLAD YOU'RE OKAY. I HEARD MAGNUS FIXED YOU UP.
HE DID! IT WAS SO AWESOME. AND HE SAT BY ALEC'S BED ALL NIGHT TO MAKE SURE HE WAS OKAY.
BLUSH
I DON'T REMEMBER ANY OF IT...

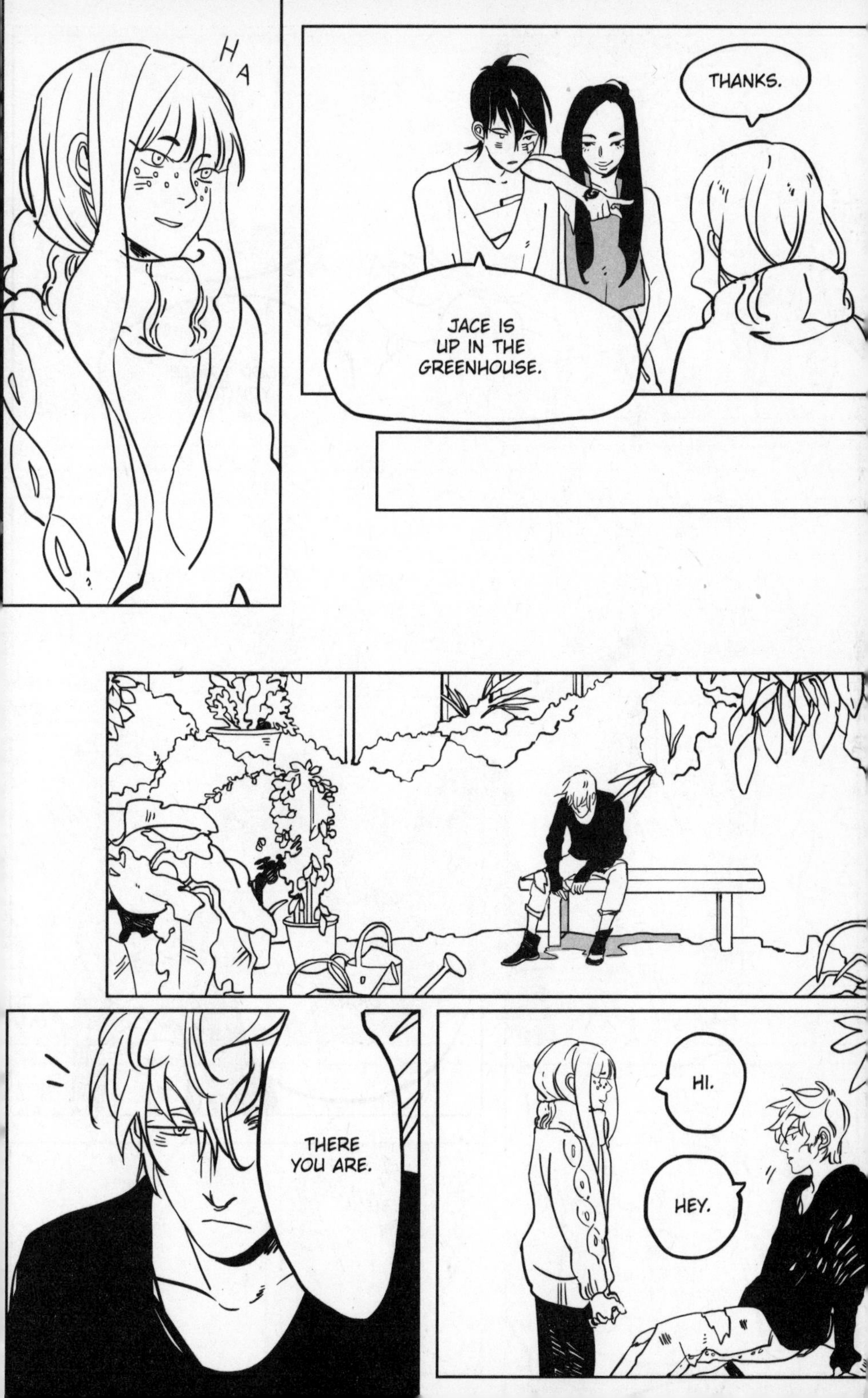
HA
THANKS.
JACE IS UP IN THE GREENHOUSE.
THERE YOU ARE.
HI.
HEY.

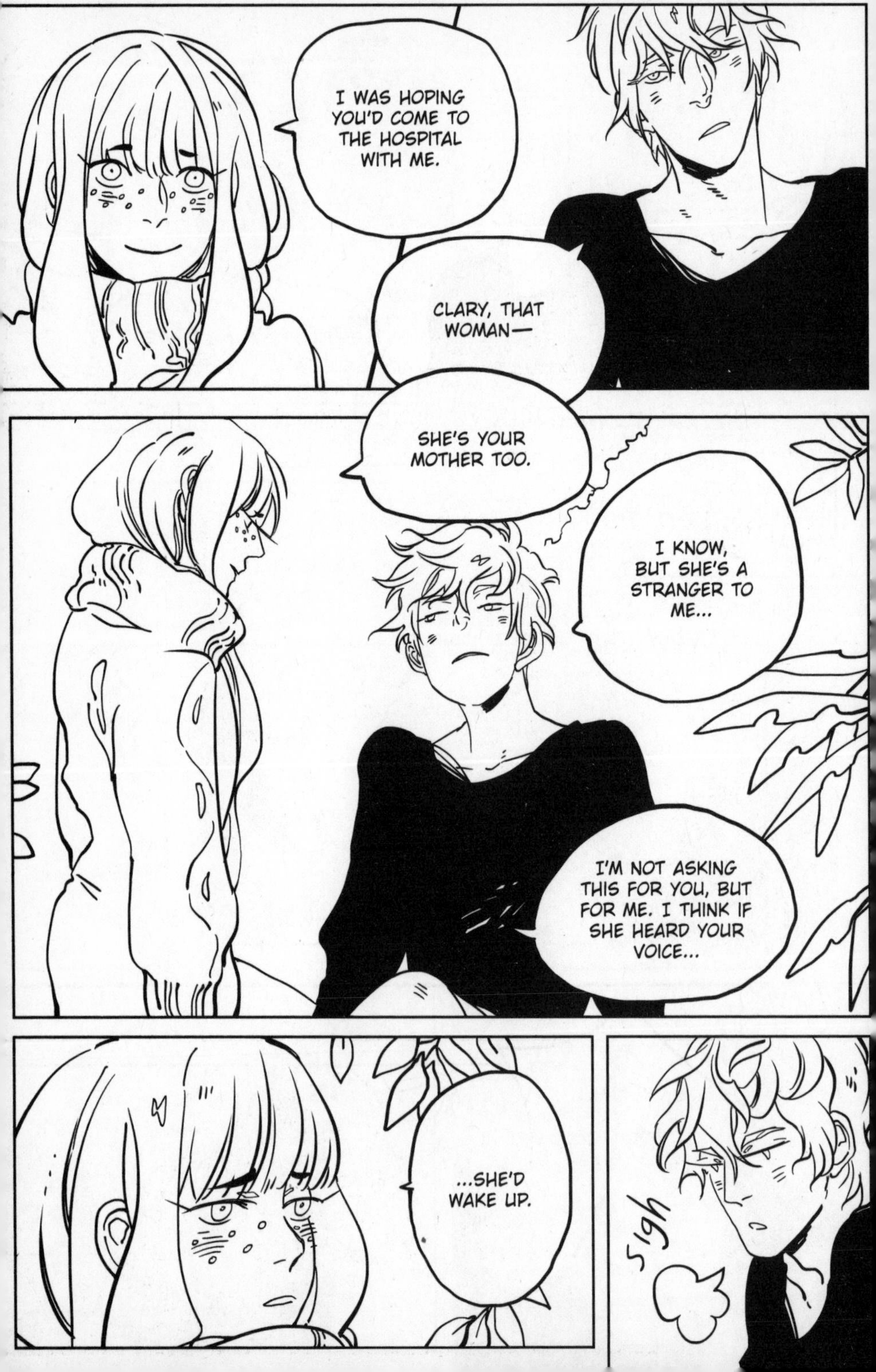
I WAS HOPING YOU'D COME TO THE HOSPITAL WITH ME.
CLARY, THAT WOMAN—
SHE'S YOUR MOTHER TOO.
I KNOW, BUT SHE'S A STRANGER TO ME...
I'M NOT ASKING THIS FOR YOU, BUT FOR ME. I THINK IF SHE HEARD YOUR VOICE...
...SHE'D WAKE UP.
sigh

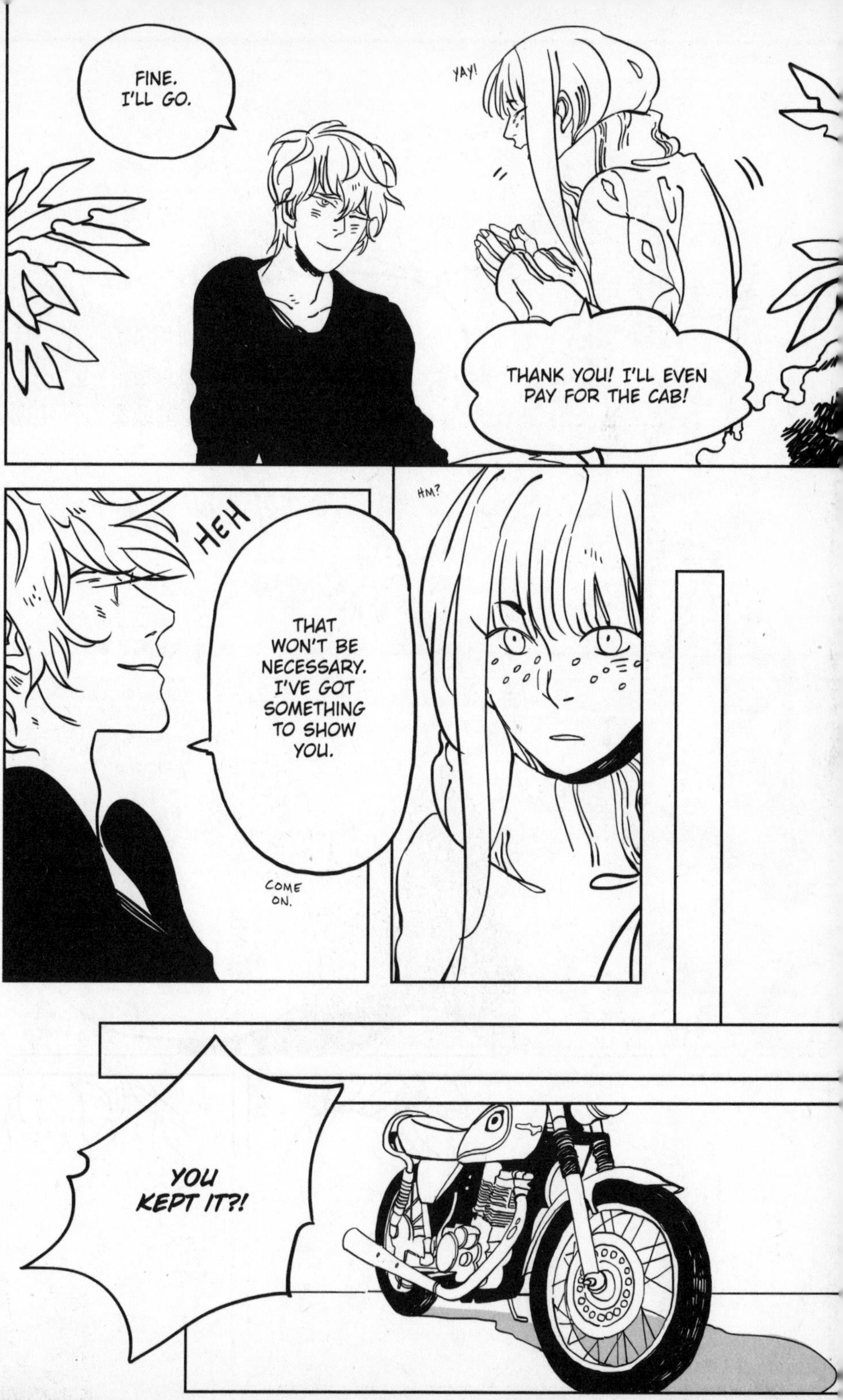
FINE. I'LL GO.
YAY!
THANK YOU! I'LL EVEN PAY FOR THE CAB!
HEH
THAT WON'T BE NECESSARY. I'VE GOT SOMETHING TO SHOW YOU.
COME ON.
HM?
YOU KEPT IT?!

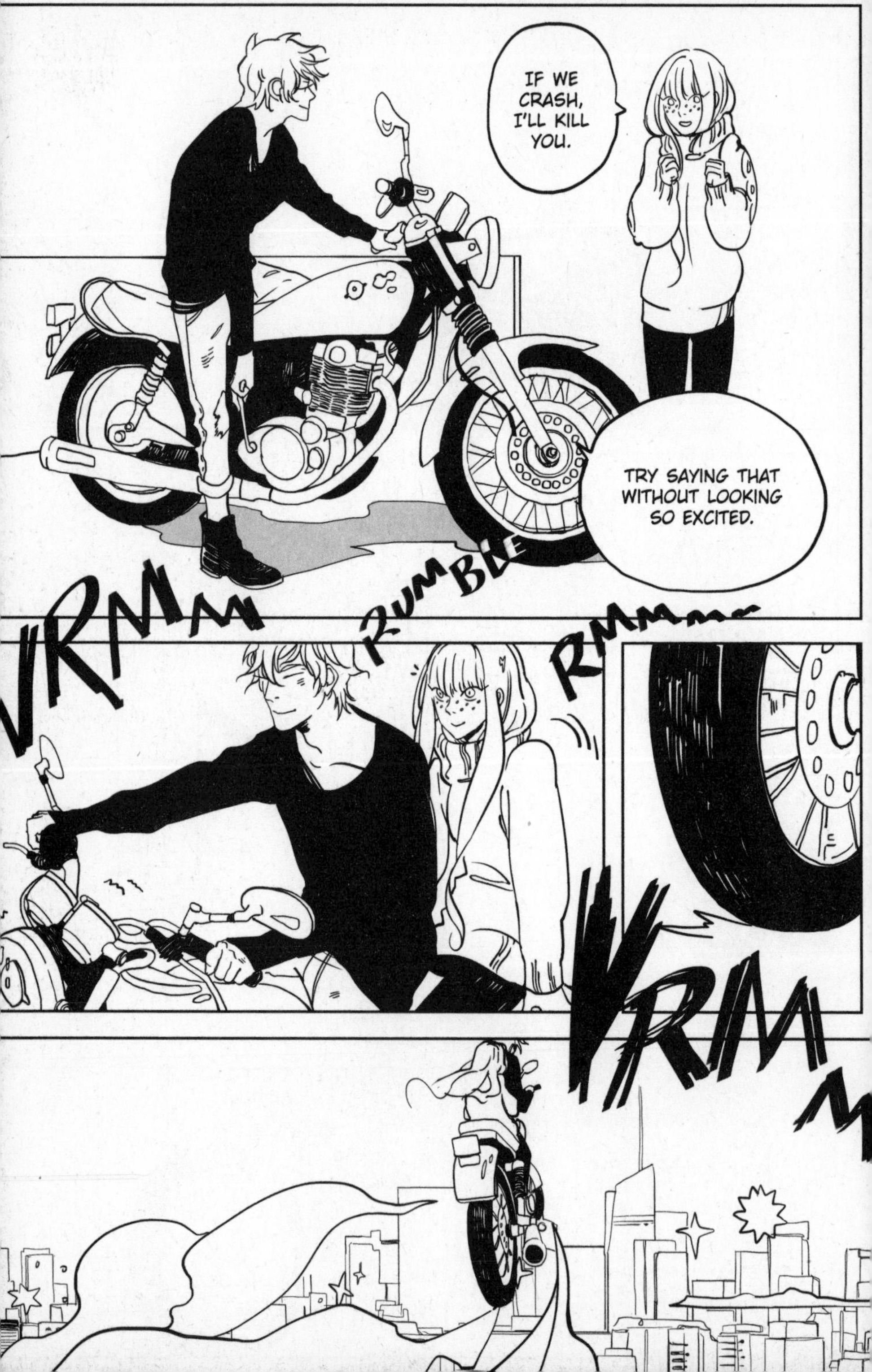
IF WE CRASH, I'LL KILL YOU.
TRY SAYING THAT WITHOUT LOOKING SO EXCITED.
VRMM
RUMBLE
RMMM
VRM

TO BE CONTINUED IN THE THIRD VOLUME OF

THE MORTAL INSTRUMENTS
THE GRAPHIC NOVEL

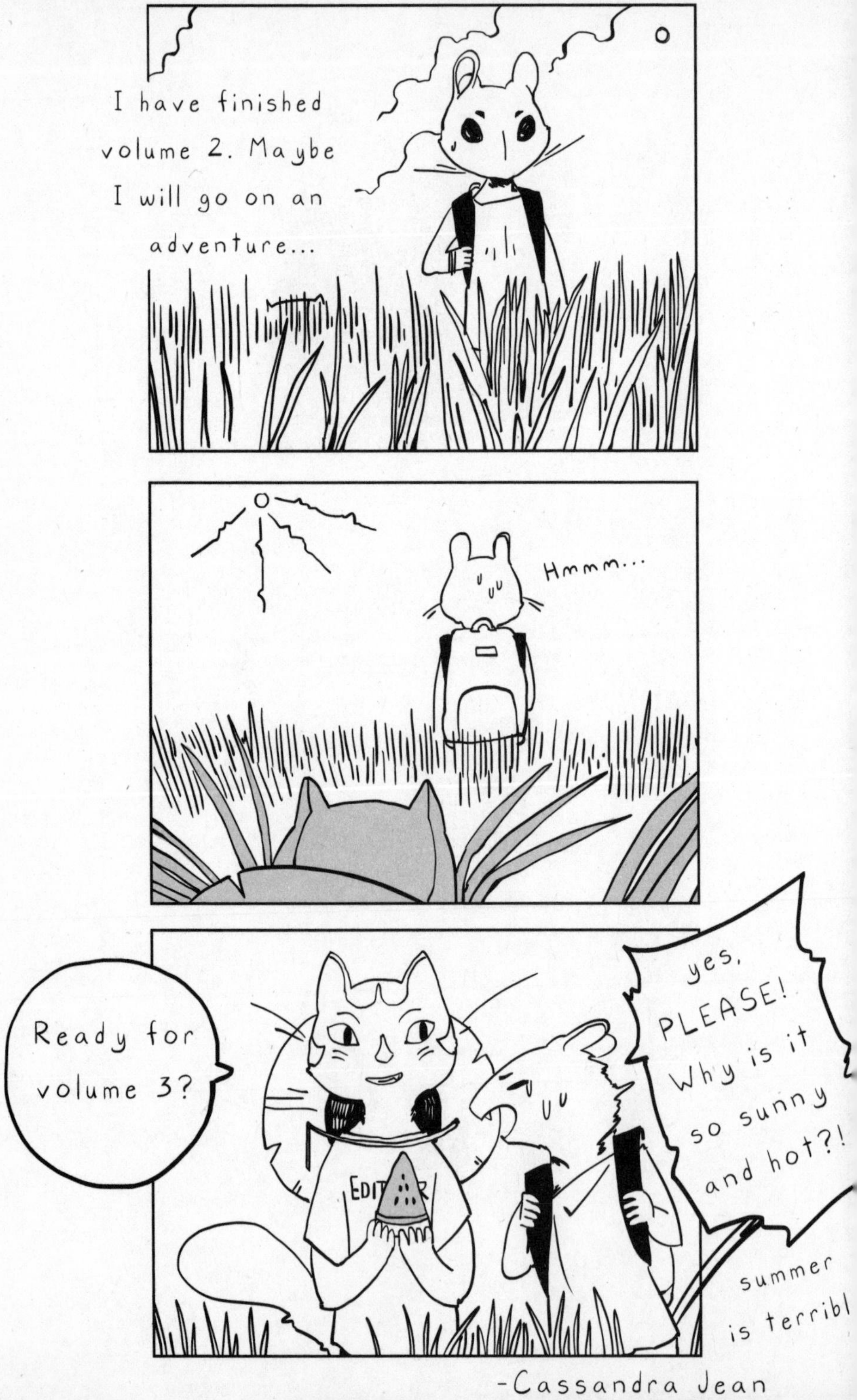
I have finished volume 2. Maybe I will go on an adventure...
Hmmm...
Ready for volume 3?
yes, PLEASE! Why is it so sunny and hot?!
summer is terribl

-Cassandra Jean

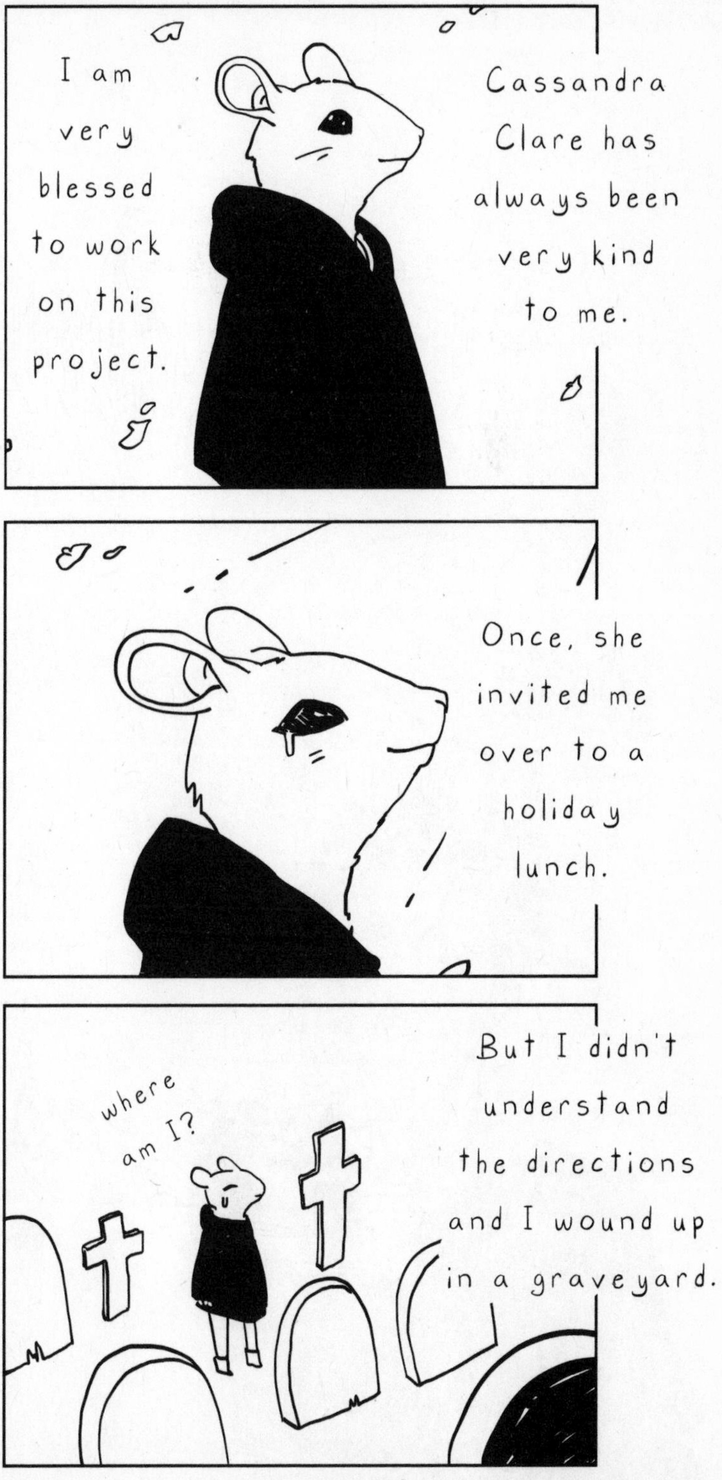
I am very blessed to work on this project.
Cassandra Clare has always been very kind to me.
Once, she invited me over to a holiday lunch.
where am I?
But I didn't understand the directions and I wound up in a graveyard.

-Cassandra Jean

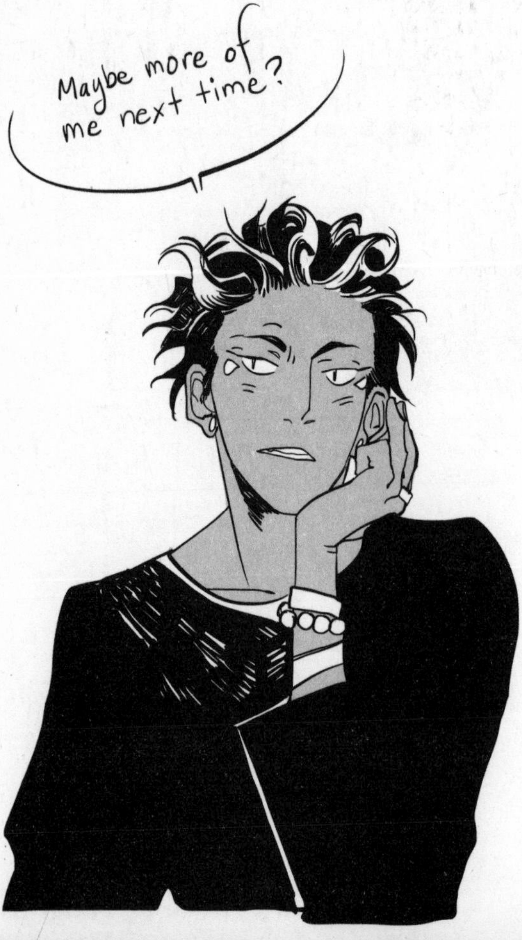
Maybe more of me next time?